EDUCATION
AND INTERGROUP
RELATIONS

*The Praeger Special Studies
Series in Comparative Education
Published in Cooperation with the Comparative
Education Center, State University of New York, Buffalo
General Editor:* **Philip G. Altbach**

EDUCATION AND INTERGROUP RELATIONS

An International
Perspective

Edited by
John N. Hawkins
and
Thomas J. La Belle

PRAEGER SPECIAL STUDIES • PRAEGER SCIENTIFIC

New York • Philadelphia • Eastbourne, UK
Toronto • Hong Kong • Tokyo • Sydney

Library of Congress Cataloging in Publication Data
Main entry under title:

Education and intergroup relations.

(Praeger special studies series in comparative education)
Bibliography: p.
Includes index.
1. Education—Social aspects—Cross-cultural studies. 2. Social interaction—Cross-cultural studies. 3. Intercultural education—Cross-cultural studies. 4. Education and state—Cross-cultural studies. 5. Educational equalization—Cross-cultural studies. 6. Comparative education. I. Hawkins, John N. II. La Belle, Thomas J. III. Series.
LC191.2.E38 1985 370.19 84-26353
ISBN 0-03-063701-5 (alk. paper)

Published in 1985 by Praeger Publishers
CBS Educational and Professional Publishing, a Division of CBS Inc.
521 Fifth Avenue, New York, NY 10175 USA

56789 052 987654321

Printed in the United States of America on acid-free paper

INTERNATIONAL OFFICES

Orders from outside the United States should be sent to the appropriate address listed below. Orders from areas not listed below should be placed through CBS International Publishing, 383 Madison Ave., New York, NY 10175 USA

Australia, New Zealand
Holt Saunders, Pty, Ltd., 9 Waltham St., Artarmon, N.S.W. 2064, Sydney, Australia

Canada
Holt, Rinehart & Winston of Canada, 55 Horner Ave., Toronto, Ontario, Canada M8Z 4X6

Europe, the Middle East, & Africa
Holt Saunders, Ltd., 1 St. Anne's Road, Eastbourne, East Sussex, England BN21 3UN

Japan
Holt Saunders, Ltd., Ichibancho Central Building, 22-1 Ichibancho, 3rd Floor, Chiyodaku, Tokyo, Japan

Hong Kong, Southeast Asia
Holt Saunders Asia, Ltd., 10 Fl, Intercontinental Plaza, 94 Granville Road, Tsim Sha Tsui East, Kowloon, Hong Kong

Manuscript submissions should be sent to the Editorial Director, Praeger Publishers, 521 Fifth Avenue, New York, NY 10175 USA

To Our Children,

Jeannette Marie La Belle
Katherine Anne La Belle
Larina Yasuko Hawkins
Marisa Harumi Hawkins

Who, in their youth, have already learned
the benefits of diversity.

John N. Hawkins
Thomas La Belle

PREFACE

It is virtually impossible to identify a nation that is not characterized by some degree of diversity based on ethnicity, social class, or caste. It is in this context that we speak of the "intergroup arena" and focus on the educational sector. This book discusses educational policies and practices in selected nations as they relate to a typology of intergroup relations. The purpose of the volume is to assess through case studies the complex interaction among class, culture, and educational policies in fostering or inhibiting cultural and economic equality. In our judgment, such studies are of use to scholars in the fields of educational foundations, comparative and international education, sociology, and anthropology of education, race relations, multicultural education, and politics of education. In addition, it is felt that policymakers and educational practitioners are in need of a comparative, international perspective on intergroup relations and education.

The first chapter of the book presents a conceptual framework and an intergroup relations typology. The typology attends to two sets of factors: the integrative processes by which groups interact in society and the particular educational policy areas. The integration processes take into account the aims and directions of the groups involved as each seeks to pursue its separate structural and cultural interests. The mechanisms by which the integration process is implemented -- coercion, interdependence, and consensus -- are also considered in determining how the dominant group fosters its definition of societal integration. Six educational policy areas are of interest because of their recurring importance to societal integration: degree of school centralization; access to education; articulation (coordination and progression between the skills imparted at one level in the school system to those imparted at the next) and tracking (assignment of specialized curricula and the degree to which tracks are permeable); curriculum; training, selection, and placement of administrators and teachers; and language policies.

The conceptual framework discusses the integrative processes and the educational policy areas within particular historical contexts across time. These particular contexts were used to develop a heuristic typology of four intergroup relations in an attempt to attend to how group membership affects socioeconomic roles, the mode and level of participation in institutional decisionmaking, and the extent to which issues of cultural identity and values are associated with group boundaries. One axis of the typology is power as reflected in political and economic resources. The other axis is the culturally defined status and prestige that shape ethnic hierarchies as well as ethnic group boundaries. Education is assumed to be important in this cultural and structural interaction because it functions as a selection and sorting device for the dominant gr oup and, along with other institutions, serves to maintain the system in its current state.

This typology is outlined in Chapter 1, elaborated and "tested" by twelve case studies, three clustered under each of the four societal types, and is further discussed in the conclusion in Chapter 14. The cases have been prepared by scholars intimately familiar with those nations chosen. Where possible, scholars from each nation were identified to write the cases, and all cases are based on original data and field work. By juxtaposing the cases against the typology, it is hoped that the complex area of education and intergroup relations will be somewhat more ordered.

We would like to acknowledge the contributing authors for taking on the task of adapting their own style to our conceptual framework; each has done an admirable job, and while not always agreeing with the typology, has illuminated its strengths and weaknesses in a scholarly manner. Here at UCLA colleagues and studies alike have contributed to the preparation of this volume in various ways, particularly Professors Val Rust and Don Nakanishi. We would like to especially acknowledge one of our doctoral students, Ms. Sharon Hare, who painstakingly checked each manuscript for style and coherence and whose editorial skills were invaluable. The preparation of the manuscript in final form could not have been accomplished without the skill and care provided by Ms. Margaret Lockwood and Ms. Christine Carrillo and her staff in the UCLA Communications Processing Center. As in the past, we are also indebted to Ms. Judith Takata for her fine graphics work. Finally, we would like to acknowledge Philip Altbach for his support throughout this project and for gently chiding us to at least attempt to keep to some publication schedule.

CONTENTS

LIST OF TABLES AND FIGURES

LIST OF ACRONYMS

APRA	American Revolutionary Popular Alliance (Peru)
BOAL	Basic Organization of Associated Labor (Yugoslavia)
CNE	Christian National Education (South Africa)
DES	Department of Education and Science (England)
GDP	Gross domestic product
INEP	Institut Nationale de Formacion Professionelle (National Institute of Professional Training, Haiti)
JCP	Japanese Communist party
JSP	Japanese Socialist party
KADU	Kenya African Democratic Union
KANU	Kenya African National Union
LEAs	Local Education Authorities (England)
MOE	Ministry of Education (Japan)
NEC	Nucleo Escolar Compesino (Peru)
SECPANE	Servicio Cooperativo Peruano-Norteamericano (Peruvian-North American Cooperative Service)
SSC	Secondary School Board Examination (India)
SIPRI	Stockholm International Peace Research Institute
UNESCO	United Nations Educational, Scientific and Cultural Organization

The Praeger Special Studies
Series in Comparative Education

General Editor: *Philip G. Altbach*

EDUCATION
AND INTERGROUP
RELATIONS

1

EDUCATIONAL POLICY ANALYSIS AND INTERGROUP RELATIONS: INTERNATIONAL AND COMPARATIVE ANALYSIS

Thomas J. La Belle
and Peter S. White

In many countries it has become increasingly common for educational planners, administrators, and practitioners to attend more carefully to the demands of ethnic, class, caste, and other minority or subordinate groups for increased access to and participation in schools. Schools are thought to be important institutions in this regard, as they are perceived by minority groups as vehicles of social mobility and cultural identity and as enabling individuals and groups to become involved in new ways in the wider society. From the dominant group's perspective, schools are also important because they are one of the principal mechanisms that help to control and shape the nature of the relationship among groups and the rate of change in a given society. Our interest is in the educational policies of societies that are characterized as bi- or multiethnic. Specifically, this chapter presents a framework within which those policies can be discussed as aspects of broader governmental approaches to intergroup relations and societal integration.[1] The contributors to this volume were asked to test the framework in the preparation of their case studies with a view to its further development and utility.

We view policy as the need to make practical choices among conflicting alternatives for purposes of optimizing outcomes. Hence policies emerge from both historical and empirical as well as technical and rational considerations and are basically political in nature; they must be analyzed in a specific social and cultural context. Although policy analysis

1

typically involves attention to policy formulation, adoption, implementation, and outcomes, this chapter will address only the area between adoption and implementation; that is, we will examine policy as it is expressed through legal codes, guidelines, regulations, and the like.[2]

The somewhat limited focus we have set is the result of the need to conceptualize in a tentative but manageable way the area of educational policy analysis relative to intergroup relations. It is a task that has yet to be done at any level, as Paulston has noted.[3] In effect, we are attempting to present here an analysis of education and intergroup relations that will establish a research agenda for the gathering of more extensive empirical data rather than attempting to synthesize all that is presently known about the effects of educational policies on intergroup relations. This enables us to concentrate on a nation's or group's statements of intent and the social groups that advocate particular points of view and participate in making decisions. As will be noted in the discussion that follows, policy in a multiethnic society cannot, by definition, involve one group alone. Hence we point to the need to take into account the needs and interests characteristic of each group that is party to the relationship, and the role and function of the school as a principal institution within which intergroup relations are manifested.

Because all societies are characterized by forms of vertical and horizontal segmentation, social groups emerge that function as frames of reference for members of each society. These societal groupings are based on both cultural and structural attributes. Cultural segments are often referred to as ethnic groups in that they represent an attributed or self-proclaimed identity that involves certain religious, linguistic, or other collective symbols or representations.[4] Structural groups, on the other hand, are often referred to as social classes or castes, as they are based on the group's relative access to or possession of political and economic power or resources. Here the focus is on the relationships among these groups in areas of government, education, occupation, and so on.

We will use the terms "dominant" and "superordinate" to signify "that collectivity within a society which has preeminent authority to function both as guardians and sustainers of the controlling value system, and as prime allocators of rewards in the society."[5] "Subordinate" will be used to indicate those groups that lack such authority. As societies sort out their social groups into superordinate and subordinate positions based on cultural, political, and economic characteristics, the result is a differential form of societal participation in accord with cultural and structural group membership.

How these various groups interact within the boundaries of a single society or political entity is referred to as integration. Drawing on Schermerhorn, we emphasize the dynamic nature of integration; it is not a state of being, but rather "a process whereby units or elements of a society are brought into an active and coordinated compliance with ongoing activities and objectives of the dominant group in that society."[6]

Although Schermerhorn rightfully accords a great importance to the active role of a society's subordinate groups, we maintain that within our focus on policy expression, rather than policy outcomes, it is in fact the respective superordinate or dominant group that deserves primary attention. It is this group in the society that sets the integrative agenda, so to speak, determining the desirable long-range goals for the subordinate group(s) as well as for itself. As such, policy statements and policy implementation, even in a multigroup setting, are virtually the monopoly of the superordinate group alone.

Our interest, then, is in how one particular social institution -- formal education -- functions in this process of integration in societies with different patterns of segmentation along cultural and structural lines. By examining superordinate approaches to integration in a variety of settings, we hope to introduce a greater contextual sensitivity to the discussion of education vis-a-vis subordinate or minority groups. That is, we expect to show how the same policy -- whether bilingual education, vocational training, separate facilities, and so forth -- may well have very different implications according to the particular structural and cultural relationship between two or more given groups.

We see the process of integration as consisting of two interrelated aspects. The first is suggested by Schermerhorn's paired concept of centripetal and centrifugal tendencies. A centripetal tendency refers to a group's cultural and structural trends toward common, society-wide lifestyles and institutional participation, whereas a centrifugal tendency would manifest itself in a group's attempts to retain and preserve unique cultural attributes as well as to seek greater autonomy politically and economically. When the superordinates and subordinates share a tendency, whether centripetal or centrifugal, Schermerhorn indicates that an agreed-upon form of integration is likely to take place. If the tendencies differ -- one group seeking closer ties and the other seeking autonomy, for example -- the integrative process is likely to be conflictual in nature. It is the tendency of <u>both</u> groups -- the congruence or difference of aims -- that must be taken into account.

Building on Schermerhorn's outline, we would suggest that a group's centripetal or centrifugal tendencies be discussed not in overall terms but rather in the group's separate structural and cultural interests. In our educational analysis, this permits us to account for what often appear to be contradictory trends in the superordinate group's stance vis-a-vis educational policies. A policy of cultural centrifugality might, for example, encourage each group's language to be used as the instructional idiom at the local level. Simultaneously, however, the standards for proceeding through the educational system and the mechanisms for decision making might be quite uniform and centrally coordinated or controlled. This latter policy would be an example of structural centripetality, as the desire of the superordinate group would be to incorporate the school and its participants into the nation-state's economic and political spheres. It is possible, then, to have both centripetal and centrifugal policies present in the same educational system and for each tendency to have identifiably separate structural and cultural aspects. Although such dual orientations may or may not be seen as contradictory by policymakers, for analytical purposes it is well to remember that they do exist simultaneously.

Because all societies use education to some extent for the centripetal purposes of ensuring the survival of the nation-state, they can be said to be acculturating ethnic or other population groups. Acculturation is used here in a distinct way from the concept of assimilation. Assimilation refers to a process that is dependent on a positive orientation by both groups toward one another.[7] Hence, whereas acculturation does not require out-group acceptance, assimilation requires an identification with the out-group.[8]

In addition to centripetal and centrifugal tendencies, we suggest that the process of integration has a second aspect, one that we call "integrative mechanisms." These are the general approaches employed by superordinate groups to implement their definition of societal integration. The three mechanisms we have found applicable to intergroup relations are coercion, consensus, and interdependence. Like the centripetal/centrifugal tendencies, more than one of these mechanisms may be employed in a single intergroup relationship; one mechanism may be preferred for structural relationships within the society, whereas another mechanism is favored for purposes of cultural relations.

Coercion will be used here to describe superordinate actions that rely on the application of military or police forces or nonconsensual economic, social, or political pressures for their implementation. Such action may be either centripetal or centrifugal in intent. Coercion usually takes place in cases where the ethnic groups or social classes are oriented to the attainment of incompatible or mutually exclusive goals.[9]

A second integrative mechanism employed by superordinate groups is the establishment of consensus among all the various groups into which the society is divided. Consensus is often seen as the natural outcome of a set of values -- cultural, economic, political -- that is held in common by two or more groups.[10] Like coercion, consensus can be centrifugal as well as centripetal. As one example, culturally distinct groups could share a set of political or economic values, say socialism, that would contribute little to intergroup consensus on cultural-policy matters but that would facilitate societal integration at the structural level.

Interdependence, the third integrative mechanism, is somewhat wider in its utility to superordinate groups than is consensus. It is essentially a structural relationship in which groups or segments of those groups function within a common network of economic and social order -- factory work, marketplaces, and so forth -- without necessarily sharing any cultural or political values[11] or without agreeing upon the fairness of the network itself. As such, interdependence for integration may be equally applicable across a whole range of structural relationships, from those of sharp inequality between groups to those where groups are equal in power and thus more jealous of their cultural prerogatives.

From this perspective, education is not, of itself, an integrative mechanism in the relations among ethnic, social, and other groups in segmented societies. Instead, schools are one institution through which those mechanisms take concrete form. Similarly, schools cannot automatically be assumed to be agents of subordinate group assimilation within the superordinate system. As we have suggested, superordinate groups are as likely to employ education for centrifugal purposes as for centripetal ones; indeed, acculturation rather than assimilation appears to be a more common strategy even where centripetal tendencies are the mode. Hence our attention is on school policies as the expression, within particular relationships between groups, of the tendencies and mechanisms that shape societal integration in multigroup settings.

POLICY AREAS

Six areas of educational policy were chosen for more detailed examination, in part on the basis of our a priori assumptions as to their importance in integrative efforts and in part on their recurrence in our review of descriptions of schooling in multigroup societies. The first area is that of the relative centralization of a society's school system.

One dimension of centralization is the extent to which the state controls the right to education; another dimension is the extent to which the central government, rather than local or regional authorities, exercises that right. The second policy area, access to education, consists of the pattern of initial enrollment in schools (What are the opportunities and facilities for the various groups to get their children onto the first rung of formal education?), the internal processes of schooling that aid or hinder the advancement of different groups through school completion, and the nature of the facilities or barriers to advancement between levels of formal schooling.

The third area of interest in educational policy is articulation and tracking. By articulation we mean a coordination and steady progression between the skills imparted on one level and those imparted on the next. In discussing tracking, we mean two things: one, the point in schools at which students in multigroup societies begin to follow highly specialized (for example, vocational) curricula, and, two, the degree to which those tracks, whether academic or vocational/technical, are permeable. That is, can students switch tracks, and if so, until what point?

The fourth policy area, curriculum, includes all regulations governing the content of particular courses of study or of levels of schooling in general. The fifth area, personnel, refers to the policies that detail the recruitment, training, selection, and placement of teachers and administrators. Our interest here is in the extent to which personnel policies reinforce (or, conversely, break down) the cultural and structural bounds between groups. Finally, language policies are those regulations that govern the selection and use of the media of instruction and materials for the schools.

In sum, we have said that our interest is in analyzing the contribution of formal education to cultural and structural integration in societies composed of distinct ethnic and social groups. Such an analysis involves the bipolar concepts of centripetal and centrifugal orientations as held by superordinate populations and as manifested in educational policies. Within each orientation, a distinction can be drawn between cultural and structural attributes, and we point to the integrative possibilities of the acculturation, as opposed to the full assimilation, of subordinate populations.

Hence it is our intention to emphasize the simultaneous existence of centripetal and centrifugal tendencies in multi-group societies even though the overall thrust in a given society may be toward either. We have assumed this position based on an analysis of educational programs in several societies where centripetality through imposed acculturation for consensus at higher levels of society is often accompanied by centrifugal tendencies toward cultural autonomy at other levels. Such an approach also enables us to employ a combination of consensus and conflict analyses irrespective of the particular societal configuration encountered.

A TYPOLOGY OF INTERGROUP RELATIONS

In the analysis of formal educational policies for intergroup relations, we were faced with the need to develop a heuristic typology of societies based in part on the concepts outlined above. Even though our interest is with educational policies rather than with differentiating among types of intergroup relation per se, it was necessary that we attempt to account for the wide between-country variation that we observed in educational policies as they related to majority/minority or subordinate/superordinate relations. A policy indicating a centrifugal tendency in one intergroup context, for example, often enough indicated centripetality elsewhere.

In the construction of a workable typology of intergroup relations, our approach has been to generate inductively the typology from societal case studies taken primarily from the literature. Our two principal variables were referred to earlier as structural and cultural characteristics of societal segmentation. Culture refers to collective symbols as well as the rules by which the system operates, and structure refers to the mode of participation characteristic of a particular population, especially the group's access to decision making and to economic resources.

The typology that we propose here extends to how group membership affects socioeconomic roles, the mode and level of participation in institution decision making, and the extent to which issues of cultural identity and values are associated with group boundaries. As with other typologies, these characteristics must be analyzed within a particular historical context where between-group transactions may be viewed across time. One axis of the typology is power as reflected in political and economic resources. The other axis is the culturally defined status and prestige that shape ethnic hierarchies as well as ethnic group boundaries (see Figure 1.1). Education is important in this cultural and structural interaction because it functions as a selection and sorting device for the dominant group, and it serves to maintain the system in its current state.

When the formal institution of education is viewed in this cultural and structural interface of societies characterized by differing patterns of intergroup relations, two principal areas emerge: the school's contribution to cultural and structural maintenance and the school's role in carrying out a society's selection process as it relates to social mobility. Insofar as both these functions serve to bring a society's subordinate groups into active compliance with the goals of the superordinate group, the school can be seen as serving an integrative role. These two aspects of the contribution of education to integration within different intergroup relationships can be observed in the six policy areas outlined previously: dimensions of centralization, access to schooling, articulation and tracking within and between levels of school, curriculum, the selection of school personnel, and the language of instruction adopted for classroom use. Following the description of the four intergroup types, we will draw on examples of specific policies to illustrate the utility of a typological approach to understanding the integrative role of education in multiethnic societies.

TYPE A: CULTURAL AND STRUCTURAL SEGMENTATION IN A VERTICAL RELATIONSHIP

Type A intergroup relations are characterized by two or more groups whose ethnic differences are highlighted and reinforced by the near monopoly of cultural prestige, political power, and economic power exercised by one group over the other group(s). This verticality in the groups' relations is particularly evident in the tacit (but in some cases explicit) mutual exclusivity in the society's system of role and functions. That is, the superordinate group fills the powerful and rewarding positions in the system with members of its own group and systematically assigns subordinate group members to society's lowest occupational and social positions. Superordinate members rarely, if ever, occupy low-status positions, and, conversely subordinate members may be legally or traditionally proscribed from holding positions in the upper echelons of society's structures.

FIGURE 1.1
Types of Intergroup Relations

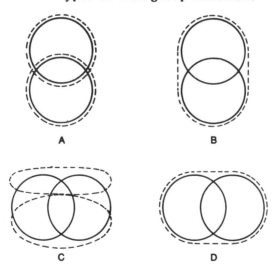

Type A: Cultural and structural segmentation in a vertical relationship. Type B: Cultural segmentation and structural commonality in a vertical relationship. Type C: Cultural and structural segmentation in a horizontal relationship. Type D: Cultural segmentation and structural commonality in a horizontal relationship. ——— indicates cultural boundaries; ----- indicates structural boundaries.

Under these conditions, ethnic diacritica assume special salience because they tend to become the overt criteria by which membership in socioeconomic strata, as well as cultural groups, is defined. Ethnicity and class, then, appear to be nearly congruent in type A situations. Congruence does not necessarily imply hermeticism, however, even where "race" or phenotype are among the important features of group identification. Moving from one group to another may be possible, albeit on an individual rather than group basis and on terms that demand assimilation rather than acculturation alone.

The relative permeability of between-group barriers, and by extension the role of educational policy in maintaining the barriers or promoting movement across them, can in large part be traced to the superordinate group's definition of appropriate societal integration. Given the strict verticality of a type A relationship, integration is likely to be interpreted narrowly. It could range from a simple crystalization of existing group differences to the selective absorption of relatively few individual subordinate group members into the superordinate sphere. In the case of simple crystallization, policies in both the cultural and structural realms tend toward centrifugality; the superordinate group seeks to keep the subordinate group(s) as distinct as possible. The promotion of local customs and languages is one type of cultural policy to further that end. In the case of selective absorption, a centripetal tendency in cultural policies (such as insistence on use of the superordinate language by all citizens) may be accompanied by centrifugality in structural matters (maintenance of traditional landholding patterns). This would allow for the kind of individual, rather than group, incorporation a superordinate group would find acceptable within a type A relationship. Clear examples of type A relationships can be found in Peru (Indian/non-Indian), Haiti (Creole/mulatto), and South African (black/white).

Type A relationships are not tranquil or stable by any means. The margination and rigid domination characteristic of type A ties frequently engender revolt and dissent on the part of the subordinate groups. Extralegal means are most often employed because the legal system of political expression is, like the superordinate occupational system, closed to the nonelites. Armed uprisings in highland Peru and rural Haiti have been recurrent phenomena in the history of those two countries, as have instances of black dissent and, more recently, open conflict in South Africa. Amidst this intergroup disparity and divisiveness, what are some of the general mechanisms by which superordinate groups attempt to impose their definition of integration and its attendant policies on subordinate groups in type A societies?

Maintenance of the status quo, which favors the superordinate group, usually requires the frequent application of coercive measures against the subordinate group. This make take the form of military coercion to counter the subordinate group's centrifugal structural tendencies (for example, demands for greater autonomy or even separation), as in the case of the blacks in South Africa or the land revolts in highland Peru. It can also manifest itself as political or economic pressure against the subordinate group's centripetal structural or cultural tendencies, that is, the group's efforts to join the superordinate society on a more equal footing. South African apartheid, the maintenance of traditional landholding patterns in Peru and Haiti, and the denigration of the Creole language in Haiti are all superordinate responses to the possibility of group-based changes (for example, upward mobility) in the social hierarchy.

As Schermerhorn points out, however, coercion alone cannot hold together a society indefinitely.[12] An alternative strategy has been to highlight, sometimes to the point of mythification, the very real, albeit unequal, political, economic, and social interdependence that binds the groups together in one society. That is, the superordinate group actively points out the beneficial aspects of the status quo for the subordinate group(s) and, in turn, acknowledges (in part) the contribution that group(s) makes to the nation. South Africa has, in fact, made the interdependence approach the official policy in its "homelands" strategy of separate but closely cooperating "nations" based on race and ethnicity within the present borders of the country.

A second noncoercive strategy of forging internal unity in type A relationships has been a reliance on consensus building. Building consensus through intergroup agreement on specific issues is difficult and usually of short duration in type A relationships because of the inherently one-sided nature of the benefits to be distributed. First, the "agreement" is usually issued unilaterally by the superordinate group, albeit with some consideration of the subordinate group's demands. Second, the agreement or consensus eventually breaks down because it is tailored to fit the needs of the superordinate group. The limited extension of lower-level urban employment opportunities to blacks in South Africa and the job ceiling encountered there point to the short life expectancy of specific ameliorate reforms aimed at consensus building in type A relationships.

TYPE B: CULTURAL SEGMENTATION AND STRUCTURAL COMMONALITY IN A VERTICAL RELATIONSHIP

Intergroup relations characterized as type B involve two or more distinct ethnic groups, one of which is clearly dominant politically and/or economically and whose traits tend to be used as the criteria against which all societal behaviors are judged. The nature and extend of an individual's participation in society, then, differ in accord with group membership. In contradistinction to a type A relationship, however, ethnic group diacritica in type B are not hermetic in the sense that they do not simultaneously prescribe a closed set of low-status occupations appropriate to subordinate group members. Occupation or role per se is not one of the salient distinguishing features of ethnic group membership, and the nature of socioeconomic participation is not completely congruent with ethnic group boundaries.

Although most of society's low-status positions are, in fact, filled by members of the subordinate ethnic group(s), they can also be occupied by members of the superordinate group. Similarly, access to roles at the top of the hierarchy in a type B situation is open to some subordinate group individuals, albeit with a greater expectation that these individuals will adopt at least some of the ethnic-related as well as class-related value orientations of the dominant group. In short, type B situations are more permeable than are type A, but there is still a superordinate group that can be expected to protect its prerogatives. Under these conditions, societal integration as a strategy of the superordinate group vis-a-vis the subordinate group rests primarily on the extension of relative benefits within the existing occupational and role structure; the underlying assumption is that the economic system's cross-group inclusiveness provides sufficient structural access to all society members.

The policies adopted by the superordinate group to bring about integration in a type B context are essentially centripetal in their intent. In the cultural realm, emphasis is on the superordinate group as a society-wide model, for example, exclusive use of the superordinate language and a concomitant silence on the subordinate group's experience or culture. Where the subordinate culture is recognized, it may be only in a historical or folkloric manner, or it may be used as a "bridge" to the approved culture. Certain types of bilingual education or multicultural curricula in the schools fall into this latter category. Structural policies in type B contexts are likewise centripetal in their overall tendency. If only to maintain the status quo, the superordinate group attempts to incorporate others into the prevailing economic and institutional system and in doing so often acts to eliminate any vestiges of autonomous subordinate group activities.

The general tendency toward centripetality, however, does not contradict the existence of other policies that reinforce the association between ethnic group membership and occupational status. Education is clearly an area in which the overall trend can be centripetal and inclusionary (for example, universal enrollment of training for modern sector jobs) and yet in which particular policies (rising educational requirements for higher positions) can effectively limit the extent to which the centripetal trend functions for the subordinate group as a whole.

Although intergroup relations in most countries can be broadly characterized as type B, particular illustrations include the Burakumin in Japan, the Maori in New Zealand, and the West Indians in Great Britain. Each provides clear ethnic and other distinctions between the groups and each offers incomplete congruence between group membership and role in the structural system. Whereas type A role relationships are clearly differentiated and divided along ethnic lines with little immediate prospects for change, the socioeconomic participation by subordinate group members in type B relationships provides some evidence of potential social mobility. This more open system manifests itself in school policies, where at least token steps are often taken to increase equality of opportunity in and through the educational system.

Central to the type B situation, then, is the relatively greater permeability in the lines between groups. Structurally, this is manifested in the subordinate ethnic group's access, albeit limited, to higher status positions in the society -- a sharp contrast with the virtual subordinate enclosure characteristic of type A. It is not uncommon for some superordinate group members in type B situations to share the low-status positions occupied by most subordinate group members, thus introducing social class as an important modifier of ethnic diacritica in the allocation of positions within the type B society. Even so, the movement is typically from the lower group toward the upper rather than an equal movement between groups. This is most evident in Japan, where the between-group permeability implies access of the Burakumin to nontraditional positions such as factory work but not the employment of non-Buraku in the tanning, butchering, and other trades considered beyond the pale. In Britain the one-way permeability is less obvious because of the blacks' recent immigrant origin. They move directly into the lower and middle positions (manual labor and industry) long occupied by British workers; there is no countermovement, as such, if only because the subordinate group has no particular structural area with which it has been historically identified.

In type B relationships this centripetal tendency -- that is, toward structural incorporation of subordinate groups -- highlights the importance of consensus building as a strategy of societal integration. Consensus relies on a tacit between-group agreement on the societal goals pursued by the superordinate group, an agreement facilitated in type B contexts by government policies and social structures that appear to hold out the possibility of eventual equality and enhanced social and economic status for the subordinate ethnic group. Although the provision of social services (health, education, and so on) has a distinctly paternalistic flavor where, as in type B, the relationship between groups is vertical, such actions further reinforce the perceived legitimacy of the dominant group.

The emphasis on building consensus between groups, usually on terms set by the dominant partner in the relationship, is apparent in the centripetal tendency of cultural policies in all three of the type B relationships examined here. At most, official policies ignore the subordinate cultures; there may be no move to suppress them but neither is there support for their maintenance. New Zealand is an occasional exception to this pattern -- occasional in the sense that the dominant policy has alternated between complete assimilation of the Maori into the Pakeha/European culture and support for the Maori's unique cultural attributes.

Intergroup relations of the type represented by Japan, Britain, and New Zealand imply a definition of societal integration predicated on the ultimate absorption of the subordinate population into the structural and cultural system of the superordinate group. The relative stability of these relations over time, and their maintenance by strategies other than coercion, are due in no small part to the size of the superordinate group as well as its firm control of practically all the important levers of social control. More important, however, are the openings to some of the benefits of the dominant group, whether as a result of unintended forces in the society (urbanization and industrialization) or as a result of policies of the dominant group itself. At the same time, we have noted that Maori, Burakumin, and West Indians remain as distinct ethnic groups that occupy predominantly lower-status positions in their respective societies. In part, this can be traced to resistance in the nonofficial sector: hiring practices, discriminatory housing patterns, racial prejudice, and so forth.

TYPE C: CULTURAL AND STRUCTURAL
SEGMENTATION IN A HORIZONTAL RELATIONSHIP

Intergroup relations that we classify as type C are somewhat more complex than either type A or type B, largely due to the importance of both vertical and horizontal lines between groups. That is, the two or more groups can be distinguished on the basis of differences in ethnic and cultural attributes, but no one group enjoys a monopoly of political or economic power or cultural and social prestige. This is not to imply that the various ethnic groups are necessarily equal in all dimensions of between-group influence or that the groups are perfectly balanced demographically or in their geographic extension. Nevertheless, enough balances are present in the relationship -- whether historical, cultural, or geographic -- to characterize it as horizontal, even where one group may be ascendant in several aspects of societal activity. The ascendant group, if indeed there is one, is simply not so powerful as to be able to impose its will completely on the other groups.

The between-group cultural differences are commonly accompanied by a separation of the groups by residence and by the roles they occupy in society. This separation can go as far as self-imposed segregation, but more often it resembles a kind of parallelism; groups may reside in different parts of the same urban area, for example, and occupy structurally interrelated and socially equivalent, but clearly distinct, positions in the economy.

It is not the ethnic and residential patterns or rough horizontality in these relationships, however, that separate them from others in our typology. Instead, it is the sharp distinctions along caste and class lines within each group -- cutting across the ethnic differences -- that give the type C situation its unique features. In this regard there is a tendency toward an elite-mass bifurcation in the society as a whole that places the upper socioeconomic strata of each ethnic group together for purposes of political and economic control. Because these class and caste lines cut across the ethnic groups, both the upper and lower strata retain their cultural and linguistic identities. This suggests that the ways in which the groups participate socioeconomically may be only weakly associated with their ethnic group membership per se. That is, the elites of each group can maintain their culture-based differences while participating in a common web of roles and relationships with other elites. The respective masses of the different groups may likewise participate in a common set of roles that cuts across ethnic lines, or each may have roles more related to its ethnic group identity. In either case, the roles and occupations of the lower strata are less prestigious and attract fewer socioeconomic benefits.

The integration of a society characterized by type C intergroup relations is, like the society itself, a delicate balance of group and class/caste interests. The cultural or ethnic heterogeneity of the superordinate socioeconomic group and the variability in the extent to which the subordinate groups are structurally differentiated from each other allow for a range of integrative strategies and group tendencies in type C contexts, especially as regards structural policies. Depending on other factors specific to each case, it may be in the interests of the elites to promote a centripetality in which subordinates, regardless of ethnic group membership, are brought into greater occupational uniformity among themselves, for example, urban industrial positions. Under other conditions -- perhaps where the elites are more contentious or less sure of their own hold on society -- integration would be defined as the maintenance of any existing role differences between the subordinate sectors of the various ethnic groups. Increased occupational specification by ethnic groups would then allow for greater control by the respective elites and would make more difficult the development of cross-group commonalities or solidarity among the subordinates. A centrifugal structural tendency of this sort, coupled with the given cultural differences between groups, would approximate a dynamic description of Furnivall's plural society.[13]

It is in the area of cultural policies that we would expect to find a greater uniformity among cases of type C relationships, due largely to the rough equivalence or balance that exists among a type C society's component ethnic groups. No one group is so powerful, or its prerogatives so attractive, as to successfully impose its own ways as a model for other groups. Instead, there is an agreement, whether tacit or explicit (and not uncommonly won only after much conflict), to allow the various ethnic groups relative autonomy in perpetuating themselves and their unique identities. Within each group and across the society as a whole, however, there is an unstated class-based centripetality in action; the sharp differences between elites and masses are commonly reflected in a bias toward the elites' standards of culture, language, dress, religion, and so forth, and educational policies in these areas assume that an assimilation to elite perspectives (if not elite position) is the ultimate goal.

In some respects each of our type C cases -- Malaysia, India, and Kenya -- leans toward one or another of the other types in our framework. Yet their greater complexity relative to other types of relationships outlined here, and their horizontal rather than strictly vertical coordination, clearly set them apart from type A or type B. Nowhere in type C is there the one-group hegemony seen in Peru, Haiti, Britain, Japan, and elsewhere. Nor do the ethnic groups in the type C examples exhibit the same degree of internal cultural and structural homogeneity that is broadly characteristic of the major groups in the other types. In short, type C is more extensive and more open perhaps to conceptual ratification than the other types we have offered to this point. For that reason, rather than despite it, type C stands as a separate and unique set of relationships within this framework.

Mechanisms for societal integration in type C relationships appear to vary according to the elite group's socioeconomic emphasis on structural and cultural centripetality. In Kenya, where there is extreme official aversion to the recognition of ethnic differences and a continuous effort to ignore them institutionally, consensus building is the most prominent strategy. Rival ethnic-based political movements have been absorbed into the ruling Kenya African National Union, while regional government -- a potential locus of ethnic power -- has been virtually stripped of authority. At the same time, the elites have agreed to pass over local (group-specific) languages in favor of two nonindigenous languages -- English and Swahili -- for all official purposes except minor local transactions. The interelite cooperation has "beheaded" any ethnic-based separatist moves and thus obviated the need for open coercion. The tendency in Kenyan integration is clearly centripetal and is toward an elite-centered version of a transethnic and essentially urban Kenya.

Malaysian integration is also very centripetal, but opposition to it among the masses of the Indian and Chinese groups has forced the governing elite, predominantly Malayan, to resort to coercion as the principal integrative mechanism. Opposition has also generated a second, more conciliatory response: a cultivation of existing ties of interdependence. Because the Chinese still control the urban economy of Malaysia, the Malaysian elite has had to grant certain concessions, for example, continued control of ethnic-specific education, in order to retain the support of the Chinese leadership. It is interdependence, in fact, that we would expect to see in a case such as Malaysia; it is a mechanism that, more than others, implicitly recognizes some degree of both autonomy and balance among the groups.

India, in contrast, appears to rely on a strategy of interdependence to promote national integration. The size of the society's component ethnic groups, their long history in the Indian subcontinent, and their concentration in specific geographic areas all work against any attempt at consensus as the principal integrative mode. As such, the contributions of all ethnic groups and all social classes are highlighted as evidence of a unified nation. Ironically, the most recent instance of India's fairly rare use of open coercion for integration was in response to a centripetal tendency among outcaste groups; their efforts to gain recognition at the university level met with violent elite group reaction.

TYPE D: CULTURAL SEGMENTATION AND STRUCTURAL COMMONALITY IN A HORIZONTAL RELATIONSHIP

We classify relations between groups as type D when they are characterized by two or more groups that are roughly equal in prestige, political power, and economic power and that participate in a single structural system of roles and positions. The equality may best be thought of as a balance between the groups rather than a strict parity in each aspect of national life. One group may well control much of the political apparatus, and another group predominates in business, trade, industry, or agriculture. Nor do all groups necessarily enjoy equal historical or cultural prestige within the country; like political and economic power, prestige is one dimension among several in the intergroup balance. The important consideration is that no one group is ascendant in all areas; every group has enough leverage in at least one dimension to be able to modify or veto substantially the initiatives of the other group(s). It should be pointed out that the balance among groups that characterizes type D situations is rarely a direct function of demographics; rather, large imbalances commonly exist between the size of one group and the size of the other(s).

Interestingly, although the equality of the groups and the inclusive structural system would suggest a high degree of between-group permeability, in a type D relationship we find instead relative stability in group size and membership. With no one ethnic group stigmatized or perceived as completely subordinate, there is little if any incentive to cross group lines. The possible advantages of assimilation to another group are usually offset by disadvantages in abandoning one's own group. Participation in a particular sphere of national life, for example, urban industry, may be correlated with membership in a particular ethnic group, but entry to that sphere by members of other groups is not predicated on a change in ethnicity or group identity.

This structural permeability, and its independence from a need for a concommitant cultural permeability, are in part an outgrowth of the unitary role system characteristic of type D relations. In most cases the system is essentially industrial, with related activities (agriculture, commerce, and so forth) that are closely tied to industry and the industrial urban centers. There are no autonomous, self-sufficient economic sectors that serve as group-specific enclaves or "internal colonies." The mutual dependence is such that members of all groups are drawn, although not always proportionately, into nearly all the society's various activities.

The complexity of centrifugal forces is evident in our examples of type D countries. In Yugoslavia, for example, there is a strong sense of between-group cultural differentiation attributable in part to distinct political-historical development and to differences in rates and types of economic development. This subjective basis for between-group differentiation can be seen in the two major languages (Serbian and Croatian), which are very similar except in their alphabets, and where even religious bonds between groups (for example, Croatians and Slovenes) do little to diminish the sense of distinctiveness. In Yugoslavia the centrifugality is moderated by strong ideologically based commitments to national unity (a structural unity rather than a cultural assimilation or amalgamation) held by the ethnic group or groups that are numerically predominant and/or in a more powerful economic or political position.

In Belgium, there are complications of a long-term shift in demographic and economic power from the Walloons to the Flemish and the links of one group -- the Walloons -- to a language and culture of wider European and world prestige. Switzerland presents the same general picture of different historical-political development for each group, but with language lines (as in Belgium) sharply drawn. Here, however, each group is linked to a wider European language and cultural community.

The centripetal tendencies are somewhat weaker in Belgium, as neither of the two major groups is identified with a specific centralizing ideology, nor, at the present, do either have sufficient power (economic or political) to impose effectively an entirely satisfactory model on the other. Unlike Yugoslavia, where certain ethnic groups have long been more powerful than the others, in Belgium there is a shift in progress, from the predominance of the Walloons to that of the Flemish. As a consequence, former centripetal tendencies in Wallonia have shifted to centrifugal ones, whereas the opposite has occurred in Flanders.

Type D relationships rely on both political and economic interdependence to maintain internal cohesiveness. The political interdependence is evident in varying degrees of government decentralization, with factors of size or location allowing the smaller group(s) in the union to protest or even disrupt the unacceptably centralizing aspirations of the union's larger group(s). The experience of the Croats in Yugoslavia and the Walloons in Belgium seems to bear out the crucial role played by the power of the smaller group(s) in defining the working relationship between groups. The power of the larger group(s), on the other hand, may be the important variable in setting the overall goals of the relationship, for example, political union and defense against external forces.

In the European type D countries, patterns of industrialization and cross-group migration for jobs serve to strengthen the interdependence of the ethnically defined groups and to put that relationship on an economic as well as political footing. Such patterns also serve to exacerbate latent intergroup rivalries, as one region or one ethnic group (usually the larger) often appears to be benefiting excessively from government or private sector policies, whereas the other region(s) and ethnic group(s) -- typically the smaller -- add economic deprivation to long-standing complaints of political domination. Belgium and Yugoslavia are prime examples of this dynamic.

There are two important facets of economic interdependence in type D societies. One, the national economy itself is fairly well integrated and coextensive with the society itself. That is, there are few if any economic units or activities that operate in isolation from the wider economy's system of supply, demand, and control (for example, subsistence farming). In European countries of the type D model, this integration is, as we have noted, part of an advanced state of industrialization and, in Yugoslavia, state-supervised agricultural production.

The second important facet of economic interdependence in type D societies is the participation of members of all ethnic groups in virtually all aspects of the economy as a whole. That is, occupational categories are not defined by ethnicity. Although one group may be more heavily represented in one or more sectors (such as the Croats in Yugoslav industry, the Macedonians in Yugoslav agriculture, and the Serbs in Yugoslav bureaucracy), we find a good deal of cross-ethnic recruitment, which makes these economic sectors relatively permeable. It is usually a process that can be directly sponsored by the government in the interests of intergroup balance.

These four types of intergroup relations form the basis for the remainder of the chapters in this volume. Each was written with the preceding framework in mind, and each deals with education and intergroup relations in one of the countries mentioned here. As indicated earlier, authors were asked to test both the viability of the framework and the placement of a given country in a particular intergroup relations type.

The goal has been to consider the issue of education and intergroup relations in both a comparative and an international perspective, thereby highlighting common educational policy issues in different cultural and structural contexts. The concluding chapter highlights the various concerns raised by the authors and makes further specific remarks regarding both the framework and the countries studied.

NOTES

1. This article is based on Thomas J. La Belle and Peter S. White, "Education and Multiethnic Integration: An Intergroup Relations Typology," Pt. 1, Comparative Education Review 24, no. 2 (June 1980): 155-73.

2. A complete analysis of these policy categories falls outside the range of our discussion here. Treating all policy-related concerns, especially from a cross-national perspective, would entail a book, or two, rather than one chapter; more importantly, we doubt that such a treatment would significantly contribute to the type of general framework we propose.

3. R. Paulston, "Ethnicity and Educational Change: A Priority for Comparative Education," Comparative Education Review 20, no. 3 (October 1976):269-80.

4. Schermerhorn describes an ethnic group as "a collectivity within a larger society having real or putative common ancestry, memories of a shared historical past, and a cultural focus on one or more symbolic elements defined as the epitome of their peoplehood." See R. A. Schermerhorn, Comparative Ethnic Relations (New York: Random House, 1970), p. 12. These characteristics may be entirely self-ascribed by the collectivity itself, regardless of how other societal groups perceive them; the traits are not necessarily objective. Conversely, socially significant diacritica may be assigned to the collectivity by others, regardless of the validity of such purported characteristics to the referent group itself.

5. Ibid., pp. 12-13.

6. Ibid., p. 14.

7. R. Teske, Jr., and B. Nelson, "Acculturation and Assimilation: A Clarification," American Ethnologist 2 (1974):351-68.

8. This distinction is an important qualifier to Schermerhorn's model, as he seemingly employs the term "assimilation" to address both processes. In fact, however, it is best to view the centripetal tendencies of both the superordinate group and

the subordinate group as either assimilation or acculturation. That is, subordinate group members may acculturate to the superordinate system in that they are able to adapt to its demands and function in its roles without necessarily abandoning their own distinct cultural identity. Assimilation, in contrast, requires that the acculturation be accompanied by an adoption of the superordinate value and identity systems and that the superordinate group approve that adoption. Both acculturation and assimilation are centripetal in nature but distinct in their implications for integration in a multigroup setting. As we suggest later in a review of specific examples of intergroup relations, there are relatively few instances where we are able to discern educational policies that are used for assimilative purposes. Instead, the emphasis is more commonly on legitimizing the nation-state, a process that to us is akin to acculturation rather than assimilation.

9. F. Barth and D. Noel, "Conceptual Frameworks for the Analysis of Race Relations: An Evaluation," <u>Social Forces</u> 50 (March 1972): 333-48.

10. Ibid.

11. R. Paulston, <u>Conflicting Theories of Social and Educational Change: A Typological Review</u> (Pittsburgh: University of Pittsburgh Press, 1976).

12. Schermerhorn, <u>Comparative Ethnic Relations.</u>

13. J. S. Furnivall, <u>Colonial Policy and Practice: A Comparative Study of Burma and Netherlands India</u> (Cambridge, Mass.: Harvard University Press, 1948).

PART I

CULTURAL AND STRUCTURAL SEGMENTATION IN A VERTICAL RELATIONSHIP

2

SEPARATE AND UNEQUAL:
A DISCUSSION OF
THE BANTU EDUCATION ACT,
1953 AND BEYOND

M.E. Kinberg

We are our history. Possibly in no other country is that statement as true as it is in South Africa. Thus, to apply to South Africa the concepts of intergroup topology in the examination of education and multiethnic integration as posited by La Belle and White, a brief recounting of the country's history is essential.

The first European settlers, 90 Dutchmen sent out by the Dutch East India Company to provide a "victualling station" for its ships in the Far East trade, landed at the Cape of Good Hope on the southern tip of Africa in 1652. They were met by the nomadic Hottentots and the remnants of the Bushmen tribe. These first negative experiences of contact with the indigenous peoples have persevered, in terms of the long-range effect of the Afrikaner's perception of the role to be played by nonwhites in the country's societal structure.

Far more formidable black tribes came down from the north to colonize the eastern half of what is today South Africa. These tribes, being farmers and cattle raisers as well as hunters, had a more complex social and political structure. They possessed iron weapons and tools and, in the case of the Zulu and Swazi tribes, were organized into chiefdoms and even kingships.

The apex of these black nations came during the reign of Shaku-Zulu, who, in the 1820s, was king of a domain larger in size than Napoleon's entire empire. And, until the 1880s, the black tribes were often a match for the combined British and

Boer (a name taken by the whites of Dutch descent) armies fielded against them.

But it was those first contacts with the Hottentots and Bushmen that remained paramount in the mythic mass culture of Afrikaners. They believed that their forebears had settled a vacant land, and they felt this made them as much natives as the blacks.

In terms of Schermerhorn's view of integration as "a process whereby units or elements of a society are brought into active and coordinated compliance with on-going activities and objectives of the dominant groups in that society," another facet of the historical equation that helps account for the confrontational nature of South African society today is the role played by the dominant Dutch Reformed church.[1] This church, which is almost exclusively Afrikaner, accepted, and to this day accepts, racial segregation as divinely ordained.

In the last part of the eighteenth century, the Dutch East India Company sickened and died. But by the time it did, its Cape station had become the base for Afrikaner expansion to the north. For a brief period of time, the 12,000 plus disputatious Afrikaners ruled themselves in freedom. The first British occupation followed in 1795. It had relatively little effect and eight years later was ended by the Treaty of Amiens. Four years later, in 1806, the British returned and recaptured the Cape, nominally from Napoleon's Dutch allies. The British takeover was seen as conquest by the Afrikaners. Thus for years to come and even up to the present time it served as one of the seeds sowing British-Dutch differences.

The Great Trek, which took place in the 1830s, is another major group memory of the Afrikaners. In part it was a response by Afrikaners to encroaching British rule, in part a natural movement north to new lands, much as the American settlers inexorably moved west. Hundreds and even thousands took part. They faced and fought the Zulu, the Matabele, the Sotho, and even tribes with treaty ties to the British.

The British agreed to Voortrekker demands for independence and recognized the Transvaal Republic in 1852 and the Orange Free State in 1854. This, in effect, began the division of South Africa into four provinces: Transvaal, Orange Free State, Cape, and Natal. The first two were predominantly Afrikaner; the latter two mainly English-speaking and more liberal in their outlook toward blacks.

In 1867, alluvial diamonds were found along the Orange and Vall rivers. The first diamond mines worked at Kimberley appeared three years later. In 1886, gold was discovered at the Witwatersrand. All three lucrative areas were in the Boer republics. The Afrikaners had fought and schemed to subjugate the black tribes in and along the borders of their country. Soon, to avoid the fate they had visited upon the blacks, they were to fight a war against the British.

The Boer War lasted from 1899 to 1902. Both sides fought bitterly, and the British created the world's first concentration camps to which entire Afrikaans families were moved. With Britain at that time near the zenith of its world power, the war's outcome was foreordained. The Boer defeat can be viewed as an early South African example of the La Belle-White integrative mechanism of coercion: "superordinate actions that rely on the application of military and police forces . . . for their implementation."[2] The discovery of mineral wealth also triggered the integrative mechanism described by La Belle-White as "interdependence . . . essentially a structural relationship in which groups or segments of those groups function within a common network of economic and social order -- factory work, marketplaces, and so forth -- without necessarily sharing any cultural or political values. . . ."[3]

The rapid growth of the diamond and gold industries, both before and after the Boer War, drew migrant black labor to the burgeoning towns of Kimberley and Johannesburg and to the mines that were making the white entrepreneurial class incredibly rich. This infusion of black labor was vital, and created a class of workers both migrant, with its roots in the tribal reserve, and also fully urbanized and "detribalized," living permanently in and around the cities and towns. The permanent African population, which soon numbered in the hundreds of thousands, tended to forego tribal customs and even tribal language in favor of becoming a new type of African with dependence on an urban, characteristically Western way of life. Nonetheless, they remained economically and politically disfranchised.

Here we see the creation of a dependent black population, best described by La Belle and White's description of interdependence, where the relationship between the groups is one of "sharp inequality." For the purposes of the discussion of South African black education in terms of the intergroup relations typology, it is important to remember that the disfranchisement happened in the late nineteenth and early twentieth centuries.

After a pause, for World War I, in the three-cornered (British, Afrikaner, black) strife, the fairly liberal regime -- for South Africa -- of Afrikaners Jan Smuts's and Louis Botha's South African party (ruling South Africa from 1910 to 1924) was succeeded by J. B. M. Hertzog's Nationalist party, formed in 1912 after he broke with Smuts and Botha. As the leader of the conservative Afrikaners, Hertzog concerned himself with preserving the group identity of his constituency, which he saw under attack by both blacks and the British. The dominant issue for Hertzog was institutionalizing ways in which the subordinate black majority "may be legally or traditionally proscribed from holding positions in the upper echelons of society's structure."[4]

White supremacy was bolstered by the Mines and Works Amendment Act (1926) that afforded sheltered employment for "poor whites" -- mainly Afrikaner -- in the state-controlled iron and steel industries, while excluding blacks from skilled jobs in the mines, and by the Native Administration Act (1927) that gave the executive wide powers over the individual. By 1933, when the effects of the world depression forced Hertzog into an alliance with Smuts, he succeeded in raising the Afrikaner to a position of political dominance and through it to near parity economically with the British.

These results are clearly representative of the second of Schermerhorn's "paired concepts" of centripetal and centrifugal tendencies in the integrative process. They are centrifugal in that they serve the superordinate (minority) group's efforts "to retain and preserve unique cultural attributes, as well as politically and economically to seek greater autonomy."[5] In the six years of the Smuts-Hertzog government, the increasingly superordinate Afrikaner minority sought to increase its power in parliament in order to reverse the flow into the cities of blacks from the land reserves granted them.

In Cape Province, the most liberal of all the country's provinces, Africans actually had the vote. In 1936, the Representation of Natives Act removed the Cape Province African voters from the common roll and limited them to three elected white members who were to represent them in the lower house; it also restricted Africans throughout the country to four elected white members to the senate. A Native Laws Amendment Act (1937) was aimed at preventing the influx of more Africans into the cities by making it mandatory for municipalities to segregate African and white residents. Thus with this act were born the townships -- those vast expanses of slum housing placed well away from the towns and cities from which black residents go out each day to work.

Other regulations and laws went further to create what La Belle and White describe as type A intergroup relations, characterized by "two or more groups whose differences along ethnic lines are highlighted and reinforced by the near monopoly of cultural prestige, political power, and economic power exercised by one group over the other group(s)."[6] As a result of the new edicts, in one year alone "500,000 Blacks were convicted of statutory and municipal offenses."[7]

Again, a war slowed the pace of segregation laws. This time, in World War II, there was far more opposition. In the war with Hitler's Germany, Smuts's motion to support Great Britain won by only 80 votes to 67. In 1943, Smuts was victorious in the elections, but the Nationalist party, now under the leadership of D. F. Malan, took all 43 of the opposition seats. As the war drew to a close, the Nationalists consolidated their position as the political instrument of Afrikanerdom.

The war hastened South Africa's economic expansion, an expansion in which the superordinate Afrikaner group participated to an increasing degree, causing the near disappearance of the "inferiority" of the Afrikaner to the English-speaking portion of the 4 million white population. But expansion brought into the cities the feared flood of blacks. By 1960, the census showed that more than 3.5 million blacks, nearly a third of the total black population, were located in the major cities and towns. They were enticed there by higher wages, which, while far inferior to whites', exceeded the income of rural blacks.

With the elimination at last of the centuries-old subordination of the Afrikaner to the British, the stage was set for the Nationalist party's ascendancy to power. One of the party's main preoccupations was the maintenance and escalation of legal barriers against the subordinate majority who desired closer ties, thereby creating an integrative process foreordained to be conflictual in nature.

As the 1948 election neared, even Smuts's verbal support of segregation was not enough to meet the challenge of the hardening line of Malan and the Nationalist party, which for the first time named and proposed a methodology for "apartheid." The election brought the Nationalist party back into power, a power increased in every election to date. True to its historically ingrained view of South African society as one in which "the superordinate group fills the powerful and rewarding positions in the system with members of its own group, while subordinate-group members are systematically assigned to the lowest occupational and social positions," the Nationalists turned "polite," de facto segregation into avowed, legalized "apartheid" through the passage of a pantheon of racial laws.[8] These included the population register fixing the racial category of every South African; the outlawing of marriages and unions out of wedlock between whites and nonwhites; the removal of "undesirable" blacks from towns by granting sweeping powers to officials; the buttressing of regulations reserving the more desirable jobs for whites; the partitioning of urban as well as rural areas into zones in which members of only one race can own or occupy property or conduct business; the "pass" law requiring all blacks to carry identity books; the enforcement of segregation not previously applied, as in buses, trains, post offices, libraries, motion picture houses, and theaters in the Cape Peninsula; and the removal of blacks from any meaningful representation in national or provincial legislatures.

Nowhere has this policy been more rigidly applied and enforced or more deeply felt than in the field of education. The "conflictual nature" of the South African educational process stems from the black subordinate majority's perception of the divergence of aims between it and the ruling white superordinate minority. Africans manifest a centrifugal tendency to maintain their cultural and ethnic heritage but not at the cost of losing changes for meaningful enhancement in industry, business, and the arts. Viewed in socioeconomic terms, that is the cost exacted by the Bantu Education acts passed by the Nationalist government.

The attention paid to education, and the nature of the laws passed to control black education, is influenced in part by the Christian National Education (CNE) movement, which enjoys a powerful influence within the Nationalist party and Afrikaner society. This is one aspect of the La Belle-White typology of intergroup relationships as it "attends to how group membership affects socioeconomic roles, the mode and level of participation in instructional decision making, and the extent to which issues of cultural identity and values are associated with group boundaries."[9]

The movement began in Holland in the middle of the nineteenth century. It first appeared in South Africa in 1876 as an effort by Afrikaners to protect themselves against the powerful influence of the English language and culture. In effect, the Afrikaners saw themselves as the subordinate group and the English-speaking whites as the superordinate group. Christian National Education was an expression of those Afrikaners to maintain centrifugal movement in terms of the integrative process by which groups interact.

As the "threat" of the English language and culture waned, the Christian National Education ethos was turned toward the question of education as a whole and, particularly, if one reads between the lines, education deemed suitable for the truly subordinate group of blacks.

In 1960, the CNE restated its policy in the following terms:

> In full preservation of the essential unity of history we believe that God . . . has willed separate nations and peoples, and has given to each nation and people its special calling and tasks and gifts. . . . We believe that next to the mother tongue, the national history of the people is the means of cultivating love of one's own. . . .[10]

As it relates to blacks, the policy statement called for promotion of "separate but equal" education. The old tribal customs were to be restored and, in the urban areas, resurrected, and as one of the ways to preserve and strengthen separateness, the use of tribal languages was to be enforced in education.

Again, the foregoing represents the viewpoint of only one of the two groups involved -- the Afrikaner superordinate group. The aims of the black subordinate group are best summed up by a black South African as

> a quest for integration into the democratic structure and institutions of our country . . . one of the most effective ways of achieving this is by education -- an education essentially in no way different from or inferior to that of other sections of the community.[11]

Thus, on the one hand, where education is concerned, there is the centrifugal tendencies of the white Afrikaner and, on the other hand, the centripetal tendendies of the black

African. The inevitable result is to cause "the integrative process to be conflictual in nature."[12] In terms of education the inevitable clash is vitally important to the cultural and structural interaction of two groups "because it functions as a selection and sorting device for the dominant group and along with other institutions serves to maintain the system in its current state."[13]

The clash was delayed not only because the Nationalist ascendancy into overwhelming power was not achieved until 1948 but also because, until the first of the educational apartheid laws was passed in 1948, African education in South Africa was mainly carried out through the church and its mission schools. As late as 1950, these schools numbered 5,213, with a total enrollment of 746,324 (approximately 40 percent of African children of primary and secondary school age). In 1951, 84.5 percent of all education for all blacks, Coloureds, and Asians was obtained through church schools.[14] A characteristic of the pre-1953 position was the multiplicity of schools and the widely varying approaches by the diverse religious denominations in control.

From the late 1940s there had been criticism from Afrikaners and Africans of the mission schools; the former felt the syllabus was too "bookish" and would result in "Africans whose views would not be in line with South African tradition and thought."[15] The Africans, although cognizant of the values of mission education for their children, were concerned about teacher shortage and uneven standards of education from one mission school to the next.

In the period (1953-59) during which the major legislation creating apartheid education was passed, for every European in South Africa there were five non-Europeans. Of this subordinate majority of non-Europeans, 84 percent were Africans. The results of the apartheid acts were summed up in the Institution of International Education Report No. 2:

The most fundamental feature of the South African educational system is that it is segregated into four racially distinct subsystems and that the three subsystems for nonwhites are grossly inferior to the one serving whites. The segregated character of the system is prescribed by South African law, and the inferior quality of black education is primarily attributable to the fact that the government short-changes it. Just a few statistics can sum up the consequences of this kind of discrimination. A white child has 100 times as much chance of becoming a university graduate as an African child; the government spends approximately 10 times as much money on each white school child as it does on each African pupil; 47.7 percent of white men have finished high school, while only 0.8 percent of African men have done so; although there are more than four times as many Africans as whites in South Africa, there are only 5,400 Africans who are university graduates, while the number of white graduates approaches 200,000.[16]

These facts and figures clearly indentify South African education as type A: cultural and structural segmentation in a vertical relationship where "policies in both the cultural and structural realm tend towards centrifugality, the superordinate group seeks to keep the subordinate group as distinct as possible."[17]

The movement by the Nationalist party to extend apartheid to education began in January 1949. Shortly after coming to power, Prime Minister Malan appointed a Commission on Native Education under the chairmanship of Dr. W. W. M. Eiselen. The first two terms of reference given to the commission were

(a) the formulation of the principles and aims of education for Natives as an independent race, in which their past and present, their inherent racial qualities, their distinctive characteristics and aptitude, and their needs under ever-changing social conditions are taken into consideration;

(b) the extent to which the existing primary, secondary and vocational education system for Natives and the training of Native teachers should be modified in respect of the content and form of the syllabuses in order to conform to the proposed principles and aims, and to prepare Natives more effectively for future occupation.[18]

The commission labored for nearly two years and reported back to parliament in 1951. Its detailed recommendations, one of which was that Bantu education should have a separate existence, created by the matrix by which the Bantu Education

Act of 1953 was formed. There were no black members on the commission, but Africans were allowed to be heard, and it was noted that their evidence "showed an extreme aversion to any education specially adapted for the Bantu."[19]

During parliamentary debate of the government's proposed Bantu Education Act, Dr. H. F. Verwoerd, minister of native affairs (later one of a succession of Nationalist prime ministers), stated that

> . . . good racial relations could not exist when education was given under the control of people who created wrong expectations among the Bantu. . . . (Bantu) education should have its roots entirely in the Native areas and in the Native environment and in the Native community. . . . The Bantu must be guided to serve his own community in all respects. . . . Education must train and teach people in accordance with their opportunities in life. In terms of the Government's plan for South Africa, there is no place for the Bantu in the European community above the level of certain forms of labor.[20]

The Bantu Education Act of 1953 dealt only with the very broad outlines of the new system. It was left to the responsible minister to make regulations covering all other matters. Main points of the act included the following: Control of black education was centralized by taking all responsibility and authority away from the four provincial administrations and giving it solely to the central government. It made it illegal for anyone to establish, conduct, or maintain a black school unless it had been registered with the central government authorities or exempted from registration by those authorities. Registration was to be at the discretion of the minister of native affairs, who might impose conditions on individual schools. If stipulated conditions were not complied with, registration could be canceled or if after an inquiry by the Bantu Affairs Commission the minister decided a school was not in the interests of the black people.

The minister was empowered to establish regional or local boards, or, alternatively, control might be entrusted to a Bantu authority. Any school board or commission might be disestablished if the minister deemed it expedient. The minister was given extremely wide powers to make regulations governing the control of schools, conditions of service for teachers, syllabuses, media of instruction, school funds, and many other matters.

The act and the ways in which it was implemented fall clearly into the type A vertical relationship, where the restrictions put on black education were the response of the superordinate group "to the possibility of group-based changes, for example, upward mobility, in the social hierarchy."[21]

Centralization of control, which in a different society could be seen as a centripetal tendency, is, in the case of South Africa, clearly centrifugal. The country is divided into four provinces. Until the centralizing process was begun under Prime Minister Malan and his successors, each province was allowed considerable home rule. It would not be too wide off the mark to compare them to the states of the United States. In their attitudes toward the black subordinate majority, the provinces tended to be shaped by their history, that is, the two "Afrikaner" provinces, which retained the old names of the Orange Free State and the Transvaal, were less liberal than the "English" Cape and Natal provinces.

We have seen that until parliamentary action in 1948, blacks and Coloureds in Cape Province were allowed a measure of political involvement unknown elsewhere in the country; it follows that the educational patterns for blacks in the two "English" provinces, and particularly the Cape, were equally liberal. Had the provincial administrations been allowed to retain control of education, the application on a nationwide basis of a standardized and politicized approach to African education would have been impossible.

La Belle and White cite six educational policy areas that are of interest "because of their recurring importance to societal integration" -- "(1) the degree of school centralization; (2) access to education; (3) articulation (coordination and progression between the skills imparted at one level in the school system to those imparted at the next) and tracking (assignment of specialized curricula and the degree to which tracks are permeable); (4) curriculum; (5) training, selection, and placement of teachers and administrators; and (6) language policies."[22] The degree of centralization and the sociopolitical reasons for it have already been dealt with here. In terms of the La Belle-White typology, this rigid centralization is certainly designed to make education function "as a selection and sorting device for the dominant group and along with other institutions serves to maintain the system in its current state."[23]

In the South African case, the language policy area, which was the symbolic focus of nationwide social unrest in 1976, can be considered the most critical of La Belle and White's six dimensions of education. Language policies have been the most divisive of all the reforms carried out under the Bantu Education Act. They are, by far, the clearest indication of Nationalist intent to pursue integration via what La Belle and White categorize as "interdependence . . . (which) may be equally applicable across a whole range of structural relationships, from those of sharp inequality between groups, to those where groups are equal in power and thus more jealous of their cultural prerogatives."[24]

In the case of South Africa, it is the first of the relationships that obtains -- sharp inequality. In my interview with George Palmer, former editor of the <u>Johannesburg Financial Mail</u>, he addressed the imposition of teaching in the black tribal languages as

being yet another example of education being used to further the Nationalist government's policy of race separation with the avowed intention of forcing the blacks to accept the open-end continuance of their subordinate role in the societal-economic structure of the country.

In a multiracial society like South Africa with a multiplicity of home languages, the spread and adoption of a common language would obviously improve communications between the various groups and remove one of the main barriers between them. . . . Since language differences can only heighten the perception of national and ethnic differences, and since the government's main tactic for ensuring the continued hegemony of the Afrikaner is by applying the principle of divide and rule, it was logical to expect the South African government to apply this to education and to adopt, as a first principle, separate education and language streams for the English, the Afrikaner and for each of the African groups as well as the Asian and the Coloured community.

The government clearly perceived the previous use of English as the lingua franca as a factor tending towards the adoption of common interests and common goals [the centripetal tendency] particularly political ones, among otherwise culturally fragmented groups.

Therefore one of the first steps was to switch to the black tribal languages as the media of instruction for blacks. There is an even deeper reason for the adoption of fragmented tribal languages: the identification of tribal members with their own groups and culture rather than with the culture of the white man since the greater the identification of black culture with the white, the more powerful the aspirations of the black to close the gap.[25]

Access to education, the second of La Belle and White's six points, represents a far more complex issue. Figures show that since implementation of the Bantu Education Act, a far higher percentage of black children have attended primary schools and matriculated into black high schools. This is especially true in the decade between 1971 and 1981.

In 1971 a total of 2,936,862 African children were attending school, but by 1981 this number had jumped to 5,083,307, representing an increase of 73.1 percent over the decade.[26] In 1970 only 9.42 percent of African children attending school were in secondary school, but by 1980 this proportion had reached 16 percent.[27] Although this growth in the proportion of high school students would seem to support the government's contention that its policies are intended to benefit the black population, deeper investigation raises serious doubts. "The growth is impressive, but the absolute numbers are much less so, in that relatively few students who enter the first year of school eventually finish Standard Ten."[28] Furthermore, as the number of candidates increased, the failure rate jumped. "In 1979, 73.5 percent of those sitting for the Senior Certificate exam passed while in 1980 and 1981 only 53 percent passed."[29]

South Africa's total population in 1980 was 27,319,980. Of these, 4,496,439 were whites, representing 16.46 percent of the total population. Africans totaled 19,471,630, or 71.27 percent of the total population. The remaining 3,351,920 were the Coloured and the even smaller Indian minorities.

In 1980, the government set up the De Lange Commission, a multiracial committee to investigate South African education. George Palmer feels that the 1981 report of the De Lange Committee on Education represented a revolution in educational policymaking in South Africa by recommending acceptance of the principle of equality as follows: "Principle I: Equal opportunities for education, including standards in education, for every inhabitant, irrespective of race, color, or sex, shall be the purposeful endeavour of the State." It also recommended "a single ministry of education . . . to effectively meet the need for a national education policy" aimed at "equal opportunity," "equal quality and standards," and state subsidization of private education.

The proposed new constitution, by making education an "own affair" for each race's (white, Coloured, and Asian) legislature, does however appear to rule out acceptance of the single unifying department of education that the De Lange group recommended. Palmer says that, nevertheless, the commission, chaired by a prominent Afrikaner, represents a watershed in semiofficial thinking on black education and is light-years away from the ideological and financial straitjacket imposed by Verwoerd in the 1953 act.

The commission issued its Report and Recommendations in 1982. It found that 64.5 percent of the total public spending on education was going to the 16.46 white percentage. In contrast, only 16.4 percent of the education budget was being spent on the 71.27 African percentage of the population. Translated in rand and based on the 1981-82 education budget of 556 million rand: 385,620,000 rand was being spent to education the children of the 4,496,430 whites and 91,184,000 rand was being spent to educate the children of the 19,471,630 Africans.

The broad and telling implications of this enormous disparity between expenditures for white and African education indicate why so few black students complete high school or qualify to attend the universities. Disparity permeates the entire system. Moreover, it explains the bitter resentment among blacks about the quality of education and why it is the most pressing issue on the agenda, as the subordinate black majority seeks to break out of the role assigned to it by the superordinate white majority.[30]

The result of the disparity in funding can best be shown in the differences in pupil-teacher ratios between white and black schools. In the white schools, the average is one teacher for every 20 pupils. The average ratio for African primary and secondary schools is one teacher for every 48 pupils. A 1977 survey of teachers in the township of Soweto showed that in the largest single group of classrooms the ratio was one teacher to between 51 and 59 students. In six of the classrooms, the ratio was one to more than 100.[31]

Allen Boesak, the black theologian and chaplain at the University of the Western Cape, summed up the reasons for the high priority accorded education: "The logic is simple, forthright and devastating; conditions are the way they are because we have inferior education. We have inferior education because we are regarded as second- and third-class citizens in the country of our birth."[32]

The recommendations of the De Lange Commission and the government's response to them clearly follow the dicta of Bowles, Carnoy, Gintis, and others as paraphrased by La Belle and White: "Here the schools do, in fact, serve clearly identified elite -- social and cultural -- in a largely exclusionary role; most subordinate-group members are . . . offered an educational content that leads to either early failure or later and limited assimilation."[33]

Although the De Lange Commission called for replacement of the present segregated systems with a single system of national education where there would be choice for those who wished to attend racially mixed schools, the recommendation was firmly shelved by the government on the grounds that it constituted an abandonment of the principle of apartheid. Thus the whole rise in the number of black students and the new schools being built for blacks (in 1983, 12 new classrooms were reportedly added each working day) seems hollow in the eyes of the people. A black township newspaper, The Sowetan, describes these new schools as "empty dreams." "They aren't really schools," said Wilkinson Kambule, former high school principal. "They are just places to accommodate children."[34]

Articulation and tracking in the rigidly enforced curriculum of the black school system are clear examples of the La Belle and White typology in the type A formula for multi-ethnic integration: cultural and structural segmentation in a vertical relationship. This was made clear in the 1954 statement to parliament by then minister of native affairs, Henrik Verwoerd. We have quoted part of his address previously; here we quote those sentences that apply directly to articulation and tracking:

Speaking of the past, he accused black teachers of

the desire to show off their knowledge of English culture and, possibly also, their inability to distinguish concepts from terminology (which) contributed to an irresistible desire to convey knowledge to their pupils in the same words in which they had received them.

It is clear that an education provided in this form must stand isolated from the life of Bantu society. It prepares them not for life within a Bantu community, progressively uplifted by education, but a life outside the community and for posts which do not, in fact, exist. . . .

The crux of the whole problem is that there will have to be the strictest supervision to ensure that our Union regulations are fully complied with and that departures from them do not take place as in the past.

The curriculum, therefore, envisages a system of education which is based on the circumstances of the community and aims to satisfy the needs of that community. Besides the usual subjects already mentioned (the three R's, the beginning of the study of Afrikaans and English), religious instruction, handicrafts, singing and rhythm must come into their own, that is self-evident.[35]

Under the Bantu Education Act, compared to the pre-1953 situation, there has been greater coordination and progression between the skills imparted at one level in the school system and those imparted at the next. But, as indicated by Verwoerd's lengthy statement in parliament, there has been a purposefully reduced level of potential attainment and a much higher degree of tracking. The tracks run forthrightly to the goal of maintaining the superordinate minority's dominance over the subordinate majority, through a policy of separate and restrictive education designed to perpetuate the master-servant relationship between white and black.

Training, selection, and placement of teachers and administrators are also rigidly controlled by government departments overseeing black education. At least seven different departments and sub-departments in the government's enormously complex structure control and finance racially differentiated education in South Africa.

In creating qualified staff for the black schools, one problem is perpetuated because of the low level of education for the black population from which the majority of teachers in black schools and universities come. Another source of difficulty is in attracting teachers from among the relatively few well-trained Africans because of the inferior salaries, much lower than those for white teachers.

For instance, in 1980 an African male teacher with four years of post-secondary training started at 382 Rand per month, while a white of exactly comparable qualifications started at 542 Rand. African women teachers receive even less at the same level of quali-fication. The government has declared its intention to progressively eliminate discrimination in wage levels for African teachers, but considerable gaps still exist.

The academic qualifications of primary and secon-dary teachers in African schools are depressingly low. Only 20 percent have completed high school, although most teachers have had some teacher training. Only a tiny fraction (2.6 percent) hold university degrees. On the average, each high school has only about one uni-versity graduate. Only seventy-six percent of high school teachers have completed high school. A survey conducted by the African Teachers Association of South Africa in 1979 showed that of the 491 teachers staffing African teacher training institutions, only 35 percent had qualifications beyond a high school dip-loma, and many teachers were less qualified than their pupils.[36]

Another factor mitigating the recruitment of the "best and brightest" Africans into teaching is the right of one or another of the government departments to remove as it sees fit teach-ers and administrators "for cause," without recourse. The re-sult has been to ensure that the majority of teachers hew closely to the simplistic line of education called for and installed by Verwoerd and the government -- guaranteeing that African education is not tainted with any centrifugal tendencies in the integrative process "whereby units or elements of a society are brought into active and coordinated compliance with on-going activities and objectives of the dominant group in that society."[37]

Until 1959, the government's design for African education seemed to take no cognizance of the university "loophole" in segregated education. Of the institutions in 1955 that ranked as universities, one was largely a correspondence school and nonresidential (the University of South Africa), one was al-most entirely a black institution but in theory open to all races (Fort Hare Native College), and the remaining eight were divided between Afrikaans-speaking universities (Pretoria, Stellenbosch, Orange Free State, Potchefstroom) and English-speaking universities (Witwatersrand, Cape Town, Natal, and Rhodes).

Lee Marquard points out that

> . . . since language, politics, and religion are all connected in South Africa, it is generally true to say that the Afrikaner universities are nationalist and are supported by the Dutch Reformed church. The English-speaking universities are much more cosmopolitan, and the Afrikaner would say, irreligious and "liberal."[38]

What is certain is that through the years the English-speaking universities have proved far more open and hospitable to qualified blacks. The majority of Afrikaners and the faculties of their universities could be characterized as believing in totally separate higher education facilities for whites and blacks; the majority of English-speaking South Africans and the faculties of the English-speaking universities were open to mixed university enrollment (so long as the number of blacks did not increase too dramatically!).[39]

In 1959, the year that was to prove fateful for higher education in South Africa, white enrollment at South Africa's universities totaled 35,095.[40] Few if any blacks attended the Afrikaans-speaking universities. In the three major English-speaking institutions, the so-called open universities, nonwhite enrollment was as follows:

University	Coloureds	Asians	Africans
Cape Town	461	133	39
Natal	50	489	187
Witwatersrand	30	193	74

In the two other non-Afrikaner universities, nonwhite enrollment was as follows:

University	Coloureds	Asians	Africans
Fort Hare	70	100	319
Total in Resident Universities	611	915	619
University of South Africa (nonresident)	211	601	1,252
Total Nonwhite Enrollment in the Five Universities	822	1,516	1,871

As early as 1953, the government had turned its attention to the question of unrestricted enrollment in the universities. Once again it appointed a commission, the Holloway Commission, to "investigate and report on the practicability and financial implications of providing separate training facilities for Non-Europeans at universities." The need for, or desirability of, such separate facilities was not included in the commission's terms of reference.

The commission's report was published in February 1955. Mainly for financial reasons, the commission rejected suggestions that new universities for nonwhites-only should be established in the near future. Once again, a government-created commission had not brought back for the coercive mechanism of integration the report the government wanted to hear. Despite the commission's conclusions, the Separate University Education Bill was introduced in parliament in March 1957.

There was strong public reaction against any infringement on the autonomy of universities. Protest meetings were held, petitions were drawn up, and throughout the country processions of students and academic staff took place. The University of the Witwatersrand pledged "to uphold the principle that a university is a place where men and women, without regard to race and colour, are welcome to join in the acquisition and advancement of knowledge and to work for the restoration of university autonomy."[41]

The government had aroused an element of South African society that saw integration in centripetal terms, at least with regard to higher education. The bill encountered "procedural difficulties," and the entire question was referred to yet another parliamentary group, a Commission of Inquiry.[42] Even before the commission made its report, work began on two new segregated colleges for Africans in the African homelands.

In 1959, the Nationalists passed a bill called the Extension of University Education Act. It, together with the University College of Fort Hare Transfer Act, "sounded the death knell for higher education in South Africa."[43] Under the Extension of University Education Act, it became a criminal offense for any nonwhite students to register without the consent of the minister of education at any of the previously open universities. Instead, the act provided for the establishment along racial and ethnic lines of separate universities for nonwhites. These lines were drawn not simply between the three different groups (African, Coloured, Indian) but also between different sections or tribes within the African group. In August 1959, two colleges for Africans were officially established: the University College of the North for students of the Sotho, Pedi, Vanda, and Tswana-speaking tribes and the University College of Zululand in Natal for Zulu-speaking students. Fort Hare was to become exclusively a college for Xhosa-speaking Africans. There was to be a Western Cape University College for Coloureds and an Indian college in Natal.

Anthony Delius, a South African journalist, described the motive behind this latest move in educational apartheid:

Afrikaners are being as fair as they possibly can be given their historical view of the situation in South Africa. They wish for everybody what they wish for themselves -- to live in large but closed family circles and suffer no foreign interference. [A reflection of the group memories of the "laager," the circling of the ox-drawn wagons to defend against native attack and of the years of struggle for identity against the British.] Only, for the time being, the Afrikaners demand absolute control of the process of forming the circles for everybody.[44]

Black students, admittedly in very few numbers, heretofore could look forward to attaining admittance to the open universities, where they would take their courses in English and live and study together with whites. The process required no consent from government authorities. Now, with the passage of the 1959 act, black students were obliged to attend what were virtually tribal colleges located far from the major towns and cities and where the severely limited curriculum was taught in their tribal languages.

Many African leaders protested that these languages are not suited to a large number of academic disciplines. Although the technical vocabulary of Afrikaans is superior to Xhosa or Zulu, even the Afrikaner universities lean heavily on English in some studies. With the language problem, there were serious doubts whether the new government-controlled apartheid colleges would gain acceptance as qualified institutions of higher learning.

La Belle and White describe integration by coercion as "superordinate actions that rely on the application of military and police forces or nonconsensual economic, social or political pressures for their implementation."[45] The enforcement of apartheid in higher education utilizes all these aspects of coercion.

The black universities were to be controlled by white councils with the separate black council having an advisory role only. Both students and staff would be subject to stringent restrictions unknown at the white universities. Under the act, the minister of native affairs may establish or disestablish a nonwhite university or college by placing a notice in the <u>Government Gazette</u>. Also, the principal is appointed by the minister, as is the senate. A clause in the bill concerning the appointment of staff states: "The power to appoint, promote, transfer or discharge persons employed at any University College shall . . . be vested in the Minister, who may delegate any or all of the said powers to the Secretary" (that is, the secretary for native affairs). Furthermore, these powers of appointment and dismissal can be delegated to any officer of the Native Affairs Department. Under the heading of "misconduct" there are no less than 17 clauses explaining just cause for dismissal. Among these, a professor or lecturer can be deemed guilty of misconduct if he "publicly comments adversely about the administration of any department of the Government, or of any province, or of the territory of South West Africa"; or if he "disobeys, disregards, or makes willful default in carrying out a lawful order . . . or if by word or conduct displays insubordination"; or if he discloses information in the course of his duties. He is guilty of an offense if he "propagates any idea . . . calculated to impede . . . the activities of any Government Department." If a family member is charged with misconduct, he would be tried by a tribunal nominated by the secretary for native affairs. At the trial he is without a legal representative. If convicted, his only appeal is to the minister of native affairs.[46]

Before they can enter such a college, the students are subjected to careful screening. The minister may refuse admission to any of them "if he considers it in the interests of the university college concerned to do so."[47] He also has the power to determine where each student shall receive instruction and where he shall reside.

Rules were published, too, for the admission, control, and dismissal of students at the two new colleges. Regulations less usual than those found normally at universities were, for example, the following:

1. Students would not be allowed to leave the college precincts without permission from the Hostel Superintendent or a representative duly authorized by the Rector.
2. Any student organization or organizational work in which students were concerned would be subject to the prior approval of the Rector.
3. No meetings might be held in the groups of the college without prior permission from the Rector.
4. No magazine, publication, or pamphlet for which students were wholly or partly responsible might be circulated without the permission of the Rector in consultation with the Advisory Senate and the Senate.
5. No statement might be given to the Press by or on behalf of the students without the Rector's permission.
6. The Rector might, after consultation with the Advisory Senate and the Senate, suspend or dismiss a student who, in the opinion of the Rector, had infringed these regulations or any particular regulation or had been guilty of misconduct.[48]

The government had the power to decide dates for enrollment at universities after which black students of specified groups would be prohibited unless given the minister's written permission.

Students wishing to take courses not available at the college catering to their own ethnic group could apply to take these courses at another Bantu university college. If not available, the subjects were to be taken by correspondence through the University of South Africa, unless in exceptional cases the minister of Bantu education decided the student could attend an open university. Some courses not available at the Bantu university colleges by 1968 -- nine years after their creation -- were "engineering, architecture, quantity surveying, town planning, linguistics, drama, music, fine arts, numbers of modern languages, comprehensive courses in classics, etc."[49]

During the 1960 session of parliament, the minister of Bantu education announced that of the 190 applications he had received from Africans wishing to enroll at white universities, he approved but four; two ultimately gained admission, one to study music at Cape Town and one for a postgraduate arts course at the University of the Witwatersrand. The minister added that seven applicants wishing to study engineering at the University of the Witwatersrand had been refused because, in the minister's opinion, there were as yet "no prospects of employment for qualified Bantu engineers." Therefore these applicants were simply told they might not study engineering, as no alternative facility existed at the ethnic colleges.

In 1966, a government commission reported that there were an estimated 1,000 jobs in South Africa waiting to be filled by qualified engineers. In his budget speech in the tribal homeland (black reserve), Chief Matanzima reported that industrial development was held back through the severe shortage of skilled workers, for example, that private white engineering firms were being contracted, as no trained Africans were available.[50]

La Belle and White sum up the situation pertaining to South Africa as typical of type A societies, in that

> control of schools is vested in the central government, and access to all levels of schooling, as well as the patterns of articulation and tracking, coincide with ethnic group boundaries. Specifically, subordinate groups have less opportunity to enter school and less chance of competing successfully in them. The geographic distribution of school sites works against . . . the blacks in South Africa. . . . These initial structural barriers are then compounded within the few subordinate-group schools by lack of materials, poorly trained personnel, and a hidden tracking towards low-wage skills.[51]

The only way South Africa's apartheid policy of education differs from this model is that the government saw no reason to keep the tracking hidden. And for years, despite protesting voices, the policy of separate and hugely unequal education for the black subordinate majority brought no meaningful repercussions.

La Belle and White also quote Schermerhorn, pointing out that coercion alone cannot indefinitely hold together a society.[52] After years of acquiescence to their own educational deprivation, and despite the availability to the government of all kinds of coercion and repression, including the extreme methods of banning and arrest without trial, in 1976 the blacks rose in protest.

In May of that year in the township of Soweto outside Johannesburg, black schoolchildren struck against their schools in what started as a three-week protest against the enforced use of Afrikaans in the curriculum. Their choice of issue was as much political as educational. Afrikaans is the language of the government, the language of the superordinate group, which, by its education acts, sought to maintain the status quo by forcing the subordinate black majority to remain separate and outside the mainstream of South African life. Education, because of its function as a "selection and sorting device for the dominant group . . . to maintain the system in its current state," became the rallying point.[53]

The state mobilized its forces of coercion, but the children refused to return to their segregated schools. Instead, on June 16, 1976, the young people led a protest march confronting heavily-reinforced and armed police. The confrontation, its roots in the historical imperative of 300 years, was at hand; its immediate cause, that of education.

It is widely believed that had the police stood their ground the young students and their supporters, after the meeting and speech making, might well have dispersed. Instead, the police opened fire at the height of the demonstration, and the situation was transformed. The children countered police coercion with mass counterviolence whose like and scale had not before been seen in South Africa. Into 1977 the boycott of apartheid schools continued. By April 1977 an estimated 100,000 black students were actively taking part, and the boycott had spread to the campus of the black university. Students' demands included the following:

1. Immediate scrapping of the present system of education. It was devised to subject the recipients to perpetual subjugation.

2. Unconditional opening to people of all races all educational institutions.
3. Immediate improvement in the working conditions of teachers to make the teaching profession attractive to the best and most talented.
4. Free and compulsory education for every child of school age up to, and including, high school.[54]

The demands, vigorously put forward at Fort Hare University, were countered by the white rector. He ordered the university closed. Police stood guard. Students left the campus.

The first deaths occurred in May 1977. In Cape Town two blacks, one a 15-year-old boy, were killed when police opened fire at stone-throwing pupils. In the incident, six others were wounded. Despite this, the boycotts continued. It is estimated that more than 600 blacks, mainly young students, were killed by government forces during the disturbances of 1976 and 1977.[55] According to official estimates, during and after the demonstrations 5,000 young blacks fled the country. Of these, about 2,000 are believed to have volunteered for military training with underground antigovernment movements. Some returned to South Africa on sabotage missions.

The South African government was shocked into remedial action. As La Belle and White posit, when coercion alone can no longer hold together a society, alternative strategies employed by the superordinate group include "building consensus through intergroup agreement on specific issues (usually of short duration because of their one-sided nature)."[56] Yet again, the government appointed a commission -- the Cillie Commission, to investigate the riots at Soweto and other black townships from June 16, 1976 to February 28, 1977. The commission's report, published in 1980, found that the outbreak of rioting on June 16, 1976 was caused by a combination of factors:

> The application of the policy on the medium of instruction (the teaching of Afrikaans and in part in Afrikaans) which gave rise to misunderstanding the dissatisfaction among the people of Soweto; the scholars' planned and organized resistance to the policy of the medium of instruction; the ineffectual official handling of the resistance; and the inability of department officials and police to foresee the imminent rioting and to take countermeasures.[57]

Consequently, expenditures on African education have more than doubled since 1977. The per capita expenditure for black students in 1977-78 was 52.86 rand. In 1981-82, it had risen to 111.36 rand. However, even after this rise, it is a fact that ten times as much is still spent on each white student as for each black.

Another breach in apartheid education has been quietly allowed since the riots of 1976 and 1977. In direct conflict with the tenets of the Bantu Education Act, private schools that accept students of all races have been established. This de facto integration began when diplomatic relations opened with the black state of Malawi. The ambassador's children must go to school; it would be diplomatically inappropriate for the school to be Bantu. A black diplomat from the United States followed suit. He was soon followed by entire black embassy staffs from the four tribal homelands that had been given nominal independence and nationhood. The solution was to establish private, nonsegregated schools. Although tuition fees are a means of deterring most black parents from sending their children to these schools, by 1982 there were several thousand black students enrolled in these private multiracial schools. The economic barrier was lowered by the offering of scholarships, often underwritten by progressive South African businesspeople and by multinational companies with interests in the country.[58]

Several thousand is minute when compared to the millions of black students who must still be a part of the substandard segregated school system. Nevertheless, the government's overlooking of these schools represents a breach, however small, in the solid wall of apartheid education.

As La Belle and White point out, policy in a type A group relationship may often follow two contradictory lines at the same time. This is true of the present educational policy in South Africa and may well indicate a struggle within the superordinate ruling class as to the future of black education. On the one hand, there is the precipitous rise in per capita expenditure for black education and the permissive attitude toward the illegal, nonsegregated, private schools. On the other hand, the government has announced a plan to alter its policy determining how many black students can attend South Africa's four English-language universities. In 1982, among a total of 36,732 students at these universities, just over 1,000 were black students. An article in the New York Times outlines the new plan, which further restricts black attendance at the English-language universities, and the reaction from the universities involved.

> The proposal, under which the government would institute a quota system determining the overall number of blacks that can be admitted to the universities, is provided for in draft legislation that Parliament is scheduled to debate when it reassembles next week.
>
> The proposal has revived an issue that has frustrated the four universities since 1959, when the Government introduced a law imposing apartheid on the English-language campuses.
>
> In a statement issued last month, the senate of the largest of the four universities, the University of the Witwatersrand, Johannesburg, condemned attempts "to compel the university to become an instrument of the Government's policy of discrimination against students on grounds of race."
>
> The three other universities, Cape Town, Rhodes in Grahamstown, and Natal, with white campuses in Durban and Pietermaritzburg and a black medical school in Durban, have also taken issue with the Government.
>
> University officials admit the plan to replace the case-by-case permit system with a blanket racial quota may streamline bureaucratic procedures. But they nevertheless reject it on moral grounds.
>
> Commenting on the Government proposal, James Moulder, special assistant in the office of the vice chancellor of the University of Cape Town, said, "Even if the quota allows us to admit 80 percent blacks, it would be totally abhorrent and unacceptable."[59]

At the time of this writing, the quota plan has not been voted into law. That does not mean it will not be. Nor does it mitigate this fresh evidence of the government's dedication to maintaining and solidifying apartheid education in the face of riots, white opposition, and growing black militancy.

How, then, in a final overview, does education in South Africa conform or confound the typology created by La Belle and White? The authors set out to codify and provide a framework that would aid analysis of the ethnic group interactions related to various educational policies. We have seen that although South Africa may seem a primary example of the type A society, where "integration is likely to be interpreted narrowly . . . (with) policies in both the cultural and structural realm tending toward centrifugality," on closer investigation the situation is more complex and fluid. There is an inexorable force that, in this writer's opinion, will eventually bring about substantive changes for the better in black education. This is the force of economics in the face of which even the most resolute Afrikaner Nationalist may eventually have to give way. It cuts across the typology of educational and societal repression to the pragmatic need for the upgrading of black training in order to ensure economic growth.

South Africa's Nationalist Manpower Commission (an agency of the South African government) has recently concluded that the expansion of South Africa's economy requires rapid growth in numbers the commission terms "high level manpower." The commission argues that most advanced economies have a much higher proportion of high-level personnel in the work force than does South Africa, and this constitutes a serious deterrent to South Africa's economic growth. The commission asserted:

It is clear that the highest priority is increasing the contribution of non-White groups to the country's high-level manpower, since the contribution that can be made by Whites is apparently already largely utilized. South Africa will not be able to realize its development potential and offer all its people an acceptable standard of living if the country persists in trying to recruit its high level manpower from the White population group; in fact, if we continue to do so, a relative deterioration may be expected in the course of time.[60]

In the long term, in this second half of the twentieth century, no highly industrialized nation can afford to keep a sizable majority of its population undereducated. South Africa is a highly industrialized nation and, as such, is feeling the adverse effects of the 1953 and 1959 education acts. The result is an inevitable confrontation between the emotional-political-fanatical adherents of apartheid and the pragmatic, economic beliefs of the rest of the population. In the conflict between history and the demand for the "good life" may lie the answer to what course multiethnic integration will take in South Africa.

NOTES

1. Thomas La Belle and Peter S. White, "Education and Multiethnic Integration: An Intergroup-Relations Typology," Comparative Education Review 24, no. 2 (June 1980):155.

2. Ibid., p. 156.

3. Ibid.

4. Ibid., p. 158.

5. Ibid.

6. Ibid., p. 157.

7. Encyclopaedia Britannica, vol. 20 (William Benton, 1968), p. 974.

8. La Belle and White, "Education and Multiethnic Integration," p. 158.

9. Encyclopaedia Britannica, p. 157.

10. F. E. Auerbach, The Power of Prejudice in South African Education (Cape Town, 1965). p. 112.

11. D. G. S. M'Timkulu, "The African and Education," Race Relations Journal 16, no. 3 (1949), quoted from Muriel Horrell, A Decade of Bantu Education (Johannesburg: South African Institute of Race Relations, 1964), p. 157.

12. La Belle and White, "Education and Multiethnic Integration," p. 155.

13. Ibid., p. 157.

14. Helen Kitchen, ed., The Educated African (New York: Praeger, 1962).

15. Ibid.

16. David R. Smock, Black Education in South Africa (Belgium: Institute of International Education, January 1983).

17. La Belle and White, "Education and Multiethnic Integration," p. 158.

18. Muriel Horrell, Laws Affecting Race Relations in South Africa 1948-1976 (Johannesburg: South African Institute of Race Relations, 1978), p. 297.

19. Ibid.

20. Ibid.

21. La Belle and White, "Education and Multiethnic Integration," p. 159.

22. Ibid., p. 157.

23. Ibid.

24. Ibid., p. 156.

25. George Palmer pointed out that the 1953 Bantu Education Act had the immediate result of increasing the number of blacks in school, though mainly at the lower primary level.

Various administrative devices were used to make this possible without increasing expenditure, but most had the effect of decreasing even further the quality of black education. The state's contribution to black education was in fact pegged at 61.5 million pounds sterling until about 1967. Palmer had this to say:

> The theory behind the pegging, advanced by Verwoerd, was based on a Christian National Education pamphlet of 1948 which argued that, beyond a certain contribution from the white taxpayer, the blacks must contribute the rest from taxes paid by them.
>
> However, you could not get much more tax out of a very poor community and this dilemma was debated for a decade. When it was seen to fail, the government said in effect, "O.K., let's stick to a ceiling of R13 million (the equivalent then of 6.5 million pounds), but we'll finance black university education from other sources, and the white administrative staff in Pretoria as well, so the R13 million will go further."
>
> However, the per capita spending on black education actually dropped in the decade 1953-63 because of the increase in numbers. Classes got bigger and bigger and the dropouts multiplied. The salaries of black teachers remained unchanged from 1947 to 1963 -- labeled "Teaching for a servant's pay."
>
> In the early seventies, this ceiling on expenditure on black education was abolished and the disparity between per capita black and white spending has been decreasing.

26. C. T. Verwey, R. R. Brazelle, and F. J. Wilkinson, eds., Education and Manpower Production (Blacks), no. 2 (Bloemfontein: University of the Orange Free State, 1982), p. 2. Quoted from Smock, Black Education in South Africa, p. 32.

27. Human Sciences Research Council, Investigation into Education, of the Work Committee: Education Financing 17, (p. 18; 11), p. 15. Quoted from Smock, Black Education in South Africa, p. 31.

28. The South African school system covers 12 years: Substandards A and B and Standards 1 to 10. Standard 5 if the final year of primary school. At the end of Standard 8 the junior certificate is awarded, and at the end of Standard

10 the senior certificate or matriculation is awarded upon successful completion of the examinations. Only those passing these examinations with the highest scores have any chance of matriculating into the universities.

29. Smock, Black Education in South Africa.

30. George Palmer said

the gap in per capita spending on education between white and black peaked at 18:1 in the early seventies. Since about 1975, the gap has been narrowing and is now down to 10:1 in the so-called white areas. Indeed, spending on black education has recently increased sharply -- in the last three budgets (1981-82, 1982-83, 1983-84) it has in fact risen by a larger percentage than has defense spending.

In the early seventies the government realized the white labor force was drying up, hence the concentration on numbers rather than quality, reducing the dropout rate and the emphasis put on secondary education. This led to a major financing policy change. Since 1979, the state has borne the capital cost of black secondary schools in black townships. Prior to that, school budgets were balanced with loans from the government at the prevailing interest rages. Those loans had to be repaid via a 38-cent per month levy on rents in Soweto and R2 in Sharpeville and the Vaal Triangle townships.

The levy is now used for financing school facilities such as libraries, and over the past few years the number of schools in Soweto has more than tripled.

The education system is still segregated but, within the framework of apartheid, the government has decided to put a lot more money into black education. And the business community is realizing not only the need for more money to be spent on education but for a system that does not result in people coming into employment with vastly different educational standards.

31. Smock, Black Education in South Africa.

32. Quoted by David Smock, from Kenneth Hartshorn, "The Unfinished Business: Education for South Africa's Black People," Optima, July 30, 1981, p. 25.

33. La Belle and White, "Education and Multiethnic Integration," p. 160.

34. Joseph Lelyveld, "Pretoria and Black Education: Status Change?" New York Times, November 1982.

35. F. Verwoerd, "Bantu Education -- Policy for the Immediate Future," statement in the senate of the South Africa parliament, June 7, 1954 (Pretoria: Information Service of the Department of Native Affairs, 1954), p. 17.

36. Smock, Black Education in South Africa, p. 8.

37. La Belle and White, "Education and Multiethnic Integration," p. 155.

38. Leo Marquand, People and Policies of South Africa (London: Oxford University Press, 1952), p. 230.

39. Ibid.

40. Statistics for these tables taken from Brian Bunting, Education for Apartheid (London: Christian Action, 1978), p. 19.

41. Horrell, Laws Affecting Race Relations in South Africa.

42. Ibid.

43. Bunting, Education for Apartheid, p. 19.

44. Anthony Delius, "The Educated African," from "Separate but Equal on the Veld," The Reporter, December 24, 1959, p. 273.

45. La Belle and White, "Education and Multiethnic Integration," p. 156.

46. I. B. Tabata, Education for Barbarism in South Africa (London: Pall Mall Press, 1960), p. 71.

47. Ibid.

48. Government Notices 1765, 1959, and 1445, 1960; Horrell, Laws Affecting Race Relations.

49. Muriel Horrell, Bantu Education to 1968 (Johannesburg: South African Institute of Race Relations, 1968), p. 127.

50. Bunting, Education for Apartheid.

51. La Belle and White, "Education and Multiethnic Integration," p. 159.

52. Ibid.

53. Ibid., p. 157.

54. Report of the Commission of Inquiry 1976-1977, in Survey of Race Relations in South Africa (Johannesburg: South African Institute of Race Relations Publication, 1980).

55. Lelyveld, "Pretoria and Black Education."

56. La Belle and White, "Education and Multiethnic Integration," p. 156.

57. Report of the Commission of Inquiry 1976-1977.

58. Ibid.

59. "South African Universities Oppose Plan to Set Up Quotas for Blacks," <u>New York Times</u>, April 9, 1983.

60. National Manpower Commission, "Highlevel Manpower in South Africa" (Pretoria: Department of Manpower Utilization, 1980), p. 12. Quoted from Smock, <u>Black Education in South Africa</u>.

3

EDUCATION
AND WHITE/MESTIZO-INDIAN
RELATIONS

Jorge M. Nakamoto, Peter S. White,
and Thomas J. La Belle

Peru is South America's third largest and fourth most populous country. It is divided into three clearly defined geographic areas, each of which runs the length of the country from north to south. The coastal region is a narrow strip of desert, between 25 and 100 miles wide, along Peru's 1,200-mile Pacific shore. Rising sharply from the desert are the Andes mountains, reaching altitudes of 18,000 feet, part of the rock wall that forms South America's western spine from Venezuela through to Chile. In central and southern Peru, the Andes split into roughly parallel chains, widening out and leaving between them a series of valleys and basins at 10,000 to 13,000 feet above sea level. The eastern third of Peru is lowland jungle, one edge of the enormous Amazon plain that covers the central part of the continent.

More than a physical characteristic, however, Peru's geographic regions are a kind of shorthand for the other significant divisions -- historical, cultural, economic, and ethnic -- that so profoundly fragment the country. The heavily urbanized coast has always been Peru's administrative and political center, especially the capital of Lima, and it is now the country's industrial center as well. Coastal agriculture, in contrast to agriculture elsewhere in Peru, is export-oriented (sugar and cotton in particular) and is organized into large-scale semi-industrial plantations that operate year-round on irrigated land. The coastal population is overwhelmingly white or mestizo, with small Japanese and Chinese groups in the urban centers and a black segment concentrated in cities near the former sugar plantation areas. Spanish is the language of the coast, with Peru's indigenous languages virtually unknown here.

The Andean highlands are home to Peru's largest ethnic minority, the Quechua- and Aymara-speaking Indians, descendants of the Incas who ruled most of western South America before the arrival of the Spaniards in the sixteenth century. The Indians live in rural areas of the mountains and high plateaus, where they combine herding and small-scale agriculture (potatoes, corn, barley, and similar crops). Landholding patterns vary widely. Most Indians own small plots of land and have access to community-owned pastures. The huge haciendas to which Indian communities were forcibly attached during the Spanish colonial period and most of the nineteenth and twentieth centuries have been broken up by the agricultural reform of 1969. But Indian agriculture remains family-centered, producing just enough to feed the family and to provide a small surplus for sale in the towns and cities. The low productivity, in the face of a growing national population, is evidenced by Peru's recent need -- for the first time in its history -- to import potatoes and corn for internal consumption.

Although Spanish is now increasingly the lingua franca of the highlands because of growing cities and the spread of national mass media, Quechua and Aymara remain the native languages of the area's population. Likewise, other Western and Spanish cultural elements have gained a foothold in Andean indigenous culture over the centuries (most notably Catholicism) without displacing or assimilating the strong native roots of the Indian culture. It is this cultural and economic tension between coast and highlands, whites and Indians, that is the axis of intergroup relations in Peru.

The jungle remains the country's marginal, half-forgotten region. It is physically isolated and only sparsely populated. The jungle's many small native groups, dependent as they are on hunting and gathering, play no role in Peru's economic life. Their isolation and dispersed habitat have also served to protect their cultures and languages more effectively than has been the case of the highland Indians. The jungle does occupy a dominant place in the national economy, but through one resource, oil, rather than the area's population. And, like most of Peru's valuable, exportable resources, the oil is controlled by the coastal elites through the national government.

In order to assess properly the implications of educational policies in the intergroup relations of Peru, it will be necessary first to give a historical overview of the development of state-sponsored education in Peru. Then, against this background, educational policy areas, as indicated by La Belle and White, will be examined in the aftermath of Peru's most recent comprehensive national educational reform of 1972.

THE INCA EMPIRE

The Inca Empire originated from its capital, Cusco, at the end of the fifteenth century through military conquest and subjugation over a vast Andean region. At the time of Pizarro's arrival in 1531, the Inca Empire covered present-day Peru, Bolivia, the northern part of Chile and Argentina in the south, and Ecuador and southern Colombia in the north.

The emperor (the Inca) was considered the "Divine Son of the Sun" and sole ruler of the empire; only his closest relatives shared with him the power of the state. His rule was achieved through the nobility, a privileged social class that imposed its domination with a well-organized army, an efficient and complex administration, and an ideologic conception that considered the sun as the principal deity. The nobility was composed of members of the Inca's lineage and noble members of conquered groups. It also included those who, because of distinguished services rendered to the state, were granted passage to the elite group.

In contrast, the commoners were organized through the ayllu systems, which were communities of extended families dedicated to common work for production. Because the economy of the empire rested exclusively on agriculture, the Inca state demanded that the ayllus specialize in crop production. And the needs of each ayllu were met through an organized crop-exchange system. The excess production was retained by the state and redistributed only in times of war or natural catastrophe.[1]

Neighboring groups were brought into the empire forcibly, through military invasion. Integration consisted of acquiescence to the Incas' imposition of their own administrative, economic, and religious order. Typically through coercion and control rather than through voluntarism, the Incas were able to keep the empire intact.[2] The emphasis was centripetal with little centrifugal movement permitted, and the goal was interdependence for mutual advantage. Subordinate groups were used for their labor to produce a surplus and to ensure economic stability.

While the hope in the long run was clearly a consensus around common values and norms, the short-run effort relied primarily on rigidly ordered direction from the top. This paralleled the control over the means of production, which belonged to the state; private property and currency were nonexistent. The state distributed land and seeds to the ayllus, which in turn, under a system of draft labor called mita, were obliged to work the land assigned to the nobles as well as to produce goods for the state. Consequently, all forms of education and cultural transmission were strictly related to the socioeconomic configuration of the empire.

Formal education was reserved exclusively for the nobility. Noble youths from every region conquered by the Incas were brought to the capital city of Cusco to study in an institution called yachaywasi. Because the students came from different regions and did not speak a common language, the immediate preoccupation was the teaching of the Quechua language as well as the history and religion of the Incas. Other specialized courses, such as astronomy, geography, mathematics, and military tactics, were taught in accordance with the potential function of the students as administrators, military, or religious leaders of the empire.[3]

The education of the commoners was informal and based on the production needs of the ayllu and the empire, that is, agriculture, public construction, mining, and so on. Some specialized tasks like artistic jewelry or ceramic making, however, required some nonformal education in specific settings where systematic contact between teacher and apprentice was encouraged to create continuity for the production of specialized goods.

The commoners, completely excluded from formal education, were educated by the ruling elite through a coercive process of socialization. The population, production, and supplies of the ayllus were systematically tallied by the state to detect and punish those who failed to comply with their expected function in society. Through this mechanism, the commoners learned their place and duties in the empire; and in turn, it compelled them to transmit to new generations the values and norms demanded for the perpetuation of the Incaic social order. In this regard, education throughout this period was elitist, despotic, and authoritarian, merely reflecting the interests of the ruling class.[4]

THE COLONIAL PERIOD

Spanish colonial rule in the Andes was facilitated by its similarity, in several key respects, to traditional Inca authority and the Inca concept of integration. Both were highly centralized, but both also depended on the cooperation of the local elites of conquered groups. Also, the Spanish and Incas alike placed their greatest administrative emphasis on the organization and control of labor, primarily for agricultural production, but also for mining, some manufacturing, and personal service. Both demanded the conquered groups' outward conformance to the state religion, but both tolerated some local religious syncretism, and neither wanted or expected the full assimilation of subordinate ethnic groups into the ruling group. Finally, the Spanish continued the Incas' practice, in all areas of society, of rigid differentiation between elites and masses.

Three major caste/class groups were differentiated on racial grounds alone: the criollos (Creoles), or Spanish-descended whites (blancos), who lived mostly in Lima; the mestizo, or mixed bloods, who usually served the Creoles or worked in the lesser bureaucracy; and the Indian from the highland, or Sierra, who was exploited by both the Creoles and the mestizos.[5]

Societal integration of subordinate groups under the Spanish was less bent on complete assimilation than under the Incas, even though the Spanish were rigidly centripetal in their economic, political, and cultural affairs. Economically, there was emphasis on forced labor and taxes, and all linked to state-sponsored institutions like the hacienda system. Dependence rather than interdependence was dominant, as the intent was one of facilitating Spanish wealth. Politically, some local control was permitted as with the Inca, but again only within the new hierarchy with the Spanish at the top. Culturally, the centripetal ways of the Spanish can be seen in their religious expectations and language practices. Religiously, the Spanish tolerated no localized deities, however subordinate, and emphasized individual conviction and compliance. Linguistically, in contrast, the Spanish permitted, and encouraged, local languages to be used in daily and even religious discourse because they found that requiring Spanish was not needed for effective control.

Coercion was clearly the dominant integrative mechanism employed by the Spanish, attested to by the conquest, forced labor, and forced conversion to Catholicism. By the very end of the colonial period consensus can be said to have become part of the Spanish integrative system, but this was more of a result of the ability of the subordinates to cope with Spanish dominance than a trade-off against basic coercion.

The education of the Indians under the Spanish was limited to the teaching of religion in the native language and the imparting of other social norms for the "extirpation of idolatry."[6] Some parish schools were built in the large towns and encomienda lands, but the costs were paid by the Indians (through labor contributions) and by the landholders. In an effort to create a nexus between the conquered population and the new order, the Spanish crown mandated the establishment of special urban schools for the native elites -- the regional curacas (community leaders). The objective was to create an educational system where Indian leaders learned to govern the native population in accordance with the interests of the crown.[7]

During the colonial period, secondary education, even for the Spanish, was virtually nonexistent. The few schools that appeared were originally designed as seminaries, and only when the first generation of Creoles and mestizos began to demand access to the educational monopoly of the elite were these institutions transformed into secondary schools. The neglect of intermediate schools was due to the more immediate need for priests and lawyers, who until then were only trained in distant Spanish universities. Thus, as early as 1551, Dominican priests helped to found in Lima the University of San Marcos, and soon after, other religious orders followed suit in the region. These universities adopted the Aristotelian scholasticism that prevailed in Spain, with such courses as metaphysics, Latin, rhetoric, and theology as basic requirements for any professional career. Access to higher education, however, was restricted to the children of the crown's officials and to the select few who could prove they were descendants of the conquistadores.

In sum, education throughout the colonial period was quantitatively and qualitatively oriented toward the maintenance of the status quo and exclusively for the upper class. The marginal education of the Indians served merely to reinforce their religious socialization for humility and obedience to the exploitative measures implemented by the Spaniards. Even though the Spanish crown and some members of the clergy attempted to improve the lot of the Indians through royal mandates for political and educational reforms, such mandates were rarely enforced -- understandable in light of the crown's own contradictory objectives of Christianizing the Indians and exploiting them to secure revenues.[8]

POST-INDEPENDENCE

It has been said that the revolutions that led Spanish America to its independence were the work of a few,[9] and it must be added that the revolution also benefited the few, that is, a minority elite ruling class. This phenomenon is clearly evident in Peru, where its independence in 1821 did not alter the social structure originated by the Spaniards. One of the most important factors of the independence movement in Peru was the determination of the minority Creole population to gain political and economic emancipation from Spain. Throughout most of the colonial period, the Spaniards monopolized the higher administrative posts of the government and thought of themselves as being superior to the Creoles, whose sole political power was in the localized municipal institutions.[10] Hence, when in the 1820s Peru declared its independence from Spain, the Creoles merely took over the privileged position of the deposed Spaniards while the indigenous Indian population found its already precarious position exacerbated by the new dominant group.

Following independence, the struggle for political hegemony among Creole groups led to a period of revolts, military rulers, and constitutions that lasted for nearly 50 years. The governing of Peru became exclusively dependent on the support of the only two nationally organized institutions: the army and the church. The power of the first was achieved during the long wars of independence, whereas the latter reasserted its power through a spiritual reconquest of the new elite. In spite of their power, however, confusions and disorder characterized Peru's political and economic systems during this period. All forms of education, as in the colonial period, remained in the hands of the church.[11]

By the end of the nineteenth century, Peru's precarious economic situation was exacerbated by the Pacific War (1879-

83) between Peru and Bolivia on one side and Chile on the other. Until the Pacific War, the social, political, and economic configuration of Peru had never been seriously questioned. The dominant Creole class considered its culture as the national culture of Peru and at the same time treated the Indian culture with disdain. The existence of a Peruvian state was taken for granted, and the relation between the dominant class and the indigenous population was not considered antagonistic but rather complementary. Only through catechization and miscegenation with the "superior" race was the Indian able to find a remote possibility for upward mobility.[12]

The disaster of the war, in which many Indians were forced to enroll in the army, prompted some members of the Creole class to denounce openly the condition of the pauperized Indian population. Foremost among the critics was Manuel Gonzales Prada, a writer and a poet, precursor of the pro-Indian movement indigenismo. Gonzalez Prada accused the government of philanthropic hypocrisy for its ineffective indigenous policies, and challenged the positivist vision of the Indian with its "scientific" rationale for the maintenance of Indian inferiority.[13]

After the Pacific War, large amounts of British and U.S. capital began to be invested in export industries and in railway and highway construction. The presence of foreign capital provoked the displacement of some traditional Creole economic groups and the emergence of new middle-class groups. Until the war, the coastal agricultural industries had drawn their labor force from coastal black slaves and Chinese coolies. When such a labor force was closed in 1873, the now economically displaced coastal elite renewed its interest in the neglected Indians of the highlands as an efficient source of labor and goods for the growing coastal cities. The Indians' attachment to their land and traditional ayllu customs, however, was an obstacle to the elite's own economic reconstruction. Thus government rhetoric to "modernize" and diversify the economy led to the establishment of private ownership programs in place of communal ownership. For the Indians the consequences were drastic. The communal ayllu lands were turned into latifundios (large landholdings) and eventually incorporated into the growing Creole-owned hacienda economy.[14] With the support of corrupt officials, massacres of Indians suppressed all forms of physical resistance by the indigenous population to these new forms of exploitation, and landless Indians were recruited for forced labor under official vagrancy laws.[15]

The nineteenth century can be characterized as an extension of the coercive, centripetal policies for integration common to the colonial era. Contrary to the early postindependence period, and its rhetoric of egalitarianism through the elimination of official recognition of indigenous communities, in practice the Indian sectors were not treated alike structurally or economically. To the contrary, the practice was basically centripetal as communal lands were splintered and the Indian was incorporated as wage labor, thereby continuing the ties to debt peonage. Because it was tied to the legal and military coercion that maintained structural dependence, even "modernization" had the effect of keeping the relationships between groups as they had been. In order to control Indian unrest, schools with condescending and paternalistic religious orientations, as in the colonial period, were built in the haciendas and major rural towns.

In the urban areas, public education was limited to a small sector of the growing mestizo population and only in the form of primary education. Secondary and higher education continued to have the aristocratic and elitist orientation adopted from the French schools in the educational reform of 1875.[16] The schools' differentiation was reproduced by the social status and financial remuneration of teachers, which strongly favored the secondary level. Primary education teachers were viewed relative to their altruistic and apostolic role in society, and their labor was considered a social service.[17]

THE TWENTIETH CENTURY

Even though the cries of Gonzalez Prada and others were ignored by government officials, his social denunciations contributed to raising the awareness of the Creole about the condition of the Indians in the highlands. Eventually, an indigenista movement composed of Creole intellectuals began to actively defend the Indian population through an organization known as the Pro-Indigenous Association, founded in Lima in 1909. Its major objectives were to lobby for the Indian, to provide legal assistance to the ayllus, and to promote the study and diffusion of information related to the social improvement of the Indian race.[18] The association's efforts, however, were thwarted by the elite-controlled government.

Unlike Gonzalez Prada, who argued that the essence of the Indian problem was neither racial nor pedagogical but instead social and economic, the Pro-Indigenous Association's prescribed solution for the liberation of the Indian was based on humanitarian, moral, and Christian idealism. Thus, the association fostered attitudinal rather than structural changes in the society.[19]

It was in the late 1910s when Gonzalez Prada's accusations about the condition of the Indians began to be debated in the political arena. This sudden concern was precipitated by two main factors: the emergence of a new progressive indigenous movement inspired by the Soviet and Mexican revolutions and the pressures on the class structure due to increased penetration of international capitalism.[20] It was in this political climate that in 1919, backed by the army and with the support of the young indigenistas and the rising new middle groups, Augusto B. Leguia, a former president (1908-12), seized the presidency. Upon taking office, Leguia promulgated a new constitution and decreed a series of laws dealing openly with the Indian question. For the first time a government officially recognized the indigenistas' protests about the condition of the Indian. In an echo of previous paternalistic policies, however, the indigenous population was considered primarily a valuable labor force. In his presidential address, Leguia declared:

> Two-thirds of our population are comprised of Indians, yet, the Indian is a shocking victim of the serfage of the past . . . and inconceivable abuses of the present. The Indian works . . . and is responsible for almost all of our production, and he is perhaps the only soldier of the national army. . . . The Indian is everything for Peru, and in return he is treated as a serf. This cannot continue . . . to defend the Indians signifies to defend our economic life which he promotes.[21]

Nevertheless, Leguia's pro-Indian rhetoric served simply as a screen for the continued exploitations of the indigenous population. Road conscription and vagrancy laws in the highlands were enforced more violently than before, and the Ministry of Development's Indian affairs section, intended to supervise the implementation of laws protecting the indigenous population, was co-opted by the gamonales (landholders) for their own interests.

It soon became evident that Leguia had played upon the interests of the emerging urban middle-class groups and young indigenistas simply to gain power, after which those opposing his policies were persecuted and exiled.[22] Leguia's dictatorial measures, however, stimulated the creation of two political parties related to the indigenista movement: APRA (American Revolutionary Popular Alliance) and the Socialist party, which in 1929 became the first Peruvian Communist party. APRA, through its founder, Victor Raul Haya De La Torre, proposed Latin American unity against U.S. imperialism and expropriation and nationalization of all lands and industries owned by foreign conglomerates. For APRA, only the emerging middle groups could take the leadership of Peru. The Socialist party, represented by its founder, Jose Carlos Mariategui, prescribed socialism as the only solution for the ills of Peru. National development required a revolutionary effort in which the majority of the population, the Indians, would play an important role in alliance with the urban proletariat in the creation of a new Peru.[23]

Although tactics might differ, Leguia's approach to integration was characteristic of much of what followed in the twentieth century. The elite looked to indigenous labor as one of its primary natural resources and thus began to advocate interdependence rather than dependence through facilitating greater access to education, better paying jobs, and the like. Similarly, coercion was to give way to consensus, as cultural centripetality was based not on isolation but on the education and general exposure of Indians to national norms. In effect, integration in the twentieth century was to use indigenous labor as the basis of a work force that would facilitate economic growth while incorporating indigenous peoples into the mainstream through their exposure to the dominant group's lifeways. Formal schooling became the principal mechanism to achieve this form of interdependence based on consensus among the active though subordinate participation of the Indian.

Leguia's plans facilitated such goals, as his intent was the Americanization of Peru[24] not only by attracting U.S. capital to the Peruvian industries but also by adopting its educational system, which had already been attempted under his first presidential term. Thus, under Leguia a 1920 educational reform law was promulgated that called for the creation of regional offices of education throughout the nation and the implementation of vocational education as a second cycle for

primary and secondary schools. The urban and rural vocational schools were differentiated in content. The urban
schools, designed for the marginal working class, emphasized
practical knowledge and domestic tasks for the local industries and commerce; whereas for the rural areas, basic agriculture, animal husbandry, and home crafts were emphasized.
It was evident that the dual urban/rural school system
perpetuated dependent relationships by preventing working-
class children and Indians from access to the elite monopoly
of professional careers. As Mariategui indicated in his critique of the U.S. oriented reform

> Politically, the historical process meant the fall of a
> feudal oligarchy because of its inability to become
> capitalist. In the sphere of education it meant an
> educational reform inspired by the example of the most
> prosperous and highly industrialized nation.
> Therefore, the 1920 reform is consistent with the
> country's historical evolution. But, like the political
> movement which it paralleled and to which it was
> linked, the educational movement was sabotaged by the
> continued and widespread existence of a feudal regime.
> It is not possible to democratize the education of a
> country without democratizing its economic and its po-
> litical structure.[25]

It was, however, the failure to include the majority indigenous population in Leguia's educational plan that provoked major criticisms from the two political parties that
emerged from the indigenista movement. APRA argued that
the problem of the Indian was predominantly social and that
their "redemption" could be accomplished only by integrating
them into the capitalist system and Western culture. It also
advocated a uniform and equal education for all under a state
monopoly and separated from church control. The Socialist
party through Mariategui stressed that the time for a liberal
and democratic revolution led by the bourgeoisie had already
expired because they had already become dependent agents of
capitalist imperialism. Mariategui believed that only through
a "revolutionary" school could Peru realize the ideals of
democracy.[26]

As is apparent, independence did not bring educational reforms on behalf of the indigenous population, and, as Mariategui noted, when the state referred to the Indians in its edu-

cational programs it treated them as an inferior race.[27] Throughout the Leguia period rural education meant promoting mobile schools, granjas escuelas (farm schools) and internados indígenas (Indian boarding schools), for controlling Indians and reducing Indian uprisings. These rural schools were used to instruct the Indians in citizenship, personal hygiene, basic Spanish, religion, and Peruvian history. The cooperative spirit of the Indians was encouraged for labor exploitation (road construction, school and house building) and above all for agricultural production for the haciendas.[28] Thus Leguia's pro-Indian laws not only failed to improve the condition of the indigenous population but in fact worsened it. Further evidence of Leguia's disregard for the Indians is the fact that only 291 of the thousands of Indian communities in existence were granted official democratic rights.[29]

Leguia's 11 years of dictatorship came to a halt through a military coup d'etat when the worldwide depression and Peruvian government corruption left the country with an almost empty treasury. A new constitution adopted in 1933 declared primary education free and compulsory, and in 1935 a Ministry of Education was created to administer all forms of public education except universities. Despite these new measures, education for the Indians continued to be minimal. The 1940 census showed that almost 60 percent of the population was illiterate and that more than 51 percent of the population lived in areas that had no school or other educational facilities. The expansion of schooling was exclusive to the urban areas and available only to a small portion of the population -- about 40 percent of the school-age population. Secondary education remained under the control of the church. There were 148 secondary schools in all Peru, but only 45 of them were government schools. The students enrolled in private Catholic schools were predominantly children of the Creole class; government subsidies for their maintenance were routinely included in the national educational budget.

After the overthrow of Leguia, the military junta called for national elections. The lack of organized political parties due to Leguia's repressive government made Haya De La Torre, the APRA candidate, a favorite to win the election. But one of the leaders of the revolts against Leguia, General Sanchez Cerro, was elected president. He attempted to offer a conciliatory approach to his political opponents, abolished Leguia's road conscription and vagrancy laws, and ordered the enactment of a new constitution that was promulgated in

1933. Sanchez Cerro, however, was not able to improve the critical financial situation inherited from Leguia's term. His austerity measures for national economic reconstruction alienated the traditional economic groups. Labor unrest and APRA and Communist party opposition were counteracted by repressive police state measures. To aggravate the crisis, boundary disputes led to a war against Colombia, and in the course of it, in 1933, Sanchez Cerro was assassinated.[30]

In 1939, following a six-year dictatorship, Manuel Prado, a representative of the elite industrialists and large landholders was elected president. Prado, an ardent supporter and admirer of the United States, signed a trade agreement treaty in 1940 and, as a result, maximized production in all industrial sectors.[31] In concert with the economic activities of the nation, a new organic law of education was decreed in 1941 that in many ways resembled Leguia's law of 1920. It emphasized a type of technical education that reflected the geographic characteristics and economic needs of each region. Construction of these schools was restricted to the urban and rural areas where industrialists and hacendados were required to provide schooling for the children of their workers.

The Indian population, confined to the ayllus and remote areas of the highlands, were not included in the new reform. Instead, through the Bureau of Indian Affairs, brigadas culturales (cultural brigades), composed of teachers and volunteers, were organized for literacy training. After the initial interest by the government and before the program could make any headway, however, the brigades were disbanded.

Following Prado's term, Jose Bustamante was elected president in 1945. His main educational policy was to declare free public secondary education and to place a new emphasis on rural education. Under his rule, through a special decree, the government mandated the creation of the first 20 Núcleos Escolares Campesinos (NECs) in the highlands. The organization of the NECs called for the creation of a central school of six grades and numerous sectional schools of three grades in remote rural areas.[32]

The NECs emerged as a result of a Peruvian-Bolivian agreement signed in 1945 to seek educational solutions for the Indian population. The outside technical assistance and financial support for the program was provided by the U.S. government through the Servicio Cooperativo Peruano-Norteamericano (Peruvian-North American Cooperative Service), or SECPANE, which became an official agency of the Ministry of Education. The relative success of the NEC concept in Bolivia during the 1930s, along with the Peruvian experiences in mobile schools and cultural brigades in the 1940s, made the programs very promising. However, the remoteness of the NECs and a lack of financial incentives for teachers became problems and were among the reasons why the program was not expanded.[33]

The political plans of Bustamante were cut short when a military group headed by General Manuel A. Odria seized the government in 1948. Odria's dictatorial intentions were confirmed two years later when he ran as an unopposed candidate, won the election, and proclaimed himself constitutional president of Peru.[34] Under Odria's dictatorship, an ambitious educational plan financed by a special fund collected from tax revenues was begun. The major innovation of the reform was the construction of schools, particularly of the grandes unidades escolares, exclusively designed for the urban areas to meet the demands of the growing mestizo and cholo (lower-middle and working class) populations. The purpose of these schools was to integrate primary, secondary, and technical education in one physical plant, thus eliminating the small and crowded schools dispersed throughout the cities.[35] Throughout these years, however, most of these schools were only able to integrate the last two years of primary education, and in most cases, technical schools gradually faded away. In the rural areas, the NEC system was expanded with the support of SECPANE, and some modest results were achieved in literacy training and community mobilization for self-reliance. The program did less well in fomenting changes and transformation that would eliminate the Indian's marginal position in the social order.[36]

In 1956, Odria called for elections as a result of a large foreign debt and financial difficulties. APRA consolidated its reformist-rightist stance by aligning with Manuel Prado, who was elected president for a second term.[37] Prado's policies for economic recovery were based on concessions to the export-oriented industries: agriculture, mining, and fishing. His alliance with the large landholders led to more exploitation of the Indian population. Guerrilla activities, stimulated by the recent Cuban revolution, as well as worker strikes and Indian revolts protesting against government policies, were violently repressed by well-organized "antiterrorist" campaigns enforced by the Peruvian armed forces.[38]

Prado sought the assistance of SECPANE to conduct a national assessment of the Peruvian educational system. The census was meant to be used as a basis for the creation of a new organic law of education. The new law, however, never came into effect. Prado continued the expansion of the educational system, opening new schools and upgrading the existing secondary schools. To control the expansion of education, five regional centers were created to supervise primary education, and eight new rural normal schools were founded in the larger cities of the interior.[39]

Near the completion of Prado's presidential term in 1962 the national election for his successor failed to produce a candidate with an electoral majority. Before congress gathered to select a new president, and ten days before the end of Prado's constitutional term, a military junta invalidated the election and seized the presidency. The military junta ruled the country for only one year and for the most part under martial law. In its short term, it established the beginning of a nationwide agrarian reform plan. The junta developed an ambitious plan for constructing low-cost housing in the urban areas, and in an attempt to decentralize the Ministry of Education, two educational regions were created, one in Lima and the other in the northern coastal city of Chiclayo -- each one with independent administrative and academic control.[40]

The junta called for national elections in 1963, and Fernanco Belaunde Terry, the populist candidate, was elected as the new constitutional president of Peru. The Belaunde presidency (1963-68) attempted to continue the agrarian, educational, and other reforms initiated by the junta but encountered political opposition from APRA and others.[41] Through U.S., UN, and private philanthropy the Belaunde government introduced a secondary school reform and built schools in the remotest areas of the country to increase access and extend the influence of the national government.[42] While dropout rates remained very high at the youngest age levels, the existence of formal education was associated with the increasing appearance of Spanish-speaking urban factory and service workers. In effect, this period saw the narrowing of the traditionally broad social definition of "Indian" to one of monolingualism in Quechua alone, and increase dependence on class-based criteria to differentiate among population segments. The opportunity for social and economic advancement in the country changed little, however, as Indian identification determined to a large extent one's status in the society.

Education served these ethnic divisions ideologically and practically through the extension of schooling to the lowest socioeconomic sectors. While the traditional dichotomy of mestizos and Indians continued to be blurred and accompanied by the growth of the urban <u>cholo</u> population, there nevertheless remained, as there are today, sharp social and economic lines between the minority urban/Spanish-speaking/industrial-commercial/U.S.-European-oriented segment of the population and the majority segment working in the agricultural highlands, speaking Quechua, dressing and living in traditional indigenous/colonial patterns, and not participating in national politics. The blurring has been due to the cumulative impact of industrialization, rural migration, land and political reforms, intranational communication, and so on -- all of which have tended to create a broad middle group of factory and service workers, small businessmen, bureaucrats, and commercial peasants whose allegiances are more national, creole, and urban than ethnic or community based.[43]

The opposition to Belaunde, plus the near bankrupt economy he headed, led to another coup d'etat in 1968. This time, however, the new military junta began its rule by adopting measures that, until then, only the leftist groups had been suggesting in their programs. These included agrarian reform, nationalization of foreign-owned industries, and sweeping educational reforms. Because people inside and outside of Peru were unaccustomed to leftist military regimes, there was a great deal of confusion about the government's ideological and practical orientation. Some conservatives and some leftists groups identified Peru as a new Cuba. Others, again including leftists, described the regime as "bourgeois reformists," fostering state capitalism that was pro-oligarchy and pro-imperialist.[44] Nevertheless, the military junta implemented a revolutionary agrarian reform with egalitarian goals. For example, before the 1968 coup d'etat, 75 percent of arable land was owned by less than 1 percent of the minority-elite landowners. By 1979, almost one-fourth of rural families had ownership of almost 20 percent of the land.[45]

While the junta clearly put forth the first fresh look at Peruvian society since the Leguia regime of the 1920s, its rhetoric often surpassed and conflicted with its ability to implement reforms. Like other governments before it, for example, the military junta explicitly recognized and even extolled the differences among cultural groups, with special emphasis on the characteristics and contributions of the indigenous population. Although it attempted to take these differences into account for policymaking, in actual practice its eagerness to unify the country and create a new nationalism that included all sectors found the Indian treated as a social structural segment of society rather than as an ethnic or cultural segment. Thus, as the government's agricultural reform effort drew much of its policy rhetoric from pre-Columbian models of communalism and communal cooperation, its actual programs treated members of rural sectors as a campesino (peasant) class with emphasis on the lands distributed rather than on the adaptation of agricultural reforms to particular culturally defined population segments.

The difficulty in matching rhetoric to practice is perhaps best seen in the 1972 educational reforms carried out under the military government. Attempts to eliminate the evils of the hacienda system were not sufficient to ensure Indian self-sufficiency, a skilled work force, and a loyal citizenry, so education played a major role in the revolutionary scheme to create a new society.[46] The educational reform was the first major reform since the 1920 law and the broadest in Peruvian history, especially as it related to subordinate group education and intergroup relations. The reform emphasized community education and the nuclearization of schooling. The process was designed to be highly participatory, with students, parents, and teachers forming an educational community designed to provide permanent and lifelong education inside and outside the schools. The community-based núcleo was to be the center of the process.[47] Although the ideas of individuals like Mariategui, Freire, and Illich, among others, were drawn on to guide the educational policy rhetoric -- including an emphasis on combining humanism and the world of work, overcoming social class bias in the educational levels, and so on -- the total configuration never materialized and often sounded like a more flexible but highly bureaucratized formal school system.

As the rhetoric on agricultural reform and education of the leftist military regime continued to flow, pressures from economic difficulties and the more conservative right began to emerge. By 1974, even though much of the former financial debt associated with Belaunde had been paid off, the military government could not secure credit from U.S. and

European banks. By 1975, as General Morales Bermudez assumed the chair of the junta, the revolutionary fervor of the junta began to turn to the right. The economic plan of Velasco had not been working, and combined with the credit difficulties, there was a need to devalue the Peruvian currency. Inflation increased and the now conservative government began to return expropriated industries to their former owners. Public reaction to these latter steps through riots, looting, and strikes -- found an equally strong reaction by the government, which declared a state of emergency and suspended all constitutional rights. Continued repression by the government accompanied by strikes and other actions by large segments of the population led the junta to call for a national election in 1980.[48] Belaunde Terry, deposed in 1968, again became president.

Even though the few educational reforms that had been put into place during Velasco's term have been gradually dismantled, they remain the latest and most sweeping statement of educational intent in the country. To illustrate intergroup relations in the educational sphere, therefore, we will draw primarily on the 1972 educational policies -- not necessarily practices -- in assessing education's contribution to overall efforts to foster interdependence and consensus.

Administratively, the educational system remains highly centralized, with all curricular, personnel, and financial decisions made at the ministerial level in the national capital. This is not out of step with traditional Spanish American colonial or postindependence governments where state and local units are more appendages of the central office than autonomous or semiautonomous units. Their basic purpose is to carry out orders from above on a localized level. Each school may have a local committee of parents, but the schools operate more as support groups for fund raising or teacher assistance than in any functional way to make decisions regarding curricula, teacher hiring, and so on. Within a type A society like Peru, this top-down centralization favors urban, dominant groups because they formulate policies, staff all administrative positions, and live and work in close proximity to the places where decisions are made. Although the 1972 reform proposed a different decision-making structure involving local participation in what would be the equivalent of local school districts, the rhetoric still preserved the decisional boundary-setting functions for centralized bureaucrats who offered no decentralization of financial, curricular, or other basic educational issues.

Although school decentralization is not a direct response to ethnic group relations, it is indicative of how the government incorporates local input into the structure and function of an important social service agency. The local nucleos were intended to strengthen the link between the ministry's policy-setting activity and the actual implementation of curricula in the community. Similarly, the nucleos were intended to offset the power of teacher unions by bringing parents into the actual running of schools. These policies, however, were detected as a means for the government to exercise its continuing control over education by co-opting parents as proponents of its policies. This seems apparent because parents are not elected to participate in the núcleo governance structure, and the elected bodies have no real power to alter the educational process. This demonstrates the centripetal basis for the use of education in intergroup relations in Peru, as individuals are incorporated structurally into the total configuration of apparent decision making without the loss of central power or control by the principal decision makers.

The maintenance of central control in the Ministry of Education and in favor of the dominant mestizo population can be seen in other aspects of the 1972 reform. Access to education, for example, reflects a centripetal structural and cultural bias as educational success under the reform required a greater assimilation of dominant group values and norms. In the reform, access to education was not based on expanding facilities or training large numbers of teachers. For example, relatively little attention was paid to the historical disparity between the overt qualifications of urban and rural teachers or to the placement of the best qualified teachers in urban areas.[49] Rather than attending to these kinds of practical issues, the reform emphasized a change in the way education was to be thought about and conceptualized. Access therefore was not something associated with increasing the number of desks or classrooms. It was more concerned with relating life-long opportunities for learning, emphasizing participation in the learning process, expanding and making more flexible the curricula, taking advantage of workplaces and existing public facilities as learning sites, and decreasing the emphasis on formal credentials relative to other experiences as the basis for school entry. Whereas such policies inevitably created greater and different kinds of educational opportunities for indigenous populations, their impact did not shift power or control to such segments. Instead, both structurally and culturally the policies required that indigenous sectors learn skills that required their leaving their traditional jobs and lifeways for those associated with more urban mestizo patterns of behavior.

Even though the reform had these implications for those who would be schooled, most rural dwellers were subject to factors that hindered access and school completion rates. These included direct and hidden costs, foregone income qualitative factors in teaching, physical plants and materials, and the hidden tracking toward labor immobility.[50] Although enrollment figures were encouraging for rural and minority areas, data for school completion indicated continuing low levels of success for lower social classes in general and minority/indigenous groups in particular.[51] The strong parallel system of private lay and religious schools from kindergarten through university continued to exist under the reform in most cities but did little to alleviate problems of access or completion for the majority. This is because private schools retained the right of selective admission even though they offered the same courses of studies and were regulated by the same administrative structure that monitored the public system. Free structures and examinations for admission have the effect of restricting access to private schools to the upper classes despite a requirement that 10 percent of admissions must be by scholarship. Such scholarships have not extended as far as the indigenous minority population.

Although the reform called for a more localized and sensitive basis for curriculum planning, including the portrayal of Peruvian life as a diverse and varied one, the curriculum's major goal was to forge a nation-state with common symbols for all population sectors. Again, this can be seen as an attempt to centripetally bring indigenous populations into the mainstream rather than to permit and encourage them to develop their own symbols and hence a centrifugal force for greater autonomy. Local variation in curricula was never able to overcome the strong centralized bias toward urban middle and upper-class experience and interest. When the curriculum was balanced with more substance drawn from the background and contributions of the minority indigenous populations, the result was typically superficial attention to folklore and simplistic cultural behaviors (clothing, food). As no separate financial resources or technical assistance was available to local communities for use in the preparation of localized curricula, reliance was on the national, standardized, often academically oriented curriculum prepared centrally. Similarly, the emphasis on preparation for work in the reform was difficult to adapt meaningfully to particular locales in the absence of resources, resulting in another mechanism to push the indigenous sector out of its cultural milieu and into urban areas.

As part of the curriculum, considerable attention has been given to the use of indigenous languages for school instruction. Despite a 1975 law mandating the rapid phasing in of Quechua or other appropriate primary languages of instruction in indigenous areas and their use as secondary languages in urban areas, Spanish remains the language of dominance in classrooms. Apart from experimental programs in isolated highland areas, the use of Quechua and Aymara appears to be limited to ad hoc judgments as to their need and appropriateness by individual teachers. Only in the experimental programs is such instruction accompanied by Quechua, Aymara, or other language-specific curricular materials and supported by teacher training programs.[52]

The language policies adopted as part of the reform demonstrate the dominant group's interest and recognition of non-Spanish speakers and take steps to increase the relevance of curricula to foster greater retention in schooling. At the same time, such primary language instruction is not contemplated as a means to centrifugally enhance indigenous power or status. Instead, it is used as a mechanism to facilitate the indigenous population's transition into the mainstream and to learn Spanish. Even though the learning of Spanish is often the preference of learners and their parents, the preference typically results from a recognition that Spanish is necessary in a type A situation. The language of instruction issue, therefore, is an additional example of how the educational system fosters structural integration of indigenous peoples as producers and consumers in the national economy and polity. It also suggests that the dominant group can permit some cultural centrifugality through educational practice but only as a means to forge ultimately a society based on centripetal white-mestizo, urban values.

CONCLUSION

The foregoing indicates that education policies in Peru are an accurate reflection of the white-criollo group's overall approach to intergroup relations in the society: the maintenance of its own dominant cultural position, the Indian's acceptance of that dominance as legitimate, and the limited access of individual Indians to the dominant group but at the cost of rejecting their own group identity.

Over the past 80 years, the extension of schooling to Indian areas has been the dominant group's principal means of promoting intergroup consensus and interdependence. It has done so, however, against a backdrop that facilitates the coercive and dependent exploitation of the Indians as a group within the national economic and political system.

The Peruvian case generally confirms the outlines of the type A society suggested by La Belle and White,[53] especially as regards the strict verticality of intergroup relations and the underlying reliance on the threat of coercion for society integration. But the case of Peru also suggests that type A, as proposed, is limited in its utility to describe accurately individual multiethnic countries. Although La Belle and White provide no multiethnic examples, it is interesting to note that a more complex model would be needed to portray Peru fully. In particular, Peru's numerous ethnic and language minorities -- blacks, Chinese, Japanese, jungle Indian groups -- do not all fit into the cultural and structural bounds of the subordinate group circle used to illustrate the type A relationship. The Japanese-Peruvians, to take one example, share most of the structural attributes of the whites-criollos (urban commerce, state bureaucracy, political participation) while maintaining a separate cultural identity that incorporates both Japanese and Peruvian elements. Furthermore, this distinct Japanese-Peruvian cultural identity would be diagrammed as more nearly horizontal to the dominant group's sphere than directly subordinate to it, as is the case with the Indians.

The application of the model to a multiethnic situation also raises the issue of whether it is possible to deal with white-Indian relations alone in Peru without attention to cholos. These people straddle the country's main ethnic divisions; although they display cultural and structural attributes of the Indians and whites-criollos, cholos are not recognized as belonging to either of Peru's major ethnic groups. More importantly, there is some evidence that cholos and mestizos are not merely a transitional category, on the way from Indian-ness to assimilation into the white-criollo group, but rather a stable and permanent new ethnicity in the country.[54]

Finally, the Peruvian case is more complex than the stark type A model in that the structural overlap between the dominant and subordinate groups (the kind of occupations that can be held by members of either group) is actually much larger than type A suggests. As much as one-fifth (3.5 million) of the Peruvian population falls into the middle ground -- sharing with Indians the subordinate structural characteristics of depending on agriculture in an increasingly urban society but identifying in language, dress, and so forth with the dominant white-criollo group's cultural norms.

The role of public education in maintaining the subordinate relationships of Indians to whites in Peru also conforms in most respects to what La Belle and White suggest in a type A case. Namely, in a sharply stratified society, all aspects of publicly-sponsored education remain in the hands of the dominant group. Specific policies reflect its agenda for the subordinate group, allowing little or no room for the subordinate group's expression of its own structural or cultural interests. The instructional language policy, the centralization of decision making, the urban-oriented curricula, and the extension of limited levels of schooling to Indian areas are all responses to dominant group demands. In none of these four policy areas has Indian control been allowed to prevail. Thus, in a type A society like Peru, education may be a vehicle for the mobility of certain subordinate group individuals but not for the subordinate group as a whole. Further, even this limited mobility requires an individual's complete break with the Indian culture and structural characteristics, if not full assimilation into the white-criollo group.

The example of Peruvian education also illustrates how, in a type A society, physical access to schooling may act to reinforce a subordinate group's position -- especially when combined, as in Peru, with one-language and common-curriculum policies. In effect, rural schools in Peru provide white-criollo access to Indians, for purposes of socialization and training, rather than access for Indians to wider societal benefits.

Another important point brought out by the Peruvian case is that subordinate group participation in the educational hierarchy, as with the parental voice on the local nucleo boards, does not have to be accompanied by effective decision-making power. Indian parents have no more control over the schools or educational personnel now, under the 1972 reform, than they did before. What Indian "participation" may actually accomplish, however, is to build the kind of consensus about the role of schooling that favors the continued domination of the white-criollo group.

NOTES

1. J. A. del Busto, Perú incaico (Lima: Librería Studium S. A., Editores, 1978).
2. B. Cobo, History of the Inca Empire, trans. and ed. Roland Hamilton (Austin: University of Texas Press, 1979).
3. D. Valcarcel, Historia de la educación incaica (Lima: Universidad Nacional Mayor de San Marcos, 1961).
4. E. González C. and V. Galdo G., "Historia de la educación en el Perú," Historia del Perú, vol. 10 (Lima: Editorial Juan Mejía Baca, 1980), pp. 11-123.
5. R. G. Paulston, Society, School and Progress in Peru (Oxford: Pergamon Press, 1971).
6. Carlos D. Valcárcel E., Breve historia de la educación peruana. (Lima: Colección Ciencias Histórico Sociales, Editorial Educación, 1975).
7. González and Galdo, "Historia de la educación en el Perú," pp. 61-70.
8. R. A. Humphrey, "The Fall of the Spanish American Empire." History, October 1962, pp. 244-54.
9. Ibid., p. 248.
10. V. J. Ortecho V., El derecho a la educación (Trujillo, Perú: Impreso en Gráfica "El Liberal," Editorial Amaru, 1972).
11. Paulston, Society, School and Progress in Peru, p. 33.
12. A. Alfageme and M. Valderrama, El debate sobre la cuestión agraria y el problema indígena nacional a comienzos del siglo xx. (Lima: Universidad Católica, 1977).
13. Ibid., p. 3.
14. F. Chevalier, "Official Indigenismo in Peru in 1920: Origins, Significance, and Socioeconomic Scope," in Race and Class in Latin America, ed. Magnus Mörner (New York: Columbia University Press, 1971), pp. 184-96.
15. W. Kapsoli, Los movimientos campesinos en el Perú 1879-1965 (Lima: Delva Editores, 1977).
16. L. G. Arista M., El curriculum y la dependencia educativa peruana, Colección Mundo Latinoamericano (Lima: Editorial litográfica La Confianza, 1973).

17.   E. Barrantes, Pedagógica (Lima: Universidad Nacional Mayor de San Marcos, 1966).

18.   Alfageme and Valderrama, El debate sobre la cuestion agraria y el problema indígena y nacional a comienzos del siglo xx, pp. 6-7.

19.   Ibid.

20.   Ibid., p. 38.

21.   Ibid., p. 34.

22.   Chevalier, "Official Indigenismo in Peru in 1920," p. 184.

23.   C. I. Degregori, "Indigenismo, clases sociales y problema nacional," in Indigenismo, clases sociales y problema nacional (Lima: Ediciones Celats, 1980, pp. 17-51.

24.   E. Ballón, C. Pezo, L. Peirano, and Y. G. Valdez, Educación básica laboral: proceso a un proceso, no. 9 (Lima: Desco, 1978.

25.   J. C. Mariátegui, 7 ensayos de interpretación de la realidad peruana, 26th ed. (Lima: Biblioteca Amauta, 1973), pp. 118-19.

26.   Degregori. "Indigenismo, clases sociales y problema nacional," pp. 41-48.

27.   Mariátegui, J. C., 7 ensayos de interpretación de la realidad peruana, p. 106.

28.   Arista, El curriculum y la dependencia educativa peruana, pp. 46-48.

29.   Chevalier, "Official Indigenismo in Peru in 1920," p. 194.

30.   R. Rivera S., Historia del Perú-República 1822-1968, 2nd ed. (Lima: Editorial Juridíca, 1974).

31.   F. Bourricaud, Poder y sociedad en el Perú contemporaneo (Buenos Aires: Editorial Sur, 1967).

32.   M. Aréstegui M., Nuclearización educativa: teoría y práctica (Lima: Impreso en los talleres de ITAL-Perú S.A., 1976).

33.   Ibid., p. 38.

34.   Rivera, Historia del Perú-República, pp. 237-44.

35.   Aréstegui, Nuclearización educativa, pp. 46-50.

36.   Ibid., pp. 33-46.

37.   C. Pezo, E. Ballón, and L. Peirano, El magisterio y sus luchas: 1885-1978 (Lima: Desco, 1978), p. 103.

38.   Kapsoli, Los movimientos campesinos en el Perú 1879-1965, p. 117-44.

39.   Gonzáles and Galdo, "Historia de la educación en el Perú," p. 103.

40. Rivera, Historia del Perú-República, pp. 266-69.

41. R. L. Clinton, "Military-Led Revolution in Peru: A Postmortem," Latin America Review, no. 15 (1980):148-205.

42. R. Paulston, "Educational Stratification and Cultural Hegemony in Peru," Journal of Developing Areas, April 1971, pp. 401-15.

43. D. Sulmont, Los movimientos populares en el Perú. Programa Académico de Ciencias Sociales (Lima: Pontificia Universidad Católica, 1983).

44. A. Quijano O., "Contemporary Peasant Movements," in Elites in Latin America, ed. S. M. Lipset and M. Solari (New York: Oxford University Press, 1967), pp. 301-40.

45. E. H. Epstein, "Peasant Consciousness Under Peruvian Military Rule," Harvard Educational Review 52, no. 3 (August 1982):280-300.

46. E. H. Epstein, "Education and Peruanidad: 'Internal' Colonialism in the Peruvian Highlands," Comparative Education Review 15, no. 2 (June 1971):188-201.

47. A. Salazar Bondy, La educación del hombre nuevo: la reforma educativa peruana (Buenos Aires: Editorial Paidos, 1975).

48. E. S. Huber, "The Peruvian Military Government, Labor Mobilization and the Political Strength of the Left," Latin America Research Review 13, no. 2 (1983):37-93.

49. G. Alberti and J. Cotler, Aspectos sociales de la educación rural en el Perú (Lima: Instituto de Estudios Peruanos, 1972).

50. N. Gall, La reforma educativa peruana (Lima: Mosca Azul Editores, 1976).

51. Centro de Información Estudios y Documentación, Perú: la reforma educativa en una sociedad de clases (Lima, 1980).

52. Gall, La reforma educativa peruana.

53. T. LaBelle and P. White, "Education and Multiethnic Integration: An Intergroup-Relations Typology," Pt. 1, Comparative Education Review 24, no. 2 (June 1980):155-73.

54. A. Quijano, Dominación y cultura: lo cholo y el conflicto cultural en el Perú (Lima: Mozca Azul Editores, 1980).

4

EDUCATION
AND INTERGROUP RELATIONS
IN HAITI

Anthony Layne

The republic of Haiti is the poorest country in the Western Hemisphere. Data provided by the Inter-American Development Bank indicate, among other things, the following: Gross domestic product (GDP) per capita in Haiti is about U.S. $267 in 1980 dollars; GDP per capita has grown annually at an average rate of about 0.3 percent over the past two decades; prices have been at a very high level; infant mortality per 1,000 live births is about 150; and the rate of illiteracy is about 80 percent.[1] On the basis of Haiti's poverty alone, the study of education and intergroup relations in this Caribbean country is of special importance.

The special importance of the Haitian case becomes even more readily apparent when two additional factors are taken into account. First, this densely populated but small country-- with a population of 5 million on a total land area of 27,750 square kilometers--has the distinction of being the world's first black-ruled republic and the second country in the Americas to gain its political independence. During the Haitian Revolution (1791-1803), the bloodiest slave uprising the world has ever known, mulattoes and blacks united to drive the French colonial masters from what was then the French colony of St. Domingue. No sooner had the two allies rid themselves of their common enemy than they engaged in a fratricidal war that has continued to this day.

The mulattoes comprise at most about 5 percent of the population and are persons of mixed European and African descent; the blacks comprise about 90 percent of the population and are the descendants of the African slaves who worked on the sugar plantations of St. Domingue. Fundamentally, the struggle between these two ethnic groups has been a contest to determine which would fill the power vacuum left by the former French colonial master and to determine which would control the country's very limited economic resources. Haiti's limited economic resources can be readily appreciated from the fact that three-quarters of the land area is occupied by three very high ranges of mountains.

The second factor contributing to the significance of the Haitian case is the peculiar mixture of forces acting upon its geopolitical surroundings. Apart from Haiti's extreme poverty, its extremely violent history of interethnic relations, and its topography, there is the fact that Haiti is a mere 17 kilometers away from communist Cuba. Haiti's geopolitical significance has been amply demonstrated in the military occupation of that sovereign country by the United States (1915-35) and by the abiding interest that the United States has had in forestalling in the black republic any repetition of the Cuban model. What is more, Haiti has been virtually isolated from the mainstream of international affairs, as the major capitalist powers, notably France, have never actually forgiven the Haitians for the way they won their political independence.

The main purpose of the present study is to show that education in Haiti has served the interests of the mulatto minority, a minority that has had a virtual monopoly of cultural prestige and economic and political power. Our analytical framework is that suggested by La Belle and White in which Haiti is classified as a type A country, that is, a country in which cultural and structural segmentation has taken place in a vertical relationship.[2] Attention will be given first to the cultural, economic, and political interaction between the mulattoes and the blacks. This contextual information is indispensable for acquiring an adequate understanding of the major forces that have had an impact on educational policy itself.

CULTURE, CLASS, AND POWER: CULTURAL CENTRIPETALITY VERSUS CULTURAL CENTRIFUGALITY

To the uncritical eye, Haiti is a culturally unified society in which mulattoes and blacks relate on a roughly equal footing to each other. Both groups speak Haitian Creole, making, in a statistical and emotional sense, that language the national language. Both groups profess to follow the official religion, Catholicism. Both groups have gained international renown for their love of the arts, especially painting. Both groups have traditionally been small farmers, for large plantations symbolized the French colonial planter and master. These apparently centripetal tendencies in cultural relations mask the more fundamental centrifugal or conflictual forces at work and the strict verticality of the relationship between the two ethnic groups in question.

Two areas of cultural interaction may be singled out for special attention because of their critical importance in the deep-seated segmentation of culture within the power structure. The two areas are religion and language. As mentioned, Catholicism, the religion of the former colonial master, is the official religion of Haiti. Voodoo, or Vodun, however, has been for the predominantly black mass of the population the unofficial religion. An authoritative study of Haitian voodoo, including its essential characteristics and social functions, can be found in Simpson.[3] What needs to be highlighted is the fact that voodoo is an animistic, polytheistic religion brought by the black slaves from Africa and that it initially had revolutionary overtones in Haiti. The black slaves made it unmistakably clear in their voodoo ceremonies that they planned on destroying the whites and all their posessions.[4] The early rulers of independent Haiti feared that the blacks would use voodoo against them in the same way that it had been used against the whites.* This mulatto superordinate group soughtto carry out a centripetalist cultural policy by insisting that both ethnic groups adhere to the Catholic religion. But voodoo had such a strong hold on the minds of the Haitians that some of the early rulers (1804-43) secretly consulted

---

*The Haitian Revolution, for instance, was started by the black slaves in the north in an elaborate voodoo ceremony that terrified the whites.

that is, voodoo priests, and they were imitated by their successors.

Cultural segmentation became more strikingly evident after 1860. In that year the mulatto-dominated political directorate signed a concordat with the Holy See that was to last for 100 years. The concordat of 1860 regularized the Catholic hierarchy in Haiti, reaffirmed Catholicism as that country's official religion, and gave the Catholic church special privileges (including special privileges in education). During 1915-34, that is, during the U.S. occupation of Haiti, the Americans sometimes destroyed the voodoo temples and rigorously carried out the law against voodoo, either by imposing heavy fines on the houngans or by subjecting the houngans to the corvee (forced labor in the construction of roads).

A new offensive was launched against voodoo during 1941-46, the last five years of a mulatto political regime that had monopolized public office since 1915. That offensive culminated in the "movement of the rejectees" when many houngans renounced any connection with voodoo. In spite of the combined onslaught of the political directorate, the Catholic church, and the occupation authorities, voodoo is still practiced by most Haitian blacks and by some members of the mulatto elite, even if practiced privately.[5] In order to survive, however, voodoo has had to rid itself of what the whites, the mulattoes, and some members of the professedly Catholic-educated black group have considered its most pagan feature, namely, the dance of the sacrifice (of animals).

In the area of religion, the centrifugal tendency by the blacks, as a group, has been countered, therefore, not only by the denigration of voodoo but also by the use of coercion to force the blacks to accept the superordinate Catholic religion. In the area of language, the mulatto-dominated ruling class also adopted a centripetalist policy but with much less vigor than in the area of religion. Haitian Creole (hereafter called Creole) is spoken by both the mulattoes and the blacks; it is the only language of blacks in rural areas and most blacks in the urban zone. However, the official language of Haiti is French, which, like Catholicism, reflects the continued dominance of the culture of the former colonial power in a country whose population is overwhelmingly of African descent. French is used exclusively in all formal public situations, including the entire formal educational system.

The number of persons who are able to read, write, understand, and speak French -- that is, who are fluent in French --

is, at the very most, about 100,000, in a population of 5 million.[6] The Haitians fluent in French, in the words of Berry, are the "aristocracy of literacy" and have been separated from everybody else, primarily by their fluency.[7] Some members of the "aristocracy of literacy" are proud of their colonial past and have spoken in glowing terms of the need to perpetuate in Haiti the dominance of the language and culture of France. For instance, in 1938 in Paris, the Haitian ambassador to France, M. Constantin Mayard, praised the continued dominance in his country of French institutions, literature, legislation, and the Paris-oriented educational system.[8] As Moore has observed, it has been the preeminently mulatto elite who, ever since the liberation, have ensured that their members be educated in Catholic and private schools and frequently in France itself.[9]

The subordinate black group has largely internalized the notion that Creole is a sign of ignorance, poverty, and inferior status. French has been used by the "aristocracy of literacy" as a mechanism for maintaining distance from the "natives," and it is precisely for this reason that while the blacks consider French to be the "language of double-dealing and corruption," they still wish their children to be fluent in French.[10] To be sure, there are some blacks who are fluent in french and have been selectively absorbed into the mulatto-dominated superordinate sphere, a phenomenon that conforms with a very narrow interpretation of integration. It is in this context that one begins to understand why there has been no opposition by the political directorate to a movement that originated during the 1920s to put Creole on an "equal" footing with French.

Segmentation and Centrifugality in Economic Relations

On the small farms in Haiti, the centripetal influence of the cultural norm has been negated or contradicted by the conflict over the distribution of fertile land in a country that has relatively little. The black peasants have not changed their centuries-old practices of living in mud huts with thatched roofs (cailles); traveling by donkey; cultivating their lands with such traditional African agricultural implements as the hoe, the machete, and the dibble; and growing food for their own consumption, as well as growing some coffee and cotton for sale. The problem is that many of the black peasant holdings can no longer support the relatively large families that depend on them. Major reasons for this condition include population pressure on the limited supply of land from fragmentation of holdings through the traditional division of their lands by peasant fathers among their sons, soil erosion, and frequent droughts.[11]

While black peasants have been forced to climb barren northern hillsides in a futile search for arable land, the prime agricultural area has been monopolized by the mulattoes and by American companies. The mulattoes have generally maintained the same lands owned before the liberation. They have, however, maintained their holdings as small farms, perhaps due to the uprising against the white plantation owners during the revolution. The foundation laid for the one or two large plantations owned by American companies was established during the U.S. occupation, when authorities rescinded the 1804 law prohibiting foreign whites from owning land in Haiti.[12] Moreover, the mulattoes continued to dominate the import-export trade, while other economic sectors (particularly agricultural processing, mining, construction, and assembly-type operations) were dominated by American, French, and Canadian companies.[13]

The most dynamic of the economic sectors, manufacturing, will probably continue to be dominated by foreign companies, according to the Inter-American Development Bank:

> The Haitian Government is considering the adoption of a new investment code that consolidates the present benefits and includes tax exemptions, tariff exceptions for imports that are re-exported, guaranteed repatriation of a percentage of the profits, and tariff protection for industries that satisfy 75 percent of the local demand and meet certain quality and price standards.[14]

In the industrial sector, labor costs are concentrated in and around Port-au-Prince and have been the lowest in Latin America and the Caribbean.[15] The minimum daily wage scale for industrial workers was raised by government decree from U.S. $0.70 prior to the year 1971 to U.S. $1.00 in 1971, from U.S. $1.30 in 1974 to U.S. $1.60 in 1977, and from U.S. $2.20 in 1979 to U.S. $2.64 by 1981. In the face of rampant inflation, the already low purchasing power of the urban industrial workers during 1971-77 alone was reduced by 45 percent.[16] In addition, some unscrupulous industrialists have circumvented the minimum wage rate by paying workers, especially females working at home, on a piece-rate basis, resulting in daily wages as low as U.S. $1.00.[17]

Verticality Through Force

The cultural and economic inequalities have been maintained largely through the use of force. The period of 1843-1915 was one of military adventurism and incessant political upheaval that benefited the mulattoes primarily as well as their ally, the army.[18]

The American military occupation enabled the mulattoes to govern not only from 1915 to 1934 but also through 1946. Control of the government from 1946 by the blacks was accompanied by political corruption, the reliance of black presidents on the advice of the mulattoes and the United States, and the intervention of the Haitian army whenever the urban blacks screamed for the blood of those they originally hailed as saviors.[19]

The democratic process was never really established after 1957, when Haiti's first elections under universal adult suffrage were held. President Francois "Papa Doc" Duvalier declared himself president-for-life in 1964. With the help of his dreaded paramilitary organization, the Tonton Macoutes, Papa Doc ruled Haiti with an iron fist. He died in 1971, and the presidency-for-life was passed on to his son, Jean-Claude Duvalier. Jean-Claude disbanded that dreaded organization, only to replace it with the Leopards, "his special private battalion which is standing by to move against any dissenter."[20] It must be emphasized, however, that the continued cultural and structural subordination of the blacks to the mulattoes has not been maintained exclusively through the use of force, for the educational system has been an important institution that has helped build the minimal measure of consensus necessary for the society to survive, while simultaneously carrying out a rigidly selective function.

SEGMENTATION, VERTICALITY, AND EDUCATIONAL POLICY

In this study special attention will be given to three areas of educational policy: curriculum, access to education, and educational articulation. Let us begin with the curriculum, bearing in mind the dominance of French cultural values and traditions, the rigidity of the class structure, and the political subordination of the blacks.

Cultural Centripetalist Policy and the Curriculum

The heavy classical and academic emphasis in the curriculum in Haitian urban schools has been part of a tradition firmly established before the reign of the mulatto ruler Petion (1807-16). Petion opened a single public school, a high school. In that public high school (lycee) all the subjects taught in secondary schools in France were made available to those mulattoes not sufficiently wealthy to provide an education in France for their children. Those subjects were Latin, French, English, other modern languages, mathematics, navigation, ancient and modern geography, religious and ancient history, and drawing.[21]

French, the superordinate language, was used as the medium of instruction in all schools, and in the urban areas, a curriculum modeled on that in France gained strength with the signing of the concordat of 1860. The concordat authorized the Catholic clergy to establish their own schools and placed a number of urban public primary schools under the management of the Catholic church. The schools built by the Catholic church were better constructed, better equipped, and better staffed than the public schools. They catered to the children of the mulatto elite and widened the sociocultural gap that already existed between the mulattoes and the blacks.[22] What needs to be highlighted is the centripetalist educational policy of excluding the voodoo religion from the curriculum and of using French as the medium of instruction at the expense of Creole.

Educational policy was also designed to facilitate the selective absorption of a handful of blacks into the superordinate sphere. There was in fact one curriculum for schools in the urban zone and another for the rural areas. There were no secondary schools in the rural areas, the black zone. The primary school curriculum in the rural areas was heavily oriented toward agricultural rather than academic education. The rural schools became increasingly fashionable after the Ministry of Education was established in 1843. They were located on plantations, had annexes of land where marketable crops were produced with a view to making those schools self-financing, and were given legal backing by the law of 1848.[23]

The use by the mulattoes of an academically oriented urban school system to preserve their dominance through the selective absorption of a few blacks into the superordinate sphere was challenged by the Americans during the occupation. The new American political bosses believed that Haiti was too poor to afford the luxury of an academic education that made no contribution to the agricultural production of a predominantly agricultural society. They also feared that with the dearth of opportunities for professional employment, too much academic education in the urban areas would give birth to revolutionaries.[24] The Americans clearly had their fingers on the pulse of Haiti, for the so-called "revolution of 1946" was spearheaded by a group of impoverished and disaffected black professionals who had not been absorbed and neutralized by the power structure.

During the occupation, the Americans took control of rural education, increased its vocational content, and financially starved the upper branches of the Haitian urban educational system when the local ruling class resisted what it considered to be the "Anglo-Saxonization" of its hallowed Paris-oriented urban school system.[25] Among other things, American control of the purse strings was used to bring about the closure of the school of medicine at Port-au-Prince.

After the occupation, the curriculum in Haiti's educational institutions reflected the cultural impact of France and the United States but little or nothing of the cultural impact of Africa. The mulattoes used their monopoly of political power from 1934 to 1946 to increase the vocationalization of public primary education, both urban and rural, along the lines set by the Americans. The black elite, on assuming control of the government in 1946, reinstated the old French curriculum and rid itself of both the previous reforms as well as the reformers.[26] The rivalry between the two political factions within the dominant local political class did not imply a transformation of the educational and other major institutions to serve the interests of the massive black population. Rather, it has been a manifestation of political factionalism within the ruling class over the most effective means of achieving structural centripetality, while simultaneously keeping the Blacks qua group in a subordinate position.

Today, at all three levels of the formal educational system, there are institutions that provide academic education and institutions providing vocational and technical education. These institutions run comparatively parallel to one another at the different educational levels and are designed to serve differing ethnic populations. The rural areas, still having few lycees or colleges, are provided with primary education, predominantly agricultural. The courses of study at the State University of Haiti in Port-au-Prince are no longer exclusively literary and academic. American cultural and economic penetration have contributed to the inclusion in the university curriculum of such "practical" areas of study as the social and behavioral sciences, business administration, engineering, and applied linguistics. The most popular fields of study at the University of Haiti are nevertheless still medicine and law, reflecting the continuing high prestige of the "learned professions" and the commitment of students in these fields to staying in or gaining access to positions of power.

ACCESS TO EDUCATION AND EXCLUSIONARY POLICY

In the 1979-80 academic year, or some 175 years after independence, the net enrollment ratio for primary schooling in Haiti was 35 percent, and the gross enrollment ratios for secondary and tertiary education were, respectively, 12 and 1 percent.[27]

Several factors have contributed to the restriction of access to education favoring a very small portion of the population. First, education has had a very low priority for government spending. Haiti spends about U.S. $4.00 per inhabitant on education, as compared with the Latin American average of U.S. $73.[28] About 7.8 percent of the minimally estimated U.S. $238.1 million in external financial assistance granted to Haiti up to fiscal year 1980-81 has gone to education.[29] Public expenditure on education has been low since the liberation.

During the occupation, the Americans cut back on educational expenditure, and the mulatto political directorate continued this policy after the Americans' departure. Duvalier disregarded the education of the blacks and consistently reduced expenditure on education, with a consequential reduction in the size of school age (5 to 19) enrollment. For instance, during 1960-61 to 1966-67, the enrollment ratio for the school age group fell consistently from about 25 to 16.7 percent.[30]

Second, in addition to the low public expenditure on education, the grim prospects for black access to education have been compounded by the expensive nature of prive schools in Haiti. The cost of tuition alone in colleges ranges from U.S. $20 to $30 per month. The vast majority of black parents can ill afford to spend much money on the education of their children. The private schools, the most expensive and most prestigious of which are the Catholic schools, account for almost 70 percent of the primary schools and for more than half of the primary school enrollment. The private schools account for 80 percent of the secondary schools and for 75 percent of the secondary school enrollment. The Catholic schools still carry out the divisive function that they commenced from the signing of the concordat, and directors of some public schools have been known to send their own children to the Catholic schools.

Third, most of the small number of children of school age who are fortunate to gain admission to the public primary schools do not complete the primary school cycle. Repetition rates in the various primary grades averaged 50 percent at the start of the 1960s.[31] Repeated grade repetition leads to dropout. The current dropout rate in the public schools is about 50 percent in the primary grades and is even higher in the secondary grades, whereas the situation in the private schools is "somewhat better."[32] In the rural areas, only 2 percent of pupils admitted to school complete the primary cycle.[33]

The official explanation of the high dropout rate is given in terms of overcrowded classes, underqualified and "generally underpaid" teachers, and "poor" administration.[34] This type of explanation is superficial and simplistic. A more powerful explanation needs to take into account the following factors:

● The impact of low public educational expenditure on the physical accommodation for pupils and on the teaching staff.
● The insistence on the use of the French language, which most blacks do not understand
● The need of some black parents to keep their children in the labor force in order to supplement the familial income
● The perpetuation of a ruthless system of selection at every grade level within the school system, as well as for admission to the postsecondary technical institutes and the university.

In short, the real explanation lies in the use of the schools to serve the interests of the mulatto elite in a manner that is relentlessly exclusionary and that preserves the verticality of the power relationship.

Any lingering doubts about the largely exclusionary role of the schools in reinforcing the vertical relationship may be dispelled by examining the selection process in the final stage of academic secondary schooling. In 1979-80 there was a secondary school enrollment of 91,247 students, and of these 87,680, or 95.9 percent, were in general or academic education.[35] Of the 87,680 pupils in secondary general education, 9 percent were in the Rhetorique, and 4 percent were in the Philosophie. The Rhetorique is the sixth or penultimate year of the academic cycle, and the Philosophie is the seventh and final year. Entry to the Philosophie requires successful completion of the Rhetorique. Students who successfully complete both these examinations are awarded the baccalaureate certificate, a requirement for admission to the State University of Haiti.

Grade repeaters in secondary general education in 1979-80 totaled 4,118. Of those repeaters, 10 percent were in the Rhetorique and 2 percent in the Philosophie. The Rhetorique, a highly selective examination, reinforces the pattern of grade repetition. In 1979-80 the repetition rates in grades 1 to 4 of secondary general education ranged from 3 to 5 percent.[36] In 1979-80 the number of students enrolled at the State University was very small, 3,801 to be precise. Almost half of those students (49 percent) studied medicine, pharmacy, odontology, and law; 9 percent were in higher teacher training.[37] The low number of students in higher teacher training seems to contradict somewhat the government's stated desire for more highly qualified and trained teachers. Moreover, although Haiti's economy has been predominantly agricultural, only 4 percent of the students studied to be agriculturalists or veterinarians.

Patterns of Articulation and Tracking

The patterns of articulation and tracking have coincided with the ethnic boundaries between the mulattoes and the blacks. Primary schooling is a dead-end for the rural blacks. Secondary schools are concentrated in the cities, and this helps explain why the handful of rural blacks who manage to complete the primary cycle soon lose whatever gains they have made in speaking French. In the urban zone, the mainstream of academic education, for the mulattoes in private institutions and for a small proportion of blacks, has been functionally separate from similar education in the public academic schools.

There are about a dozen vocational secondary schools. These schools have programs running roughly parallel to the programs in the lycees and colleges. Both the academic and the vocational programs have a first or lower cycle of four years. The lycees and colleges, however, have a second or upper cycle of three years, and the vocational secondary schools have second or upper cycles ranging from two to four years. The lower cycle of vocational secondary schooling has been designed officially to provide training for semiskilled workers. The upper cycle has been designed to provide training for skilled workers and middle-level technicians.

The secondary vocational programs are aimed at channeling urban blacks of humble circumstances into occupations at the lower levels of the occupational and income ladder. However, privileged students, some of them with the baccalaureate certificate, have been making use of these relatively new programs. Such opportunistic students have little intention of entering low-wage jobs and seek to add technical know-how to the advantage they already possess in academic training. Regardless of the successful efforts of a few in achieving upward mobility, most blacks in the urban zone have suffered from the disadvantage of selection at the end of primary schooling for low-wage jobs and from the inability to secure places in the upper cycle of the vocational programs even if they qualify for such places.

In 1973 the Institut National de Formacion Professionelle (INEP) was created by the government to carry out a number of functions, including the coordination and standardization of the numerous vocational and technical programs. The INEP evidently has had its hands full, given the willingness of some elements in the ruling class to use these programs to their advantage. Moreover, several of the programs are sponsored by international funding agencies. Some of these agencies have had their own views on what is best for Haiti, and the government does not appear to be happy with them:

The degree of co-operation between the Haitian authorities and the donors of aid leaves something to be desired in many instances. The government hopes that this co-operation will be strengthened and rationalized in order that the external assistance may be better adjusted to the realities of the country, and that the assistance will be granted on the most liberal terms.[38]

Additional problems of coordination have resulted from the various administration departments splitting up responsibility for education. The American occupation authorities, who took over complete control of the Department of Agriculture, created a Technical Service and a Central School of Agriculture to serve as coordinating agencies for rural education. The Department of Public Education was left in Haitian hands. The black elite, who came to power in 1946, returned the responsibility for rural education to the Department of Public Education. Today, the administration of the educational system is still divided between different bodies. The Department of Agriculture has responsibility for all of the vocational agricultural schools, as well as for the Faculty of Agronomy and Veterinary Medicine at the University of Haiti. The Faculty of Medicine and Odontology is administered by the Department of Public Health. In principle, the Department of National Education looks after what is left. The private schools have functioned as autonomous units from the time of the concordat.

The low level of coordination of the formal educational system has been a function of political factionalism within the ruling class, rather than a result of any fundamental disagreement within that class as to the class or ethnic group whose interests should primarily be served by the educational system. Viewed from the top down, educational policy has been centripetal, with those fortunate few students who have successfully jumped over the multiplicity of hurdles in the process of educational selection by having conferred on them a "rite of passage" into the privileged cultural and structural circle of the dominant group. Small wonder, then, that the rate of illiteracy continues to be one of the highest in the world.

Francois Duvalier, on coming to power in 1957, launched what professed to be a country-wide campaign against illiteracy. Haiti's illiteracy rate is still about 75 percent, and the vast majority of it is in the rural areas. Regardless of what one may think of neighboring Cuba's communist road to development, the fact is that Cuba has shown that illiteracy can be defeated in a very short space of time, provided there is the political will to mobilize the masses to achieve that particular goal. Given the experience of Cuba, Chancy may very well be justified in claiming that the continued existence of Haiti's phenomenally high rate of illiteracy has been consciously maintained by the ruling class to make social and economic institutions function in their capitalistic interests.[39] Although it is difficult to demonstrate the deliberate perpetuation by the ruling class of this mass illiteracy, it is evident that the mass illiteracy has been functional in maintaining the exploitative structures that have been examined in this study. The functionality of mass illiteracy for the exploitation of the black majority helps to explain the granting by government of subsidies to private schools for the well-to-do, while the National Literacy and Community Office has been granted only that amount given to higher education. It also helps to explain why primarily until 1972 only 27 percent of the teachers in the rural areas had earned diplomas compared with 35 percent in the urban areas.[40] In addition, it helps to explain the scarcity of equipment and books, the scarcity of audiovisual aids and means of transport, the ineffectiveness of the monitors, and the general indifference of the population to the literacy campaign.[41]

CONCLUSION

In Paris, in September 1981, the representatives of the Haitian government made the following statement, which reveals that the political directorate is aware of the fundamental causes of the continued suffering of the blacks and of the need for the structural transformation of the economy:

Whereas in the past the distribution of incomes was governed mainly by market forces, with the consequence that the incomes of the poorest population groups have not kept pace with the rate of inflation, investments have benefited principally the well-off and the standard of living of many families has actually declined, it is proposed to rectify the situation by a number of measures, viz: (a) the redistribution of cultivable land; (b) the redirection of investments into activities offering greater benefits to the poor population groups; (c) the adjustment of prices in a manner benefitting the poor; (d) fiscal reform.[42]

On the educational front, it was proposed to ensure primary education for all by the year 2000, to reform the secondary school system, to promote technical and vocational training, and to stimulate technical and scientific research at the university level. The blacks in Haiti have grown accustomed to having their rulers make and then break promises. It is difficult to see how the proposal for radical economic reform can be reconciled by invitation with the contemplated intensification of industrialization. The educational reform proposals will mean very little unless they are linked to radical policies on religion, language, the system of land tenure, the private schools, and the class structure in general. Revolt in Haiti has led to repression and to further revolt and repression. Bombs are beginning to explode once more in the streets of Port-au-Prince. Unless drastic action is taken to remove the long-standing inequalities between the mulattoes and the blacks, these two groups may well discover themselves to be the protagonists in a second Haitian revolution but on opposite sides of the firing line.

Conceptually, the value of this study has rested on its moving beyond a traditional consensus or functionalist view of ethnic integration to one that examines the interplay between centripetal and centrifugal forces in the shaping of the integration process. The strict verticality of the power relationship between mulattoes and blacks in Haiti has been maintained primarily through force, but force has not always been necessary because of the function of selective absorption performed by the educational system. As the contradictions in Haitian society continue to work themselves out, it may eventually become more appropriate to analyze the Haitian case along the other more sophisticated dimensions of the La Belle-White typology. At this time, however, Haiti is a clear case of the naked use of power by a minority to keep the majority in cultural and structural subjection, a clear case of what may be considered the old colonial show under new management.

NOTES

1. Inter-American Development Bank, 1980-81 Report, pp. 274, 395.

2. T. La Belle and P. White, "Education and Multiethnic Integration: An Intergroup-Relations Typology," Pt. 1, Comparative Education Review 24, no. 2 (1980):155-73.

3. G. E. Simpson, Religious Cults of the Caribbean: Trinidad, Jamaica, and Haiti, enl. 3rd ed. (Rio Piedras, P.R.: Institute of Caribbean Studies, University of Puerto Rico, 1980), Pt. III.

4. C. L. R. James, The Black Jacobins, 2nd ed. rev. (New York: Random House, 1963), p. 18.

5. R. W. Logan, Haiti and the Dominican Republic (New York: Oxford University Press), pp. 180-81. See also O. E. Moore, Haiti: Its Stagnant Society and Shackled Economy (New York: Exposition Press, 1972), p. 119; and M. Hippolyte-Manigat, Haiti and the Caribbean Community (Kingston, Jamaica: Institute of Social and Economic Research, University of the West Indies, 1980), p. 49.

6. Hippolyte-Manigat, Haiti, pp. 57-58.

7. P. Berry, "Literacy and the Question of Creole," in The Haitian Potentials: Research and Resources of Haiti, ed. V. Rubin and R. P. Schaedel (New York: Teachers College Press, 1975), p. 86.

8. James, The Black Jacobins, p. 393.

9. Moore, Haiti, p. 114.

10. Berry, "Literacy and the Question of Creole," pp. 87-88.

11. F. Latortue, "Reflections on the Haitian Labour Force," in The Haitian Potential: Research and Resources of Haiti, ed. V. Rubin and R. P. Schaedal (New York: Teachers College Press, 1975), pp. 230-31. See also D. Marshall, "The Haitian Problem," in Illegal Migration to the Bahamas (Kingston, Jamaica: Institute of Social and Economic Research, University of the West Indies, 1979), pp. 3, 4.

12. E. G. Balch, "Notes on the Land Situation in Haiti," in Occupied Haiti, ed. E. G. Balch (New York: The Writers' Publishing Co., 1927), pp. 74, 75. See also A. C. Millspaugh, Haiti Under American Control 1915-1930 (Boston: World Peace Foundation, 1931), p. 153; and Marshall, "The Haitian Problem," p. 4.

13. Hippolyte-Manigat, Haiti and the Caribbean Community, pp. 127-40.

14. Inter-American Development Bank, 1980-81 Report, p. 279.

15. Ibid. See also Hippolyte-Manigat, Haiti and the Caribbean Community, pp. 113-18.

16. Femmes Haitinnes (Montreal: Maison d'Haiti, 1980), p. 14.

17. Ibid., pp. 17-18.

18. Balch, "Notes on the Land Situation in Haiti," p. 9. See also M. Dorsinville, "Haiti and Its Institutions: From Colonial Times to the Present," in The Haitian Potential, ed. by Y. Rubin and R. A. Schaedel (New York: Teachers College Press, 1975), pp. 201-05.

19. B. Diederich and A. Burt, Papa Doc: The Truth About Haiti Today (New York: McGraw-Hill, 1969), chap. 6, 7.

20. I. Hawkins, The Changing Face of the Caribbean (Bridgetown, Barbados: Cedar Press, 1976), p. 203.

21. K. Vielot, "Primary Education in Haiti," in The Haitian Potential: Research and Resources of Haiti, ed. V. Rubin and R. P. Schaedel (New York: Teachers College Press, 1975), p. 116.

22. Ibid., p. 18.

23. Ibid., p. 117.

24. Z. Baber and E. G. Balch, "Problems of Education," Occupied Haiti, ed. E. G. Balch (New York: The Writers' Publishing Co., 1927), pp. 93-94, 103-04.

25. Ibid., pp. 105-06.

26. Vielot, "Primary Education in Haiti," pp. 128-34.

27. UNESCO, Statistical Yearbook 1982 (Paris, 1982), table 3.2.

28. Ibid., tables 2.12 and 4.1.

29. United Nations Conference Secretariat, "Summary of the Country Presentation for Haiti," United Nations Conference on the Least Developed Countries, Paris, September 1, 1981, p. 12.

30. M. Chancy, "Education et Developpement en Haiti," in Culture et Developpement en Haiti: Symposium (Montreal: Lemeac, 1972), p. 138.

31. Vielot, "Primary Education in Haiti," p. 137.

32. United Nations Conference Secretariat, "Summary of the Country Presentation for Haiti," p. 10.

33. M. Chancy and C. Pierre-Jacques, "Problems Scolaires et Conditions Socio-economiques des familles," in Enfant de Migrants Haitiens en Amerique du Nord (Montreal: Centre de Recherches Caraibes, Universite de Montreal, 1982), p. 43.

34. United Nations Conference Secretariat, "Summary of the Country Presentation for Haiti," p. 10.

35. UNESCO, Statistical Yearbook 1982, table 3.7.

36. Ibid., table 3.9.

37. Ibid., table 3.12.

38. United Nations Conference Secretariat, "Summary of the Country Presentation for Haiti," p. 11.

39. Chancy, "Education et Developpement en Haiti," p. 147.

40. Ibid., p. 142.

41. Ibid., p. 137.

42. United Nations Conference Secretariat, "Summary of the Country Presentation for Haiti," p. 5.

PART II

CULTURAL SEGMENTATION AND STRUCTURAL COMMONALITY IN A VERTICAL RELATIONSHIP

5

BLACK AND BROWN UNDER THE WHITE CAPITALIST ENGLISH CROWN

Mark B. Ginsburg
and Judy K. Sands

In this chapter, on the relations among English residents of Asian, West Indian, and other origins, we label "other" as those nonbrown and nonblack (that is, white) people who have less recently migrated to England. We thus try to avoid referring to whites as English or indigeneous and to browns and blacks as immigrants.

In order to understand the contemporary relations among these three groups, each of which exhibits degrees of internal variation, we first trace the historical colonial relations and then briefly discuss the educational system that developed prior to the main immigration of blacks and browns to England.[1] Next we discuss educational and other relevant policies implemented after intergroup relations shifted from a colonial to a metropolitan context.

These discussions will provide an opportunity to assess the utility of La Belle and White's typology of intergroup relations[2] (see Chapter 1) with respect to England. This assessment will examine relations among whites, blacks, and browns, allowing us to ascertain whether they coincide with "type B: cultural segmentation and structural commonality in a vertical relationship." In addition, we shall gauge the extent to which educational policy in the following areas has resulted from the interaction of "centripetal" and "centrifugal" tendencies evidenced by the dominant (white) and subordinate (black and brown) groups:

- Access to education
- Articulation of and tracking within the system
- Curriculum content
- Language of instruction
- Degree of administrative centralization

Finally, we attempt to refine and clarify La Belle and White's discussion about "integrative mechanisms" by reference to recent Marxist analyses of the state -- a concept of central importance when examining policy determination. La Belle and White sometimes seem to adopt a liberal view of the state as a neutral structure vis-a-vis various class, ethnic, and gender groups, but in their definition of integrative mechanisms they imply that the state is simply and directly an expression of the superordinate group's interests.[3] In contrast to both approaches, we view state policy and action, following Poulantzas (see the bibliography at the end of this book), as being "determined by the necessity to reproduce capitalist relations in general" and the state as being infused with the contradictions of capital.[4] This view is perhaps most clearly articulated by Offe and Ronge:

> What the state protects and sanctions is a set of rules
> and social relationships which are pre-supposed by the
> class rule of the capitalist class. The state does not
> defend the interests of one class, but the common in-
> terests of all members of capitalist society.[5]

Remembering that capitalist political economies are inherently unequal -- profit or surplus value being obtained by capitalists via the exploitation of workers -- it should be clear that Offe and Ronge's position is not that the state is neutral but that it does not always operate in the specific interest of members of the capitalist class, nor does it always negatively affect all workers.

Such an approach predicts that, because of more frequent crises stemming from tensions and contradictions in capitalist political economies, the state increasingly intervenes to restore some (unequal) balance between capital and labor to facilitate and ensure the accumulation (of surplus value) process. The interventions, through which the state protects and sanctions the rules and social relationships presupposed by a capitalist economy, occur via two sometimes confluent channels, which, drawing selectively from Athusser, could be termed ideological and repressive.[6] The school system might be seen primarily, but not solely, as an "ideological state apparatus," whereas the legal system, focused both within the borders (misconduct of citizens) and at the borders (war and immigration matters), might be viewed as a "repressive state apparatus." Thus our analysis will focus on other elements besides educational policy in the working of the state -- a focus encouraged by La Belle and White's broader treatment of the concept of integrative mechanisms.

HISTORICAL CONTEXT OF COLONIALISM

Relations among whites, blacks, and browns began approximately 400 years ago. These relations were conditioned by the actions of an imperialist and colonialist British state that provided the infrastructure for Britain's economic development. As Hall observes

> Britain's rise to mercantile domination and the processes of generating the surpluses of wealth which set economic development in motion were founded on the slave trade and plantation system of the Americas in the seventeenth century. India provided the foundation of Britain's Asian Empire in the Eighteenth.[7]

West Indies

First "discovered" for Europeans by Columbus in 1492, the islands of the West Indies are as varied in their histories as in their development patterns. With the expansion of British colonialism into this area a plantation economy was implemented, and white indentured servants, indigenous Amerindians, East Indian indentured laborers, and, to a greater extent, black slaves were imported to meet labor needs. Well situated in the New England, West Indies, West African trade route, some white businessmen garnered considerable wealth through the marketing of sugar and slaves.

The West Indies were the pride of the English because they were excellent revenue-producing territories. Intervention into the domestic affairs of the area was nonexistent until 1833, when the Act of Emancipation freeing all slaves ended both the slave trade industry and the plantation economy's supply of cheap labor. In addition, a decline in the sugar market undermined the West Indies' only other profitable export.

Educational responsibility was assumed by the British government in 1833. The Sterling Report, commissioned in that year, recommended that education be made the responsibility of religious orders, although historically they had not encouraged or participated in the education of blacks. The British granted 30,000£ per year to support religious educational efforts, an annual allocation until 1840, when the sum began to decline.[8] In 1845, the grant was abruptly stopped and responsibility for education was shifted to the territorial legislatures, which remained unsympathetic to the cause of mass education. However, by this time the infrastructure for mass education had been established and the churches continued to play an integral role.

In the second half of the nineteenth century all of the islands, except the Bahamas, Barbados and Bermuda, became crown colonies, formalizing their economic interdependence (in a subordinate position) by relinquishing their political autonomy. Crown colony status allowed the West Indies access to grants from England to assist in educational provision, though these grants were severely cut at the turn of the century in order to facilitate England's economic retrenchment program.[9]

It is instructive to examine the situation in Jamaica, the island that would eventually contribute more than 60 percent of the West Indian immigrants to Britain.[10] Before 1879 Jamaica had no system of secondary education. The development of secondary schools appears to have stemmed from the demands of the white "plantocracy" for postprimary education for their children, who in days of greater prosperity had been schooled in England, and the colonial power's needs for personnel to staff lower level, local administrative positions. As Cogan notes

> The system was seen as a means for educating just enough non-whites to establish an indigenous middle class which could keep the bureaucracy running. The masses were still required as labor on the plantations of the wealthy landowners, and it was the intent of the ruling parties to see that such labor was available.[11]

The masses, if they received any schooling at all, experienced a curriculum that was designed to prepare them (both with respect to skills and attitudes) for such work. A very selective examination process determined access to secondary schooling, and its fees further restricted entry for the children of landowners, white or "colored." Only 1 percent of an age cohort entered secondary school by 1911, and the percentage figure remained below 5 until 1957, when Jamaica assumed full internal self-government (prior to becoming independent in 1962).

The educational system throughout the West Indies remained stagnant until 1940, when a report was issued by a royal commission. This commission, which was called to investigate a workers' rebellion in the West Indies, outlined educational needs, called for major reforms, and advocated extensive financial assistance to launch new programs. Parliamentary action was immediately taken to increase educational spending; however, all monies were withheld to finance the war effort, which was dominating world attention, including that of the West Indians, who joined the British in battle in the belief that they too were British.

The conclusion of World War II brought the beginnings of adult suffrage, popular government, and the opening of England's doors to the British West Indians.[12] Sixty-two percent of the population could read and all but 23.6 percent of the population over 10 years of age had received some formal education. However, only 2.76 percent had any secondary education and only .22 percent had received professional training.[13]

Indian Subcontinent

The British East India Company set up its first trading station in 1612 during a period in which the Muslim absolute monarchy of the Mogul Empire was beginning to break down, Hindus were asserting some power, and other Western European trading companies were becoming established. By 1757 the company had gained control over most of India.[14] As Carnoy relates, the original purpose was the "pursuit of monopoly, profits through plundering India's goods and selling them in Europe. . . . The traders had the British flag behind them, and even organized their own police force for the purpose."[15] Until it gained control, the company actively supported the educational work -- Christianizing and "civilizing" -- of the missionaries. Afterwards the missionaries' work was restricted because it was seen to undermine the company's attempts "to win cooperation from Moslem and Hindu elites in establishing its legal and governmental power."[16]

A policy of "orientalism" was put into place, establishing colleges for Indian elites, while also "enlisting traditional Brahmin and Moslem scholars to codify and translate laws based on the most extreme religious separatism and orthodoxy."[17] This buttressed the position of indigenous elites, while establishing their allegiance to the British and thus enhancing British power to exploit economically, through taxation and plundering, India.

The confluence of two developments in England helped to redirect education in India. With their emerging power, capitalists sought "to smash the East India Company's trade monopoly and open up India for selling goods . . . and some Protestants wanted to see India educated and morally cleansed from its own religious decadence and from the Company's corruption as its 'just' reward for British rule."[18] Thus, in 1813, the company's monopoly was reduced, and in 1833 its trading powers were abolished and its status was changed to administering the government of India. In the same charter acts, the company was obligated, to spend 100,000£ annually on education of Indians (1951), and missionary work was again to be allowed.

The aristocratic nature of schooling became increasingly Anglicized, yet was only provided to a small elite group of Indians who would become low-level civil servants (at lower salaries) in the colonial administration.[19] While this Anglicism policy did lead to the development of secondary schools and colleges, it never realized the downward filtration of English-language education to the masses as T. B. MacCaulay in his Minute of 1835 stressed. Instead, to facilitate "the production of raw cotton for export to Britain," efforts (described in the Wood Education Despatch of 1854) were made to develop "vernacular education," using native languages, "which would teach the peasants accounting and farming techniques and (hopefully) win more political support for the colonial government at the same time."[20] The grants-in-aid scheme included in the Wood Despatch only stimulated the growth of primary schools to a limited extent because only the more affluent families and communities could afford to provide for the supplementary costs.

Thus even as education and other administrative decision-making was being decentralized in 1919 and 1935, only one-sixth of the Indian children were attending primary school.[21] And Sargent reports only 10 percent of the population was literate when India was granted independence in 1947.[22]

This brief sketch of the colonial relationships among whites, blacks, and browns is important in our attempt to understand the more recent interethnic relations in England.[23] By increasing wealth in the metropole at the expense of the periphery, the colonial relationship created conditions that strongly encouraged migration to England.[24] Colonialism also affected the self-perceptions of the formerly colonized people as well as English whites' perceptions of these "immigrants." As Raynor explains, Jewish and Irish immigrants of the late nineteenth century "were received as hostilely as any of the recent arrivals from the New Commonwealth. But in the case of black immigrants, the old imperial links that bound the former colonies to the mother country have ensured the existence of a reservoir of popular racism."[25] Parekh suggests that racist ideas, which developed to buttress the political and economic subjugation of "colored" people, portrayed a "human hierarchy," with white English highest, followed in descending order by Europeans, Asians, and Africans (and thus black West Indians).[26]

Before examining current educational policies and the more general experiences of black and brown groups migrating to England about 1950, it is necessary to set the scene in England, as much of what these groups encountered in the school system was constructed before their arrival.

AN EDUCATIONAL SYSTEM IS DEVELOPED IN ENGLAND

Before 1870 schooling in England was the province of church and other voluntary organizations.[27] In the Education Act of 1870 Parliament authorized the creation of local school boards to oversee the provision of publicly supported, universal, compulsory, elementary education up to age 11.[28] With the growth of capitalist enterprises, elementary education was directed at the working class, reflecting an orientation Johnson describes as follows:

> Concern about authority, about power, about the assertion (or the reassertion) of control. This concern was expressed in an enormously ambitious attempt to deter-

mine, through the capture of the educational means, the patterns of thought, sentiment and behavior of the working class.[29]

The 1902 Education Act established the "first nationally coordinated system of education . . . for England and Wales."[30] A National Board of Education was created, and English was designated the language of instruction in schools funded through local education authorities (LEAs), as the local school boards were renamed. Anglican and Catholic schools, which had been denied local tax support in 1870, were given access to such funds.[31] Concomitantly, LEAs were empowered to offer secondary education, a move that responded to middle-class demands.[32]

Elementary and secondary education continued as two separate overlapping and contradictory systems primarily for the working class and middle class, respectively, until the 1944 Education Act. This act, which continues to serve as the "legal basis for the educational system," articulated, or systemetized, the provision of schooling.[33] Primary and further education was designed to sandwich selective entry, secondary education: grammar, secondary modern, or technical schools. Thus Tawney's manifesto for the Labour government to provide "secondary education for all" was achieved but in the tripartite fashion urged in the Norwood Report.[34] Religious studies were made the only compulsory subject, and nondenominational (but Christian) corporate workshop was included as part of the process of schooling in county (LEA) and voluntary "aided" or "controlled" schools.[35]

Centralization of educational decision making was increased by the replacement of the National Board of Education with the Ministry of Education.[36] According to the 1944 act, the minister of education was to serve the following broad functions:

to promote the education of the people of England and Wales and the progress of institutions devoted to the purpose, and to secure the effective execution by local authorities, under his [or her] control and direction, of the national policy providing for a varied and comprehensive service in every area.[37]

Furthermore, the number of local education authorities was reduced from 315 to 170.

Thus, on the eve of increased "colored" immigration, England had an education system that:

1. Provided access for all residents to state education, compulsory from ages 5 to 15 (raised to 16 in 1973), and free (plus a living allowance) through further education.
2. Was articulated, although only the grammar school "track" was linked to university entry.
3. Offered a curriculum stressing male, Western, middle-class and gentry values, ideas, and world views.
4. Had a requirement that English be the medium of instruction, although Welsh, for example, could be a subject in the curriculum.
5. Was characterized by a compromise between centralized and decentralized decision making but moving toward centralization.

The independent schools -- with high percentages of students who are children of elites, attend university, and attain elite status themselves -- should also be mentioned, in that students of Asian and, particularly, West Indian origin have always been underrepresented in these "superior training institutions."[38] This educational structure evolved incrementally through the interaction of social classes, religious groups, teachers' organizations, and political parties at the local and national levels.[39] In a sense, the black West Indian and brown Asian do not feature in these developments, either as participants or as the focus of the process. In another sense, however, they do; the wealth enabling England, among other things, to create such a school system was derived from the colonial exploitation of people in other lands. As Hall reminds us, "The imperialist chain . . . has bound the fate of millions of workers and peasants in the colonial hinterlands to the destiny of rich and poor in the heartlands of English society."[40]

THE FIRST TWO DECADES IN THE METROPOLITAN CONTEXT

Prior to 1950, few immigrants came to England from the West Indies or the Indian subcontinent.[41] This changed as a result of the 1948 British Nationality Act, which enabled any member of the British Commonwealth to enter freely, settle down, and find work.[42] "Finding work" is the key, as the primary motivation of the act was to supplement the work force with relatively cheap labor to fuel the post-World War II economic expansion. As Sarup notes: "[I]n the 1950s, immigrant labour was brought in to do the very worst jobs. The immigrants came to major urban areas and filled jobs which white workers did not want, jobs which meant low earnings, working in unpleasant conditions and unsocial hours."[43]

Thus, although there was no interest in encouraging large-scale immigration, the view that emerged -- that blacks and browns had sneaked into the country when whites' backs were turned -- misrepresents the facts, at least for capitalists and national politicians.[44] There were "murmurs of protest," perhaps because of racist ideas developed during the colonial era or because, as King observes, "There has always been something in the British make-up which allowed the English to imagine a privileged retreat . . . into the peace and privilege of his own estate."[45] The protests may also have derived from the fact that, although industry needed a cheap source of surplus labor, not all white Englishmen reaped (at least initially) the benefits of the growing economy; for example, the rationing of potatoes, bread, and other food begun during the war "continued well into the 1950s."[46]

The immigration of both brown Asians and black West Indies to England and elsewhere was spurred by the unequal economic development in the metropole and periphery under colonial rule and neocolonialism. However, the two groups arrived in England with somewhat different orientations and plans. Those emigrating from the Indian subcontinent were more likely to arrive with plans to return home with their accumulated wealth after spending five to seven years, although for a variety of reasons, they usually could not achieve their objective in this period.[47] Those emigrating from the West Indies more often came with the desire to become integrated into the mainstream of English society, at least partly because they conceived of themselves as English in culture.[48] As Singham explains: "When he arrives in Great Britain for the first time, the West Indian feels at last that he has come home."[49] Nevertheless, both groups "ended up in the same isolation from the influencing social institutions to allocate resources for them," a situation that, although granting equal voting rights and statutory protections, prohibits national influence by such a small population.[50]

The relatively small size of the black and brown populations should be emphasized; in 1971 they constituted approximately 3.5 percent of the residents in England.[51] Annual rates of immigration about 1955 and 1961, respectively, were 27,000 and 66,000 for those from the West Indies and 5,800 and 23,000 for those from the Indian subcontinent.[52] The cautionary note about the use of the term "immigrant" should be reiterated, however, in that more than 45 percent of blacks and browns living in England were born there.[53]

The number of blacks and browns in England has not grown to any substantial proportion because immigration was severely restricted by immigration acts in 1962, 1968, and 1971. The 1962 Commonwealth Immigration Act cut off immigration to people who did not already have immediate family members or employment waiting in England. This and subsequent acts have been seen as an indication "that England could only tolerate a limited number of people with cultures different from that of the White Briton" and have been described as "racist in effect and probably racist in intent."[54]

Although during these two decades numerous race relations policies and programs were established to promote better race relations and reduce growing tensions, one must question whether these represented fundamental efforts to create a multiracial society or merely actions to keep a lid on the "racial problem." There had been "race riots" in Nottingham and Notting Hill in 1958, and during the 1960s, Enoch Powell and other politicians became more vocal in referring to blacks and browns as the "enemy within" and in encouraging "repatriation" of "colored immigrants." However, Hall makes two important, related points indicating that the racism explanation must be coupled with an understanding of the economic. First, in the sixteenth century Queen Elizabeth I, faced with problems of food shortage and a shortfall of government resources, decreed that blacks (then living in England as a consequence of "England's growing involvement in the slave trade") "be sent forth from the land." Hall also notes that the 1962 act was introduced "as the economic downturn begins and youth culture surges forward."[55]

Even before blacks and browns became the scapegoat to be sent away to solve the economic and social crises, the most immediate problem facing those who recently immigrated was social integration in terms of opportunities in employment and housing.[56] As previously noted, these new immigrants were employed primarily in the least desirable, unskilled and semiskilled jobs, and thus initially they did not compete with white workers. As Ogbu explains, West Indian immigrants, even more so than their Asian counterparts, "confronted a job ceiling. . . . The jobs held by the immigrants were generally inferior to those held prior to immigration," a situation that "cannot be explained primarily in terms of their . . . level of skills."[57] Upward mobility was minimal at best because of competition with whites and racial discrimination in hiring practices. Browns and blacks may be described as an underclass, residing at the bottom of a dual labor market, whereas Asians from the Indian subcontinent exhibit a slightly more favorable profile.[58] This variation derives from a small but important Asian stratum of shopkeepers and professionals, many of whom immigrated with the necessary credentials after mass immigration was restricted in 1962.[59] Thus, even in the 1966 census, of all immigrant groups in Britain, those of West Indian origin had the lowest proportions of employees as managers, professionals, and nonmanual workers.[60]

The Race Relations Bill of 1965 addressed discrimination by government contractors, but it was the 1968 Race Relations Act that made discrimination on the basis of race, color, or ethnic or national origin unlawful in employment.[61] The latter act expanded coverage to the areas of employment recruitment, training, promotion, dismissals, and employment terms and conditions. The Race Relations Board, however, produced results that can only be classified as a "little less than derisory."[62]

By the beginning of the 1970s, unemployment in England was increasing, and blacks and browns were a disproportionate share of those forced to go on the dole.[63] They remain the last hired and the first fired.[64] Moreover, as Sarup contends, a racist ideology similar to that which helped to justify colonial domination has been drawn upon to legitimate blacks and browns being put out of work.[65]

In terms of housing, it "is clear from a number of studies that West Indian and Asian people tend to live in lower-standard housing than the rest of the population."[66] Both blacks and browns initially settled in inner-city housing in deteriorating condition. This can be partly explained by private party discrimination in home sales, a practice not proscribed by law until the 1968 Race Relations Act. However, as Rex's studies in the Birmingham area indicate, local government also played a direct role in segregating and concentrating blacks and browns.[67] For example, in Sparkbrook, a "secondary housing system" involving "overcrowding" under brown landlordships, was both supported and harassed by local authorities. And in Hardsworth local authority mortgages were given to "colored immigrants" who purchased deteriorating properties, and building societies would neither loan money to whites for such purposes nor loan money to blacks or browns in other areas of the city.

Housing in England can be classified into three categories: owner occupied, rentals from local councils, and rentals from private sources. By 1978, blacks were more likely (45 percent) to be in the council rental category than the general population (30 percent), whereas browns were underrepresented in this category (10 percent) basically because they exceeded the national average in the owner occupied classification.[68] Note, however, that even with such differences, both blacks and browns remain concentrated in low-quality housing in redlined areas of conurbations.

EDUCATIONAL POLICY IN THE METROPOLITAN CONTEXT

During the 1950s and 1960s, the major educational policy issues generally revolved around the unequal achievement of different social classes and specifically in terms of comprehensive secondary schooling, positive discrimination, and educational priority areas. The policies that emerged were influenced by an alliance of the Labour party, organized teachers (especially the National Union of Teachers), and sociologists of education.[69] As Silver claims: "The sociologists of the 1950s and 1960s profoundly altered the agenda of social policy discussion. They made social class, as a concept and a set of social issues, as basic to British debates of the 1960s as race has become for the United States."[70] This focus on social class may be part of the reason for the "benign neglect," a kind of laissez-faire national educational policy, with respect to blacks and browns.[71] Color or race was rarely the focus of attention because blacks and browns were relatively powerless groups that could be seen as "only one part of an undernourished educational system for the poor of any 'colour.'"[72]

It has been argued that the massive influx of black and brown school-age children during the 1950s and 1960s caught English school systems unprepared to deal with their special needs. The existing "basic deficiencies and inequalities in the

educational system" only further served to hinder advance-
ment of these children by narrowing their opportunities.[73]
The system's basic inequalities were brought to light in the
Crowther Report, the Newsom and Robbins reports, and the
Plowden Report.[74]

Race-related educational policy during the 1960s developed
primarily from the 1964 second report of the Commonwealth
Immigrants Advisory Council, which recommended dispersal
of immigrant students where they composed more than 30 percent of a school's population. This policy, stimulated by fears
of white parents, was formalized in the 1965 white paper of
the Department of Education and Science (DES), but was not
pushed by the department nor accepted and implemented by
the LEAs. Further, English as a second language was advocated for non-English-speaking children in a 1963 DES
pamphlet, "English for Immigrants."

Second-language programs gained acceptance among LEAs,
but as in the case of the use of Welsh, the second language is
used as a bridge to English, and, for example, students cannot
take A-1 level exams in Hindu or Urdu.[75] It is important to
note that these programs applied only to the brown populations, as the Creole-speaking blacks were classified as English
speaking. Additionally, the Plowden Report addressed, though
briefly, many of the unique problems that these children encountered in the educational system. These issues, however,
were not directly addressed by educational authorities until
1973.[76]

As noted above, the 1950s and 1960s in England were characterized by a consensus, at least among whites. According to
Raynor

> The whole period was one in which the avoidance of
> crisis became a priority for successive governments
> . . . and this social peace was achieved by the incor-
> poration of organized labor on the one hand and orga-
> nized capital on the other into what was increasingly
> [viewed ideologically as] a pluralist and corporate
> state.[77]

However, even before the end of the 1960s this consensus,
which had embraced both major parties and most education-
ists and had encouraged the development of comprehensive
schooling and the provision of compensatory education programs, began to break down.[78] In the wake of the 1973 oil

crisis, the recession deepened, and prospects for any sustained economic growth came to an abrupt end. Critiques, for example, in the "black papers" were directed toward comprehensive schooling, progressive education practices, and teaching standards.[79] This conservative backlash in education was in some sense captured by then Labour Prime Minister James Callaghan's Ruskin College speech (October 1976) and in the subsequent (spring 1977) staging of the "Great Debate."[80]

In the context of an economic crisis, represented as a fiscal crisis of the state, funding for education and other social services was reduced. Concomitantly, education was being redefined and restructured, as evidenced in the "Green Paper," which identified and elaborated the issues raised in the Great Debate.[81] Education was called upon to be the efficient servant of a corporately managed economy, while the locus of education decision making was moved away from school-level educators to noneducators at the county level -- a move facilitated by the 1974 local government reorganization and the adoption of corporate management techniques -- and to the Department of Education and Science (which replaced the Ministry of Education in 1964) at the national level.[82]

During most of the 1970s race remained on the periphery of national educational policy discussions. The James Report, on teacher training, stressed the need for teachers to develop an understanding of the multicultural society in which they work.[83] In 1974 the Parliamentary Select Committee on Race Relations and Immigration rejected the concept of black studies as "partial and divisive," but "recommended the establishment of a central fund, to which local education authorities could apply to meet the special needs of 'immigrant' children and adults."[84] In response to this report, the government issued a White Paper that rejected not only the idea of the special fund but also the idea of "singling out immigrant children from all those who have suffered from educational disadvantage."[85]

The Bullock Report urged that black and brown teachers be recruited to enhance race relations in schools and emphasized a commitment to compensatory education.[86] In the same year, the DES tried to avoid complying with "a draft directive of the European Economic Community that children of migrant workers receive instruction in their mother tongue," though English as a second language had already been implemented in many LEAs previously for browns, but not blacks.[87] The 1976 Education Act compelled LEAs to submit comprehensive reorganization plans, and it spelled out a structure for providing special education in county or special schools for handicapped youngsters. The latter element was drawn from an ongoing inquiry that was subsequently published as the Warnock Report.[88] In neither case was there an allusion to the situation of blacks and browns.

The issue of educating blacks and browns did not surface in Callaghan's Ruskin College speech, nor was it listed as a topic for the 1977 regional conferences orchestrated as part of the Great Debate, although one of the sections of the Green Paper does address "minorities."[89] The discussion in the Green Paper is general, calling for tolerance, respect and a "sympathetic understanding" of different cultures. This document also recognizes the "special cultural and educational needs" of some black and brown children and expressed the "wish . . . to alleviate as fully as possible inequalities of opportunity."[90]

In 1978, the DES established a Committee of Enquiry into the Education of Children of Ethnic Minority Groups. In 1979, the committee issued its first report, the Rampton Report, which highlighted the severe underachievement of children of West Indian origin.[91] Margaret Thatcher's Conservative government delayed the distribution of the report and requested the resignation of the committee's chairperson.[92] The government's response has probably ensured that this report would be both the committee's first and its last.

In the late 1970s, university fees were dramatically increased for overseas students, who composed approximately 10 percent of the student population.[93] This move has been criticized as being racially biased, although it did not have a direct effect on the neglible number of "indigenous" black and brown students.

OTHER RECENT DEVELOPMENTS

During this same period, other relevant developments were occurring outside the educational system. In 1976, Parliament passed a new Race Relations Act, the substance of which continued in the tradition of the 1965 and 1968 acts. On the law enforcement front, the trust was toward what Hall et al.[94] have aptly termed "policing the crisis."

[C]onsensus developed in Britain for the more coercive apparatuses to have increased dominance. The authors begin by considering how mugging became a black crime, how "mugging" came to equal "blacks."[95] Furthermore, Sarup noted, the researchers found that, at the level of structures, there is a symbiotic relationship between the police, the judiciary and the media. . . . Mugging was described in emotive terms such as "violent lawlessness.". . . Under the guise of concern with public order an attempt is being made to discipline blacks. There is increased surveillance; black youths are arrested on suspicion and daily face police harassment and intimidation.[96]

These dynamics have been supported ideologically and structurally by the National Front (a rightist Political Party) and others on the extreme political right and certainly are not related to the increased level of unemployment, especially among young people generally and even more so among black and brown youth.

In 1980 and 1981, what have been called "the first race riots in English cities since 1958" took place.[97] The Scarman Report, which focused on the violence of April 10-12, 1981, in Brixton, identified many of the causes as inherent in the political, economic, and social features of English society.[98] As Raynor notes

The report scrutinized closely the policing patterns in the area; the training and tactics of police and their lack of community relations and accountability. It called for a better coordinated policy from the government in order to deal with the problems of racial disadvantage and for a more vigorous effort in enforcing the law against racial discrimination.[99]

However, Raynor continues

Disturbing evidence exists that lessons learned from the Scarman Report are already being forgotten, particularly by the police. The recent [March 1982] decision to break down some of the categories of offenses . . . by color of assailant is one small indication of the way racist assumptions have been allowed to intrude into public discussion.[100]

Even more recently (January 1, 1983), a new Nationality Act was implemented. This law, enacted as promised by the Thatcher government, basically withdraws British citizenship rights from the children of former East African and Malaysian colonials, who opted for British overseas citizenship when independence was granted. A second category, citizens of British dependent territories, which includes residents of Hong Kong, Bermuda, Belize, and the Virgin Islands, retains British citizenship; however, the right to reside in England has been withdrawn. Clearly, the door that was opened in 1948 to blacks, browns and other "colored" residents of the former British Empire has now been securely closed.

CONCLUSIONS

In assessing the utility of La Belle and White's typology, one first observes that brown-white relations seem to be adequately represented by their type B: cultural segmentation and structural commonality in a vertical relationship.[101] Whereas there are social class, religious, and regional intragroup differences in culture among both whites and browns, the intergroup cultural differences are substantial. Structurally, browns in England appear to be integrated, although usually in a subordinate position, in the political and economic sphere.

Characterizing black-white relations, however, is more problematic. First, at least with respect to the economy, blacks seem to be subordinate to whites in a structurally segmented, vertical relationship, a situation similar to that characterized by type A. The blacks' experience is less likely to match the "assumption . . . that the economic system's cross-group inclusiveness provides sufficient structural access to all society's members," an assumption that La Belle and White use to distinguish relations of types A and B.[102] At best, the blacks' situation can be described as "selective absorption . . . into the superordinate spheres" associated with type A.[103] To a greater extent than browns, the black population in England make up a "sub-proletariet, a new dark-skinned underclass beneath the white social order."[104] "West Indians in Britain . . . occupy the most inferior positions in a system of color-castes."[105]

Second, cultural segmentation seems less valid in labeling black-white than brown-white relations. As Ogbu concludes:

"West Indians are linguistically and culturally closer to the white British than are the . . . other colored immigrant groups; they speak English as their language, practice Christianity and share other aspects of British culture."[106] The one equivocation to this statement pertains to the issue of language, in that is has been argued that "standard English is a language considerably different from Jamaican Creole."[107] The point, however, is that Creole differs from the standard English used as the medium of instruction in schools in England, as well as in schools in the contemporary West Indies, in a manner similar to the distinction between the white English working-class speech variant and that associated with the English middle- or upper-class variant preferred in school.[108] Thus, and more generally, it can be documented that the imported and developed West Indian culture(s), with the possible exception of Rastafarianism, has much in common with white English culture, but with respect to the working class rather than the middle class or elites.[109]

The utility of the La Belle and White typology for predicting the nature of educational policies varies over the five areas. With respect to the first two areas, access and articulation/tracking, the situation in the state school system in England coincides with the prediction of type B.

1. Access is initially broad for all groups in the state sector schools, which are free and compulsory.
2. The state sector education system is fully articulated: primary -- secondary -- further and higher. In state sector secondary schools tracking, which has gradually changed form as the selective, tripartite system has been reformed along comprehensive lines, appears to favor (in terms of gaining higher education and higher status jobs) those students who accommodate to white, aristocratic culture.

But if we include the private, prestigious independent sector schools in our analysis, the access and tracking areas resemble those associated with type A, especially for students of West Indian origin -- differential access and tracking favoring the dominant group.

Moreover, the systematic features were in place by 1944, prior to the arrival in England of any significant number of blacks and browns. Therefore, to account for the existence of these features one would need to examine the centripetal and centrifugal tendencies not of whites, blacks and browns but of different white groups: Protestant versus Catholic, Welsh versus English, and bourgeoisie versus proletariat.

With regard to the third educational policy area, curriculum, the English scene coincides with the prediction of type B.

3. The curriculum seems to be oriented primarily to super-ordinate culture, that is, that tie not only to white but also to elite and male values, ideas, and views of the world. Some elements of Asian and West Indian cultures are also being incorporated in a small way, perhaps for purposes of co-opting or deflecting separatist movements.

A stronger centripetal tendency of the dominant group is deflected slightly by the weaker centrifugal tendencies of brown and black groups and also by those of subordinate whites, both working class and female.

Language policy in English schools is in line with that predicted for type B relations.

4. Language policy specifies English as the medium of instruction, although Asian languages, but not West Indian dialects/languages, are being used in a bridging or transition fashion.

Language policy as it pertains to Asian languages can be explained, as with the curriculum area, in terms of a strong centripetal tendency by white elites being partly counter-balanced by a weaker centrifugal tendency among browns. It is assumed that in shaping this policy, the more economically advantaged (professionals, technicians, and the like) browns play a major role both by arguing (centrifugally) for the distinctiveness and legitimacy of Asian languages, as well as by asserting (centripetally) the need for a quick transition to English. The latter tendency may be conditioned by the high status accorded to English by many elites on the Indian sub-continent, a status deriving at least in part from dynamics (described earlier) during the colonial period.

For blacks, the explanation of school language policy is less clear. We will assume, perhaps contentiously, that Creole "differs from the standard English of the British schools in vocabulary, grammatical structure and intonation" and will circumvent the controversy as to whether the difference should be described in terms of dialect or language.[110] The centripetal tendency of white elites either is not countered by blacks or, assuming some centrifugal tendency, the centripetal tendency in this case is much stronger. On one hand, we have cited evidence that those emigrating from the West Indies viewed themselves as English who were returning home. Thus there may have been, and continues to be, little tendency for them to assert (centrifugally) their linguistic differences. One may wonder, however, why other cultural differences are publicized in attempts to incorporate West Indian songs, dances, and festival celebrations into the school setting in England. On the other hand, we have discussed how Creole and the working-class speech variant differ in analogous ways from standard English. This suggests that elite whites' centripetal tendency or their resistance to the blacks' centrifugal tendency may be stronger than in the case of browns. Allowing bilingual transition programs with Hindi, Urdu, or even Welsh is not tantamount to undermining the structure of class-based English-language stratification, which is such a salient feature of British life.[111] Recognizing the legitimacy of Creole and, thereby, of working-class speech variants would seem to do so.

The fifth area, administrative centralization, provides difficulty for the analysis. According to La Belle and White's typology, education systems existing in the context of type B interethnic group relations are predicted to be "highly centralized."[112] We conclude, however, the following:

5. Administratively, while the state sector school system is not (yet) highly centralized, it appears to be moving in that direction.

The relatively decentralized administration of the educational system in England and Wales presents obvious problems for the typology. Centrifugal tendencies, the opposite to which are predicted to dominate for type B (as well as types A and D) relations, at least until recently, do seem to account for the existence of a highly decentralized system, though the relevant intergroup relations involve social class, religious, and nationalist (Welsh and English) groups rather than whites, blacks, and browns. And the recent, dramatic move toward administrative centralization does not appear to be attributable to a strengthening of centripetal tendencies in white and black and brown relations. Nor can this rapid movement toward centralization in England be predicted by Archer's theoretical model (but see her caveat), despite its success in making sense out of the historically strong decentralization of the education system.[113]

What we have found particularly helpful in understanding the centralizing dynamics are recent Marxist discussions of the state. Such theorizing, as outlined in the introduction, postulates a notion of the state that is seen to intervene increasingly in human experience not only through education but through other apparatuses as well.[114] These interventions are precipitated by crises in the world capitalist system and are directed at restoring some (unequal) balance between capital and labor to facilitate and ensure the accumulation (of surplus value) process. Offe and Ronge explain: "Since the state depends [indirectly through mechanisms of taxation] on a process of accumulation which is beyond its power to organize, every occupant of state power is basically interested in promoting those conditions most conducive to accumulation."[115]

It is also important to note that state intervention is not without side effects. According to Habermas, this trend toward administrative structures replacing the liberal exchange relations of the market has resulted in a crisis of legitimation for the state, a crisis that may be deflected ideologically by attempting to redefine the problem as located elsewhere than the economy and the state.[116]

This is not to suggest a passivity of actors inside or outside the state apparatus, nor a sort of deterministic functional explanation of institutional dynamics. Rather, this logic defines the boundaries within which human action takes place, part of the "rules and resources" that both constrain and enable human action.[117] Thus the state should be viewed as relatively independent from the economy. As Urry contends: "[t]he state . . . is never simply omnipotent, nor does it simply react to the needs of the economy. . . . Rather, the state itself is seen as actively seeking to establish and sustain a particular constellation of social forces."[118]

In reviewing the experiences of blacks and browns under British colonial rule, we observed the state intervening to foster the economic activity that benefited white Britons, although some were benefited much more than others. The state, through taxation, educational, and other policies, ensured the underdevelopment of the periphery, while facilitating economic and other forms of development in the metripole. In England, the state increasingly has assumed responsibility for educating future workers, attempting to provide them with the requisite skills, as well as attitudes, to reproduce capitalist relations of production with respect to both technical and social dimensions. This education takes on a more progressive trend when profit rates are not under pressure, but recent trends indicate a turn toward a narrower notion of education as a "training" of workers.

When the prospects for economic growth were good, the state encouraged immigration to build an urban army of surplus labor. As economic growth stalled, immigration was increasingly shut off. This trend was later complemented by another aspect of the repressive state apparatus -- policing -- to counter a development, among black and brown youth after they were forced into "temporary" unemployment, of an enduring culture of disassociation from labor. We also observed the state intervening in race relations and educational policy to improve the situation for blacks and browns. This counterbalanced the clearly racist policies in immigration and policing. We should note, nevertheless, how minimally such efforts have altered the lived experience of blacks and browns, perhaps helping to legitimate the state as neutral more than positively affecting the lives of these groups. Notice also that at the same time greater concerns were being expressed about the schooling of blacks and browns, cuts in educational and other social service expenditures were being implemented.

During the June 1983 election campaigns in Britain, which resulted in an overwhelming Conservative majority in Parliament and a continuation of the Thatcher government, neither race nor education appeared to be a major issue. This is a helpful reminder of the broader dynamics in which race relations and educational policy are centralized. With reference to the mid-1970s, Hall states

> This is not a crisis of race. But race punctuates and periodizes the crisis. Race is the lens though which we see that a crisis is developing. . . . Race is only one of the elements in this wider ideological crusade to "clean up" Britain, to roll back the map of progressive liberalism and to turn the clock of history back to the time when the world was "safe for the ordinary Englishmen."[119]

And we might refine this by saying, when the world was more conducive to capital accumulation under the white English crown.

NOTES

1. S. Allen, New Minorities, Old Conflicts: Asian and West Indian Migrants (New York: Random House, 1971), pp. 88-96.

2. T. La Belle and P. White, "Education and Multiethnic Integration: An Intergroup Relations Typology," pt. 1, Comparative Education Review 24, no. 2 (1980):155-73.

3. Ibid., p. 156.

4. M. Sarup, Education, State and Crisis: A Marxist Perspective (London: Routledge and Kegan Paul, 1982), pp. 68-69. See also J. Holloway and S. Picciotto, State and Capital: A Marxist Debate (London: Edward and Arnold, 1978).

5. C. Offe and V. Ronge, "Theses on the Theory of the State," in Education and the State, vol. 1 Schooling and the National Interest, ed. R. Dale et al. (Sussex: Open University and Falmer Press, 1981), p. 78.

6. See various sections of L. Althusser, "Ideology and Ideological State Apparatuses," Lenin and Philosophy (London: New Left Books, 1971).

7. S. Hall, "Racism and Reaction," in Five Views of Multi-Racial Britain: Talks on Race Relations Broadcast by BBC-TV (London: Commission on Racial Equality, 1978), p. 25.

8. J. Figuero, Society, Schools and Progress in the East Indies (Elmsford, N.Y.: Pergamon Press, 1971).

9. N. Atkinson, Educational Cooperation in the Commonwealth--An Historical Study (Salisbury, Rhodesia: University of Rhodesia, 1972).

10. J. Ogbu, "West Indians in Britain," in Minority Education and Caste: The American System in Cross Cultural Perspective (New York: Academic Press, 1978), p. 242.

11. J. Cogan, "Jamaica: Education and the Maintenance of the Social-Class System," in Politics and Education, ed. R. M. Thomas (New York: Pergamon Press, 1983), p. 176.

12. Figuero, Society, Schools, and Progress in the West Indies.

13. G. Cumper, The Social Structure of the British Caribbean (Millwood, N.Y.: Kraus Reprint Co., 1972).

14. S. Mukerji, History of Education in India (Barada, India: Acharya Book Depot, 1966).

15. M. Carnoy, Education as Cultural Imperialism (New York: David Mckay, 1974), p. 86.

16. Ibid., p. 90.

17. Ibid., p. 93.

18. Ibid., p. 96.

19. B. McCully, English Education and the Origins of Indian Nationalism (New York: Columbia University Press, 1940).

20. Carnoy, Education as Cultural Imperialism, p. 104.

21. Mukerji, History of Education in India.

22. J. Sargent, Society, Schools and Progress in India (Oxford: Pergamon Press, 1969), p. 49.

23. Allen, New Minorities, Old Conflicts, p. 89. See also B. Parekh, "Asians in Britain: Problem or Opportunity," in Five Views of Multi-Racial Britain: Talks on Race Relations Broadcast by BBC-TV (London: Commission on Racial Equality, 1978); J. Rex, Race, Colonialism and the City (London: Routledge and Kegan Paul, 1973).

24. Sarup, Education, State and Crisis, p. 96.

25. J. Raynor, "Race and Education: Interpreting British Policies in the 1960s and 1970s," in Different People: Studies in Ethnicity and Education, ed. E. Gumbert (Atlanta: Center for Cross-Cultural Education, Georgia State University, 1983), pp. 79-80.

26. Parekh, "Asians in Britain," p. 37.

27. E. King, Other Schools and Ours, 5th ed. (New York: Holt, 1979).

28. A Corbett, "Education in England," in Education in Great Britain and Ireland ed. R. Bell, G. Fowler, and K. Little (London: Routledge and Kegan Paul, 1973), pp. 2-8.

29. R. Johnson, "Educational Policy and Social Control in Early Victorian England," 49 Past and Present (1970):96-119. See also G. Grace, Teachers, Ideology and Control (London: Routledge and Kegan Paul, 1978).

30. King, Other Schools and Ours, p. 184.

31. Ibid., p. 227.

32. D. Wardle, The Rise of the Schooled Society: The History of Formal Schooling in England (London: Routledge and Kegan Paul, 1974), p. 13.

33. Corbett, "Education in England," p. 2; M. Archer, Social Origins of Educational Systems (Beverly Hills, Calif.: Sage, 1979), p. 196.

34. R. Tawney, Secondary Schools for All (London: Allen and Unwin, 1922); Norwood Report of the Board of Education's Departmental Committee on Curriculum and Examinations in Secondary Schools (London, 1943).

35. R. Butler, "The Politics of the 1944 Education Act," in <u>Decision Making in British Education</u>, ed. G. Fowler, V. Morris, and J. Ozga (London: Heinemann, 1973).

36. Archer, <u>Social Origins of Educational Systems</u>, p. 578.

37. As quoted in King, <u>Other Schools and Ours</u>, p. 185.

38. S. Shaffer, "England and Wales: Muted Educational Confrontations in a Parliamentary Democracy," in <u>Politics and Education</u>, ed. R. M. Thomas (New York: Pergamon Press, 1983), pp. 211-34. See also Ogbu, "West Indians in Britain."

39. Archer, <u>Social Origins of Educational Systems</u>.

40. Hall, "Racism and Reaction," p. 25.

41. Allen, <u>New Minorities, Old Conflicts</u>.

42. Raynor, "Race and Education."

43. Sarup, <u>Education, State and Crisis</u>, p. 94.

44. F. Wirt, "The Strangers Within My Gate: Ethnic Minorities and School Policy in Europe," <u>Comparative Education Review</u> 23, no. 1 (1979):33. See also Parekh, "Asians in Britain," pp. 47-48.

45. Parekh, "Asians in Britain," p. 39; King, <u>Other Schools and Ours</u>, p. 196.

46. King, <u>Other Schools and Ours</u>, p. 196.

47. Parekh, "Asians in Britain," p. 40.

48. G. Male, "Multicultural Education and Educational Policy: The British Experience," <u>Comparative Education Review</u> 24, no. 3 (1980):291-301; J. Rex, "Race in the Inner City," in <u>Five Views of Multi-Racial Britain: Talks on Race Relations Broadcast by BBC-TV</u> (London: Commission on Racial Equality, 1979), p. 18.

49. A. Singham, "The Political Socialization of Marginal Groups," in <u>Majority and Minority: The Dynamics of Racial and Ethnic Relations</u>, ed. N. Yetman and C. Steele (Boston: Allyn and Bacon, 1972).

50. Wirt, "The Strangers Within My Gate," pp. 36-38.

51. Parekh, "Asians in Britain," p. 40.

52. Male, "Multicultural Education and Educational Policy," p. 291.

53. A. Little, "Schools and Race," in <u>Five Views of Multi-Racial Britain: Talks on Race Relations Broadcast by BBC-TV</u> (London: Commission on racial Equality, 1978), p. 57.

54. Male, "Multicultural Education and Educational Policy," p. 291; Raynor, "Race and Education," p. 81.

55. Hall, "Racism and Reaction," pp. 23, 28.

56. Singham, "The Political Socialization of Marginal Groups."

57.   Ogbu, "West Indians in Britain," pp. 257-58.
58.   The Runnymede Trust and the Radical Statistics Race Group (RTRSRG), Britain's Black Population (London: Heinemann Educational Books, 1980), p. 59.   See also P. Doeringer and M. Piore, Internal Labor Markets and Manpower Analysis (Lexington, Mass.: Heath, 1971); J. Rex and S. Tomlinson, Colonial Immigrants in a British City: A Class Analysis (London: Routledge and Kegan Paul, 1979).
59.   E. Rose, Colour and Citizenship: A Report on British Race Relations (London: Oxford University Press, 1969).
60.   Ogbu, "West Indians in Britain," p. 259.
61.   Allen, New Minorities, Old Conflicts.
62.   Rex and Tomlinson, Colonial Immigrants in a British City.
63.   RTRSRG.
64.   Little, "Schools and Race."
65.   Sarup, "Education, State and Crisis," p. 98.
66.   RTRSRG, p. 73.
67.   Rex, Race, Colonialism and the City; Rex and Tomlinson, Colonial Immigrants in a British City.
68.   RTRSRG.
69.   D. Finn, N. Grant, and R. Johnson, "Social Democracy, Education and the Crisis," Working Papers in Cultural Studies 10 (1977): 147-98.
70.   H. Silver, "Education Against Poverty: Interpreting British and American Policies in the 1960s and 1970s," in Poverty Power and Authority in Education, ed. E. Gumbert (Atlanta: Center for Cross-Cultural Education, Georgia State University, 1981), p. 19.
71.   D. Kirp, Benign Neglect: Race   and   Schooling   in Britain (Berkeley: Graduate School of Public Policy, University of California, 1977); D. Kirp, Doing Good by Doing Little (Berkeley: University of California Press, 1979); Male, "Multicultural Education and Educational Policy"; Wirt, "The Strangers Within My Gate."
72.   Wirt, "The Strangers Within My Gate," p. 36.
73.   Rose, Colour and Citizenship, p. 25.
74.   HMSO, Fifteen to Eighteen, Crowther Report to the Ministry of Education, Central Advisory Council for Education (London, 1959); HMSO, Half Our Future, Newsom Report of the Central Advisory Council for Education (London, 1963); HMSO, Higher Education, Robbins Report (London, 1963); HMSO, The Plowden Report: Children and Their Pri-

mary Schools, Report for the Central Advisory Council for Education (London, 1967).

75. Shaffer, "England and Wales."

76. Plowden Report; Male, "Multicultural Education and Educational Policy."

77. Raynor, "Race and Education," p. 80.

78. M. Ginsburg, G. Wallace, and H. Miller, "Professionals Responding to Reduced Financial Resources and to Increased Government Control," paper presented at the World Congress of Sociology, Mexico City, August 16-21, 1982.

79. C. Cox and A. Dyson, eds., Right of Education: A Black Paper (London: Critical Science Society, 1969); C. Cox and R. Boyson, eds., Black Paper (London: Dent, 1975); C. Cox and R. Boyson, eds., Black Paper (London: Maurice Temple Smith, 1977).

80. M. Ginsburg, R. Meyenn, and H. Miller, "Teachers, the 'Great Debate' and Education Cuts," Westminster Studies in Education 2 (1979):5-33.

81. Department of Education and Science, Education in Schools: A Consultative Document, Green Paper (London: HMSO, 1977); J. Donald, "Green Paper: Noise of Crisis," Screen Education 30 (1979):13-49.

82. B. Simon, "Marx and the Crisis in Education," Marxism Today, July 1977, pp. 195-205; Ginsburg, Wallace, and Miller, "Professionals Responding to Reduced Financial Resources"; G. Wallace, H. Miller, and M. Ginsburg, "Teachers Responses to the Cuts," in Contemporary Education Policy, ed. J. Ahier and M. Flude (London: Croom Helm, 1982), pp. 109-38; B. Salter and T. Tapper, Education, Politics and the State (London: Grant McIntyre, 1981).

83. HMSO, Teacher Education and Training, James Report (London, 1972); Male, "Multicultural Education and Educational Policy," p. 292.

84. R. Giles, The West Indian Experience in British School (London: Heinemann, 1977), p. 152.

85. Department of Education and Science, Educational Disadvantage and the Needs of Immigrants (London: HMSO, 1974); Raynor, "Race and Education," p. 89.

86. Department of Education and Science, Language for Life, Bullock Report (London: HMSO, 1975); Male, "Multicultural Education and Educational Policy," p. 297; Finn, Grant, and Johnson, "Social Democracy, Education and the Crisis," p. 93.

87. Raynor, "Race and Education," p. 89.

88.   HMSO, <u>Report of the Committee of Enquiry into the Education of Handicapped Children and Young People</u>, War-nock Report (London, 1978); Department of Education and Science, <u>Educating Our Children: Four Subjects for Debate</u>, Background Paper for Regional Conferences, February and March 1977 (London, 1977); Department of Education and Science, <u>Education in Schools</u>; Ginsburg, Meyenn, and Miller, "Teachers, the 'Great Debate' and the Education Cuts." p. 10.

89.   Male, "Multicultural Education and Educational Poli-cy," p. 299.

90.   "Extracts from the 'Green Paper,'" <u>Times Educational Supplement</u>, July 7, 1977, pp. 5-8.

91.   HMSO, <u>West Indian Children in Our Schools</u>, Ramp-ton Report, Committee of Enquiry into the Education of Chil-dren of Ethnic Minority Groups (London, 1981).

92.   Raynor, "Race and Education," p. 90.

93.   King, <u>Other Schools and Ours</u>, p. 257.

94.   S. Hall, C. Critcher, T. Jefferson, et al., <u>Policing the Crisis: Mugging, the State, and Law and Order</u> (London: Mac-millan, 1978).

95.   Ibid.

96.   Sarup, <u>Education, State and Crisis</u>, pp. 62-64.

97.   Raynor, "Race and Education," p. 75.

98.   HMSO, <u>The Report on the Brixton Disorders</u>, CMND, 8427, Scarman Report (London, 1981).

99.   Raynor, "Race and Education," p. 84.

100.   Ibid., p. 85.

101.   La Belle and White, "Education and Multiethnic Integration."

102.   Ibid., p. 161.

103.   Ibid., p. 158.

104.   Sarup, <u>Education, State and Crisis</u>, p. 96.

105.   Ogbu, "West Indians in Britain," p. 276.

106.   Ibid., p. 243.

107.   Shaffer, "England and Wales," p. 223.

108.   Ogbu, "West Indians in Britain," p. 248.   See also B. Bernstein, "Social Class, Language and Socialization," in <u>Class, Codes and Control</u>, vol. 1 (London: Routledge and Kegan Paul, 1971).

109.   For concurring perceptions by some white working-class adolescents, see P. Willis, <u>Learning to Labour</u> (London: Saxon House, 1977).

110.   Ogbu, "West Indians in Britain," p. 251.

111.   King, <u>Other Schools and Ours</u>, p. 233.

112. La Belle and White, "Education and Multiethnic Integration." p. 162.

113. Archer, Social Origins of Educational Systems, p. 790.

114. C. MacPherson, "Do We Need a Theory of the State?" in Education and the State, vol. 1 Schooling and the National Interest, ed. R. Dale et al. (Sussex: Open University and Falmer Presses, 1981); Salter, Education, Politics and the State; Sarup, Education, State and Crisis.

115. Offe and Ronge, "Theses on the Theory of the State," p. 79.

116. J. Habermas, Legitimation Crisis, trans. T. McCarthy (London: Heinemann, 1976); J. Habermas, "Conservatism and Capitalism," New Left Review, June 1979, p. 115.

117. A. Giddens, Central Problem in Social Theory (Berkeley: University of California Press, 1979).

118. J. Urry, The Anatomy of Capitalist Societies (London: Macmillan, 1981), pp. 35-36.

119. Hall, "Racism and Reaction," pp. 31-34.

6

MAORI EDUCATION

Ian Maclaren

During Great Britain's greatest expansionist era, the nineteenth century, almost invariably trade followed the Union Jack, and education, the Bible. The Committee of the Church Missionary Society decided in 1814 that pioneer missionaries in heathen lands must open schools where native children could be "trained in the knowledge of those divine Truths, by which, under the blessing of God, they would be rendered useful members of Society, and heirs of glorious immortality."[1]

Policy quickly became practice, in the Church Missionary Society's newest mission field, northern New Zealand, with the opening in 1816 of a missionary school in the Bay of Islands. In this, as in all other New Zealand missionary schools until 1847, instruction was in Maori. Adults as well as children attended because of the great value literacy had for many Maori, especially those with no traditionally ascribed status. The refusal of the missionaries to teach English, however, caused resentment when the limitations of literacy in Maori became apparent.

After Great Britain formally annexed New Zealand in 1840 and the first settlers arrived, the missionaries accepted the need to change their policy of language. With government aid they established a network of mission schools in whose curriculum religious education, industrial training, and instruction in the English language were compulsory. Hopes of "removing barbarism and promoting civilization" through these schools, were, however, dashed by the North Island settler-Maori land wars.[2]

The wars ended the missionaries' educational monopoly, as the victorious settler-politicians, skeptical of the civilizing value of isolated, denominational boarding schools, replaced them (in the Native Schools Act of 1867) with government-aided secular village day schools "scattered broadcast over the country" and controlled through the Department of Native Affairs. Intergroup relations became, in La Belle and White's terminology, type B.[3] Traits of the dominant Europeans were the criteria against which all societal behaviors were judged. Knowledge of the English language was made "an indispensable requisite in all Native schools in receipt of Government aid."[4] This requirement is claimed to have "marked the beginning of the policy of prohibiting the use of Maori in the schools. . . . Maori language became the 'enemy.'"[5]

Further educational provision was made for Maori children in the national Education Act of 1877. During the debates on the 1877 bill, some parliamentarians argued that because the Native Schools Act had already established schools for the "children of the aboriginal native race and half-castes or children of indigent parents," Maori children should be denied entry to the national public schools. Fortunately for the future of race relations in New Zealand, the mid-1870s temptation to allow racial enmity leading to educational sanctions was overcome. "Nothing in this Act," section X of the act reads, "shall be binding on any Maori; but any Maori shall be at liberty to send his child to a public school under this Act."

In 1879 the Department of Education assumed responsibility for all publicly funded Maori schools. For the next 90 years the department's Native Schools Branch (Maori was not substituted for "native" until 1948) directly controlled Maori schools.

For the Maori people, the Native Schools Branch came into being at a particularly difficult time. Beaten in battle and punished by the confiscation of land, many Maoris, both physically and psychologically, retreated from the European advance. Withdrawing into the mountainous, heavily forested, and inaccessible areas of the North Island, they showed little interest in having their children educated in government schools.

These understandable reactions to defeat led to despair: "The white man looks on the men, the trees and the birds and they wither and die. I and my people are like dead trees in a forest clearing. One falls and another falls and soon we shall all be gone."[6] At the turn of the century, the young Apirana Ngata, destined to become an outstanding politician and scholar, described his people as "battling bravely, nobly against the fates . . . braced with the hope that the day may yet be won . . . yet gladly dying with the knowledge that though their race is lost, it had died hard, bravely and nobly."[7]

Education was seen as facilitating the speedy absorption of surviving "noble savages" into the general population -- "to bring an untutored but intelligent and high-spirited people into line with civilization."[8] European school buildings and European families were introduced into Maori settlements by the Native Schools Code of 1880 "to serve as . . . examples of a new and more desirable mode of life."[9] The goal was assimilation: "The Maoris will ultimately become Europeanised."[10]

The curriculum to hasten this "civilizing" process was predictably centripetal in orientation. It was a diluted six-year version of the national eight-year primary school curriculum. Emphasis was on the teaching and constant use of English. A former inspector of native schools commented in 1930: "From early times . . . English has been recognized as the cardinal subject of the Native schools curriculum."[11]

The 1880 code, drawn up by J. H. Pope, the newly appointed inspector of native schools, permitted the use of the Maori language in the junior classes as an aid to teaching English, but later any use of the Maori language was seen as educationally and linguistically undesirable. In 1903 Pope commented that the earlier practice of teaching English "through and by means of Maori" had proved unsatisfactory; the only way to teach English was through English.[12]

Although Pope tried very hard to make the native schools village centers (to which adults as well as children could come for agricultural, technical, and health instruction), their European atmosphere and the stress they put on learning English repelled rather than attracted the Maori people. At the turn of the century, more than 90 percent of the Maori population still spoke only Maori at home.[13]

Between 1909, when a revision of the 1880 code made the curriculum of the native schools very similar to that of the public schools, and 1929, when it became identical, Maori children in both native and public primary schools did less well academically than their Pakeha peers. Lack of school progress came to be regarded as a characteristic of Maori children.

Just as the prediction that schooling would transform the Maori into brown-skinned Pakehas was proving false, so too was the prediction that the Maori race was doomed. From its 1896 low of 39,000, the Maori population increased to 56,987 in 1921 and to 63,670 in 1926. Although this unexpected resurgence occasioned instances of overt racial hostility by hitherto tolerant Pakehas, especially during the depression 1930s, little real conflict between the races was feared as long as the Maori stayed in isolated country districts. And it was the intention of the Department of Native Affairs to keep them there: "The future of the Maori is indubitably bound up in the soil . . . the policy today is to assist the Maori to develop and farm his lands."[14] To bring educational policy in line with evolving economic and social policies, the Department of Education in 1930 adapted the native school curriculum to emphasize the teaching of agriculture. The native schools' task, the director of education said, was to teach "the [Maori] lad to become a good farmer and the girl to become a good farmer's wife."[15]

By fostering selected aspects of Maori culture in the native schools, the new education policy tacitly conceded the failure of the department's 50-year-old assimilation policy and gave official sanction to what many teachers had always done. The Maori now had bureaucratic permission to be proud of being Maori.

Maori studies and agriculture notwithstanding, the new curriculum introduced by the Regulations Relating to Native Schools, 1931 was more conservative than innovative, particularly in its continued emphasis on English as the medium of instruction. The director of education ignored a request from teachers that the Maori language be included in the native school curriculum because, he said, "the natural abandonment of the native tongue inflicts no loss on the Maori."[16] Ultimately, he believed, the subordinate Maori population would be absorbed into the structural and cultural system of the superordinate Pakeha group.

Many Maori parents and contemporary Maori leaders shared the director's view. They acquiesced in what Maori leaders 40 years later were to call "cultural genocide" because they believed knowledge of English would bring them equality with the Pakeha.[17] When, in 1936, Peter Fraser, minister of education in the newly elected Labour government, asked Sir

Apirana Ngata to tell him "what your people expect of our schools system," the reply was unequivocal. "Dear Mr. Fraser," Ngata answered, "the question you pose is one that I have raised with my people . . . and the reply has always been the same -- we send our children to school to learn the ways of the Pakeha."[18]

Ngata's response was to be expected, given New Zealand's type B pattern of societal integration. Most Pakehas and many Maori saw only historic or folkloric value in Maori culture and were in general agreement with a Maori medical practitioner, Dr. Wi Repa (one of but 35 Maori until 1945 to earn a university degree), who told a gathering of teachers from native schools that "the modern life of the Pakeha is the only one. The Maori method is worthless. . . . Maoris must conform or go under. The sooner we become European the better."[19]

Department of Education officials did not agree, although ten years earlier they would have. Rather, they wrote in the official New Zealand Education Gazette:

> Instead of trying to make the native people like (our-
> selves), the better plan might be to recognize the social
> realities of the Maori and then to assist him to make
> the necessary adaptations to new conditions. This com-
> pletely new conception acknowledges the values inher-
> ent in the native culture, and the right and need for
> any people to be actively cooperative in adjustments to
> new conditions.[20]

While the call to acknowledge "the values inherent in the Native culture" fell largely on deaf ears, there was acceptance of the need "to recognize the social realities of the Maori and then to assist him to make the necessary adaptations to the new conditions," and the Department of Education decided to establish three native secondary schools.

Until 1941 the Department of Education, being content to award able Maori children scholarships at certain denomi-national boarding schools, had made in Maori areas no direct provision for secondary schooling. Departmental influence over these denominational schools was limited, but their con-trolling authorities generally accepted the official view that secondary education for the majority of Maori children should be of a practical nature. Parents, however, often disagreed. "When I suggest an agricultural course, parents want their boy to take matriculation," the headmaster of Te Aute College, a leading Maori denominational school, complained.[21]

The stress on agricultural education for Maori youth continued into the 1930s, although it should have been apparent to education policymakers that growing numbers of under-educated and largely unskilled young Maori were already drifting to the cities. The 1936 census showed that almost half of New Zealand's 82,000 Maori were under the age of 21.

The provision of state secondary schooling in a predominantly Maori region, the isolated east coast of the North Island, was proof of the Labour government's determination to honor its 1939 promise to ensure "that every person, whatever his level of academic ability, whether he be rich or poor, whether he live in town or country, has the right, as a citizen, to a free education of the kind for which he is best fitted and to the fullest extent of his powers."[22] It was also a partial, if belated, recognition of "the social realities of the Maori."

Local Maori elders and officials differed about the nature of the curriculum most appropriate for the minister of education's "bold new experiment."[23] The elders wanted an academic bias, but they got the departmental officials' preference, a manual-technical one. The officials pointed out that highly talented and motivated children could still attend the more academic boarding schools. Nor was instruction in agriculture dropped altogether because it was hoped that such courses, by "according status and dignity to the work of the farmer," would help deter rural depopulation.[24] The new manual-technical curriculum was intended to ensure that if the young Maori did leave the communal security of their tribal districts to seek work in the predominantly Pakeha towns and cities, they would have some skills appropriate to the lower status positions most would occupy.

Poorly equipped and often, because of World War II, indifferently staffed, these new secondary schools were regarded locally as "second grade," good enough only for children whose parents could not afford to send them away to a boarding school.[25] Not until 1945 did they develop respectability and a much needed academic purpose in response to the introduction of a new, broad-based national secondary examination, the school certificate, for which the rural high schools could prepare candidates.

But still, as the Department of Education extended educational opportunities for rural Maori families, increasing numbers of young Maori moved into the towns. In 1936, 14,212

Maori or 17.3 percent of the total Maori population, were town dwellers; by 1945, the figures rose, respectively, to 25,414 and 35.0 percent. To help these internal migrants enter the mainstream of the country's social and economic life without a sense of inferiority, the schools, once regarded as a principal means of Europeanizing the Maori, were now required to attempt almost the opposite; they were to assist in "restoring to the Maori his pride of race, initiative and self-confidence."[26]

Between 1936 and 1945 a burst of legislative activity, leaving on the statute books only such discriminatory legislation as was deemed to favor the Maori, brought the Maori to equality with the Pakeha. Educational equality in practice, however, was not so easily achieved, even though the need was made urgent by the rapid growth in the Maori population (between 1936 and 1951 it increased from 82,326 to 115,740) and the large-scale mixing of the two races in a close urban environment.

By 1955 pressure mounted to have all Maori service schools transferred from central department to regional education board control. Spokesmen for the boards and the primary teachers' organization, the New Zealand Education Institute, reminded the department that a permanent dual system had never been intended; clause XVIII of the original Native Schools Code of 1880 encouraged the transfer of native schools to board control. Proponents of a uniform administration system for all primary schools pointed out that, in 1950, 56.8 percent of Maori pupils were in education board schools as against 37.8 percent in Maori service schools and 5.9 percent in denominational schools, that the curriculum of the two types of schools had been the same since 1929, and that the teachers, similarly trained, moved freely between the two services.

Senior Department of Education officers, concerned with the generally slow scholastic progress of Maori primary school children, were sympathetic but cautious; they knew that in rural Maori districts the Maori service schools, built often on gifted land as required by earlier legislation, were looked upon somewhat as an extension of the marae, the center of community life. Maori service school teachers, of whom, in 1955, 46 percent were themselves Maori, also believed that special welfare and curricular and language needs of their pupils would go unnoticed in board schools.

The department's response to the dilemma in Maori education was to set up a National Advisory Committee on Maori

Education (on which there was, for the first time nationally, Maori representation). Its recommendations, all accepted, led, first, to an increased emphasis on Maori arts and crafts, history, and language in all primary schools and to the appointment of teachers and college lecturers in Maori studies; second, through the appointment of an officer for Maori education, to much greater departmental responsibility for the educational and general welfare of Maori youth in secondary as well as primary schools; and, third, to agreement that Maori service schools gradually, after "full consultation . . . with the local Maori people" and with compensation for gifted land, be transferred to regional education board control.

Attitudes towards the transfer of Maori service schools differed. The department's concern was to meet the special needs of Maori children wherever they were being taught; the director and his minister were adamant that no Maori service schools would be coerced into merging with the public system. Some education boards, by advocating immediate transfer, created resentment among tradition-conscious Maori leaders, who preferred direct departmental control. However, the National Advisory Committee's insistence that Maori and Pakeha basic educational needs be identical, and that the association of the two peoples should be encouraged, made transfer of control inevitable.

The transfer began in 1956, and in 1967, the centennial year of the Native Schools Act, when the number of pupils in Maori service schools had dwindled to about 7,600 (52,000 Maori pupils were in board schools), the National Advisory Committee urged the Department of Education to complete quickly the transfer process. Accordingly, on February 1, 1969, control of the remaining Maori service schools was transferred to the regional education boards.

Despite predictions of an "avalanche of criticism," the merger progressed smoothly, principally because by 1969 there was clear evidence that the particular needs of Maori children were recognized and were being catered to, in part at least, in the New Zealand state school system.[27] A Maori had been appointed assistant to the officer for Maori education. Pre-service training courses prepared teachers to discuss and teach things Maori, not only to give the increasing numbers of Maori children a background of their own culture and traditions but also to make Pakeha children more aware and appreciative of the distinctive contribution of the Maori people to New Zealand life. The department's publications branch helped by preparing a series of specialized bulletins and manuals.

Having committed itself to strengthening Maori culture, the department had then to accept the corollary and agree to encourage teaching of the Maori language in secondary schools. A departmental committee on the teaching of Maori was asked to prepare language texts for secondary schools and to advise on the correct form of the language, which, by the 1950s, was the primary language of a decreasing number of older people in rural areas. There is a degree of irony in the fact that the Department of Education, whose director in 1931 had said, "The natural abandonment of the native tongue involves no loss on the Maori," was now embarking on what proved a continuing language rescue operation.

The speed with which most of the recommendations of the 1955 National Advisory Committee were acted upon reflected an increasing unease about the position the Maori held in New Zealand society. While in the immediate postwar years it was almost heresy to suggest that New Zealand race relations were anything less than perfect, many people sensed a developing brittleness. The enforced migration into urban centers of job-seeking rural Maori with limited education or work skills revealed disturbing pockets of latent anti-Maori prejudice.

Appropriately, in 1960, the Department of Maori Affairs, traditionally responsible for the general welfare of the Maori people, attempted to analyze "the Maori problem." After surveying, as statistically and objectively as possible, the fields of education, employment, crime, health, housing, and welfare, J. K. Hunn, the secretary for Maori affairs, concluded that, whatever New Zealanders might wish to believe, the Maori were indeed a depressed ethnic minority whose members could easily become an unemployable proletariat.[28]

Hunn emphasized the importance of education in maintaining the validity of New Zealand's postwar claim of a country housing two races but only one people: "It is the one thing, more than any other, that will pave the way to further progress in housing, health, employment and acculturation."[29] Hunn found that Maori children, after years of apparently equal educational opportunity, were in fact underrepresented proportionately in senior secondary school classes and that this underrepresentation became more marked at the postsecondary level.[30] The small number of Maori undergraduates -- only 89 in 1956 when their proportional representation should have been 741 -- particularly disturbed Hunn, and he urged the government to establish a Maori Education Foundation to provide scholarships for Maori secondary and postsecondary students.[31]

Although an underfunded foundation created by act of Parliament in 1961 failed to "transform the educational scene within ten years," as Hunn had predicted, its activities did make more New Zealanders aware of Maori educational handicaps, at the same time encouraging Maori parents to take greater interest in their children's schooling.[32] Because the foundation's original intention of creating an educated elite did not find favor everywhere, its aims were broadened.[33] Particular attention was given preschool education in order "to strengthen Maori home life and the language, general knowledge and experience of children in their crucial pre-school years, until every Maori child is as well equipped as the European child to come to school."[34] In the 1980s the emphasis has moved to secondary education.

The main outcome of the Department of Maori Affairs' public examination of its own stewardship was to stimulate discussion about the plight of the Maori people. At the same time this appraisal implicitly acknowledged the truth of a number of unfavorable charges made in 1958 by visiting American ethnopsychologist David P. Ausubel.[35] A spate of more specialized inquiries by teachers' groups, business and manufacturing organizations, and other government departments followed; all were forthright and constructive and all expressed concern that the scholastic gap between Maori and Pakeha children, identified and quantified by Ausubel and Hunn, seemed to be widening.

The Commission on Education, constituted in February 1960 "to consider the publicly-controlled system of education in relation to the country's present and future needs," decided that it must go beyond its specific terms of reference and make education of the Maori the subject of special inquiry.[36] With a plethora of statistics, the commission drove home the stark points already made by Ausubel and Hunn. Particularly alarmed by the width of the scholastic gap between Maori and Pakeha children, the commission, besides making specific recommendations -- more Maori entrants to teachers colleges, more suitable reading materials, additional advisers, nursery classes in the more remote areas, residential trade-training courses for Maori apprentices from country areas -- called for government-supported research into the social, linguistic, and pedagogical causes of underachievement. Responsibility for monitoring progress and ensuring that Maori opinion was sought and considered was to rest with the National Advisory Committee on Maori Education.[37]

This official recognition that the Maori held views about their children's schooling worthy of attention was long over-due; for decades periodicals in the Maori vernacular had been recording talks between Maori leaders and Pakeha leaders at which Maori educational and vocational aspirations had been explained -- and ignored. Long before the revelations of Ausubel, Hunn, and the Commission on Education, the Maori knew there were inordinate gaps between home and school, between school and vocations, and between levels of achievement of Maori and Pakeha children. They therefore welcomed research-backed recommendations leading to the narrowing of these gaps. "The tide of progress is sweeping on and we must go with it," an orator said. "Education is to be the future paddle of our canoe."[38]

Consideration of the relationship between schooling and social environment and of the consequences for schooling of the depressed socioeconomic strata of many urban Maori families and the subsequent poor schooling offered led the Commission on Education to conclude: "Too many [Maori children] live in large families in inadequately sized and even primitive houses, lacking privacy, quiet, and even light for study: too often there is a dearth of books, pictures, and educative material, to stimulate the growing child."[39] Research evidence confirmed the accuracy of these generalizations. In addition, research of the perceptions of lower status Maori people regarding the purposes and values of formal education has shown that parents with limited occupational horizons seldom encouraged their children to excel at school.[40] This is not the result of what Hunn described tersely as "parental apathy" but simply of the parents' failure to realize that for the school to be effective, they, too, have a role to play.

Less obvious cultural factors also impede children's school progress. Unless they emerge from highly acculturated homes, Maori five-year-olds beginning school have very different personalities than their Pakeha classmates. These typical Maori five-year-olds enter school with a sense of self-depreciation acquired from parents and relatives; consequently they are often immobilized by intense feelings of whakama (embarrassment and shyness) when they find themselves in a strange environment.[41] The students' embarrassment, the Commission on

Education was told, is itensified by language difficulties experienced in school. Unable to communicate easily with the teachers and to grasp what they are saying, too many Maori children readily are classified in teacher jargon as "non-achievers." As they grow older, they and their teachers, between whom classroom relations at the intermediate and secondary school levels become strained, agree on one thing -- their fifteenth birthdays cannot come too soon. Consequently there are eighteen-year-old Maori youths, currently unemployed, whose reading levels are those of second-year primary pupils.

The Commission on Education, aware of Maori pupils' deficiencies in English, toyed with suggesting that in some Maori-speaking districts infant classes could be taught in Maori, but then concluded, as education authorities had done since 1847, "it will be wiser to choose English, the language of the community at large, as the teaching medium from the outset."[42] It did suggest, however, introducing Maori as a second language in the second to last year of the eight-year primary school if qualified teachers were available.

Since the commission's report in 1962, debate about the status of the Maori language in New Zealand primary and secondary school curricula has continued. The 1971 report of the National Advisory Committee on Maori Education, reconstituted to ensure the majority of members were Maori, echoed the Commission on Education's proposal. Nine years later, a note of desperation creeping into its recommendations, it spelled out in more detail what was needed. First priority in such a language rescue operation, the committee suggested, is to establish the policy decision to extend Maori-language and studies programs to all primary schools.[43] Although such a decision has not yet been taken, in 1977 the department relaxed its English-only policy and agreed to use Maori as the medium of instruction for the first four years in a small rural primary school in Ruatoki, a district where Maori still remains the language at the home for a majority of pupils.[44] Three similar primary schools have since begun bilingual teaching in Maori and English. Two secondary schools also have bilingual classes.

Officially, there is now far greater support for the teaching of and about Maori in schools, both primary and secondary, than at any other time in the history of the national school system. This new policy is timely because, as the National Advisory Committee on Maori Education said in

1980, "Maoris need the support of Pakehas to help them keep their language and culture alive."[45]   Twenty years earlier, however, it was the Commission on Education's judgment (as it had been Sir Apirana Ngata's 20 years previously) that the ultimate future of Maori language and culture lay entirely with the Maori themselves.[46]

Many New Zealanders still believe this to be the case, and whereas there is a real desire in the central Department of Education to encourage the teaching of Maori in the nation's schools, its officers know that any attempt at any level in the school system to make the Maori language a compulsory subject would be flying in the face of public opinion.   A bill, introduced in the New Zealand parliament in 1980, which proposed conferring a right for speakers of Maori to use their native language for certain public or official purposes, was rejected.   Nevertheless, in 1980 the National Advisory Committee on Maori Education urged the department to draw up a timetable for implementing the "systematic teaching of Maori," first in six-year primary schools, then in the two-year intermediates, and finally in the secondary schools.   The department's response was to employ more itinerant teachers of Maori.   In 1981 the director-general of education reported to his minister that 40 itinerant teachers of Maori involved 600 primary schools, 1,100 classroom teachers, and 38,000 children in "learning and teaching Maori."   Maori was also taught to 14,740 pupils in 182 secondary schools.[47]

Although the National Advisory Committee wants a more vigorous implementation of a "Maori for all" program, the department is cautious, not wishing to outstrip public support. (See Tables 6.1 and 6.2.)

Efforts -- national, regional, or local -- to close the education gap between Pakeha and Maori secondary school children are, however, well received.   But though increasing numbers of Maori pupils are passing public examinations, the gap between Maori and Pakeha achievement levels and ratios remains disturbingly wide.   There are still too few Maori undergraduates.   Although Polynesians make up 15 percent of greater Auckland's population in 1980 only 5 percent of the students at the University of Auckland (enrollment 14,000) were Maori or Islanders.

Enhanced achievement levels depend on improved retention rates.   Too many Maori children leave school at age 15 to join the ranks of the unemployed or, all too frequently, the imprisoned. (In 1980, 80 percent of the inmates of a large North Island youth prison were Maori.)

In 1962 the Commission on Education noted that many Maori children entering secondary school (promotion to which has been automatic since 1937) were older than Pakeha entrants, the primary school subsystem's social promotion policy notwithstanding. Some teachers attributed this to the often irregular school attendance by Maori children in the first two years of school, before, as seven-year-olds, they become subject to the education act's compulsory attendance regulations. Section 109 of the 1964 revision of the education act countered this practice by lowering the compulsory entry age to six. In 1980, because only 40 percent of the Maori three- and four-year-olds were enrolled in preschool centers, the National Advisory Committee asked the Department of Education to take more initiative (preschools are outside the statutory system) in extending preschooling opportunities.

TABLE 6.1
ATTAINMENTS OF MAORI AND
NON-MAORI SCHOOL LEAVERS

ATTAINMENTS OF MAORI SCHOOL LEAVERS

Percentage With	1968	1973	1978
University entrance or better	2.6	4.3	6.9
Some school certificate or sixth form certificate	18.4	22.2	26.0
No attainment	79.0	73.5	67.1

ATTAINMENTS OF NON-MAORI SCHOOL LEAVERS

Percentage With	1968	1973	1978
University entrance or better	22.9	26.7	31.7
Some school certificate or sixth form certificate	35.9	37.6	39.9
No attainment	41.1	35.7	28.4

Source: National Advisory Committee on Maori Education, He Huarahi (Wellington: Department of Education, 1980), p. 61.

But the Advisory Committee's most urgent request was for the secondary schools to take stock of what had and was happening to their Maori pupils. In 1973 the minister of education, concerned at the apparent frequency with which certain Auckland secondary school controlling authorities expelled Maori pupils, set up a committee "to study ways of improving communication between secondary schools and parents, with special reference to Maori and Polynesian children."[48]

TABLE 6.2
RETENTION OF MAORI AND NON-MAORI PUPILS

RETENTION OF MAORI SCHOOL PUPILS

Percentage Remaining From	*1967-68*	*1972-73*	*1977-78*
Form 3-4	83.5	81.5	90.9
Form 4-5	70.5	64.8	74.0
Form 5-6	14.1	20.4	29.3
Form 6-7	12.5	13.8	14.8

RETENTION OF NON-MAORI SCHOOL PUPILS

Percentage Remaining From	*1967-68*	*1972-73*	*1977-78*
Form 3-4	96.3	96.8	97.4
Form 4-5	83.0	84.8	90.8
Form 5-6	43.4	52.7	56.8
Form 6-7	30.7	28.5	30.1

Source: National Advisory Committee on Maori Education, He Huarahi (Wellington: Department of Education, 1980), p. 61.

Difficulties in adjustment were two-way. Many secondary teachers, accustomed to the semiselective, authoritarian, prewar system, found it hard to adjust to universal secondary education. Because some tended to equate intellectual status with human worth, they had little sympathy with, or understanding of, children who did not share their goals of academic excellence, sporting prowess, and conventional middle-class behavior. Such children, especially if they were Maori, posed, some teachers considered, "disciplinary problems, teaching problems and eventually drop-out problems."[49] Particularly if these children found it difficult to accommodate to the schools' Pakeha cultural criteria, they were likely to be tracked, as La Belle and White point out,[50] into curricula leading to the lower socioeconomic roles and statuses of the wider New Zealand society. Maori youths whose abilities went unrecognized at school but who were later admitted to apprenticeship training schemes described their secondary schools as harsh and inhospitable, ruled by teachers too ready to use the cane or to humiliate them.[51]

For large numbers of urban Maori children, the secondary school entrance tests brought early humiliation. New entrants with higher scores, mostly Pakeha (ability being assess on the basis of primary school record and performance on the school's English and mathematic attainment tests), were placed in courses styled academic, professional, or general. The rest were allocated to one or the other of a number of alternative vocational courses.

In the early 1970s, concern that such organizational practices tended to confirm certain stereotypes and to institutionalize discrimination against Maori entrants -- and more recently Pacific Islanders -- led teachers and administrators in the South Auckland area, where Polynesians are the majority in most primary and secondary schools, to experiment with less conventional forms of school organization. The whanau house concept (whanau meaning "extended family") was one outcome. Emphasizing the extended family basis of the school, a whanau house (each house contains up to 250 pupils from the third to seventh forms and their teachers, classrooms, activity rooms, laboratory and common rooms) attempts to counter the alienation many children, particularly the Polynesians, feel in a large school.[52]

But it is the teacher who holds the key to the future educational success or failure of the Maori; well-trained, sensitive teachers are essential if mutual respect and understanding between Maori and Pakeha is to be enhanced. Every major education report emphasizes improving teacher education, both preservice and in-service, as the prerequisite for Maori children to improve school performance. In the mid-1960s the Department of Education, which has direct supervision of teach-

FIGURE 6.1
New Zealand Organization Education Chart

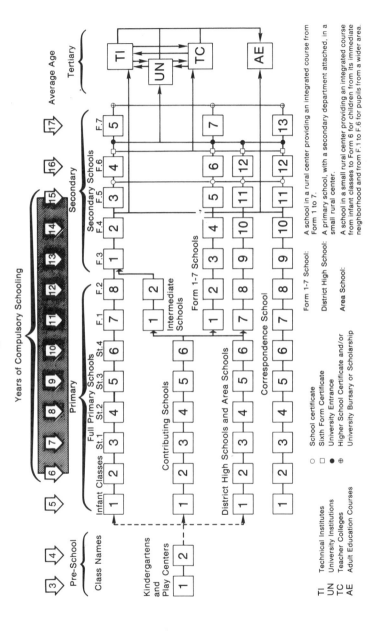

155

er training programs, suggested that teachers college offer optional Maori studies course. Perhaps because in some colleges the response was lukewarm, the Race Relations Coordinator remarked in 1977, "The ignorance of teachers of basic facts of modern Maori life is little short of appalling."[53]

The Department of Education, which since the early 1950s has preferred to advise rather than direct its semiautonomous teachers colleges, aware that Maori and Pacific Island children were an increasing proportion of the school population in 1982, exerted its full authority over the colleges' curricula. A directive setting the numbers of hours required during the three years of initial training for each curriculum area greatly increased the time allotted to preparation for teaching in multiethnic classrooms.

For many years, and with limited success, the department has sought to increase the number of Maori in the teaching service. In 1971 only 3.2 percent of primary teacher trainees and 2 percent of secondary were Maori, but Maori were 7.6 percent of the total population. In 1979, when the 290,000 Maori (66 percent under 24 years of age) were 9.1 percent of New Zealand's population, only 5.3 percent of primary teachers were Maori, even though the minister of education, following a recommendation from his teacher education review committee in 1978, instructed primary teacher recruitment committees to follow the country's two medical schools in giving Maori applicants preference when selecting the last 10 percent of their students.

The minister's decision to favor Maori candidates was in keeping with his department's policy as it evolved since 1962 when the Commission on Education reported it considered "the adoption of special measures to assist Maori pupils fully justified."[54] The 1970 and 1980 National Advisory Committee reports argued also "that to achieve the goal of equal opportunity, it is often necessary to take measures that are vastly unequal."[55] The assistant director-general of education in 1978 said the same: "There is nothing more unequal than equal treatment of pupils with special needs."[56]

The Department of Education has provided some "unequal measures." It encourages the opening of homework centers to alleviate the problem of overcrowding in Maori homes. After 1965 it allowed primary school with large Maori enrollments the "benefit of extra staffing and special staffing ratios that improve the staff both quantitatively and qualitatively."[57] When the proportion of Maori enrollments reaches 30 percent, secondary schools are also given additional staff. Departmental advisers on the education of Maori and Pacific Islanders work closely with all schools to encourage the inclusion across the curriculum of Polynesian values and content.

The Curriculum Development Division of the central department oversees the production of a wide range of curricular materials, including Maori-language tests, for use in multiethnic classrooms. Departmental support is given teachers' inservice courses held on marae where Pakeha school authorities can meet the Maori on Maori terms, thus gaining better understanding of what a multicultural society in which all New Zealanders talk to, not past, each other might be.

In 1980 the National Advisory Committee on Maori Education argued that in an education system in such a society success in national examinations should not constitute the only measure of worth of children from subordinate groups whose educational aspirations might not coincide with those of the superordinate. "In a multicultural society, it is possible to pursue other goals and to have other notions of success."[58]

Acutely aware that the many Maori dropouts are ill-equipped to succeed unaided in the Pakeha-dominated society beyond the school gates, and therefore that the education system still has undischarged responsibilities, Department of Education officers cooperate, through an interdepartmental committee, with officers of the Department of Maori and Island Affairs in developing both formal and informal types of postsecondary education.

In the late 1970s, the newly appointed head of the Department of Maori and Island Affairs, himself a Maori, launched "a massive effort . . . to inspire greater achievement by youth," which he named Tu Tangata ("the stance of the people").[59] At the heart of Tu Tangata lies the belief that Maori people have resources grossly underutilized, not least the abilities of the people themselves, a point made nearly 20 years before by the Commission on Education when it referred to the Maori pupil as "the greatest reservoir of unused talent in the population."[60] In part a morale-building exercise, partially very practical, Tu Tangata is, the secretary for Maori and island affairs says, becoming highly successful.[61]

Specially appointed community officers from the Maori and Island Affairs Department over recent years have been most active in the South Auckland area, joining forces with Department of Education advisers and school counselors to impress on Polynesian parents and pupils alike the idea that "education is the future paddle of our canoe." It is not, however, only Pakeha education that is desired; the Maori people want as well a solid Maori side, claiming that as tangata whenua ("indigenous people") they have the same rights to the promotion in the schools of their cultural heritage as the dominant Pakeha majority. Maori leaders no longer believe, as Sir Apirana Ngata did, that the passing on of Maori traditions is solely a community responsibility. "It is now the urgent task of the schools, for which the Maori people pay taxes like anyone else, to assist in this role."[62]

Maori and island affairs officers are adding their weight to the efforts of Maori Education Foundation and Department of Education advisers in reaching more Maori preschoolers, but as the economic recession of the 1980s continues and deepens, their main concern is the establishment for unemployed Maori youths of basic skills centers, called kokiri ("to advance"). To help some out-of-work urban youth grow in self-esteem and self-confidence, qualities often lacking in school dropouts, the department provides a two- or three-week stay on an ancestral tribal marae, which, with its meeting house and dining facilities, provides an ideal setting for the Maori version of a Danish folk high school.

Much of the work of the Department of Maori and Island Affairs is inevitably remedial because it is for young people who have passed through the school system but have gained little benefit from the experience. Senior educational administrators are as concerned, even alarmed, about this fact as are Maori activists, welfare workers, probation officers, and everyone else aware of the continuing educational gap between Pakeha and Maori school achievement. Understandably, multicultural education is the Department of Education's number one research priority.[63]

Research is not necessary to make one fact clear: The policy of assimilation pursued for so long is not tenable in today's schools. In its report to the minister of education following the 1974 Education Development Conference, the conference steering committee commented:

> We consider that in the past there has been too much emphasis on the Maori having to subordinate his cultural values to those of the European-oriented education system. . . . We believe that the teaching of Maoritanga [the Maori way of doing things] would

benefit both Maori and non-Maori. . . . If we are to build a truly multicultural society in New Zealand, we need schools which give due recognition to cultural differences.[64]

These observations were welcomed in the Department of Education and have been the basis for policymaking. Throughout all of New Zealand's history, Maori and Pakeha have never before spent to much time in each other's company. Better understanding and mutual respect between the two races are essential if the racial harmony of which New Zealanders have long boasted is to be preserved. Departmental administrators, aware that the school is the place to begin building this understanding and respect, that prejudiced and stereotyped ideas about Maori are still abroad in the community, are encouraging schools to broaden their criteria of educational achievement to include not only "the general competencies needed by all in a multi-cultural society, but also particular competencies valued by various groups."[65]

Although curricula in New Zealand's centralized school system will continue to be principally centripetal in orientation, and Maori scholastic success will require considerable accommodation to the cultural criteria of the dominant group, centrifugal tendencies are becoming increasingly apparent and accepted. Cultural diversity is no longer seen as a threat to the social cohesion of New Zealand society. He iwi ktahi tatou -- "We are from many tribes but we are also one people."

NOTES

1. Missionary Register 1 (1814):29.
2. British Parliamentary Papers, Governor Grey to Earl Grey, December 9, 1847 (Shannon: Irish University Press, 1969).
3. T. J. La Belle and P. S. White, "Education and Multi-ethnic Integration," Comparative Education Review 24, no. 2 (June 1980):161.
4. Appendices to the Journals of the New Zealand House of Representatives (hereafter cited as AJHR) 1868, A-4, p. 7.
5. B. Biggs, "The Maori Language Past and Present," in The Maori People in the Nineteen-Sixties, ed. E. Schwimmer (Auckland: Blackwood and Janet Paul, 1968), p. 74.

6. W. Baucke, Where the White Man Treads (Auckland: Wilson and Horton, 1928), p. 131.

7. A. Ngata, The Past and the Future of the Maori (Christchurch: Christchurch Press, 1863), p. 9.

8. New Zealand Education Gazette (hereafter cited as NZEG, February 2, 1931, p. 14.

9. Ibid.

10. AJHR (1881), E-7, p. 11.

11. NZEG, February 2, 1931, p. 14.

12. AJHR (1903), E-2, p. 18.

13. AJHR (1906), E-2, p. 4.

14. AJHR (1937), G-10, p. 3.

15. P. M. Jackson, ed., Maori and Education (Wellington: Ferguson and Osborn, 1931), p. 192.

16. Ibid., p. 193.

17. Rangi Walker, "Culture Gap," New Zealand Listener, November 3, 1973.

18. Ibid., p. 189.

19. La Belle and White, "Education and Multiethnic Integration"; see also National Education, December 1, 1940, p. 411.

20. NZEG, October 2, 1941, pp. 189-90.

21. J. M. Barrington and T. H. Beaglehole, Maori Schools in a Changing Society (Wellington: New Zealand Commission on Educational Research [NZCER], 1974), p. 190.

22. AJHR (1939), E-1, p. 2-3.

23. AJHR (1941), E-1, p. 5.

24. NZEG, May 1, 1943, p. 91.

25. Barrington and Beaglehole, Maori Schools, p. 232.

26. AJHR (1944), E-1, p. 10.

27. Evening Post (Wellington), June 25, 1968.

28. J. K. Hunn, Report on Department of Maori Affairs (Wellington: Government Printer, 1960).

29. Ibid., p. 22.

30. Ibid., pp. 24, 157.

31. Ibid., p. 26.

32. Ibid.

33. E. Schwimmer, "The Maori Education Foundation," Comment 3, no. 4 (July 1962):7-11.

34. Evening Post (Wellington), Aug. 22, 1962.

35. See D. P. Ausubel, The Fern and the Tiki (Sydney: Angus and Robertson, 1960), and Maori Youth (Wellington: Price Milburn, 1961).

36. New Zealand Commission on Education (hereafter cited at NZCE), Report (Wellington: Government Printer, 1962), p. 401.

37. Ibid., pp. 434-37.

38. W. Parker, "Maori Education," Education, no. 9 (1962):56.

39. NZCE, Report, p. 418.

40. Ausubel, Maori Youth, p. 162.

41. J. E. Watson, Horizons of Unknown Power (Wellington: NZCER, 1967), p. 27.

42. NZCE, Report, p. 424.

43. National Advisory Committee on Maori Education (hereafter cited as NACME), He Huarahi (Wellington: Department of Education, 1980), pp. 19-20.

44. La Belle and White, "Education and Multiethnic Integration," p. 163.

45. Ibid., p. 11.

46. NZCE, Report, p. 417.

47. AJHR (1982), E-1, p. 23.

48. New Zealand Department of Education, Parent-School Communication (Wellington, 1973).

49. New Zealand Educational Institute, Report and Recommendations on Maori Education (Wellington, 1967), p. 12.

50. La Belle and White, "Education and Multiethnic Integration," p. 163.

51. R. J. Bates, ed., Prospects in New Zealand Education (Auckland: Hodder and Stoughton, 1970), p. 124.

52. "New Zealand Unveils the Secondary School of Tomorrow," Education News 1, no. 4 (October 1975).

53. AJHR (1977), E-17, p. 15.

54. NZCE, Report, p. 434.

55. NACME, Maori Education (1970), p. 3; He Huarahi, p. 14.

56. Quoted on p. 4 of an unpublished report of an in-service course held at Ti Pai-O-Hauraki Marae, Paeroa (February 1978).

57. AJHR (1969), E-1, p. 28.

58. NACME, He Hurahi, p. 8.

59. AJHR (1979), E-13, p. 4.

60. NZCE, Report, p. 414.

61. AJHR (1980), E-13, p. 3.

62. NACME, He Huarahi, p. 10.

63. AJHR (1980), E-1, p. 28.

64. Advisory Council on Educational Planning, <u>Directions for Educational Development</u> (Wellington: Government Printer, 1974), pp. 52, 54.

65. "The Child and Learning in a Multi-cultural Society," <u>New Zealand Official Yearbook</u> (Wellington: Department of Statistics, 1979), p. 940.

7

EDUCATIONAL DEMANDS
AND INSTITUTIONAL RESPONSE:
DOWA EDUCATION IN JAPAN

John N. Hawkins

Education in Japan is well documented as being a major channel and access to social and institutional roles.[2] In fact, the very preponderance of formal educational credentials as a prerequisite for success in Japanese social and economic life has been singled out as a source of extreme dysfunction in Japanese society.[3] Yet it remains a fact that access to education, and especially certain selected sectors and institutions in Japan's educational structure, is a sought-after goal of most Japanese families regardless of social class, geographic origin, and, as we shall see, caste status.

This study was conducted in Japan and concentrated on the political organizations and educational demands of a persistently isolated and discriminated against group, the Burakumin. Termed "Japan's invisible race" by Wagatsuma and DeVos, this group in many respects remains a discrete subgroup in Japanese society, outside the pale of the majority and as such lacking the social and institutional connections so vital to individual mobility.[4] Although official policy prohibits discrimination against this or any other group, and although the educational system is theoretically open to all, statistically the Burakumin have not participated in or been represented in the upper levels of Japanese education and

---

An earlier version of this study appeared in <u>Comparative Education Review</u> 27, no. 2 (June 1983):204-26.

have consistently been the underachievers at the lower levels (as well as having the greater number of problem students and dropouts as identified by Japanese educational authorities.)

For this and a variety of other reasons, there is a fairly long history of active political organization and mobilization by the Burakumin to gain access to preferred institutions and to seek an end to all discrimination in Japanese society. With respect to the typology discussed in Chapter 1, the case of the Burakumin is best characterized as type B: cultural segmentation and structural commonality in a vertical relationship. The degree to which Japan fits this type will be discussed below.

We will direct our attention to recent political struggles carried out by the Burakumin and their representative organizations under the general rubric "_dowa_ education" (also called _kaiho_ education), which, directly translated, means liberation education or assimilation.[5] In an effort to redress that perceived educational discrimination and lack of equal opportunity, Buraku organizations have generated a series of specific and general demands directed to the appropriate educational and governmental authorities. There have been a variety of policy responses on the part of the educational system, and the Burakumin have reacted accordingly. Here we focus on ideological characteristics of Buraku organizations and dowa education, the nature of selected educational demands, the access channels utilized to transmit the demands to the authorities, and the resulting educational policy responses and feedback from Buraku organizations. In this initial effort we hope to clarify political and educational relations between a marginal and subordinate group and the dominant, superordinate majority in Japan.

Although a strictly systems model was not employed, data were collected and organized around concepts and strategies identified by Easton and Scribner as useful in investigating educational policies and focusing specifically on educational demands. This method of organization provided the closest approximation of the relationship between the Burakumin and the Japanese government and educational system. Easton's framework includes the major institutions of society and assumes that interest groups and institutions interact in the context of dominant and subordinate roles. The political system is the arena that is distinct because it is the only source of the "authoritative allocation of values." As such, it is recognized as possessing both power and legitimacy. In the

Japanese case the "valued" resource is education, and the political system allocates this resource according to patterned relationships between it and various interest groups such as the two Buraku organizations.

Following Easton's model, interest groups outside the political system (Buraku organizations) were formed as a result of societal stress caused by perceived inequities in the allocation of educational resources. The organizations generated input in the form of "demands" on the government and educational system. The demands were processed, converted into decisions and policy actions in the form of "outputs" that then served as "feedback" functions, and the entire process continued anew.[6] By utilizing such an orientation, this study will illuminate the process by which an outcast minority group attempted to gain access to a preferred social institution and how those in control converted demands into policy (or a lack of policy).

GENERAL BACKGROUND OF "OUTCASTES" IN JAPAN

Although the history of the origin of outcast groups in Japan is not well documented, some basic features are clear. For more than 1,000 years long association with certain ritual impurities connected usually with occupation were believed to have changed the very nature of a person so that he became defiled and polluted, and, moreover, that this pollution was hereditary and communicable. As noted by Wagatsuma and DeVos, it was a complex of "economic, social, political and ideological conditions" that led to the development of a status and attitude associated with untouchability.[7] In the ninth and tenth centuries, Japanese culture, influenced by Buddhism imported from China and Korea, merged this system of thought with local Shinto beliefs and generated occupational stratification patterns whereby certain occupations associated with blood and death -- skinners, butchers, leather workers, cremators, tomb watchers (shuku) -- were considered polluting. The rise of outcast groups was related directly to the development of Japanese guild protection arrangements (be), slavery (yakko), and the rise of a "labour market" that operated in closed corporate communities.[8]

The fusion of Buddhism (with its strictures against the taking of life in any form) and Shinto (with its notion of ritual impurity) contributed to the development of a hereditary, occupational, ritually impure outcast group, termed during the Nara period (710-784) <u>eta</u>. Individuals engaging in certain defiled occupations, as well as slaves conquered in battle, were often forced outside Japanese society. From that time, they were historically not of the majority and were forced to hold a monopoly on their inherited occupation. Racially and linguistically part of the Japanese majority, they were identified by official papers, residence patterns, occupation, and other identifiable symbols on their clothing and person. During the Edo period (1603-1867), these relationships became even more formalized and solidified, resulting in a virtual cessation of upward mobility by the groups in question.

From this early period to the end of World War II, a variety of organizational efforts were pursued by members of this group to pressure the Japanese government to enact legislation and other official edicts aimed at ending any type of discrimination toward the outcast group. In August 1871, the Meiji government officially abolished the pariah status of this group, and they were henceforth designated as "new commoners" (Shin Heimin).[9] Although their former official outcast status was removed by legislation, among the general Japanese population long-standing culturally imbedded negative attitudes toward this group remained. They lived as always in segregated communities, engaged in their historical occupations (but without the monopoly protection previously guaranteed), and continued tied to traditional social and financial networks. The net effect of such legislation was that although officially liberated, the Burakumin as a group remained poor and isolated from the mainstream of Japanese life.

In 1903, the Greater Japan Fraternal Conciliation Society was established to form a more organized political body constituting a "reconciliation movement" (Yuwa Undo). This movement represented an effort at "self-improvement" and shifted responsibility for eliminating discrimination to the Burakumin themselves. Poverty and continued discrimination led in 1922 to the "rice riots" and the subsequent formation of a more militant liberation movement called the National Levellers Association (Sueheisha). Heavily influenced by socialist and Marxist ideology, this movement abandoned the notion that discrimination existed because of deprivation and disadvantages of Burakumin, thus requiring "self-improvement," but rather that the locus of the problem lay with the majority society, and that any acts of discrimination should be met with immediate retaliation. During the 1920s and 1930s, internal factionalism split this movement, and with the rise of Japanese militarism, it, along with other left-wing associations, dispersed or went underground, not to emerge until the end of the war.

In this early period, then, it is clear that structurally and culturally the Burakumin were viewed by the dominant Japanese group as inferior and of low status, in line with our argument that eventually one group must exercise dominance over the other in a type B system. What is questionable is whether or not they represented a distinct ethnic group, or were occupationally stratified, being based on ritually distinguished occupations. This issue will emerge as the discussion of the Burakumin and the majority Japanese social structure proceeds.

The postwar organizational history of the Burakumin is complex, and only a brief summary will be presented here. In 1946, a special committee was formed to carry on the prewar political struggle and took officially the name Kaiho Domei, or Buraku Liberation League. Associated with a variety of left-wing groups, the league engaged in both local struggles (accusations of individuals practicing discriminatory activities) and national administrative struggles (aimed at both local and national governments). These activities proceeded unevenly but with significant success until 1961, when it was decided that a major national demonstration culminating with a petition to the government be launched. The demonstration, called the "Grand March of Liberation," had three major goals: improvement of social and economic conditions in Buraku communities, increased coordination and cooperation among the diverse political groups supporting the Burakumin (for example, Socialist party and the Communist party), and increased solidarity with those Burakumin not previously drawn into the struggle.

The petitions were accepted by the Japanese diet and resulted in formal government action by a special council at the ministry level (Deliberative Council for Buraku Integration, or Dowa Taisaku Shingi Kai) to investigate Buraku conditions, the subsequent submission of a report to the prime minister proposing a plan of action to end the discrimination against the Burakumin, and the effective integration of the group into Japanese society. A sort of Japanese affirmative action program developed that stated the following activities be carried out "systematically and swiftly":[10]

1. Improvement of housing and other living conditions through the construction of public facilities
2. Enactment of social welfare and public health facilities
3. Promotion of agriculture, forestry, and fishing
4. Promotion of small-scale industry
5. Improvement of working conditions and employment security through vocational training and guidance
6. Improvement of education and encouragement of higher education
7. Promotion of activities to protect people's fundamental rights
8. Actualization of any effective means for attaining all the objectives stated above

It was clear that the Kaiho Domei succeeded in successfully involving the Japanese government both financially and politically in the campaign to eliminate discrimination toward the Burakumin. The ten-year plan (1969-79) that finally emerged had as an underlying theoretical assumption that discrimination would disappear only as a result of economic and social improvement and that education be utilized as a major force for such change. Upwards of $80 million (U.S.) was apportioned for this program.

Almost immediately, however, the various political factions within the Buraku movement disagreed over the intent and implementation of the report and subsequent legislation. The primary split occurred between the Japanese Socialist (JSP) and the Japanese Communist (JCP) parties, eventually resulting in the creation of two separate organizations.[11] The reasons for the split and the complex theoretical and practical differences between the two groups are detailed elsewhere.[12] For our purposes here, the differences related specifically to education can be summarized as follows:

The JSP faction maintains that continued discrimination against the Burakumin is based primarily on the lack of civil rights and access to education and employment -- in short, the lack of opportunity. The JCP essentially contends that discrimination is a carryover from the old feudal society, continues under modern capitalism, and is essentially a class question. The JCP promotes a more standard Marxist analysis of social class discrimination and has suggested that all poor

Japanese are discriminated against, not just the Burakumin. To the JCP, the JSP faction is unjust in its accusation about the majority of Japanese and too sectarian in its support of the Burakumin. For its part, the JSP faction accuses the JCP of dishonest and splitting the ranks of the Burakumin, who still feel specifically discriminated against. The discrimination practiced against the Burakumin is of a special kind over and above that practiced against poor Japanese. Therefore, the JSP argues, special programs should be generated to assist the Burakumin specifically and to educate both the Burakumin and the overall Japanese population in general.

Ideologically, a dilemma presented itself as leaders within the Buraku movement disagreed over whether they have special characteristics (ethnic group status) or whether they are simply a politically and economically deprived member of the majority population, which puts them into a class of poorer Japanese. Both groups, however, agree on the need for greater educational opportunities and an end to discrimination in the schools. It is this educational issue that will be explored below. The study will also focus on the overriding political questions, as both groups have utilized political strategies and tactics to obtain desired goals and objectives.

THE DEMOGRAPHIC AND EDUCATIONAL CONTEXT

Although demographic statistics on the Burakumin are difficult to authenticate, various efforts have been made by both the Japanese government and the Buraku Kaiho office to detail several demographic and social aspects of the buraku population. As can be seen in Figure 7.1, of the eight official regions in Japan, six contain Buraku districts and corresponding populations. The most heavily populated district is the Kinki area (the focus of this study), followed by the Chugoku area in the south. Statistics are difficult to obtain because of the intermixing of Burakumin and non-Burakumin, land readjustments causing boundary shifts and merging of one slum area into another, and general migration patterns.[13] Other population data are similar to that of the Japanese population as a whole, with the exception that the Burakumin have a slightly higher birth rate and a population structure clustered in the range of 0 to 30 years old (about 70 percent).[14]

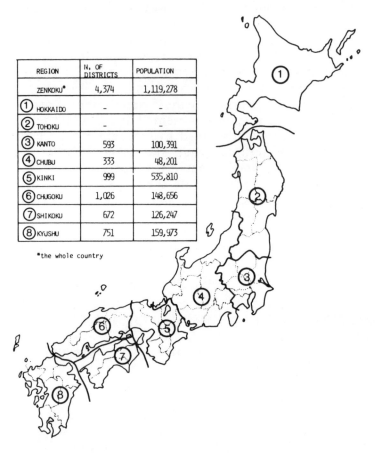

FIGURE 7.1
Population of the Eight Official Regions of Japan

REGION	N, OF DISTRICTS	POPULATION
ZENKOKU*	4,374	1,119,278
① HOKKAIDO	–	–
② TOHOKU	–	–
③ KANTO	593	100,391
④ CHUBU	333	48,201
⑤ KINKI	999	535,810
⑥ CHUGOKU	1,026	148,656
⑦ SHIKOKU	672	126,247
⑧ KYUSHU	751	159,973

*the whole country

Source: Mombusho dowa kyoiku shiryo (Tokyo: Mombusho, 1981).

Data obtained from the city of Kyoto indicate that the majority of the Burakumin are employed either in manufacturing or service industries (see Table 7.2). A 1973 survey conducted in the Osaka area (data obtained from 41,000 individuals of whom 16,097 were working outside the family or self-employed category) suggested that occupational conditions have not improved markedly for the majority of the

Burakumin.[15] Typically, occupations vary according to location. Thus, in larger cities, such as Kyoto and Osaka, the Burakumin are employed in construction (masonry), small business, leather goods manufacturing, and so on, in middle-sized and smaller cities, occupations include tanning, farming, livestock and animal husbandry, and forestry; in villages, in addition to small scale industries such as those mentioned above, more traditional industries are practiced, such as slipper making, peddling, refuse work, recovery of discarded articles, and so on. In the 1973 sample, it was found that .01 percent had reached a level of employment that could be termed professional (lawyer, physician, teacher). Seventy percent of those working were employed full time in skilled and semiskilled laborer capacity; the remainder were in temporary factory or laborer positions.

TABLE 7.1
Occupations of Burakumin in Kyoto (%)

	Buraku (Kyoto)			Kyoto (General)
	1937	1970	1977	1975
Professionals	1.4	1.9	2.4	9.3
Administrators	.3	.7	1.9	5.4
Clerks	.5	6.3	6.5	17.7
Salespersons	23.6	12.2	13.7	17.9
Farming, fishery	.6	.9	.6	1.5
Public employees	2.8	8.2	3.9	3.9
Manufacturing, industry	65.5	57.1	35.1	33.5
Insurance, services	4.7	12.7	35.9	10.8
Others	.7	--	--	--

Source: *Buraku kaiho kenkyujo* (Tokyo: Kaiho domei, 1981).

With the decline of traditional Buraku industries and the continued discrimination against the Burakumin in other job categories, the occupational picture for the future does not appear promising. Directly related to the bleak picture portrayed here is their historically low level of access to education and to the subsequent rewards educational attainment can bring in Japanese society.

A brief overview of educational conditions among the Burakumin and within Buraku districts reveals that as of 1963, compared to their parents, of whom less than 10 percent went to senior high school, about 30 percent of Buraku children in some districts were attending senior high school. This can be compared with the 60 to 70 percent attendance rate among the overall Japanese population at the senior high level. In 1973, the situation improved significantly for the Burakumin, with 64 percent attending the compulsory level, but they still lagged behind the Japanese cohort, which was close to 95 percent.[16]

Although attendance figures demonstrate some improvement over the period under discussion, other factors must also be considered. Absenteeism and wastage are high, and school performance for Buraku children is low overall (see Tables 7.2 and 7.3). University attendance is virtually nonexistent (4.2 percent graduating).[17] Due to effective political organization and struggles in recent years, additional reforms have resulted, such as Buraku children receiving increased financial subsidies from the government.

TABLE 7.2
Tanaka-Binet Test in a City Near Osaka (%)

IQ	Non-*Buraku* Children (N=274)	*Buraku* Children (N=77)
Above 125	23.3	2.6
124-109	31.8	19.5
108-93	23.3	22.1
92-77	11.7	18.2
Below 76	9.9	37.6

Source: George De Vos and Hiroshi Wagatsuma, eds., *Japan's Invisible Race* (Berkeley: University of California Press, 1972).

TABLE 7.3
Reasons for Absence by Students
in Junior High Schools (Nara)

Reasons	Non-*Buraku* Students (N=148)	*Buraku* Students (N=297)
Poverty	1	32
Work for family	0	11
Lack of parental understanding	0	9
Laziness	0	24
Physical disability	1	0
Total absent	2	76

Source: George De Vos and Hiroshi Wagatsuma, eds., *Japan's Invisible Race* (Berkeley: University of California Press, 1972).

It has been suggested that education conditions have improved in the 1980s, but precise figures remain elusive. It is quite likely that it is precisely in the area of education that the Burakumin have made significant advances and increased access to Japanese society. They have done so, it is suggested here, largely because of an effective program of generating, transmitting, articulating, and converting educational demands into public policy. This demand process, the supportive political organization structure, and the public policy output will be examined below.

THE SUPPORTING IDEOLOGY

Both of the major Buraku organizations espouse an ideological position to explain the persistence of discrimination against the group and to offer a general critique of Japanese society. Although it is in this area that the most critical differences between the JCP and JSP factions exist, both organizations employ a variant of a basically Marxist interpretation of society and culture. The JSP concentrates its critique on what it describes as a "lagging feudal culture" that has con-

tinued to influence social relations while the economic base
has changed and assumed the basic relations of capitalism.
This argument holds that while urban capitalism developed
during the Meiji and post-Meiji periods, feudal social relations
continued in rural and semirural regions. As capitalism continued to develop, eventually absorbing other sectors of
Japanese society, feudal relations adapted to the new situation
without disappearing. However, continued discrimination
against the Burakumin is not simply a problem of lagging social conciousness but rather serves, at this time, a specific
political and economic function. Japanese society and economy require a labor pool of exploited workers, so the system of
discrimination is consciously maintained to provide a referent
point justifying further exploitation of lower class people.[18]

The JCP argues that exploitation of poor people has been a
characteristic of Japanese society especially since the development of feudalism. To ease the suffering of poor peasants during the Tokugawa period, a scapegoat was institutionalized by providing still lower classes (Burakumin and Hinin)
for the peasants to discriminate against and look down upon.
Yet all suffered, as did the newly arising urban working class.
It is the position of the JCP, then, that there is nothing unusual about the exploitation of the Burakumin other than,
perhaps, its intensity. Along this line of reasoning, there is
nothing preventing a union of the Buraku liberation movement with other more general struggles for human rights, such
as those of the urban working class, the peasants, and the
struggles against the military. The discrimination practiced
against the Burakumin is but one area in Japanese society of
discrimination, which includes discrimination against the
poor, against outsiders (Koreans, Chinese, and any foreigner),
and even against the physically handicapped. Thus, any
movement to end discrimination must unite with other
antidiscriminatory movements to form a struggle against
Japanese capitalism and the supporting social structure.[19]

Each group, of course, finds great fault with the other's
theory and practice. For its part, the JSP accuses the JCP of
promoting a false "unity" that will work only to the disadvantage of the Burakumin and turn leadership and control as before over to non-Burakumin. Dowa education and dowa
struggles cannot be formulated collectively in the sense the
JCP promotes. Such a policy will only further isolate the
Burakumin and simply reflects a form of deprivation theory.
Correspondingly, to argue that the problems of the Burakumin

are not special but simply the problems of all poor Japanese ignores the extra oppression that the group has suffered for hundreds of years and the social and psychological effects of institutionalized discrimination. To argue further that the educational problems of the Burakumin can be solved within the general framework of education inhibits the development of theories to cope with the historical effects of oppression, resulting in low academic achievement and retardation of physical and mental development. In short, the educational and social problems of the Burakumin are special and should not be categorized or lumped with those of other oppressed groups in Japanese society.[20]

The JCP's criticism strikes more at what on the part of the JSP faction is considered the lack of political theory. It maintains that the JSP does not look at all the facts and tends to overexaggerate the problems of the Burakumin. Over the years conditions among the Burakumin have improved to the point that there is little difference between their political, social, and economic conditions and those of other working-class Japanese. Although the JCP concedes that the lower rungs of the socioeconomic scale are occupied disproportionately by the Burakumin, there are other Japanese as well at that level, and it should therefore be the program of any social change-oriented group to improve conditions for all individuals at this level, not just the Burakumin. Furthermore, within the Buraku group there are wide differences between some very wealthy, and exploitative, Burakumin in control of major economic enterprises and the mass of extremely poor Burakumin. Again, it is naive to lump all Burakumin into one category without distinguishing political and economic contradictions within and between the group and the majority society. To maintain that discrimination against Burakumin is a total and completely conscious policy on the part of the "ruling bourgeoise ideology" is contradictory, because it implies that all non-Burakumin belong to the bourgeoisie, and the ordinary working people are as much to blame for continued discrimination as the ruling class. The net effect of such a policy is to create a different discrimination against non-Burakumin.

From the perspective of the JCP, a characteristic tendency in the JSP's approach to discrimination is that it lacks objectivity and is unable theoretically to distinguish between specific discriminatory practices against the Burakumin and the discriminatory practices promoted in Japanese society.

There is no such thing as discrimination in the abstract, only certain kinds of discrimination with specific historical and economic backgrounds. In short, the JSP's position is slightly metaphysical and ignores the class analysis strategy so basic to Marxism.[21]

Although the ideological dispute is a real one and forms the basis for the lack of unity and antagonism that characterize JSP and JCP dowa relations, the fundamental differences in their respective positions do not appear to be irreconcilable. Both provide a critique of Japanese society that recognizes continued discrimination that is at once exploitative and demeaning. Both assert that the Burakumin historically have been on the receiving end of unusual discrimination and, whereas the JCP argues that conditions have improved, it does not go so far as to suggest that great progress has been made. In essence, the difference between the two positions is that which distinguishes between the special nature of discrimination against the Burakumin, calling for a separate and independent organization and the consequent political control over the resources that have been successfully obtained from the Japanese majority, and that which suggests a broad united front by all oppressed Japanese. These differences become more apparent if we look at some of the specific criticisms made by each group regarding the Japanese educational system and its relation to the needs of the Burakumin in particular.

In keeping with its basic position that the educational problems of the Burakumin are of a special nature, the JSP has focused its criticism of education in several areas (specific educational struggles and issue will be detailed below; this section is meant to provide a brief overview of some basic critiques of Japanese education). First and foremost the JSP maintains that it is the responsibility of each school at both the collegiate and precollegiate levels to provide a curricular program aimed at improving the self-image of the Burakumin. The study of history, politics, and economics is to provide the base from which an understanding will emerge as to the reasons for discrimination past and present. Thus dowa education courses have been designed, texts compiled, and teachers trained to offer courses of this nature. The long-range goal, however, is to move in the direction of permeating the curriculum with dowa content rather than to have separate courses. A related goal is to provide dowa courses for the general population to make them aware of the causes of discrimination, promote a more healthy image of the Burakumin, and generally raise the consciousness of the Japanese population. Dowa education should generally promote educational programs in the area of human rights and specifically focus on the human rights needs of the Burakumin.

A second major issue is that of providing adequate financial support for the Burakumin to attend quality senior high schools and colleges and universities. The financial support would be in the nature of tuition, clothing, educational materials, and a variety of other educational expenses. It is argued that one reason for low attendance rates at the senior high and college levels is the poor economic position of most Burakumin and therefore the necessity for children to begin work at an early age. Financial support alone, however, is insufficient, as the Burakumin historically have been unable to compete with the majority of Japanese on the rigorous and highly competitive entrance examinations required at both the senior high and college levels. Therefore some leaders within the JSP are now arguing for special admissions policies providing quotas to ensure an equitable percentage of the Burakumin at each level. This policy is not a solution but a temporary measure until the Burakumin are able to raise their educational level to compete with other Japanese. Although progress has been made, a parallel tutoring program is another aspect of this policy, and the lack of such facilities in the Japanese educational system is another source of discontent.[22]

The JCP critique again reflects its position that educational problems in Japanese society are of a social nature and not specific to any particular subgroup. Overall, the educational system is discriminatory because it reflects the interests and needs of the middle and upper classes. It discriminates against all poor Japanese. The educational system serves to reproduce in Japanese society existing social relations, including that held by the Burakumin through an intense system of intergroup competition. The entire educational system, then, is in need of restructuring to provide for a more cooperative school environment. All students should be allowed to work together on problems, to develop self-initiative, and to attain democratic attitudes. Parents and teachers should unite in their efforts to provide a more cooperative and collective school environment, and the medium for such an action program should be the dowa educational programs existing in many schools. Any program designed to foster collectivism should realize also that significant curricular reform is necessary. The JCP states that current texts and supporting curricular materials contain only the point of view of the ruling class's ideology and, furthermore, are not relevant to the daily needs and experiences of the majority of Japanese. They are especially unrelated to the experiences of the Burakumin and poor Japanese. Thus a complete curricular reconstruction should occur and should be a major component of any dowa educational program.

Finally, and somewhat contradictory to its previous position on social class, the JCP has argued for universal preschool education, high school education, free textbooks, educational allowances, scholarships, tuition exemptions, lower student-teacher ratios (less than 50 to 1!), fewer teaching hours, better pay, and improvement of educational facilities for teachers, and social education (adult education).[23] These suggestions are not specific to any social class but are considered general priorities for educational reform in Japan.

Criticisms related to the interaction between the Burakumin and the Japanese educational system are not all so general; it again becomes apparent as we examine some specific demands that those of the JCP are geared more toward pedagogical issues concerning most poor Japanese and those of the JSP to those specifically related to the Burakumin.

DOWA EDUCATIONAL DEMANDS

Over the years, the movement for dowa education by both organizations has generated a series of specific educational demands, usually triggered by some incident of overt discrimination. In this section we will detail some educational demands by both organizations. The demands are clustered in four areas: general pedagogical demands, demands focused on the precollegiate level, demands focused on the collegiate level, and nonformal educational demands.

One general educational issue raised by both organizations during the past ten years concerns the cost of education. Although there is no direct tuition, there are a number of indirect educational costs that the Burakumin find difficult to meet (uniforms, textbooks, auxiliary study materials, donations to the school, lunch, expenses for school trips and other extracurricular activities). Both organizations have stressed the need for government agencies to provide subsidies for the

Burakumin to meet these expenses (and, of course, the JCP argues that all poor people should receive such subsidies).[24] In 1970, the Kaiho Domei (JSP) further outlined five specific educational demands: decrease in the number of students per class to 30 through enforcement of the dual homeroom teacher system, assignment of extra teachers to work with dowa problems in the schools, guaranteed admission of all Burakumin to public senior high school, establishment of a new dowa scholarship system and an increase in the amount of existing scholarships, and guarantee of special educational measures to support the education of physically handicapped children.[25] Both organizations agree that dowa education should seek to improve the overall educational environment through financial subsidies, educational programs to increase the social consciousness of both the Burakumin and the general population, and improvement of the occupational opportunities for the Burakumin in general (although one informant stressed that somebody must engage in traditional Buraku occupations and that they should not be considered "dirty").

At the precollegiate level, a series of discrimination incidents resulted in specific educational demands by dowa organizations in the Osaka area. Incidents were often reported by students to their parents and then to the local dowa office. Usually the discrimination took the form of a remark made by a teacher regarding the low position of the Burakumin and attributing the low status to some racial or other defect in their character. This suggests that at least some portion of the Japanese population genuinely believes that there are racial or ethnic differences within Japanese society, despite anthropological evidence to the contrary. Occasionally the incident took place outside the school but more often during the course of instruction (for example, one instructor made a discriminatory remark about the Burakumin during a lecture on the origin of the samurai).

Such incidents turned the attention of the dowa office to the individual school, where, first, the accused party was denounced (kyudan) and pressure applied to remove him from his position; second, and more important, the educational conditions of the Burakumin in that specific school would be analyzed and more specific demands made upon the school and city educational administration.[26] In some cases, the new demands were relatively uncomplicated, perhaps identifying priority areas for improvement, such as providing free lunch money (failure to bring lunch money in some schools results in punishment in the form of running laps; Buraku children, it was charged, were always punished more severely), free books, and other financial subsidies.[27] In other cases, such as the Sayama incident,[28] demands included that the entire curriculum for the school district be changed to require a specific set of texts (the Ningen series written jointly by Buraku children and adults and compiled and edited by the Kaiho Domei) be adopted district-wide.

Educational demands were not limited by the pedagogical needs of Buraku children only but included their parents as well. It was felt that parents' educational levels were too low, thereby setting a bad model for their children. Thus, at least in one case, demands stressed the importance of formal alliances between Buraku parents and teachers in Buraku districts designed to raise the educational level of parents, especially in reading and mathematics. The reasoning was that if parents were better able to augment their children's formal study, the 30 percent variance between achievement levels of Buraku and non-Buraku children would disappear. Finally, once achievement levels rise, special admissions policies should be provided for Buraku children to enter the better public high schools.[29]

Educational demands for higher education are directly related to those identified for the precollegiate. It is essential to raise educational levels and reduce discrimination at the precollegiate level as a precondition to achieving success for the Burakumin in higher education. For the present, however, until Buraku children as a whole achieve at levels closer to the national norm, it is felt necessary to provide special tutoring to prepare students for the entrance examinations. Moreover, special admissions policies must be pursued to ensure equal representation in Japan's colleges and universities.

A second problem is again associated with the parents. Despite the overwhelming importance of higher education in Japan, and the direct correlation between university degrees and occupation, many Buraku parents do not see the necessity for higher education, and thus they need to be enlightened. Also, universities must begin to provide meaningful dowa education for all students and ensure that it remain an integral part of the curriculum. Finally, one of the first (1959) collegiate-level demands was the allocation of special funds for university scholarships for Buraku youth. For ten years this demand was not met. Little progress has been made in this area, and university reform will be one of the most difficult educational levels to penetrate and for which to create new programs. This has caused an increased sense of frustration, and some have suggested that the entire higher educational system be dismantled.[30]

In recent years a variety of nonformal educational wants and demands have also been articulated. Both Buraku organizations have recognized that the educational needs of Buraku children are related to other community needs. One specific need is that of information relating specifically to Buraku concerns. Thus special Buraku newspapers have been established to create awareness and pride in Buraku children and adults. One such paper, the <u>Kaiho Kyoiku</u> in Osaka, focuses on the history of the Burakumin and in particular the political struggles over the years. A variety of joint Buraku-government offices and agencies has been proposed, and some were eventually formulated. Here the need (as represented by the Claimants Union in Toyonaki-shi) may focus on child care, special demand committees for educational reform, and health care.[31] The need for university student organizations has been identified, and in many universities in the Kinki area they have been formed. These organizations are to increase consciousness raising for the university population and the Burakumin, to increase coordination of different dowa struggles, and to provide an organizational base to articulate specific educational demands at the university level. Also, extracurricular clubs have been formed at the precollegiate level that include students, teachers, and parents, as well as other community representatives. Increased participation of the Burakumin in such nonformal educational activities has been an important feature of dowa demands.[32]

We see that educational demands cluster around several important issues:

1. Financial -- both organizations identified the financial needs of the Burakumin as being first and foremost on their list of demands to educational decision makers; finances are needed for educational materials and scholarships, and special subsidies are needed for extracurricular activities, as well as resources for physical plant construction.
2. Upgrading educational skills -- a priority for the Burakumin to increase participation and achievement at all levels of schooling calls for increasing educational achievement levels to more closely approach the national

norm. To achieve this, special tutoring for Buraku children, as well as parents, is deemed essential.
3. General improvement in the educational environment -- smaller class size, extra teachers, special admissions policies for senior high schools and colleges and universities, and special educational programs for the study of dowa education have all been identified as necessary to promote equal opportunity in the field of education.
4. More systematic organizational efforts on the part of Buraku organizations and the government -- it has been noted that the educational problems of the Burakumin are related to the social and economic conditions of people residing in Buraku districts and, for this reason, demands to improve education should be linked with demands to improve living conditions, thus requiring a more effective organizational base and joint effort between Buraku groups and political decision makers.

Having once formulated priority areas for educational improvement, a complex network of channels to communicate the demands to appropriate educational decision-makers.

EDUCATIONAL ACCESS CHANNELS

Both the JCP and JSP factions have experimented with a variety of ways to gain access to the educational decision-making apparatus in Japanese society. Here, again, the case of the Burakumin in Japan is supportive of the type B society where a highly centralized educational system with wide access at all levels exists; yet distinctions exist between dominant and subordination groups. Depending on the nature of the issue, dowa organizations seek access ranging from direct relations with an individual school to the Ministry of Education (MOE) in Tokyo. Indeed, larger struggles, such as those described in the introduction, occurred at the national level and yielded policies and directives from the various ministries concerned. However, with regard to dowa education, the primary target for dowa organizations seeking access to the educational decision-making machinery has been at the city level, more specifically, the mayor's office.

A secondary target for reform has been the prefectural boards of education, which have direct authority over the municipal precollegiate level.[33] Direct lines of decision making are thus, at the municipal level: The mayor's office appoints the board of education, which directly administers, through the superintendent, municipal colleges and universities and selected precollegiate educational institutions; at the prefectural level, the governor's office appoints the prefectural board of education, which has direct authority over prefectural institutions, as well as municipal compulsory precollegiate schools. The authority wielded by municipal and prefectural governments is significant. They have responsibility for the establishment, administration, and occasionally the abolition of schools. They administer curricular reforms (under MOE leadership), appoint, transfer, and retire teachers, conduct in-service training for teachers, supervise entrance requirements for children, and determine basic policy for student-teacher-parent relations.[34]

The more complex the educational issue, the higher up the educational decision-making ladder the dowa struggle would focus. For example, the effort to have the entire student scholarship system revised for Osaka prefecture resulted in a broad alliance among various Buraku organizations (the Osaka Prefectural Council for Studies of Dowa Education and the Osaka City Council for Studies of Dowa Education formed an alliance with the Kaiho Domei chapter in Osaka to seek support from local parent-teacher and teacher union groups). Eventually, an executive committee was formed (October 1973), and 23 additional organizations joined the struggle.[35] The coalition then campaigned for signatures requesting specific revisions in the scholarship system and presented their demands to the prefectural board of education. A series of meetings were held with the staff of the prefectural section for educational institutions (Shigaku-ka) and the revision was eventually obtained. Another source of access to the prefectural level is, of course, the official Prefectural Council for Promoting Dowa Countermeasures (Osaka-fu dowa jigyo sokushin kyogikai), which is tied directly to city-level dowa organizations. For most issues, this channel is sufficient, but as has been noted, certain educational policy questions demanded a more action-oriented approach bypassing the official channels.

Although the specific organizational network employed to gain access to the educational system at the city level varies, a survey of the system in Kobe, Osaka, Ashiya, and Toyonaka reveals a general pattern. Representatives from Buraku districts, scholars and experts on dowa problems, and city personnel form an overall committee for administering dowa policies. A more complicated managerial council is formed that may consist of subsections focused on specific problems (environment, welfare, human rights, or education) and/or subsections to represent various city departments (finance, health, environment, agriculture, public works, or education). As demands are received and processed into policy, they pass through committees composed of city representatives, Buraku representatives and scholars, and experts who make revisions and finalize the first draft of a program. The program is then sent to the local Buraku district offices for discussion and then returned to the managerial council (dowa taisaku renraku chosei kaigi) for final implementation. If the issue is educational in nature, the subcommittee under the council is composed of educational personnel (parent-teacher group, teachers' union, scholars and experts, Burakumin, and city council members). It should be stressed that this is an ideal channel, yet it does not always operate smoothly. In terms of appointments to committees, there appears to be continuous jockeying for power for the purpose of gaining voting blocs. But for many minor educational issues this access channel appears to function well.[36]

Demand articulation also varies according to the issue and can range from denunciation (kyudan) of individuals who have obstructed Buraku demands or have made discriminatory remarks to formal petitions to the appropriate educational authorities. The manner of presenting educational demands also depends on the degree of receptivity the educational body or authority approached displays. In cases where educational authorities at either the prefectural or municipal level prove cooperative and make positive moves to address the issue, the demand will be presented and stressed in a consistent but non-antagonistic manner.[37] However, where educational authorities and officials in the prefectural or municipal level do not receive the demands with a sympathetic ear, denunciation and other, more drastic steps are taken.

A case in point is the struggle that occurred in 1970 in Ashiya, where five demands were presented by the local Kaiho Domei office (regarding classroom size, student-teacher ratio, scholarships, and admissions requirements) to the mayor's and superintendent's offices. The superintendent refused to accept the demands and stated that education was really the parents' responsibility. Several denunciation meetings were held. Educational officials faced parents and teachers of the Buraku districts and eventually promised to redress the grievances and initiate policy for the five areas under question. Although promises were made, the failure of the superintendent to follow through resulted in his kidnapping by the Kaiho office, which forced him to view the conditions existing in the Buraku district and the area schools. This action caught the attention of the city board of education and the media and contributed to the pressure already on the district to enact reforms. After one month, the prefectural board intervened and forced the Ashiya city board to concur with the Kaiho office.[38]

The pattern discussed above relates primarily to JSP activities during the past seven years in the Kinki area. The JCP engaged also in mass meetings and pressure tactics to achieve educational goals, but on the other hand has criticized the JSP for excessive use of violence and terrorist tactics.[39] What emerges is evidence that both the JCP and JSP have formed their own structural organizations contraposed to the dominant structural commonality of the dominant group in Japanese society, and challenging the notion that they eventually will be absorbed by the dominant society. Such practices in the Osaka area have resulted recently in several important educational decisions by the prefectural and municipal governments. To highlight the scope and degree of educational change that has occurred, this conversion of educational demands into policy will be examined next.

EDUCATIONAL POLICY AND FEEDBACK

The organizational activities of the Burakumin, the demands presented to the educational authorities in the Kinki area, and the administrative structure established by both the prefectural and municipal governments to respond to the demands have resulted in several important responses in the field of education. Although these responses vary according to prefecture and city, there have been some common areas of emphasis, as revealed by the policies generated in Osaka, Itami, and Ashiya cities. The policies can be categorized in three major areas: policies for school districts, policies for individual schools, and policies in the broad area of social education (shyukai kyoiku).

District-level policies have generally reflected the belief that the child must be assessed in all developmental terms, not just the intellectual level of achievement. Buraku children must be assured a complete educational cycle from preschool to guaranteed employment. Policies in most cities have focused on building and staffing nursery schools (<u>dowa hoiku</u>), thus providing a sort of head-start program for Buraku children. For older children and adults, policies will provide special dowa classes to foster positive attitudes toward the Burakumin and their history. At the general school level, policies have focused on the need to provide adequate nutritional and health care for Buraku children. District-wide study groups and centers for studies in dowa education are other responses and have resulted in special committees composed of representatives from the community, labor unions, business community, and, of course, the Burakumin.

Although there has been general satisfaction with the policy response at the district level, the Kaiho Domei has criticized these programs as taking too long to implement, being too little too late, and in some cases being not well suited to the general needs of the Burakumin. Thus, as of 1976, the Kaiho headquarters began a strategy to generate at the district level another set of demands to encourage public officials to complete plans already formulated and begin programs to augment and increase existing district educational programs.

At the individual school level, educational policy has rested on the assumption that in each school the role of education is to provide absolute equal opportunity to all children, as well as special measures for the Burakumin because of previous discrimination and deprivation. Programs have focused on special in-service teacher training in dowa education, study sessions for parents and teachers, and research groups to study the history of the Burakumin and compile new teaching materials. Additional programs have concentrated on implementing programs especially for the Burakumin to "guarantee scholastic achievement." Guaranteed achievement is to be ensured through a systematic study of the nature of achievement and the relationship between scholastic ability and class size, teacher-student relations, community environment, and the like. In the area of curriculum, policies have suggested that the entire curriculum be reviewed to ensure proper compliance with Buraku demands and to remove any remaining discriminatory statements or suggestions. A review of entrance examination procedures has also begun, and a program to construct more public high schools closer to Buraku districts has also been a policy response.

Although Buraku organizations have recognized that significant advances have been made with respect to positive policy responses on the part of individual schools and districts, there is frustration that, in the area of entrance examinations to preferred high schools in particular, there has been little advance. It appears that in the future educational demands at the school level will focus on the achievement issue and the national examination system. It is this area that will likely be the most difficult to reform, and at least one youth leader in the Kaiho Domei has suggested the complete dismantling of higher education in Japan and the severing of the close relations between higher education and occupation.

In addition, a series of policy responses related to the concept of social education (shyukai kyoiku) have appeared. Policies in this area rest on the assumption that the social and educational problems of the Burakumin are interrelated with the total fabric of Japanese society and thus affect everyone. As a consequence, efforts have been made to foster leaders of dowa education in the workplace as well as other social institutions. To support such a program, teaching materials have been or will be compiled to provide adequate reference materials for the study of dowa education in a variety of settings. Special news publications have been proposed and implemented in at least one city (Itami). Steps have also been taken to make more accessible social educational facilities, such as libraries, public halls, and museums, to the Burakumin as well as to encourage such institutions to provide for the general public dowa education classes. According to Buraku leaders in the Osaka area, it is this program that has advanced the least. Although educational officials and government authorities seem willing to enact policies that focus specifically at the school level, and even generate overall district-level policies, in terms of the overall community the response has not been encouraging. Officials have suggested that this falls outside their jurisdiction and that an office other than education should handle such problems. Buraku leaders are not satisfied and this will likely be a target area for new educational demands in the future.

As a final note, Japan's highest level educational research organization, the National Institute for Educational Research, in Tokyo, has not set research priorities in the educational problems of the Burakumin. Some members of the institute expressed dismay that the MOE has seen fit not to identify this area as important for educational research, but others indicated that were such an effort pursued the various Buraku organizations would not allow researchers access to the communities or sanction any empirical studies. For now, any evaluation of educational policy and the Burakumin must take place in an environment lacking empirical data.[40]

With respect to the typology introduced in Chapter 1, the following comments are in order. First, both the majority and minority groups (the Japanese in general and the Burakumin in particular) are ambivalent with respect to the ethnic question. Educated and informed segments of both groups agree that the Burakumin are not an ethnically or racially distinct group within Japanese society but of the same stock. Yet neither group will relinquish the notion that it is somehow special and different. Second, clearly one group is dominant over the other. Third, the idea that occupation or role is not a salient feature of group membership does not appear to hold true. Fourth, the concept that eventually the subordinate group will be absorbed by the dominant group will almost certainly be born out, despite the fact that there are those in both groups who will oppose the idea. Finally, the case of the Burakumin is quite clearly coincident with a type B society in that neither class nor ethnic considerations can account fully for the stratification that is documented.

The ten-year plan, announced in 1969, was extended with some revisions by the national diet to March 31, 1982. Funding has been further extended to 1986. The extension allows continuance of funding for special Buraku needs. The continuing involvement of the Japanese government with problems of the Burakumin testifies to the long-term nature of the issue. This study is clearly exploratory and, it is hoped, has revealed a general pattern of effective political organization achieving specific and general educational goals. Clearly, both Buraku organizations have wrested from a reluctant Japanese educational system a variety of educational reforms and have succeeded in directing national attention to their plight. The experience of the Burakumin is a revealing and fascinating study in the politics of educational reform and intergroup relations and, in the future, Japanese and non-Japanese scholars alike will continue to focus their research here.

NOTES

1. Research for this study, conducted in Japan during 1976, 1979, and 1981, was partially supported by grants from the Ford Foundation and the East West Center. I would like to thank Dr. Fumiko Okumura and Yoshiro Tanaka for their comments and assistance with translating Japanese sources. I would also like to thank Professor Yasutaka Tokorozawa for his assistance in the initial stages of data collection.

2. Major sources include Ronald S. Anderson, Japanese Education (Washington, D.C.: U.S. Government Printing Office); Tetsui Kobeyashi, Society, Schools and Progress in Japan (New York: Pergamon Press, 1976); Herbert Passin, Society and Education in Japan (New York: Teachers College Press, 1965); John Singleton, Nichu: A Japanese School (New York: Holt, Rinehart and Winston, 1967); William Cummings, Ikiro Amano, and Kazayuki Kitamura, eds., Changes in the Japanese University (New York: Praeger, 1979); and Theodore Brameld, Japan: Culture, Education, and Change in Two Communities (New York: Holt, Rinehart and Winston, 1968).

3. Ronald Dore, Diploma Disease (Los Angeles: University of California Press, 1976).

4. George DeVos and Hiroshi Wagatsuma, eds., Japan's Invisible Race (Berkeley: University of California Press, 1972).

5. It should be noted that although dowa is the commonly used term for educational programs and policies directed toward the Burakumin, the term kaiho (liberation) is preferred by both Buraku organizations, reflecting more accurately the conflict-oriented nature of intergroup relations in this case.

6. Frederick M. Wirst and Michael W. Kirst, Political and Social Foundations of Education (Berkeley, Calif.: McCutchan Publishing Co., 1967), pp. 12-15.

7. DeVos and Wagatsuma, Japan's Invisible Race, pp. 6-20.

8. Ibid., pp. 19-20.

9. A complete detailed analysis of the pre- and postwar political militance and organizational strategy of the Burakumin can be found in DeVos and Wagatsuma, ibid., pp. 68-88. This summary draws heavily from Hiroshi Wagatsuma, "Political Problems of a Minority Group in Japan: Recent Conflicts in Buraku Liberation Movements," Case Studies on Human Rights and Fundamental Freedoms (The Hague: Foundation for the Study of Plural Societies, 1976).

10.   Wagatsuma, "Political Problems of a Minority Group in Japan."

11.   The faction associated with the JSP continues under the name Buraku Kaiho Domei, and that associated with the JCP, formed in 1969, a group called Buraku Kaiho Domei Seijoka Kenkoku Renraku Kaigi. In this study, when referring to these two groups, we will refer to them in terms of their affiliation with either the JSP or the JCP, but it should be noted that although Buraku associations have affiliated or sought support from or the other political parties mentioned, they resist the notion that they are controlled by the parties.

12.   Wagatsuma, "Political Problems of a Minority Group in Japan."

13.   Mombush dow kyoiku shiryo (Tokyo: Japanese Government Printing Office, 1981); Dowa taisaku shingikai toshin (Tokyo, 1965).

14.   Dowa taisaku shingikai toshin.

15.   Baraku kaiho, no. 45 (September 1973).

16.   Ibid.; Organization of Education in Japan, 1971-1973, Report Presented at the XXXIVth International Conference on Education, Geneva, 1973.

17.   Buraku kaiho, no. 45.

18.   Asahi newspaper, "Views on Discrimination," March 1975.

19.   T. Ogawa, Dowa kyoiku no riron to hoho (Kyoto: Buraku mondai kendyusho, 1975).

20.   Buraku kaiho, no. 51 (February 1974).

21.   Asahi newspaper, March 1975.

22.   Interview with representatives of Kaiho Domei, Osaka, July 18, 1976, and February 3, 1981.

23.   Ogawa, Dowa kyoiku no riron to hoho.

24.   Ibid.

25.   Kaiho kyoiku, no. 1 (July 1971).

26.   Buraku kaiho, no. 57 (July 1974).

27.   Interviews with Asuka city educational representatives, July 20, 1976, and February 4, 1981.

28.   "Kyoiku wo mamoru fabo no kai," Buraku kaiho domei, Hojyo chapter, Osaka-fu, 1976.

29.   Buraku kaiho, no. 56 (July 1974).

30.   Interview with Kaiho Domei youth organizer, Osaka, July 26, 1977.

31.   Buraku kaiho, no. 36 (January 1973).

32.   Interviews with Asuka city representatives.

33. In the final analysis, it is the MOE that has direct authority over virtually all levels of education in Japan, but the various dowa organizations have found that presenting educational demands at lower levels often brings a more direct and swift response.

34. Organization of Education in Japan, 1971-1973.

35. For a complete list of such organizations, see Buraku kaiho, no. 50 (January 1974).

36. Kobe-shi dowa taisaku jigyo choki keikaku, 1973; Ashiya-shi dowa taisaku shingikai (Ashiya-shi dowa taisaku shingikai toshin, 1975); Kaiho kyoiku, ed. Zenkoky kaiho kyoiku kenkyu kai (n.d.); Buraku kaiho, no. 36 (January 1973).

37. For a description of the scholarship struggle, see Buraku kaiho, no. 50 (January 1974).

38. Ashiya-shi kaiho kyoik kenkyukai, Dai nikai Ashiya-shi kaiho kyoiku kenkyu taikai shuroku, 1975.

39. Wagatsuma, "Political Problems of a Minority Group in Japan"; Ogawa, Dowa kyoiku no riron to hoho.

40. The author attempted to conduct an empirical study of Japanese perceptions of the Burakumin (both teachers and students) correlated with test scores and encountered opposition from Buraku organizations and the Japanese Teachers Union. One remark was that such a study was too "psychological" and therefore too sensitive for teachers and students.

PART III

CULTURAL AND STRUCTURAL SEGMENTATION IN A HORIZONTAL RELATIONSHIP

8

EDUCATION AND INTERGROUP RELATIONS— AN INTERNATIONAL PERSPECTIVE: THE CASES OF MALAYSIA AND SINGAPORE

R. Murray Thomas

It is useful to consider the cases of Malaysia and Singapore together for two reasons. First, the ethnic patterns of these neighboring nations have grown from similar historical roots. Second, contrasts between the two can be nicely illustrated with the system of visual models introduced in Chapter 1. The cases are presented by historical periods: British colonialism until World War II; transition to independence, 1945-65; for Malaysia, reactions to the ethnic relations crises, 1968-70s; for Singapore, from independence into the 1980s; and ethnic conditions in the mid-1980s. As the discussion progresses, we describe changes in the patterns of ethnic relations and speculate about the changes in the patterns. Also, inspect the interactions between ethnic conditions and the education system, considering ways that ethnic patterns have affected schooling as well as ways that schooling has influenced ethnic relations.

First, however, as a preparation for analyzing the cases era by era, we can profit from recognizing the general ethnic composition of the two societies in recent years and theories about causes behind such ethnic patterns.

PRESENT-DAY ETHNIC PATTERNS

Geographically, Malaysia is divided in two. West Malaysia, which is the more populous and more modern portion of the

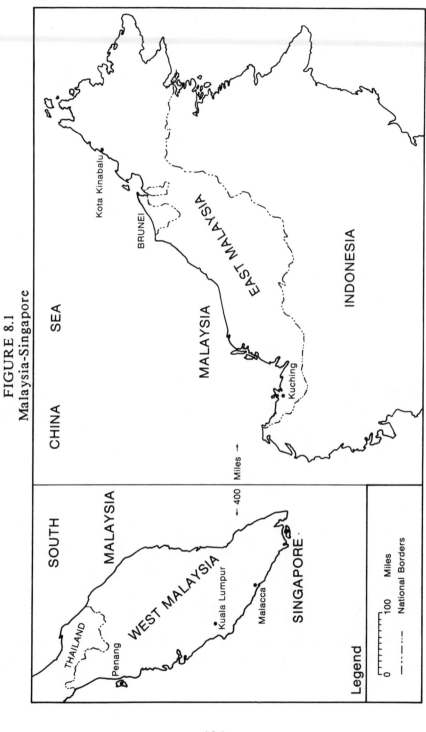

FIGURE 8.1
Malaysia-Singapore

nation, is on the Malay Peninsula, which forms the southern-most extension of the continent of Asia. East Malaysia con-sists of a wide strip of territory across the northern sector of the island of Borneo, separated from West Malaysia by 400 miles of the South China Sea. By the 1980s the population's ethnic composition (referred to as "racial composition" in Malaysia) was listed as about 55 percent Malays, 34 percent Chinese, and 9 percent Indians, with the remaining 2 percent of other ethnic stock.[1] Of the nation's total land area, 40 percent forms peninsular West Malaysia, where 85 percent of the total population lives, so that only 15 percent of the people inhabit the less developed 60 percent of jungle and mountain terrain that makes up East Malaysia.

Although the racial designation Malay tends to suggest that this 55 percent of the population is composed of an eth-nically homogeneous group, such is not the case. It is true that most of the people included in the Malay category are in-deed of Malay stock -- they speak the original Malay lang-uage, they share a common Malay culture, and most are Mus-lims. However, a portion of the people listed as Malays are actually of different ethnic origins, speaking separate languages and displaying other distinct cultural character-istics. Most of the true Malays live in peninsular West Malaysia, whereas a large proportion of the non-Malays that appear in the Malay category are members of tribal groups in-digenous to the island of Borneo -- such groups as the Dusun or Kadazan, Iban (Sea Dyak), Land Dyak, Melanau, Murut, and Bajau.

The reason for applying the single label Malay to such varied groups has been mainly political. It enables the Malays to demonstrate that they have a secure majority of the citi-zenry in comparison to the proportions of Chinese and Indians in the population. Actually, a more accurate umbrella label under which these separate ethnic groups can be clustered is bumiputera, a Malay term for "sons of the land." The bumi-putera, then, are the indigenous peoples of East and West Malaysia -- including the real Malays and the other tribes -- whose ancestors were living in the region before the Europeans, Chinese, and Indians arrived.

We turn now to Singapore, the city-state that occupies a tiny island at the lower tip of the Malay Peninsula and whose political and economic fate has been linked intimately with that of Malaysia for more than 160 years. In geographic size, Singapore is 200 times smaller than Malaysia, but in population Singapore is only six times smaller (by 1984 an estimated 2.52 million people in Singapore compared to 15.25 million in Malaysia). Whereas Malaysia is chiefly rural, including large expanses of jungle, Singapore is a crowded urban center, a nation in which half of the population lives in high-rise housing estates.

Although the major ethnic types that compose the citizenry of Singapore are essentially the same as those of Malaysia, the proportions are different. And it is chiefly this difference that caused the separation of Malaysia and Singapore into two sovereign states in 1965 after they had been amalgamated to create the newly constituted nation of Malaysia in 1963. Whereas the majority of Malaysians today are ethnically Malay (or bumiputera), in Singapore the dominate racial group is Chinese (76 percent), with the remainder of the population Malay (15 percent, primarily people from nearby Indonesia rather than from Malaysia), Indian (7 percent), and others (2 percent).[2]

The foregoing, then, are the general ethnic patterns for Malaysia and Singapore in the mid-1980s. Our task throughout the rest of this chapter is to trace the development of such patterns and their relations to education. As a preface to this task, we first preview three theories about the causal factors that could have produced and maintained such racial structures. Our attention will focus primarily on the Malays and Chinese because of their numbers and significance; we make only passing mention of the small percentage of Indians who form a politically weak segment of the two societies.

THEORIES OF CAUSE -- THE "WHY" OF ETHNIC PATTERNS

The principal source of racial and political conflict in Malaysia for at least three decades has been the Chinese domination of the economic system in contrast to the Malay control of the apparatus of government. In recent years the government has taken measures to improve the economic status of Malays, with education chosen as one of the main tools for effecting this change. Social scientists and politicians have speculated about how successful these efforts are likely to be. As guides to their speculation, they have depended chiefly on a number of theories of cause, three of which are the genetic, cultural, and structural.

According to the genetic hypothesis, racial groups differ in biological inheritance in ways that influence their intelligence and social behavior. For instance, a Malay politician and physician, Dr. Mahathir bin Mohammad, proposed in his book The Malay Dilemma that inbreeding among Malays has caused them to be inferior genetically to the Chinese in a number of intellectual characteristics.[3] He suggested that this inferiority accounts for the Chinese succeeding in the school system and in controlling the nation's economic life. Busch writes that "repeatedly, I heard this theme from Malays in Singapore, even from secondary school pupils who had never heard of Dr. Mahathir and his book."[4]

The cultural theory, in contrast, proposes that the differences in the positions of ethnic groups in economic, educational, and political affairs stem chiefly from differences in the traditional values, goals, and habits of those groups. In both Malaysia and Singapore, people hold widely recognized stereotypes about the cultural characteristics of the racial divisions. Esman has summarized these stereotypes from the perspectives of both Malays and Chinese:

> Malays regard themselves as scrupulous in their dealings with outsiders as well as one another, faithful in all obligations to their families, friends, religion [Islam] and rulers, and concerned more with the quality of human relations and with the unhurried enjoyment of simple, decent living than with material acquisition. . . . [On the other hand, Malays picture the Chinese as] hardworking, insatiably acquisitive, clever but unscrupulous in transactions outside their family, coarse and insensitive in interpersonal relations, ritually and physically unclean, unreliable in their values -- except their enduring obligation to ancestors and thus to Chinese culture and to China. . . .[5]

> [The Chinese] regard themselves as hard-working, progressive, concerned with improving their lot through their own efforts in a competitive and often hostile environment, and faithful to their family and social obligations. To the Chinese, a "typical" Malay is lazy and superstitious, without motivation to improve himself through education or hard work, preferring to subsist on handouts or patronage from relatives or the government than to earn his way through diligent work.[6]

The cultural hypothesis, then, holds that the relative positions of the ethnic groups in Malaysia and Singapore are primarily due to such characteristics as the above. The fact that many members of the particular ethnic groups do not fit their stereotype does not negate the further fact that, to a great extent, members of the ethnic groups base their social interactions on the conviction that such stereotypes are generally valid. In other words, the stereotypes, as attributions, are socially and politically significant causal factors in ethnic relations.

According to the structural theory, the ethnic groups' political, economic, and educational conditions are explained by the particular architecture of the society that resulted from British colonial policies nineteenth and twentieth centuries. The theory proposes that the different ethnic groups' life-chances were determined by the positions to which the groups were relegated in the colonial social system. Supporters of the structural hypothesis contend that British policies kept the Malays in rural areas, where educational facilities were minimal and instruction was in Malay, while the same policies encouraged the Chinese to settle in cities where advanced schooling in English was available. Thus Chinese rather than Malays were trained for more influential positions in both the colonial government and commerce.

Some analysts have marshaled arguments to support one of these theories in preference to the others. However, as Snodgrass has pointed out, such theories need not be considered mutually exclusive.[7] The truth could well lie in some combination of causes. Furthermore, as Hirschman has noted, it may be desirable to separate explanations for the origin of the ethnic patterns from explanations about how such status is maintained or reduced over time.[8] With such considerations in mind, we turn now to a brief historical account of the evolution of ethnic relations in the region.

CONSTRUCTING BRITISH COLONIES

At the height of Great Britain's empire building during the nineteenth century, British commercial interests, backed by the army and navy, gradually gained control over increasingly larger areas of Southeast Asia. At the same time, other European powers were equally anxious to gain control of the region. The Dutch finally succeeded in ruling most of the islands of the Indonesian archipelago, including the bulk of the island of Borneo. But the British persisted, and by 1826 they had incorporated three separate trading ports -- Singapore, Penang, and Malacca -- as the Straits Settlements. Much later, in 1895, four princedoms on the Malay Peninsula (Perak, Selangor, Negri Sembilan, and Pahang), which had earlier signed treaties designating Britain as their protector, were reorganized as the Federated Malay States with the centralized government under a British resident-general. Over the period 1910 to 1930, the remaining lands of the peninsula were consolidated under British governance as the Unfederated Malay States. Meanwhile, Britain had also gained control of North Borneo. All of these areas combined would form the new nation of Malaysia when it was established in 1963.

During the nineteenth and early twentieth centuries, the British exploited the economic potential of their expanding Malay holdings by developing the trading port facilities in the three Straits Settlements, by setting up extensive plantations (principally rubber and coffee), and by mining the rich tin deposits on the peninsula. The indigenous population was neither sufficiently large nor sufficiently interested in plantations and mining to provide a suitable labor force for the colonial enterprises, so the British imported laborers from China and India to do the work. In addition, other Chinese migrated to the region on their own initiative, often locating themselves in the seaport cities to set up small shops and engage in trade. Although some Indians also settled in the towns, the bulk of them became laborers on rubber estates, where many of their descendants today still work.

British policies for the governance of their multiethnic colonies were compounded of self-interest and a small measure of altruism. In the Malay States and North Borneo, the British did not rule the people directly but, instead, controlled the regions through the sultans who had governed the princedoms before the Europeans arrived. In Singapore, though the British assumed more direct control, administrative actions were often routed through leaders in the city's ethnic communities. From the time Singapore was first established in 1819 by Sir Thomas Stamford Raffles, the British encouraged the ethnic groups to live in separate parts of the city, a practice that newcomers found compatible with their own interests. Hardpressed peasants who left their homeland in China, India, or Indonesia for a better life in the British colonies felt most secure when they settled in the section of the city occupied by earlier arrivals who spoke their same language and followed their same customs. Today different sections of the city are to some extent still identified with particular ethnic strains.

Throughout the Malay States, the British policy of paternalistic protectionism toward the native peoples resulted in land ownership regulations and schooling policies that encouraged the Malays to remain in their rural settings and to continue in subsistence farming and fishing. The policies also served to prevent Chinese and Indian immigrants from controlling land and positions of political power. As a result, the immigrants remained laborers in tin mines and on plantations or else operated shops in the cities and towns. The pattern of schooling resulting from such policies became a significant cause behind the kinds of ethnic relations found today in both Malaysia and Singapore, as illustrated in the following review of the evolution of types of schools.

<u>Koranic schools</u>. The only formal education being conducted in the region when the British arrived was Islamic, principally in the form of Koranic schools in which the young learned to intone passages of the Koran and to study a bit of Arabic language and Muslim law and customs. Known today as <u>pondoks,</u> some Koranic schools still exist in Malaysia as private ventures.

<u>English-language schools</u>. The earliest Western-style schools were established by Christian missionaries after 1815. The Singapore Free School, opened by an Anglican clergyman in 1834, accepted pupils of all racial groups, with separate language streams, so that pupils could receive their instruction in English, in Malay, or in the Tamil language from South India.[9] Throughout the nineteenth century, additional English-language schools were set up in several urban centers, not by the colonial government but by Britishers acting as private groups or by such religious organizations as the London Missionary Society, the Roman Catholic church, and the American Methodist church. Although these schools were not established by the government, they were officially encouraged by means of government grants-in-aid.

Because English was the language of the colonial government and of the leading trading firms, fluency in English became a mark of prestige for Orientals. Asians who were privileged to learn English had an edge over the others in obtaining employment in government and in commerce, for it was English-speaking Asians who staffed lower positions in the government and European business establishments.

However, the facilities for learning English were very limited, as it was never the intention of the colonialists to provide universal schooling. The majority of the population continued to speak indigenous Oriental languages.

Malay schools. The colonial government's protectionist policy toward the native population was displayed in the provision of a form of publicly supported schooling in the Malay language. Beginning in the 1850s, colonial officials established rural Malay primary schools at an accelerating pace. By 1872 there were 16 schools, and by 1892 there were 189 with an enrollment of 7,218 pupils.[10]

Although Malay schools had the advantage of providing children a modest level of education in their own language, the schools failed to equip youths for government service or for the commercial sector. In order to care for Malay students who hoped to progress beyond the primary grades, some transfer schools were set up for teaching the English needed in English-language secondary schools. However, trying to acquire sufficient English in a transfer school proved difficult for rural pupils, so that using the transfer to achieve upward socioeconomic mobility became the exception rather than the rule for Malay youths.[11]

Chinese schools. Even before the Singapore Free School opened in 1834, there were at least three private Chinese-language schools in the city -- one conducted in the Hokkien dialect and two in Cantonese. And over the ensuing decades, more private Chinese schools were founded at a rapid rate. Although the British did not purposely oppose the establishment of Chinese schools, colonial authorities did little to encourage or support them. Moreover, by favoring English-language secondary and tertiary education, the colonial government effectively frustrated the educational progress of youths whose lower-school training had been exclusively in the Chinese language. Before World War II, when the only available tertiary education in the colonies was in English, it was usually necessary for students from the Chinese stream to go to China for higher education.

As time passed, a new language division developed within the colonies' growing Chinese population. On the one hand were the Chinese schooled in their own tongue. On the other were those who attended English-language schools so they might take advantage of the employment opportunities in the colonial government and business houses, as well as receive secondary and tertiary education in the colonies. The division became particularly significant following World War II, as the anticommunist business and political leaders came chiefly from the English-educated group, while the opposing communist forces were derived mainly from the Chinese-schooled segment.

The Tamil schools. To care for the primary school needs of the Indian population, British authorities permitted the establishment of Tamil-language schools, with the Indian community providing its own teachers and learning materials. From the standpoint of promoting upward socioeconomic mobility for Indian youths, the Tamil schools were of little help, as they were limited to the primary grades and did not equip pupils with language skills useful in the broader society. The schools did, however, enable children to maintain ties with their Indian heritage and with the Hindu religion.

In summary, British educational policy throughout the colonial era was primarily passive and permissive rather than active. The main active role of the government was that of furnishing modest amounts of Malay elementary schooling and of providing government subsidies to English-language and Tamil schools and to Chinese-language schools operated by Christian missionaries.

At no time was universal education a goal of colonial authorities, nor did they offer a plan for unifying the society by means of a colony-wide school system. They were satisfied, instead, to permit a modicum of schooling in the ethnic groups' own languages, thus encouraging a continuation of segregated ethnic communities in a plural society. Critics of this policy have charged that it was a device intentionally employed by the British to maintain control over the colonies by preventing the ethnic groups from gaining a sense of unity that could result in their wresting control of the region from the Europeans.

With the foregoing historical sketch of ethnic relations in hand, we are now prepared to picture the colonial ethnic structure in terms of the diagrams described in Chapter 1. Figure 8.2 is intended to represent the structure during the 1930s, which was the final decade of normal British control before Japanese military units captured the territory in early 1942. The three diagrams offered in Figure 8.2 represent an estimate of the relationships among the five main ethnic clusters in terms of economic power, political power, and educational advancement. The sizes of the circles are intended to suggest the comparative sizes of the ethnic

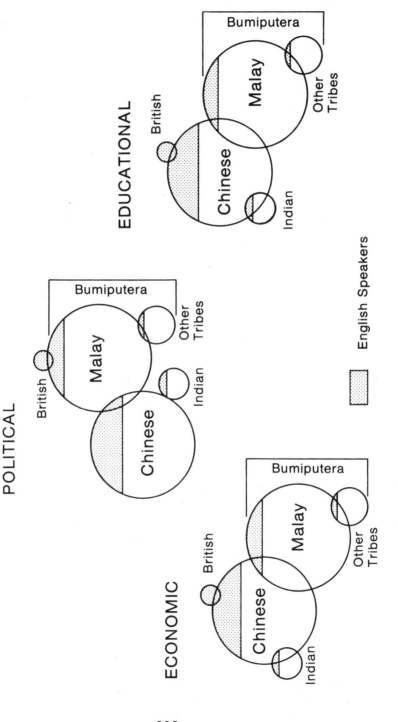

FIGURE 8.2

The 1930s: Colonial Ethnic Hierarchies for Political Power,
Economic Power and Educational Advancement

POLITICAL

EDUCATIONAL

ECONOMIC

English Speakers

205

populations. The Europeans, principally the British, at the top of all three hierarchies are the smallest in number. The Malays and Chinese are similar in number, with the "true" Malays shown as higher in political power (because the British ruled through the traditional sultans) but lower than the Chinese in economic power and educational advancement. The indigenous non-Malay tribes, mostly in North Borneo, are placed at the bottom of each diagram.

TRANSITION TO INDEPENDENCE, 1945-65

From early 1942 until late 1945, Japanese military forces occupied Southeast Asia. After they were ousted at the close of World War II, the British gradually realized that they could no longer maintain control over their former colonies. The spirit of political independence that was sweeping through Africa and Asia was bound to prevail. With this prospect in mind, British authorities planned with local political leaders for a peaceful transfer of power rather than having the people suffer the armed revolutions that the Dutch met in Indonesia and the French faced in Indochina.

In preparing to transfer, colonial authorities found themselves negotiating two key decisions with Asian leaders in the colonies. First was the matter of proper geographic boundaries that would define the independent nation or nations that would replace the existing Straits Settlements, Federated and Nonfederated Malay States, and North Borneo. Second was the question of what sort of political system should be set up in a proposed written constitution.

By 1957 such matters had been basically settled. Peninsular Malaya would be governed as a constitutional monarchy, with the head of state chosen for a five-year term from among the reigning sultans of the existing Malay States. The constitution was a compromise agreement that accorded non-Malays, chiefly the Chinese and Indians, the opportunity to become permanent citizens of the new state. But the plan favored the indigenous peoples (chiefly the Malays) by designating Islam as the state religion and Malay as the national language. English was allowed for a period of ten years as a second official language. The constitution further entrenched measures from the past that had favored Malays -- employment quotas in public services, scholarships, business licenses, and the reservation of certain lands for Malays.[12]

Whereas a transitional form of independence was thus granted the Malay States in 1957, it was not until 1963 that further negotiations resulted in the formation of the new nation of Malaysia, which was composed of all the Malay States, the Straits Settlements -- including Singapore -- and all of North Borneo except the tiny oil-rich kingdom of Brunei. Snodgrass summarized the economic and political positions of the major ethnic groups at this time, after the British had relinquished political control and were being replaced in. the economic sphere.

> Economically the Chinese were in by far the strongest position, not only because they had amassed relatively large amounts of wealth, education, and experience, but also because of their demonstrated capacity to adapt to changing circumstances and seize newly-offered opportunities. In the political arena however, the Malays had already seized the initiative, based on their historical advantage of legitimacy and their earlier development of nationalism focused on Malaya. Through their preoccupation with the fast-moving affairs in their homelands, the Chinese and Indians had bungled whatever chance they had for a major political say in post-war Malaya. When they finally decided to opt for Malaya [rather than return to China and India] it was too late to obtain anything more than a junior-partner role.[13]

The establishment of Malaysia in 1963, however, did not settle the political struggles. Both economic and political competition between Singapore and peninsular Malaysia pitted aggressive Chinese leaders in Singapore against Malay-dominated political powers in the national capital (Kuala Lumpur) and in late 1965 resulted in Singapore being ejected from membership in Malaysia. A significant cause behind the expulsion of Singapore was a desire on the part of Malays to establish in the polity a secure majority of bumiputera by ridding the nation of Singapore's dominantly Chinese population.

MALAYSIA: AFTERMATH OF THE
RACIAL RIOTS, 1968-70s

In May 1968 the strong showing of non-Malay political parties in parliamentary elections led to riots that damaged the country's former record of avoiding racial violence. As a result, through emergency powers granted under the constitution, Malay leaders instructed parliament to amend the constitution and the sedition act to make it illegal for any one to question the position of the Malay rulers or the special rights accorded Malays.

Of particular importance for the education system, the time schedule for securely establishing the Malay language as the nation's official tongue was stepped up. This meant eliminating English-medium education and replacing it, one year at a time, beginning in 1970, with the first grade of the primary school, with education in the Malay medium. Schooling in the Chinese and Tamil languages would continue in the six-year primary school, but secondary and tertiary education, by the mid-1980s, would need to be in Malay.

The changes that this policy would require in the school system are suggested by figures on the number of children who in 1963 had been in the four language-media streams of primary schools. Of more than 1 million children in the primary grades, 44 percent were in the Malay stream, 30 percent in the Chinese, 20 percent in the English, and 6 percent in the Tamil.[14] The 20 percent in the English stream -- most of them Chinese and Indian children -- would need to choose a different language medium. And if this medium was Chinese or Tamil, such pupils would still need to gain sufficient mastery of Malay as a second language during their primary school years to compete successfully in secondary and higher education, which would subsequently be offered solely in Malay.

Coupled with the hastened implementation of the language policy, Malay leaders increased educational opportunities for the bumiputera -- special schools, liberal scholarships for study both within the country and abroad, and favorable quotas for entrance into higher learning institutions. In the appointment of people to administrative posts in education, as well as in other sectors of government, ethnic status rather than education, talent, and experience became the dominant criterion. The rationale for such favored treatment has been that British colonial policies had placed Malays at a disadvantage in competing educationally and economically with the

Chinese and Indians. In other words, Malay leaders have invoked a structural theory rather than a cultural or genetic theory, in defending the present-day favored treatment of indigenous peoples. The educational advantages now being provided to Malays are proposed as intentional structural changes designed to correct injustices of the past.

There has been nothing hidden about the government's special treatment of Malays or about the reason for such favoritism. The government's intention has been expressed openly in each of the five-year plans used for charting the course of national socioeconomic development. For example, the Third Malaysia Plan, 1976-80, explained that

> to the extent that the incidence of poverty falls most heavily on the Malays and other indigenous people, the poverty redressal efforts of the government will contribute towards reducing current economic differentials among the major racial groups in the country. . . .
> The focus of policy in this regard will continue to be the need to reduce disparities in the ownership and control of wealth in the modern sectors and to diminish the concentration of employment among the Malays and other indigenous people in traditional agriculture while increasing their presence in the relatively more affluent urban sectors.[15]

The Fourth Malaysia Plan, 1981-85, pointed out that in recent years the nation's growing economic strength had been accompanied by the rising of the Malays' average income at a rate higher than that of the other ethnic groups. However, by the early 1980s the Malay average wage was still below the average of the Chinese and Indians, so "much remains to be done to remove the large income disparities" between the Malays and others.[16]

The method for achieving cultural unity has also been described in a forthright manner in the national plans.

> The evolution of a Malaysian national identity will be based on an integration of all the virtues from the various cultures in Malaysia, with the Malay culture forming its core. . . . These qualities [of tolerance, good will, and common sense] have been reinforced by the teachings of Islam and other religions.[17]

Thus, through designed structural alterations, in which the schools are assigned a very significant role, the government is seeking to effect major revisions in both the socioeconomic and the cultural patterns of Malaysian society.

SINGAPORE: FROM INDEPENDENCE INTO THE 1980s

While in Malaysia the Malay-dominated government has pursued official measures to redress what have been termed educational and economic wrongs of the past, in Singapore the Chinese-dominated government has adopted a far different attitude toward ethnic relations. The reasons behind this difference are both economic and political. In contrast to Malaysia's extensive agricultural and mineral resources, Singapore's natural resources are limited to its strategic geographic position -- its location at the intersection of Southeast Asia's main sea routes. Not only is Singapore's population unable to feed itself from its meager agricultural lands but the city must even import drinking water from Malaysia. Singapore depends for survival, then, on the ingenuity and diligence of its people and on maintaining a peaceful social climate that permits its populace to focus full attention on conducting efficient trade and industrial enterprises. But, unlike Malaysia, Singapore experiences no ethnic split in terms of who controls the government and who controls the economic system. Both are dominated by the Chinese.

The government of Singapore has been characterized by Skolnik as "paternalistic authoritarianism . . . honest, efficient, highly organized, prudish, vehemently anticommunist, and convinced of its own superiority."[18] The country's economic progress over the past two decades has been the envy of other developing countries of Southeast Asia, with the gross domestic product growing at least 10 percent a year during much of this period.

In ethnic relations, what Singapore's leaders strive for is not favored treatment of one group but rather for an integration of the various groups in a way that minimizes their differences and maximizes their commitment to common goals and loyalties. The school system has been viewed as an important instrument for promoting such integration, with a variety of measures adopted to implement the plan.

One measure has been the constant emphasis in the schools on the necessity to increase interracial amity:

A primary or secondary school student hears important government officials [who frequently visit schools], his principal, and his teachers continually telling him that Singapore is a "multiracial" state in which all of the country's cultures and languages must be respected and in which no race can disregard the political rights of any other group. . . . While several moral and pragmatic reasons for racial tolerance and cooperation are mustered, the one most heavily stressed and most deeply believed by the elite is that racial harmony is essential to the survival of the country. One argument used to convey this message to Singapore's Chinese citizens is that Chinese domination over the island's other peoples would make the country's position untenable in view of its Malay neighbors, Indonesia and Malaysia. The Malays are often told that social cohesion is the key to their economic advancement.[19]

Another measure for furthering racial integration has been the government's series of structural changes in the country's education system, particularly in relation to the four traditional instructional language streams that were inherited from colonial times -- English, Chinese (Mandarin), Malay, and Tamil. One step has been to locate classes in the same building for more than one of the language streams on the belief that familiarity among pupils of various ethnic origins breeds understanding and friendship. This effort to turn monolingual schools into multilingual ones has met with modest success, more so in government primary and secondary schools than in the city's many private (government-aided) schools.

Part of the aim behind the school integration program has been to promote the government's bilingual policy of making every student literate and orally fluent in at least two of the country's four official tongues. What this has meant in practice is that pupils are pressed to achieve fluency in English, plus their own language -- Chinese, Malay, or Tamil. At the time the nation of Malaysia was established in 1963, Singapore adopted Malay as the national tongue all citizens were to master. And after Singapore became independent in 1965, the Malay language ostensibly still held this official status. However, in reality English has become the official common tongue. In 1959 only 47 percent of children entering the first grade of the primary school were in the English stream and nearly as many (46 percent) were in the Chinese stream. By 1979 the English stream enrolled 91 percent of all primary one children, with only 9 percent in the Chinese track and a negligible number in the Tamil and Malay sections.[20]

In effect, by advocating bilingualism and promoting English as the society's common language, political leaders have avoided favoring one ethnic group over another and, at the same time, have encouraged the populace to gain fluency in the language most important in the world for international communication. However, educational planners and parents have expressed concern about the effect the shift into the English-medium schools will have on maintaining the cultural roots of the separate ethnic groups. Language unity may soon be achieved but probably at the expense of cultural traditions.

MALAYSIA: THE MID-1980s

An estimate of ethnic group relations for Malaysia during the mid-1980s is displayed in Figure 8.3 in the form of hierarchies of political power, economic power, and education. The estimate suggests that Malays continued to dominate political affairs and thereby were able to implement government policies in economic and educational spheres that favored Malays and other indigenous tribal groups. Although Malays had made progress in economic control during the 1970s, the Chinese, by the mid-1980s, were still in the strongest economic position and continued to hold many upper-level technical positions in the government.

In regard to educational opportunity and cultural emphasis, policies favoring Malays over the 1963-84 period had greatly strengthened the Malay position. Their home language had become the official instructional language in all secondary and tertiary institutions, and Malay was taught as a required subject in the remaining Chinese- and Tamil-medium primary schools. Malays continued to enjoy study both at home and abroad through liberal scholarship opportunities, and strong government support continued to be given to the secondary and higher education institutions that had been established particularly for the benefit of the bumiputera. Yet, despite these advantages, Chinese students as a group continued to be more successful academically than were Malays.

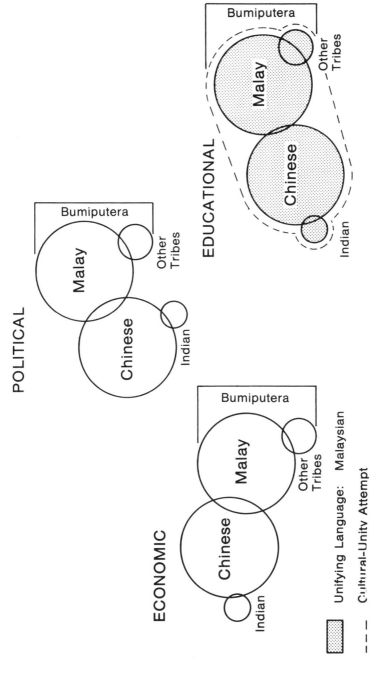

FIGURE 8.3

Malaysia -- Mid 1980s: Ethnic Hierarchies for Political
Power, Economic Power, and Educational Opportunities

POLITICAL

ECONOMIC

EDUCATIONAL

Bumiputera

Malay

Chinese

Other Tribes

Indian

Unifying Language: Malaysian

Cultural-Unity Attempt

213

The question, then, may be asked: Are the Malays likely to achieve parity with (or even surpass) the Chinese in economic and educational progress? And, if so, when will it likely occur? The answer lies, at least partially, in which theory of cause of ethnic conditions proves to be most accurate -- the genetic, the cultural, or the structural.

The genetic hypothesis, we may recall, holds that Malays are biologically inferior to Chinese in certain intellectual abilities contributing significantly to educational and economic success. If such a cause is true to any marked degree, then we might expect the Malays never to catch up with the Chinese, unless the government places such oppressive restrictions on Chinese economic and educational opportunities that there is no room for the Chinese to express their talents in either business or schooling. At present, however, the evidence to support the genetic theory is very meager and weak.

More reasonable, in terms of available evidence, is the cultural hypothesis, which proposes that compared with the Chinese, the Malays' traditional values and customs have not been well suited for success in school and in business. If such cultural characteristics have indeed contributed significantly to the economic and educational differentials between the two ethnic groups, then there is hope for the Malays to catch up with the Chinese -- if Malays enjoy special educational and employment opportunities, Malays receive attractive incentives for availing themselves of the opportunities, and school curricula are devised for Malays stressing new values and customs that foster success in a modern, technological society. Such an altered cultural emphasis in the schools would be expected to meet some resistance from traditional Malay parents and thus would produce a degree of intergenerational conflict. Whether such an educational renovation of cultural commitment can be accomplished with Malays (particularly in view of a revival of fundamentalist Islamic religious practices that has recently appeared in Malaysian society) remains a question unanswered.

The structural theory, as noted earlier, suggests that the ethnic groups' past positions within economic and schooling hierarchies resulted from the configuration of colonial society as determined by British colonial policy. This cause is the one directly addressed by the Malaysian government when implementing policies to compensate Malays for what it regards as past injustices. If the dominant cause for the racial groups' positions has indeed been structural, then the structural treatments applied in the government's series of five-year socio-economic development plans can in the near future be expected to bring Malays into parity with both the Chinese and Indians. And if the treatments are maintained past the point of parity, the Malays can be expected to achieve an increasingly dominant position in economics and education, as well as in politics.

It is my guess that the locations of the ethnic groups within the economic and educational hierarchies are a result of both cultural and structural factors. However, it is not as yet clear what proportion of the groups' conditions have been caused by cultural, and what proportion by structural, influences. As the Malaysian government's compensation policies continue to be implemented in the years to come, evidence to settle this question of cause will likely accrue.

SINGAPORE: THE MID-1980s

As we have seen, government ethnic policy in Malaysia has been founded on the proposition that until Malays have received compensatory advantages that put them on par with the Chinese and Indians at the starting line, individuals should not be allowed free rein to run the educational-socioeconomic footrace of life. In contrast, racial policies in Singapore have been founded on the belief that justice is served when all citizens are furnished equal educational opportunities that permit them to progress educationally and economically in keeping with the diligence and talent each brings to the task. Consequently, in Singapore there has been strong public financial support for all types of schools and an effort to integrate the several ethnic strains into the same school buildings and, perhaps ultimately, into the same classrooms.

My estimate of ethnic group relations for Singapore during the mid-1980s is shown in Figure 8.4 in the form of hierarchies of political power, economic power, and education. The estimate suggests that the Chinese continued to dominate in the economic and political spheres, but with only a small advantage over the Indians. In education there was a strong push toward parity among the three ethnic groups.

Adopting English as the nation's dominant language has been founded on two principal rationales. English is not the native language of any of the nation's ethnic groups, so it

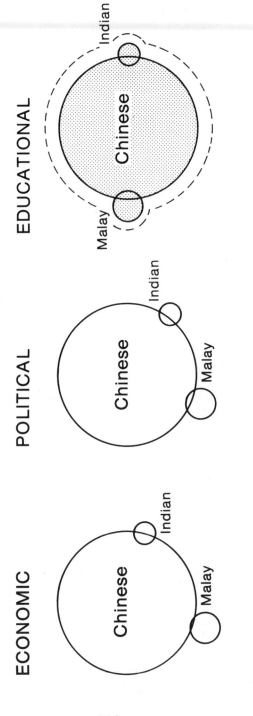

FIGURE 8.4
Singapore -- Mid-1980s: Ethnic Hierarchies for Political
Power, Economic Power, and Educational Opportunities

ECONOMIC

POLITICAL

EDUCATIONAL

Chinese

Malay

Indian

Unifying Language: English

Cultural-Unity Attempt

does not favor one group over another. And English is the most useful language for a city-state that depends for its livelihood on international commerce. Near the end of the 1970s, the schools' bilingual policy was introduced full force, with the expectation that all students would become fluent in both their native tongue and in English.

However, by the early 1980s, it seemed clear that this goal was beyond the capabilities of the less apt students, who would do well to become truly literate in one language. Therefore, by the mid-1980s, expectations for universally implementing the bilingual policy were being downgraded, so that students who seemed unable to master two languages would be permitted to pursue one language in a curriculum track suited to their talents.

In Malaysia, Malay critics of Singapore's racial policies have charged that without compensatory measures the city's Malays will simply fall farther and farther behind the Chinese in the areas of politics, economics, and education. In other words, Malay leaders contend that Singapore's equal opportunities for schooling are not equal when, for both structural and cultural reasons, the Chinese continue to be ahead of the Malays at the beginning of the race.

As in Malaysia, there remains in Singapore the question of which theory or which combination of theories best accounts for the ethnic groups' past and present positions within the political, economic, and educational hierarchies. If the main cause lies in the formal structure of the educational system, then we can expect within a few years to find Malays and Indians represented in proportions approximating the ethnic groups' proportions in the general population at all levels of the political, economic, and educational hierarchies. However, part of the cause may reside in informal structural characteristics, such as a tendency when hiring and promoting employees for those in charge of business houses and government offices to prefer their own ethnic groups. In the event that this informal structural influence continues to be strong, the progress of Malays and Indians in the economic world will be slowed.

If, however, the main cause is cultural, then we can expect to wait longer for ethnic groups to achieve parity in the three spheres, as values and habits among the ethnic groups lower in the hierarchies would need to be altered, and this takes time. And if the chief cause if genetic, then change can be expected only through interbreeding of the races.

As in the case of Malaysia, a more secure answer to this question of cause must await the results of future studies of Singapore's evolving racial patterns.

CONCLUSION

To summarize, we can review ethnic relations in the two nations in terms of the analytical categories described in Chapter 1.

First is the matter of whether the current movement in structural and cultural conditions, as fostered by government policies, is in a centrifugal or a centripetal direction. As the dashed lines in Figures 8.3 and 8.4 suggest, in both Malaysia and Singapore, government ethnic policies are intended to be centripetal in effect. The policies are designed to amalgamate ethnic groups through promoting greater cultural unity. Educational instruments used to promote centripetal movement include increased central control over both public and private schools in curriculum contents, standards -- particularly test scores -- that determine whether a student advances to the next higher school on the educational ladder, criteria for determining the academic or vocational track a student enters, teacher training and placement, and language of instruction. Centrifugal forces left over from colonial times, including a segmented private school structure and distinct divisions among language tracks and their curricula, are rapidly being eroded by government school-integration planning in both societies.

To implement their ethnic plans, the governments of both nations have employed all three integrative mechanisms mentioned in Chapter 1 -- consensus, interdependence, and coercion. In an effort to achieve consensus by peaceful means, political and educational leaders in both Malaysia and Singapore have made constant use of mass communication media -- particularly television, radio, and newspapers -- and of the formal school system to argue both the necessity for national cultural unity and the desirability of current racial policies to achieve this end.

Built into the propaganda designed to foster consensus is a persistent emphasis on the interdependence of the nations' ethnic groups, an appeal based on the conviction that the fate of each group depends on how successfully all groups cooperate in peacefully pursuing the common good. The necessity for the ethnic groups to accept the interdependence hypothesis is greater in Malaysia than in Singapore because in Malaysia the politically dominant group, the Malays, have only a bare majority, and they are still subordinate to the Chinese in the economic and educational spheres. Having the populace convinced of the desirability of interdependence is not so crucial in Singapore, where more than three-fourths of the citizens are Chinese and clearly dominate in political, economic, and educational arenas alike. Yet Singapore's leaders have stressed interdependence, apparently for a variety of reasons, including a belief that even minor racial disorders could disrupt the city's economic progress, and that anti-Malay practices would antagonize the neighboring Malay nations of Indonesia and Malaysia.

The third mechanism, coercion, has been employed in both Malaysia and Singapore to prevent any diversion from the course each government has set for achieving racial integration. People in both countries recognize that they are liable to be imprisoned and to suffer serious economic and social sanctions if they openly criticize government policies or foment social unrest.

In summary, Malaysia and Singapore represent adjacent nations that display two varieties of the type C ethnic relations structure described in Chapter 1. Over the past two decades, each government has sought to achieve ethnic integration of a sort that is to the advantage of the politically dominant racial group, yet acceptable as well to the subdominant groups. In each case, the education system is being employed as an important tool for implementing the integration plan.

NOTES

1. Arfah A. Aziz and Chew Tow Yow, "Malaysia," in Schooling in the ASEAN Region, ed. T. Neville Postlethwaite and R. Murray Thomas. (Oxford: Pergamon Press, 1980), p. 101.

2. Peter A. Busch, Legitimacy and Ethnicity: A Case Study of Singapore (Lexington, Mass.: Heath, 1974), p. 19.

3. Mahathir bin Mohammad, The Malay Dilemma (Singapore: Donald Moore Press for Asia Pacific Press, 1970).

4. Busch, Legitimacy and Ethnicity, p. 59.

5.   Milton J. Esman, Administration and Development in Malaysia (Ithaca, N.Y.: Cornell University Press, 1972), p. 20.
6.   Ibid., pp. 20-21.
7.   Donald R. Snodgrass, Inequality and Economic Development in Malaysia (Kuala Lumpur: Oxford University Press, 1980), p. 131.
8.   Charles Hirschman, Ethnic and Social Stratification in Peninsular Malaysia (Washington, D.C.: American Sociological Association), p. 79.
9.   R. Murray Thomas, Goh Kim Leong, and R. W. Mosbergen, "Singapore," in Schooling in the ASEAN Region, ed. T. Neville Postlethwaite and R. Murray Thomas (Oxford: Pergamon Press, 1980), pp. 187-95.
10.   Francis H. K. Wong and T. H. Eee, Education in Malaysia (Kuala Lumpur: Heinemann), pp. 9-10.
11.   Atan Long, Fikiran-Fikiran Tentang Pendidikan (Thoughts on Education) (Kuala Lumpur: Dewan Bahasa dan Pustaka, 1979), p. 148.
12.   Snodgrass, Inequality and Economic Development, pp. 45-47.
13.   Ibid., p. 42.
14.   Philip Loh, "Some Current Problems in Primary Education in Malaysia," Masa'alah Pendidekan (Educational Problems) 1, no. 1 (1965):20-21.
15.   Third Malaysia Plan (Kuala Lumpur: Government Press, 1976), p. 159.
16.   Fourth Malaysia Plan (Kuala Lumpur: National Printing Department, 1981), p. 4.
17.   Third Malaysia Plan, p. 94.
18.   Richard L. Skolnik, The Nation-wide Learning System of Singapore (Singapore: Institute of Southeast Asian Studies, 1976), p. 10.
19.   Busch, Legitimacy and Ethnicity, pp. 32-33.
20.   "Trends in Education," unpublished, (Singapore: Ministry of Education, 1979).

9

KENYA: THE EMERGENCE
OF AN EDUCATED ELITE

George Urch

In 1963, Kenya became the thirty-fourth independent nation on the African continent. Since then, the country, with its concern for social welfare reflected in an expanding educational system receiving the largest share of the annual budget, has been viewed generally as a benign model of political stability and economic development. However, in the past few years, Kenya has been shaken by a series of problems that have clouded its image. These include a fragile political structure facing internal strife, a vulnerable economy with a mounting national debt, and a population explosion that strains its social services. The problems have brought to light patterns of long-standing internal factionalism and the rise of a privileged elite who increasingly appear to hold political and economic power at the expense of the poor.

In the view of Kenya's critics, these powerful elite are Western-oriented, neocolonial in their attitudes and socially divorced from the masses of their countrypeople. They gained their privilege through an alignment with Europeans and the small clique of people surrounding the president's office. Membership today includes top politicians and civil servants who maintain power by using the heavy hand of civil administration to control mass participation in the political process. To enhance their class status, they promote an educational policy that uses schooling for special advantage for some, while squeezing the rural poor and exacerbating ethnic tensions.

On the other side, those who defend Kenya's development process look instead at a political course that has brought relative stability and a buoyant economy through industrial expansion and agricultural development. They argue that the system works for a growing number of citizens who participate in the political and economic process. This view sees Kenya's leadership as sensitive to rural demands and to the need to expand educational facilities in order to equalize opportunities. The interethnic cooperation that has emerged in urban areas is noted, and Kenya is viewed as a country where privilege is earned, not inherited.

These contradictory interpretations concern a nation of approximately 18 million people who identify themselves not only as Kenyans but also as members of more than 30 ethnic groups. This chapter will attempt to identify how membership in these groups affects participation in political decision making and how that participation relates to educational policies that promote or discourage equality of opportunity. Societal forces that influence the emergence of a national consciousness will be explored, as well as those educational practices that support socioeconomic class difference and ethnic division.

Special reference will be made to the typology of intergroup relations identified in the La Belle-White conceptual framework. Kenya can be viewed as a type C society, where there is clear cultural and structural segmentation along class lines that, at times, cuts across ethnic identification. The distinctiveness of the superordinate group will be viewed culturally as it attempts to define its own status and particular role and structurally as it grasps political and economic power. The distinctiveness of specific ethnic groups will also be explored as their members attempt to gain influence through ethnic identity.

POLITICAL CONSIDERATIONS

In Kenya there are more than 30 distinct ethnic groups, each with its own homeland, customs, and language. The source of solidarity in traditional Africa has been the extended family and interdependence within the ethnic unit. The network of kinship, with strong loyalty to the group, embraces all the needs and activities of life. An individual's obligations to the demands of the kin group are clearly defined and taught, providing a sense of security and identification. The group transcends the individual and ensures position in society and in history.[1] With their strong ethnic self-consciousness, many Kenyans care more about the preservation of ethnicity than the obtaining of additional goods and services from the national government.[2]

The colonial administrators saw advantages in fostering ethnic identity. By channeling political and economic dealings through traditional authorities, they were able to maintain control and influence. These administrators also attempted to define ethnic boundaries and develop ethnic specializations whereby certain groups were selected for the army and police, while others served as clerks or worked for the white settlers.

However, the colonial demand for services brought large numbers of Africans into the urban areas and into the civil service. Responding to the demand were the two largest ethnic groups in Kenya: the Kikuyu, from the central highlands close to the capital city of Nairobi, and the Luo, from the western part of the country. Both groups responded early to the opportunity for Western-style education offered by the missionary teachers. Both adapted their social structure and their culture to the emerging modern sector. The Kikuyu assumed quite early clerical positions in the colonial administration. During the Mau Mau period in the 1950s, large numbers of them were forcibly repatriated to their home areas.[3] The Luo took their place as civil clerks and found other wage-earning positions in Nairobi. In a survey taken just prior to independence, the Kikuyu, with 19.5 percent of the population, made up 23 percent of the African elite, followed by the Luo, with 14.4 percent of the population and 19 percent of the elite. During the same period 29 percent of the African civil servants were Kikuyu and 23 percent were Luo.[4]

During the colonial period the Kikuyu and Luo were also politically motivated. The earliest ethnic associations developed among the Kikuyu. The Luo were also in the vanguard of the association movement, as well as the organization of trade unions. These associations gave to the Western-educated African an opportunity to express himself politically and, to other Africans, the semblance of unity for their grievances.[5] As the leaders of the associations became more adept and conscious of political questions, they began to broaden the scope of the associations to serve as a foundation for political parties.[6] Soon the avowed aim of the new political parties became independence. One of these, the Kenya African Democratic Union (KADU), was composed of a confederation of smaller ethnic groups. The other major party, the Kenya African National Union (KANU), was dominated by a coalition of Kikuyu and Luo. With independence, political leadership passed to KANU, with the charismatic Jomo Kenyatta, a Kikuyu, as the nation's first Prime Minister.

THE MOVE TOWARD CENTRALIZATION

The awareness that a citizen's loyalty to the nation could be tested by his or her willingness to respect the authority of the government caused the new leadership to note the relations between good citizenship and political integration. For their own survival, political leaders needed to promote respect for their authority. Yet it was the new leadership that, during the struggle for independence, urged the rural population to disregard the law -- and it was the same urban-based leadership that turned away from the traditional way of life and moved toward Western values and institutions. Western education and settlement in urban centers helped to isolate them from their rural ethnic environment. Contact with colonial administrators helped them understand the metropolitan system of government. As independence grew near, the colonial administrators did not turn to the traditional chiefs and elders but to the new, Western-oriented political elite. Thus the struggle for independence shifted from a rural base to a power struggle within the political mechanism created by the colonial government.

With independence, it was clear that some type of accommodation between the Western-oriented political leaders and the traditional chiefs and elders, who still commanded the loyalty and respect of large segments of the population, was necessary. It was one thing to dominate national politics in an urban environment and another to survive under the ethnic pressure that existed.[7] There was fear that the traditional leaders, who had lost position and authority, would form centers of conservative opposition and become a centrifugal force breeding disunity. Their interests and the demands of the majority of people in the rural areas could not be ignored.

The new ruling group moved quickly to consolidate its political position. It recognized that its status was earned, not ascribed. This new elite came from different ethnic backgrounds but were bound together by class as well as by political and economic interests. The class consciousness came from their education, a special form of preoccupation with income and status, and an awareness of playing a central role in political and economic development.[8]   Because of their status they had access to economic opportunities through commerce and land ownership.   When new businesses were organized, a growing number were formed with boards of directors from different ethnic groups.   More important than ethnicity were shared commercial aims and an appreciation of individual talents and assets.[9]   The new elite also had a common interest in having the political process function in specific ways as a mechanism for control and development.

The independent constitution of Kenya called for two houses of parliament and the establishment of seven regional assemblies.   Regional assemblies were an attempt to placate the concerns of the smaller ethnic groups that feared centralized domination.   However, a year to the day after independence, the necessary legislation was in place for Kenya to become a republic.   The new republic was to be headed by Kenyatta as president, and he was to function through an executive cabinet.   Regional powers were virtually abolished.   Members of the opposition party crossed over the floor to form a one-party state.   Two years later the two houses of parliament merged to form a single-chambered national assembly.[10]   In effect, political power was now centralized within the executive branch.   To ensure that it stayed there, the president's office made two strategic moves: The power of locally elected politicians was weakened, and the power of the government controlled bureaucracy was strengthened.

With independence came an increased demand for entrance into the political system.   The initial response was to provide more positions in order to satisfy the fervor surrounding independence and to assure the allegiance of smaller ethnic groups, which were needed in the movement to create a national consciousness.   New posts were created in parliament and in regional assemblies and municipalities.   However, with an increasingly large number of politicians, it soon became clear to the key leaders and high-level civil servants that their power base could become fragmented and the new society ungovernable.[11]   The initial concern for broad participation to encourage a democratic spirit gave way to a concern for stability.   Steps were taken to restrict the number and the kind permitted to join the elite group.   Along with the abolishment of regional assemblies and the movement toward a one-party system, candidates not belonging to the ruling political party were not permitted to compete. In addition, the president chose to let his political party wither away.[12] A decision was made to rule through the governmental bureaucracy rather than the political party.

As the power of the political party declined, so did the power of the politicians who made up the legislative branch. In their place, the president strengthened his civil service with an increase in both membership and power.[13] By the 1970s all the important functions of elected local government officials had been transferred to the central ministries and to the civil service. The message to the majority of people who lived in the rural areas was clear: The politicians had lost out to the bureaucracy. When the rural people wanted more services, they turned to their district and provincial administrators, who were the major agents of the government. The major point of contact with the government for most Kenyans had become the civil service.

An important by-product of a strengthened and expanded civil service was the growing domination of one ethnic group. As the president consolidated his power base, the Kikuyu began to dominate the critical cabinet posts and top civil service positions. As a result, other ethnic groups were expelled from the ruling elite and forced to retreat to their home territories. The politicians, looking to their home bases for support, heightened ethnic consciousness among their constituents within the political framework. This centrifugal movement created autonomy of political aims along ethnic lines and negated the interdependence of the superordinate group along class lines. One outcome was an increase in tensions between the two largest groups, the Kikuyu and Luo, and the selection of political leaders on the basis of ethnicity.[14]

The ruling leadership was aware of the political fragmentation taking place, as well as of the dilemma: Their own political control must be strengthened through increased executive power, but so must the fragile network of an interdependent political elite that had evolved during the first decade of independence. They also understood the need to build national consciousness in the rural areas. Toward this end new coalitions were formed to transcend ethnic identity. Politicians from various ethnic groups were invited to join the executive cabinet, and additional elections were held to increase participation in the political process.[15] However, the most visible means used by the government to promote unity was through its educational policy.

EDUCATION AND NATIONAL UNITY

Independence had given rise to expectations among the people for both material benefits and equality of status and rights. Government leaders recognized that social and economic change geared to the welfare of the populace would occur only through strengthening the government structure to accomplish this task. Toward this end the ruling elite sought to promote a sense of common cultural purpose with nationalism as a centripetal force. National unity quickly became a primary goal, and to help in the process, the government enlisted the aid of its educational system.

The need to have the schools serve as a centripetal tool led the new political leaders to identify objectives that they believed education could accomplish. These centered on the following issues: the expansion of educational facilities to satisfy the growing demands of the people, the strengthening of control over the educational system in order to achieve government aims, and the design of a uniform curriculum to develop civic responsibility and build consensus along political lines.

The need to expand educational opportunity was self-evident. During the struggle for independence, political leaders had consistently used the theme to create a common bond. The emerging leaders spoke to the people of discriminatory and limited education under colonial rule, and they declared their determination to work toward the goal of universal primary education and an expansion of all educational facilities.[16] With independence the goal was reiterated. Jomo Kenyatta stated his intention to devote a large part of the nation's resources to educational expansion.[17] The government's sessional paper on African socialism declared the need to adopt a definite plan to achieve universal primary education and to promote the rapid expansion of secondary schools so that education could contribute directly to economic development.[18]

Soon after independence the new government appointed an Education Commission to survey the existing state of education and to advise the government on the formulation and implementation of educational policy.[19] The second part of the

Education Commission's report devoted a major section toward the planning of universal primary education, calling for 80 percent of the eligible children to be enrolled in primary schools by 1980.[20] The commission also recommended that the expansion of secondary education have the immediate highest priority in order for its graduates to contribute to the modern economic sector.

Although educational expansion was an avowed aim, government administrators wanted this to take place under their control and supervision. They viewed education not only as a major factor in national development but also as a strategic instrument for achieving it. However, shortly after independence, a threat to government control of education emerged. The traditional spirit of self-help and cooperation, which the new leaders had encouraged in order to involve the people in the development of the nation, spilled over into education. Within two years after independence, one-third of all the secondary schools in the country had been developed through self-help projects by the people in rural areas. Called Harambee schools, after the Swahili word for pulling together, they were built from funds raised in the local communities. Most hired unqualified teachers and were understaffed; few had science laboratories or sufficient educational books and materials. It was these schools that constituted a threat to government control -- and that produced graduates of little value to national development schemes.[21]

Politically, however, the Harambee schools relieved the pressure for the expansion of secondary school facilities in the rural areas. Politicians, who had encouraged self-help projects in their areas, found it difficult to urge restraint.[22] Yet leaders recognized the danger in weakening the government's authority and its development plan. They also feared that the uncontrolled multiplication of schools would draw adverse comments from the International Bank for Reconstruction and Development, to which the government had applied for money to develop a secondary school program.[23] Needed were controls that would not dampen the enthusiasm for self-help projects but that would place restraints on uncontrolled secondary school growth. Toward this end the government implemented a new external examination and dictated a restrictive syllabus used to prepare students to pass the examination.

The Kenya Junior Secondary Examination was to be given after the first two years of a four-year secondary school

program. The government planned that those students enrolled in Harambee schools who did well on the examination
would complete their last two years at a government-aided
secondary school.[24] The new syllabus prepared by the Ministry of Education suggested subjects and period allotments per
week as a guide to the Harambee schools. The English language, with emphasis on reading and oral usage, was to occupy
nine or ten periods of a forty-period week. Both general
science and mathematics were allocated seven periods per
week. History and geography were to emphasize the local
area and the nation, with each given three periods per week.
Swahili and religious knowledge were also given three periods.
These were the subjects in which the students were to be
tested.

To the extent that the Harambee spirit developed a feeling
of personal and civic responsibility, the government was hesi-
tant to slow its advance, for one of its major aims was to
build a national consciousness. The leaders realized they
needed the active support and participation of the people in
the process of nation building and they saw in the schools an
institution that could stress responsibility toward the government. To achieve these goals the Education Commission
identified as one major function of education the need to
"foster a sense of nationhood and promote national unity."[25]
The commission felt that divisive influences from the past, as
well as the present, created difficulties in the establishment of
a psychological basis for nationhood. It urged the development of an educational policy consciously directed toward the
growth of a national consciousness among teachers and students.[26]

In a statement issued to the Kenya National Union of
Teachers, the Ministry of Education emphasized the importance of building national pride and said that efforts had
been made to ensure that all school children had copies of the
national anthem and were taught to sing it either in Swahili
or English. The ministry assured the teachers union that the
history of the struggle for independence would be taught in
all schools and hoped that the teachers would give their full
cooperation in the development of a national consciousness.[27]

The use of the curriculum to stress national unity was also
explored by the Education Commission, especially in the primary schools, which constituted the terminal point in education for the vast majority of children.[28] It identified both
history and geography as obvious subjects in which the em-

phasis could be made consonant with the concern of nation building in an African context. Special emphasis was also given toward the development of a language policy, an area that has been under dispute since independence. Although the commission emphasized the advantages of English-language usage, it strongly recommended that Swahili be made compulsory in the primary schools, for it considered the general spread of the African lingua franca a specific vehicle for national coordination and unification.[29]

The government responded to the concerns of the commission, and in 1967 published its new primary school syllabus, along with instructions that it be carefully followed in all schools. The syllabus detailed a seven-year course. In language, the use of the indigenous tongue was encouraged for the first few grades with a switch to English as a medium of instruction by the fourth grade. However, the syllabus took into account the growing number of schools that used English as a medium of instruction from the first day of school.[30] From a political point of view, it was difficult to ignore the heavy demand of popular response from parents who saw in the English language an opportunity for their children to seek employment in the modern economic sector. History and civics were designed to prepare students to become useful members of their nation, capable of contributing to the general welfare of their community. The system of government was to be studied, as well as the part that ordinary citizens could play within the system. Comparative tribal history was to be taught, with stress placed on the fact that Kenya was one nation made up of people with diverse traditions and customs.[31]

The superordinate group clearly saw education as a centripetal force that could help develop, along well-defined lines, both a common national consensus and societal integration. The difficulty occurred when the large subordinate group expected more out of schooling than a common national purpose and a minor role in the economic sphere.

EDUCATIONAL OPPORTUNITY

The continuing ground swell of demand for more educational opportunity created intense political pressure requiring government response. Not long after independence, educational attainment was seen to be virtually the only means of access to position, power, and wealth. Kenyans holding prominent positions in the modern sector for the most part did so because of education rather than heredity. Initially after independence the government attempted to link educational expansion to personnel needs. However, for political reasons, it soon saw the need to increase educational opportunity.

This reality was reflected in the first five-year development plan. Discussing the need to avoid the emergence of antagonistic classes, the government document of the plan stated that differences in earned income would begin to narrow as education and training were extended throughout the nation in order to ensure that everyone's latent ability was fully recognized.[32] To help in this effort, the development plan identified long-range goals, which provided universal primary education, ensured enough places at the secondary and higher levels to educate those with recognized abilities, and organized the educational system to meet the worker needs of the country.[33] These goals were seen as necessary to satisfy the demands of the people and to contribute to the unity and cohesiveness of the nation. Education was to be an effective means of keeping citizens well informed so they could fully participate in the development of the democratic African socialist state. The goals were to be accomplished through a widespread increase in the number of primary schools and, by 1970, a 53 percent increase in the number of students beginning secondary school.[34]

The government's commitment to educational expansion was borne out in fact. Government statistics reported that enrollment in primary schools increased more than 100 percent during the ten-year period -- 1963-73 -- and the ratio of children in the six- to twelve-year age cohort who were enrolled in schools rose from 32 to 73 percent during the same period.[35] The government maintained 99 percent of these schools, set the curriculum, supplied the equipment and books, trained and assigned the teachers, and paid their salaries.

At the secondary level the number of registered schools grew from 400 in 1966 to 1,029 by 1974, with an increase in enrollment from 20,553 to 195,674 students.[36] The majority of the new secondary schools were Harambee schools built through local self-help projects. The willingness of individuals to devote personal resources for the education of their children was a growing phenomenon. The policy of the government was to attempt to absorb these schools under the Ministry of Education's jurisdiction by financing their maintenance and controlling the curriculum. By 1966, half of all Kenya's secondary schools were government-aided. However, Harambee schools were emerging so quickly that the government could neither finance nor control them all. By 1974, the proportion receiving government aid declined to 39 percent.[37] To some education officials it appeared that secondary school development was getting out of hand. The quality of the secondary schools was poor and their graduates were flooding the job market in the urban areas. If increased access to schooling had relieved some political pressure, the direction in which it was headed caused some concern.

The 1974-78 development plan reflected this concern. The plan noted the enormous increase in the cost of education since independence and the growing difficulty for those leaving the schools to gain wage employment. Acknowledging that education was the most accessible route to individual social and economic advancement, it questioned the wisdom of unlimited expansion. Such expansion had produced large numbers of individuals who were competing in the modern sector for relatively few job openings. In addition, these individuals were not equipped with the knowledge and skills required by the economy. Expansion had drawn to education an ever-increasing proportion of the nation's resources but had only succeeded in the quantitative development of the system inherited from colonial days.[38] To address these problems the plan called for the establishment of a National Commission on Educational Objectives and Policies.

The commission was convened in December 1975, and one year later issued its report to the president. At the heart of the report was the desire to modify and diversify education so as to serve the majority of students who lived in rural areas and who terminated their education at either the primary or secondary level. The report noted that education up to now had been oriented to serving the needs of the modern sector of the economy. Consequently, there had been a heavy migration to urban areas in search of nonexistent jobs and a concomitant scarcity of educated people to facilitate the growth of rural areas. One result of such a system was to produce young people who disregarded the social and cultural values of their society in pursuit of material benefits. The report recommended that education assist in the growth of rural areas and the informal sector of the economy by giving the youth the necessary skills to create self-employment opportunities.[39]

The report recommended that after the first three years of primary education the curriculum focus on preparing youth for agriculture, budgeting, family welfare, and community development. This would require the development of such subjects as agriculture, carpentry, domestic science, fish culture, pottery, basketry, forestry, and elementary mechanics.[40] At the secondary level the report stated that Ministry of Labor projections indicated that only one secondary school graduate out of ten would obtain a modern sector job. The vast majority would have to be absorbed primarily in self-employment. Toward this end the report recommended that the goals of secondary education be redefined to integrate them with rural development. This would require the diversification of the curriculum, with agricultural sciences occupying a central position. The curriculum would also give students the skills and qualities needed to create their own income-earning opportunities.[41] Such an educational program would integrate the life of the school with the local community and reduce the degree of alienation among school-leavers.

To help the schools assist in rural and community development, the commission urged that a system of job rewards and incentives be developed and more government resources be directed toward productive activities in agriculture and related industrial and commercial enterprises. The commission also placed emphasis on the use of the school to promote social and cultural values based on the nation's philosophy of African socialism and the tradition of mutual social responsibility. Social responsibility was promoted as an extension of the African family spirit to the nation as a whole, an African tradition already manifested in the numerous self-help projects that contributed greatly to the development of the nation. The commission stated that the continuing success of this tradition depended on the extent to which it was taught and adopted by the youth. The educational system was expected to play a basic role in this process.[42]

These proposals ran counter to the desires of the vast majority of people who sent their children to school. As a consequence the government's attempt to redirect its educational efforts toward the development of rural areas appeared to have little effect. The better informed saw it as a plot to keep the youth away from the cities where they could cause fewer problems. The less educated continued to develop Harambee secondary schools in the hope that their children would be the successful ones in gaining entry to the cash economy in urban areas. To discourage this, the government reduced expenditure and curtailed the takeover of the operating costs of newly developed Harambee schools.

In spite of these efforts, the secondary school system continued its rapid expansion through the growth of Harambee schools. During the period 1973-77, enrollment rose from 174,767 to 319,982, an increase of 83 percent in four years.[43] By 1977, the percentage of secondary schools financially assisted by the government dropped to 29 percent.[44] Primary education also continued to expand. When, in 1974, the government abolished school fees for the first four years of schooling, enrollment increased to 51 percent in one year. By 1977, the government stated it had enrolled 86 percent of eligible children in primary schools.[45]

The total number of students enrolled in the educational system was impressive, yet a closer look at the enrollment patterns showed significant disparities. The government's development policy had not created equal educational opportunities for all citizens. As opportunities expanded for certain sectors of the country, inequalities increased elsewhere. What became evident were patterns of regional, ethnic, and class disparity closely allied to a class-based centripetal political and economic structure. The centripetal structure was designed to monitor membership in the superordinate group. What it produced was inequality of educational opportunity.

EDUCATION AND INEQUALITY

The inequality of educational opportunity in Kenya has been well documented. Where children are born and the socioeconomic background of their families has a significant bearing on whether they enter the school system and whether they succeed in the tasks it imposes.[46] Patterns of regional imbalance appear to have been reinforced through the configurations of political power.[47] Strong ties of family and ethnic loyalty have ensured that elite offspring have access to educational opportunity, preferably in schools that are considered superior.[48]

At the primary level prior to 1974, only a few relatively wealthy regions had 80 percent of the eligible students enrolled in school. The majority of the country's agricultural districts registered far below that, with the semiarid and arid pastoral districts lagging way behind.[49] The provinces that sent the largest percentage of their children to primary school were the Central Province, the homeland of the Kikuyu, the Nyanza Province, where the majority were Luo, and the Western Province, where the Luyia lived.[50] During this period the Central Province, with approximately 15 percent of the primary school-age children, had 26 percent of all trained primary teachers.[51]

The disparity continued at the secondary level. The areas that had the largest number enrolled in primary schools produced more students qualified to enter the next level and thus applied political pressures on the government to support new secondary schools. The government was faced with a decision of whether to spread its educational resources evenly throughout the country or build schools where the demand was greatest and public clamor the loudest. The government decided that areas should receive support for secondary school places in proportion to the size of their primary system; entrance to secondary schools should be allocated according to the index of primary school graduates in each region.[52]

This decision meant that the distribution of secondary schools would bear little relationship to the distribution of the population as a whole. A good example is the Central Province, where there were more government-maintained secondary schools than provinces that had larger school-age populations.[53] By 1970 the Kikuyu, with approximately 20 percent of the African population, accounted for 38 percent of all secondary school plans; the Luyia, with 13 percent of the population, 18 percent; and the Luo, with 14 percent of the population, 14 percent.[54] The most sensitive political problem was the continuing domination of the educational system by the larger ethnic groups. This was especially the case with the Kikuyu, who continued to be overrepresented throughout the school system. In 1978, out of the fifteen "national" secondary schools maintained by the government, six were located in the Central Province and five in Nairobi.[55]

Inequalities in education could also be seen in rural and urban differences. Better staffed and more prestigious government-aided schools were almost always located in or near urban centers. Whereas rural secondary schools tended to have ethnically segregated student bodies, such was not the case in urban areas. Wealth and parental education were important determinants of who attended urban secondary schools. The small ethnically mixed elite located in cities created family environments conducive to successful school performance. English was used in the homes, books were read, and pressure was applied to ensure that children became a part of the elite through educational attainment. The urban secondary schools, for the most part, had been all-European or all-Asian schools prior to independence. They usually contained well-equipped science laboratories, good libraries, and a well-educated teaching staff. These schools charged tuition and fees that were five times higher than those of other secondary schools.[56]

The regional imbalances and preferential treatment in urban areas created political problems. Education was the single most important institution that allocated present and future societal privileges. If these privileges could not be explained, animosities would be exacerbated. The government was aware of the problem. Whenever possible the people were reminded that Kenya inherited from the colonialists an education system characterized by gross inequalities. Before independence, schools were developed in areas near white settlements and in the cities where commerce took place. Beyond these areas the establishment of schools closely coincided with missionary activity. As the principal Western educators in rural areas, the missionaries tended to settle in those places where there was the greatest response: geographically, the Central, Western, and Nyanza regions.[57] The government also pointed out the accomplishments in the expansion of educational opportunity. The elimination of school fees was one example; others were the development of primary school boarding facilities in the pastoral areas and, later, experimentation with mobile teaching units that followed the nomadic pastoralists.

However, the most often used explanation of inequalities in education focused on the nation's social ideology. Kenya was a society that rewarded hard work and merit. In the 1974-78 development plan, the government stated: "Equal incomes for everyone is therefore not the objective of this plan. Differences in skill, effort and initiative need to be recognized and rewarded."[58] This same social philosophy carried over into education. All citizens were to have an equal chance to demonstrate ability and thus be rewarded. Differences in achievement would justify inequalities and the acceptance of differentiation. Because schooling for everyone was not possible financially, a selective process was necessary, but one based on merit for everyone. All were to be judged as impartially as possible by the same procedure: Favoritism was not to be permitted; everyone was to have an equal chance to achieve; the criteria to determine ability were to be fairly applied.[59]

Since independence the government has promoted the ideology of a meritocracy so as to secure acceptance of distributive inequalities. In education the openness of the schools to students of equal ability was the test. But the growing emergence of a class-conscious elite challenged the fairness of the system and became a serious point of controversy. Examples of class and ethnic privilege in the education system were widespread. The growth of Harambee schools was one example. Their development depended on community initiative, the ability and willingness to pay, and the ability to convince the government to classify them as aided schools. This pattern favored the more developed areas with the most money and political clout. The provinces with the largest number of Harambee schools were Central, Western, and Nyanza, the same provinces that had the largest number of government-aided schools.[60]

School fees also helped to promote ethnic and class privilege. Prior to their abolishment at the primary level in 1974, the cheapest government school charged SH.60 (U.S. $6.70) per year, exclusive of clothing and equipment expenses. In urban areas the cost was three times that amount for the former Asian schools and ten times that amount at the ex-European primary schools.[61] Moreover, when school fees were abolished, an era of free schooling did not emerge. All schools collected an equipment levy of SH.10, and many primary schools imposed supplementary fees for building funds, activity costs, uniforms, and feeding schemes.[62] In some districts the cost of primary schooling quadrupled. To contravene this the president in 1978 issued a decree canceling all extra fees. Still, one field survey conducted in 1980 showed that all throughout the country schools were still charging building fees.[63]

At the secondary level, variances in the fee structure also attested to socioeconomic differences. In postindependence development plans the government identified low- and high-cost secondary day schools with different fee structures. For example, boarding schools were classified as low-, medium-, and high-cost schools, with the elite ex-European schools charging four times the amount of the low-cost boarding schools.[64] Clearly, the ability to pay for a secondary education was an important factor in determining access to education.

CONCLUSIONS

The La Belle-White typology of intergroup relations has helped to define more clearly the cultural and structural segmentation found in Kenyan society. Utilizing the type C framework, the relations between government educational goals and the attainment of political and economic power becomes more intelligible. Although there is little doubt among the people that education is associated with prestige and material rewards, the superordinate group visualizes the use of educational policy for more specific purposes. This dichotomy between the subordinates' view of education and dominant group needs has led to the emergence of three ways in which education in Kenya has functioned as an "integrative process": Education contributes to the development of cultural consensus and is used as a centripetal force to build national unity; education serves as an arena for contending with centrifugal tendencies and, consequently, a measure of educational opportunity is ensured; education is used to enhance the interdependent structured relationship among members of the dominant elite group.

Since independence the government has been clear in its intent to use education as a centripetal force to build national unity. Policy statements have consistently called upon the schools to cultivate a sense of belonging to a nation and a desire to serve that nation. Schoolchildren were to think of themselves as Kenyans interested in extending the indigenous tradition of social responsibility and cooperation to the nation as a whole. The schools were to integrate themselves more closely with the traditional value of corporate togetherness. Teachers were to help the youth understand the need for every citizen to contribute to the social ideal of Harambee. No theme has been more pervasive in educational policy statements than the need to build national unity.

Educational policy for national unity has been implemented in several ways. The large expansion of the educational system was an attempt to show how the government responded to the demands of its people. The movement toward free universal primary education was another government effort to show concern. However, coupled with the expansion was a high degree of administrative centralization and government control. Primary schools came under the jurisdiction of the central government and secondary schools were classified into four grades and aided, depending on the quality of their facilities.

The government also assumed firm control over the curriculum. In 1966 the Ministry of Education developed a Curriculum Development Center for the expressed purpose of developing national school syllabi. The new curriculum emphasized the nation's struggle for independence and the contributions of people with diverse traditions. The syllabi were designed to prepare the youth for service to their nation and community. In he area of language, the curriculum quickly moved the youth away from their ethnic tongue toward the lingua franca, Swahili and/or English. Swahili was viewed as a specific African vehicle for national unification. English was considered important to help meet national worker needs in the modern economic sector.

Ethnic identity has always been an important factor in Kenya. This identity was reinforced during the drive for independence when the colonial government prohibited a national political party. In the absence of a national movement, emerging politicians strengthened their local organizations, which in turn strengthened their ethnic unity. Ethnic consciousness was also heightened by the significant social and economic differences that existed between ethnic groups. The Kikuyu were seen as the most economically developed and politically conscious people. Their aggressiveness provoked in others antagonistic feelings, especially among those ethnic groups that bordered the Kikuyu homeland. The primary issue was land ownership and the economic position that accompanied it. The Kikuyu were pushing out constantly into land claimed by small ethnic groups.

During the struggle for political and economic domination, the Kikuyu and Luo found each other convenient allies. Because they came from different parts of the country, land was not an issue. Both groups had an earlier educational advantage and, as a consequence, greater economic advancement. Equally important, they had worked together in urban areas. Their common political consciousness made both groups more receptive to a national movement. When political power passed to them after independence, the tendency was to extend educational advantage to their own kind.

The transfer of overall responsibility for primary education to the central government meant that substantial educational grants tended to go to the provinces where the Kikuyu and Luo lived. The placement of better trained teachers followed the educational grants. When the government decided that geographic areas should receive secondary school places in proportion to the size of their primary systems, an added advantage was gained. Most government-aided secondary schools could be found in the same areas. These schools had catchment areas restricted to the province in which they were located. The government decision to have less than 10 percent of all secondary school students enrolled in schools that recruited nationally was another way to maintain the strength of the schools located in distinct ethnic areas. Clearly, the expansion of educational opportunity favored the ethnic groups that had political power.

The same political base could be seen in urban areas where ethnic appeal and economic advancement did not necessarily run a parallel course. Mutually beneficial economic groups, as well as political considerations, tended to support cross-ethnic cooperation in the urban areas. The commonality of life-style, privileged status, and shared commercial interests were an integrative force among the urban-based educated elite. This small class-conscious group understood the need to maintain this position for their children through increased educational opportunity.

To be the child of an educated and wealthy urban resident guaranteed substantial educational advantage. Private nursery schools were available, as were well-equipped primary schools with well-trained teachers. At the secondary level, the former all-European schools, with facilities unheard of in rural areas, were also situated in urban areas. Large school fees maintained the exclusiveness of these schools and ensured that places went to the children of the wealthy. The privileged students graduating from these schools were ushered on to important career ladders, which helped to perpetuate their status. For these students personal interests were closely associated with their view of being a chosen group destined to maintain political power and economic advantage.

With more and better education, the children of specific ethnic groups and the urban elite have performed well academically. Their success provides examples of what a merit system can do, within the context of the fact that they have substantial advantages over children from illiterate, impoverished rural areas. Yet, with growing numbers of rural youth in schools, more students are successfully climbing the educational ladder and proving their merit. To the extent that those opportunities continue to exist and social mobility occurs, political tension rising from inequalities in money and position can be tolerated. The picture that emerges is that of a class elite who have learned to reinforce their position while leaving the socioeconomic door slightly ajar for others to enter. How long Kenya can preach egalitarianism and practice social differentiation remains to be seen.

NOTES

1. Paul Bohan, Africa and Africans (Garden City, N.Y.: Natural History Press, 1963), pp. 171, 172.

2. Henry Bienen, Kenya: The Politics of Participation and Control (Princeton, N.J.: Princeton University Press, 1974), p. 132.

3. Mau Mau was a violent revolt against colonial rule and primarily involved the Kikuyu. Between 1952 and 1957 more than 400,000 arrests were made, and the colonial government declared a state of emergency. For more about the Mau Mau, see Donald L. Barnett and Karari Njama, Mau Mau from Within (London: MacGibbon and Kee, 1966).

4. Bienen, Kenya: The Politics of Participation and Control, pp. 135, 136. The data are based on surveys done for Who's Who in East Africa, 1963-64 (Nairobi: Marco Surveys, 1964). The criteria for the selection of the elite included income, position, and relative power of the position. Close behind the Luo in the percentage of elite and civil servant class were the Luhya, the third largest ethnic group in Kenya with 12.5 percent of the population.

5. The first African association was organized in 1920 by the Kikuyu. At one time there were more than 200 associations of various kinds. For additional information, see George Bennett, Kenya: Political History (London: Oxford University Press, 1963).

6. Africans were not permitted to form political parties until 1955, and then they were only allowed to be formed on a district basis. See Tom Mboya, Freedom and After (Boston: Little, Brown, 1963), p. 70.

7. Bienen, Kenya: The Politics of Participation and Control, p. 163.

8. Gideon C. Mutiso, Kenya: Politics, Policy and Society (Nairobi: East African Literature Bureau, 1975), p. 76.

9. Colin Leys, Underdevelopment in Kenya (Berkeley: University of California Press, 1975), p. 176.

10.   J. F. Maitland-Jones, Politics in Africa: The Former British Territories (New York: Norton, 1973), pp. 54, 55.

11.   Bienen, Kenya: The Politics of Participation and Control, p. 93.

12.   Mutiso, Kenya: Politics, Policy and Society, p. 83.

13.   Bienen, Kenya: The Politics of Participation and Control, p. 33.

14.   Mutiso, Kenya: Politics, Policy and Society, pp. 89-92.

15.   During one period every ethnic group with better than 2 percent of the population had a minister or junior minister in the president's cabinet. All together there were 36 members. See Bienen, Kenya: The Politics of Participation and Control, p. 137.

16.   Kenya African National Union, What a KANU Government Offers You (Nairobi: Press and Publicity Department, KANU, 1963), p. 4.

17.   Jomo Kenyatta, Harambee: The Prime Minister of Kenya's Speeches (1963-649 (Nairobi: Oxford University Press, 1964), p. 83.

18.   Republic of Kenya, African Socialism and Its Application to Planning in Kenya (Nairobi: Government Printer, 1965), p. 40.

19.   Kenya Education Commission Report (hereafter cited as KECR) (Nairobi: English Press, 1964-65).

20.   Ibid., Pt. 2, p. 6.

21.   Ibid., pp. 22-23.

22.   Both Jomo Kenyatta and the minister of education had laid the cornerstone for Harambee schools. See "Self-Help School Is Big Success," East African Standard, April 8, 1966, p. 5.

23.   KECR, Pt. 2, p. 23.

24.   "Kenya Pupils to Sit New Examination," East African Standard, February 11, 1966, p. 17.

25.   KECR, p. 25.

26.   Ibid., p. 28. The commission identified the three main divisive influences in Kenya as tribe, race, and religion.

27.   "Nationhood Campaign in Schools," East African Standard, May 22, 1965, p. 5.

28.   Kenya's educational ladder was typical of those found on the African continent. Less than 10 percent of primary school graduates find places in government-maintained or -aided secondary schools.

29.   KECR, p. 60.

30. Republic of Kenya, Primary School Syllabus, Ministry of Education (Nairobi: Government Printer, 1967), p. 14.

31. Ibid., p. 103.

32. Republic of Kenya, Development Plan 1966-1970 (Nairobi: Government Printer, 1966), p. xi.

33. Ibid., p. 305.

34. Ibid., p. 308.

35. Republic of Kenya, Educational Trends 1973-77 (Nairobi: Central Bureau of Statistics, 1980), p. 5.

36. Ibid., p. 56.

37. Ibid.

38. Republic of Kenya, Development Plan 1974-78 (Nairobi: Government Printer, 1974), chap. 19, pp. 2, 3. While questioning the quantity and quality of educational development, the plan abolished school fees for the first four years of primary education.

39. Republic of Kenya, Report of the National Committee on Educational Objectives and Policies (Nairobi: Government Printer, 1976), p. xviii.

40. Ibid., p. 51.

41. Ibid., p. 63.

42. Ibid., p. 5.

43. Republic of Kenya, Educational Trends 1973-77, p. 1.

44. Ibid., p. 71.

45. Ibid., p. 24. In 1974 only 8 percent of children age 13 to 16 were enrolled in secondary schools. By 1977 the percentage had risen to 13.

46. David Court, "Education and Social Control: The Response to Inequality in Kenya and Tanzania," in Education and Politics in Tropical Africa, ed. Victor Uchendu (New York: Conch Magazine, 1979), p. 26.

47. Ibid., p. 50.

48. Kenneth Prewitt, "Education and Social Equality in Kenya," in Education, Society and Development: New Perspectives from Kenya, ed. David Court and Dharam Ghai (Nairobi: Oxford University Press, 1974), p. 206.

49. John Nkinyangi, "Access to Primary Education in Kenya: The Contradiction of Public Policy," Comparative Education Review 26, no. 2 (June 1982):205.

50. Jerry Olson, "Secondary Schools and Elites in Kenya," Comparative Education Review 16, no. 1 (February 1972):48.

51. Prewitt, "Education and Social Equality in Kenya," p. 205.

52.   Mwendwa, "Constraint and Strategy in Planning Education," in Education, Employment and Rural Development, ed. James Sheffield (Nairobi: East African Publishing House, 1967), p. 280.

53.   Prewitt, "Education and Social Equality in Kenya," p. 205.

54.   Olson, "Secondary Schools and Elites in Kenya," p. 47.

55.   Republic of Kenya, Educational Trends 1973-77, p. 69.

56.   Ibid., p. 51.

57.   Ibid., p. 2.

58.   Republic of Kenya, Development Plan 1974-78, p. 3.

59.   Court, "Education and Social Control," p. 33.

60.   Republic of Kenya, Educational Trends 1973-77, pp. 4, 79.

61.   David Parkin, The Cultural Definition of Political Response (New York: Academic Press, 1978), p. 83.

62.   Republic of Kenya, Educational Trends 1973-77, p. 8.

63.   Nkinyangi, "Access to Primary Education in Kenya," p. 216.

64.   Parkin, The Cultural Definition of Political Response, p. 83.

10

EDUCATION FOR EQUALITY AND INTEGRATION OF THE ETHNO-RELIGIOUS ELITES/MASSES IN INDIA

Suma Chitnis

The issue of education and intergroup relations is essentially one of the role of educational practice and policies in fostering economic equality. It is also an issue of the manner in which education integrates or divides people who have different religious, ethnic, or cultural loyalties and identities. The former arises because modern societies aim at equality through education but seek, nevertheless, to preserve the selective and allocative functions that education systems have served. The latter arises out of the fact that although plurality is valued for the richness and liveliness that it brings to a culture, it implies separatist identities and conflicts that are difficult to manage or resolve. This chapter deals with these issues with reference to Indian society.

THE CLEAVAGE BETWEEN THE MASS AND THE ELITE

By far the most critical of all the cleavages that divide Indian society, and one that cuts across all other existing divisions, is the division between the mass and the elite. Primarily an economic division, this cleavage is evident in the disparity between the rich and the poor.

India is a poor country. With a per capita income of less than $200 a year, it is among the poorest of the poor in world comparisons. According to official estimates, 48 percent of the population, consisting of about 331 million people, live below the poverty line.[1] Some estimates place the figure much higher. Statistically defined in terms of per capita calorie consumption, life below the poverty line is a subhuman existence -- without adequate food, clothing, and shelter, without water to wash in or drink, and constant exposure to fatal or debilitating disease.

Poverty is all the more painful because of the polarization between the rich and the poor.[2] In metropolitan cities like Bombay and Calcutta, the contrasts are stark and obvious. The dwellings of the poor are hovels, without such basic amenities as toilets, water, or space to sit, stretch out, sleep, or separate the several activities of daily life. Urban poverty is further characterized by uncertainty of employment, frequent dislocation or residence under pressure from "slum-clearance programs," and total powerlessness to gain any control over the circumstances of life. By a strange irony of coexistence, the poor often live side by side with the rich, in makeshift dwellings propped up against walls of apartment houses with all the modern paraphernalia of affluence -- air conditioners, elevators, terrace gardens, and swimming pools. Standards of life for the urban rich rise higher and higher as the economy grows. So do opportunities for education and for employment as the sphere for their life and activities extends to encompass international markets and educational institutions.

In the villages, where 80 percent of the Indian population lives, poverty is less visible. Fresh air and more abundant land, which allows for better spaced housing and for primitive yet effective sanitation, make for a facade of well-being. But this facade masks a poverty that is as harsh and often worse than that in the cities. This is evident from such indicators as severe malnutrition, high mortality, landlessness, and poor wages in rural India.[3] Contrasts between the rich and the poor are also less evident in villages than in the cities, not because they do not exist but because the rich do not live in villages. They function as absentee landlords and live in the cities.

Inequality with respect to education is one of the most critical aspects of polarization between the masses and elite. It finds basic expression in the contrast between the educational level of the villages, where the masses live, and of the cities, where the elite concentrate. Although most villages in the country are equipped with primary schools, few have middle schools and even fewer have secondary schools.[4] Not that primary schools in the villages are optimally used either.

Many times parents are too ignorant or indifferent to enroll their children in school. In any case, rural poverty is so severe that children cannot really afford the opportunity costs of schooling. Forced to help their parents to eke out a marginal living, they usually drop out before they have completed the four years of primary school.[5] For those who do manage to finish primary school, going to larger towns and cities for middle school or high school education is extremely difficult.

The problem is compounded by the fact that village schools have not yet managed to become relevant to rural life. The content of the learning they offer is not relevant to rural occupations; it does not equip rural children to gain control of their situation and to effect change in rural powerlessness and poverty. Nor does it facilitate the urban transition that most villagers seek. Thus the utilization of village schools is poor, and rural literacy and schooling remain conspicuously low.

Although the disparity between rural and urban education is the most critical form of the polarization between the education of the masses and of the elite in the country, disparities within cities are equally critical and sharp. In keeping with its promise to universalize schooling, the government provides free schooling, at least up to the primary level and generally up to secondary school, throughout the country. However, it also permits private bodies to own and manage schools that charge fees, ranging from the nominal to the very high. In urban areas the law of supply and demand for schooling leads to a situation where children get sorted, by social class, into free schools and schools that charge medium or high fees. And, of course, there are those who do not even get enrolled. This is where inequality in urban schooling begins.

All schools are required to teach the same syllabus and to use the same textbooks. Their students are examined by the same agency and take the same examinations. In spite of such careful centralization for equality, differences are evident. The schools used by the well-to-do and schools used by the poor differ substantially in terms of laboratory facilities, library facilities, sports, extracurricular activities, and other programs. They differ in the character of the classroom interaction and instruction and in the quality of preparation for examinations. Above all, they differ in the ethos that they generate and the futures they project. Elite schools, with concentrations of children from upper-class homes, provide an environment where aspirations are uniformly high. All these differences show in the performance of children throughout their primary and middle school education and, more importantly, in the Secondary School Board (SSC) and other examinations that determine a child's prospects for higher education. These differences have been documented in several studies over the last few years.[6]

The differences between schooling for the elite and for the poor in the city are evident in the more elementary indicators of dropout rates and stagnation or repeated failure at school. This may be illustrated with a recent study of schooling in the city of Bombay.[7] The city is served by a Municipal Corporation that has taken responsibility for free primary school education since 1907. Out of a total of 2,036 primary schools in the city today, 1,298 are financed and managed by the Municipal Corporation. The corporation also owns and manages 51 out of the 765 secondary schools. The municipal schools are used by the low-income populations of the city. So are some of the private schools. But by and large the latter cater to the middle- and upper-middle-class elite.

An intensive study of a sample of 95 municipal schools in the city conducted in 1982 revealed that barely 20 percent of the children enrolled in the observed samples completed primary school within the stipulated four-year period. As many as 33 percent had dropped out altogether, and 40 percent were "stagnating" or repeating their classes at the various points at which they had failed. About 12 percent had changed schools due to transfer of residence. A follow-up of those who had completed primary school showed that barely 8 to 10 percent passed on to Standard VIII, which marks the termination of middle school and the point of entry into high school. In contrast, data on a cohort of elite schools covered by the study showed that there was not a single dropout case. Stagnation was marginal. Most, or practically all children, enrolled in Standard I had moved on to complete the SSC and were planning to enter college.

Poverty in different forms emerges as the principal cause for dropout and stagnation of urban children. In fact, some studies show that in the urban scramble for employment children sometimes succeed where adults fail. But in keeping the wolf from their homes, they miss out on school. Sickness, shifting residence, and other manifestations of poverty are other factors that interrupt the schooling of urban children.[8]

At the national level, the rural and the urban inadequacies in education, as indicated above, are reflected in the failure to universalize schooling. The constitution of independent India promises free and compulsory education to all children up to the age of 14. However, the census of 1981, conducted more than three decades after the launching of the first of the country's six five-year plans, indicates that only 36 percent of the population is literate. Figures for 1980-81 indicate that barely 83 percent of the population in the age group 6 to 11 years, 40 percent of the population in the age group 11 to 14 years, and 20 percent of the population in the age group 14 to 17 years are in school. The actual situation is even worse than these figures suggest. More than one study points out that school enrollment figures in the mass of state-financed schools are highly inflated because financial subsidies depend on the number of children enrolled.[9] Moreover, enrollment figures do not indicate the heavy dropout stagnation rates that mark the careers of children who fail their grades and have to repeat classes. Most estimates indicate that about 60 percent of the children enrolled in Standard I drop out before they complete the four years of primary school. Barely 25 percent finish the eight years of middle school that they are expected to by the age of 14.

Their high rate of dropout, poor level of the performance in the SSC examination, and the opportunity costs involved reduce the chances of university education for the masses. The few who manage to make it to the university usually get into those courses that lead to relatively low-status, poorly paid positions. They are rarely to be found in courses or at institutions that lead to room at the top.

In order to appreciate this point, it is necessary to recognize that India has a highly hierarchical system of higher education, consisting of a variety of educational institutions that are widely disparate in the quality of the futures for which they equip their students. At the top are the institutions of National Importance(10) and the prestigious institutions for technical and professional education, such as the institutes of management or of technology, which are deemed to be universities(12). Then come the medical colleges (111) and the colleges of engineering and technology (116). These are followed in the hierarchy by the many arts/science/commerce/law colleges (3,425) and by the colleges for teacher training (500). Not only does education at one of the 10 Institutions of National Importance or one of the 12 institutions that are deemed to be universities equip students for high-status positions within the country but it also equips them for further education at prestigious universities abroad and for competition in the international job market.

All institutions for higher education are, in principle, open to all. But studies of the socioeconomic background of students at prestigious institutions have consistently shown the upper-class and upper-middle-class composition of these institutions.[10]

Actually, the educational disparity between the masses and the elite is a British legacy, rooted in British educational policy dating back to the nineteenth century. Historical records indicate the existence of an indigenous system of mass education in India when the East India Company first established itself as a ruling power in the middle of the eighteenth century.[11] This system combined a variety of practices, ranging from household instruction to formal schooling. It was funded by native rulers as well as by wealthy landlords within each community. Designed to fit in with the caste system, it denied instruction to low caste Hindus and graded by ritual status the level of knowledge to be communicated to children of the other castes. Nevertheless, it provided to the mass of the male population between 5 and 10 years of age the basic literacy, numbers, and other skills relevant to the times.

When the British displaced the native rulers, the system lost its official support. Meanwhile, the system they established never really provided for mass education. Although the Charter Act of 1813 required the East India Company to accept responsibility for the education of Indians, the obligation was accepted purely as a political task aimed at the "dissemination of European culture" to the Indian elite and at obtaining a cadre of loyal, Western-educated Indians to serve in the administration.[12]

Several bodies pressed for education for the masses. Prominent among these were Christian missionaries, who believed that Western education would promote acceptance of Christianity in India, educated Indians, who believed that it would bring progress, and a small section of British administrators, who felt morally responsible for the nurture of the colony. The British Parliament responded to these pressures, and the Charter Act of 1854 specified that the education of the masses should be regarded as the duty of the state. But until the end of its rule in India, the British government kept evading this obligation.

The problem was partly financial. But it was also ideological. British rule in India was heavily influenced by the "downward filtration theory," or the notion that the benefits of facilities provided for the elite would somehow trickle down to the masses. Most important of all, the issue was political. Within a few decades of the passing of the act, the earlier faith that Western education would obtain loyalty and strengthen British dominion over India had been destroyed. On the contrary, it was realized that the education of the masses would only hasten the end of British rule.[13]

Thus the period between 1854 and 1947 was a tussle between the Indian demand for mass education and the British evasion. Throughout this period Indian reformers and nationalists, Christian missionaries, and sympathetic administrators worked for the cause of education in India. Because of their efforts it advanced far ahead of what it did in other African and Asian countries under colonial rule. But universalization of schooling remained a distant goal. Consequently, when the country acquired self-rule in 1947, only 16 percent of the population was literate. Barely 50 percent of the children in the age group 6 to 11 years were in school.

Even more critical to the division between the masses and the elite was the Westernization of educated Indians and their alienation from Indian culture that British educational policy brought about. At the outset, the British had encouraged learning of Sanskrit and Arabic, partly as a political gesture and partly because they continued to rule by Hindu and Islamic personal and civil law and needed the knowledge relevant to the interpretation of Sanskrit and Arabic legal texts.[14]

However, as British sovereignty became more firmly established, the outlook changed. The new attitude is best expressed in Macauley's famous Minute of 1835, which categorically states that "a single shelf of a good European library is worth the whole native literature of India and Arabia."[15] Guided by this faith, British educational policy after 1835 concentrated on communicating European science, literature, philosophy, and history to Indians. Indigenous knowledge and culture were consciously excluded. This led to the westernization of educated Indians and their consequent alienation from the masses.

There were at least two more factors that accentuated this process, the language policy and the structure of universities in the country. Although education in the vernacular languages was encouraged, the British clearly accorded greater importance to English, both as the language of administration and as the medium of instruction. Socially, a command over the English language was a major asset in that it facilitated interaction with the rulers. Consequently, those who aspired to higher education or to higher positions of any sort concentrated on mastering English and turned away from the vernacular languages. In the process, they lost communication with the masses and with the native culture. Further, the universities established by the British in India were only designed to provide education suitable for middle-level positions in the administration and in the professions of medicine and law. Indians who aspired to higher positions were expected to go on to English or European universities for further qualification. Conscious of the peripheral status of their own universities, educated Indians began to lean on the West and to lose respect for their own culture.

All this led to the division of the country into two worlds -- the Westernized, English-speaking world of the educated elite and the indigenous world of the uneducated masses. This division was reinforced by the economic and the political structure of colonialism. Throughout British rule, the country remained technologically and industrially undeveloped. The mass of people surviving by subsistence agriculture, landless labor, or menial service had little use for schooling and did not question the division.

The political leaders and architects of independent India were determined to bridge the gap between the masses and the elite. Therefore they planned for the promotion of Indian languages and culture, for the universalization of schooling, and for equalization of opportunities for higher education. However, they were also committed to technological advancement, industrialization, and economic growth and development and invested heavily in the establishment of highly specialized centers of higher learning and research in engineering, technology, medicine, and management.[16] As observed earlier, the plans for universalization of schooling and for equalization of educational opportunities have not worked out as anticipated. In contrast, the advancement of higher learning in science and technology succeeded beyond measure. India is not only self-sufficient in technologically trained personnel, but is also in a position to provide such trained workers to developed and other developing countries in the world. This a a great strength for the nation. However, the technologically educated, who gain in terms of wealth and status, invariably belong to the elite, which has had a head start in education -- and thus the gap between the masses and the elite widens.

CASTE -- THE UNIQUELY INDIAN PHENOMENON

The gap between the masses and the elite is the most critical cleavage in Indian society, but there are several others. The most important of these is caste, the uniquely Indian system by which Hindu society has been stratified and integrated for centuries. It consists of a tiered system, in which a multiplicity of strata, known as jati, are hierarchically organized in terms of the purity of their ritual status.[17] Individuals belong to the jati of the family in which they are born. Birth into a particular family is explained in terms of Karma, or life, in the previous birth. Thus the system is firmly anchored in the Hindu philosophy of karma and the transmigration of souls.

At an abstract level, jati is conceived of in terms of four classificatory categories, or castes -- the Brahmins at the top, followed by the Kshatriyas, Vaishyas, and Shudras. The divine origin of this hierarchy is symbolically explained in the Vedas, by the sacred hymn of the Purusha Sukta. It says that the Brahmins are born of the head of the Brahman, the Kshatriyas from the limbs, the Vaishyas from the torso, and the Shudras from the feet. Apart from defining positions, this symbolism indicates priesthood and scholarship as the occupational sphere of the Brahmins, statecraft, warfare, and administration of the Kshatriyas, commerce and craft of the Vaishyas, and service as the sphere of the Shudras. The jatis within the four castes are accordingly ascribed their specific occupations within the spheres appropriate for their caste category. Agriculture is the only occupation open to all.

While division is basically by ritual status and by occupation as described above, social distance between jatis/castes is maintained through prescriptions concerning endogomy and exogamy and through a complex system of rules and regulations concerning matters of daily behavior, particularly personal interactions within caste boundaries. Some of these regulations are particularly harsh. Severest of all is the requirement that the other castes keep away from the touch of the Shudras, thus forcing the Shudras into the degenerate status of "untouchables." Conformity of caste rules is enjoined as a "sacred duty." Deviance entails "pollution" -- something akin to defilement or sacrilege.

Access to education is strictly defined by caste status. Knowledge of the Vedas and of other sacred texts is considered to be a sacrament available only to Brahmins. The

Kshatriyas are allowed knowledge relating to statecraft, administration, and welfare. The Vaishyas are allowed knowledge relevant to trade and crafts. But the Shudras are considered to be so low in ritual status that they are categorically excluded from learning.

As may be expected, all this has led to the total exploitation of the Shudras. For centuries they have been the poorest and the most powerless in the country. Their first break came with British rule, as the British formally introduced the principle of the equality of all citizens before the law. Their status further improved when the British passed the Caste Disabilities Removal Act of 1850. At the same time employment in the British army, railways, and other services provided occupational mobility, and possibilities for conversion to Christianity provided another escape. European liberalism, in turn, had an impact on the attitudes of upper-caste, educated Hindus. By the middle of the nineteenth century, they were questioning caste discrimination. By the early twentieth century reformers like Gandhi had declared the uplift of the untouchables to be a moral duty, and educated Shudras like Ambedkar had organized themselves politically for their own cause.[18]

Thus, not unexpectedly, the constitution of independent India declared the practice of untouchability a crime. A series of constitutional provisions and preferential policies have been provided for the "uplift" and "protection" of the Shudra castes, now listed in a special Presidential Schedule, and therefore known as the Scheduled Castes. Most important of these is the policy of "reservations." It provides the Scheduled Castes, who constitute about 15 percent of the population, a proportionate quota of reserved seats in parliament and in the legislatures, reserved jobs in government, and reserved admissions to institutions of higher education. The latter is supplemented with a variety of supports such as freeships/scholarships, hostel facilities, and other aids.[19]

Several studies have been conducted to evaluate the outcome of the provisions for education.[20] They indicate a substantial improvement in the status of the Scheduled Castes. Nevertheless, they also show that the Scheduled Castes have not yet achieved equality in education. In most of the 22 states and 9 union territories in India, the enrollment of Scheduled Caste students in secondary school and in university continues to be smaller than their proportion in the population. In some states it is smaller in primary and middle school as well.

Their educational backwardness takes several other forms.[21] For instance, their dropout and stagnation rates at school are substantially higher than for the rest of the population. In higher education, they cluster into inferior institutions and in courses leading to relatively low-status, low-income occupations. Admitted to reserved quotas in high-status institutions, they rarely survive. For instance, data on one of the five prestigious institutes of technology reveal that in spite of the heavy concessions offered, very few Scheduled Caste students qualified for admission up to 1973. From 1973 on, the requirements were further relaxed and a concerted effort was made to fill the reserved quota. But only 5 of the 15 Scheduled Caste students who were admitted to the institutes in response to this effort survived by 1978. The others had dropped out. None of the five who survived made it to the fifth, or final, year of the course but were stagnating in the third or fourth year. Efforts to improve their performance by providing them with special instruction also failed. The pattern for successive batches is similar. Meanwhile, records indicate that some other institutions such as the Post-Graduate Institute of Medical Studies at Chandigarh have flatly refused to reserve admissions to their postgraduate courses.[22]

The situation described above indicates that the policy of reservations conflicts with the obligation to maintain high academic standards, particularly in institutions for professional education. Over the last five years it has been seriously questioned on this count even by those who are committed to the welfare of the Scheduled Castes. On the other hand, the issue of standards has been misused and exploited by a sector of the population that is unwilling to forfeit its traditional advantages and make room for the former untouchables. Their agitations, which have often taken violent form, suggest that the willingness to help the downtrodden that marked the early years of independence is now wearing off. Of course, it is possible that preferential policies were accepted then only because the possibilities for the advancement of the Scheduled Castes seemed too remote to endanger the established advantages of other Hindus. Now that the former have really advanced and are eligible through reservations for positions for which other Hindus must face hard competition, they are seen as a real threat and ruthlessly opposed. The opposition, particularly when it takes the form of violence, is, strangely, directed at the weakest sections of the Scheduled Caste population -- the urban poor and the village masses. This has been amply evident in the violence that has swept across Gujarat and Bihar over the last few years.[23]

Several other interesting features regarding the politics of inequality are beginning to surface. One of these is the new inequalities that have emerged among the Scheduled Castes. In each state one or two castes use most of the facilities and advance ahead of the others.[24] For instance, the Mahars in the state of Maharashtra, who constitute about 35 percent of the Scheduled Caste population of the state, use 80 percent of the facilities, whereas the Mangs, who constitute 33 percent, use a negligible amount. Similarly, the Chamars in many states in the country typically are advanced.

It has been observed that urban location, practice of a caste occupation that has scope in the modern economy (tanning or leather work, the traditional occupation of the Chamars), or a head start in terms of employment in the British army or railways (the Mahars of Maharashtra) are correlated with this advance. Surprisingly, castes that have advanced reject the suggestion that they opt out of the benefits of reservation and make room for those who are more disadvantaged. Their attitudes illustrate that those who have advanced wish to use the policy for further advantage. This creates a serious problem. The policy was initially promulgated for a period of ten years with the faith that the Scheduled Castes would advance far enough to make any extension unnecessary. However, it has had to be extended for three successive ten-year periods -- in 1961, 1971, and 1981. Although these extensions, granted in response to strong political pressures, are justifiable on the ground that the Scheduled Castes have not yet gained equality, they are disturbing in view of the clear evidence of the vested political interests that have grown around the continuation of reservations.

TRIBAL ISOLATION

Somewhat different, though administratively clubbed together with the problem of the Scheduled Castes, is the problem of aborigine tribes, also listed in a Presidential Schedule, and known as the Scheduled Tribes. They account for about 7 percent of the population. They are the "original" inhabitants of the land, pushed back into deep forests and remote coastal regions, as wave upon wave of conquerors invaded the country throughout the centuries. Several such tribes, isolated in small concentrations, are spread across the country in tribal villages. All but the few who have advanced through early contact with Christian missionaries live by primitive fishing, forestry, food gathering, or agriculture and practice primitive, animistic religions.

With respect to the more advanced among them, the issue for the government is exclusively political, that of handling their seccessionist demands. But with respect to the vast majority, who continue to be primitive, poor, and backward, the issue is one of providing relief from want, of absorbing them into the mainstream of life and providing opportunities for sharing in the benefits of civilization.

Education has been viewed as one of the principal mechanisms for the development and the integration of the tribals. Reservations, similar to those provided for the Scheduled Castes, have also been provided for the Scheduled Tribes in higher education. In addition, special schools known as "ashram schools" have been organized in tribal areas for tribal children. But the results are not very encouraging. The difficulties to a large extent are the same that inhibit the education of the economically disadvantaged, particularly the rural poor. But the problem is further complicated by the ethical-moral dilemma of whether the tribals should or should not be assimilated, as assimilation carries the risk of the destruction of their somewhat idyllic and highly self-respecting tribal cultures.

Educational policy has aimed at balancing assimilation with the preservation of tribal distinctiveness. Within the short limits of this chapter it is not possible to detail either the strategies used for the purpose or the outcomes achieved. But it is necessary, at least to draw attention to this special issue of equality and integration and to point out that in spite of the efforts for their education, the tribals remain backward and isolated. Meanwhile, the few who have advanced refuse to give up their preferential privileges and to use the special facilities to leap further ahead, creating the same dilemmas that have been mentioned with respect to the Scheduled Castes.

RELIGION, LANGUAGE, AND HORIZONTAL DIVISIONS

Although the majority (84 percent) of the population of India is Hindu, the country has several religious minorities: Muslims (11 percent), Christians (3 percent), Sikhs (2 percent), and others. Religious conflict, and vested interests in these conflicts, have of course been corollaries of this plurality. In fact, it is commonly said that the British harnessed conflict between the Hindus and the Muslims to divide and rule. It was this division that eventually led to the partition of the country and to the establishment of Pakistan.

Today India is constitutionally committed to secularism, defined as religious tolerance and mutuality, not as the elimination of religious consciousness or organization. In deference to this, the constitution guarantees all religious minorities the right to own and manage their own educational institutions.[25] However, the expectation is that the spirit in which this right has been granted will be honored by the minorities by their refraining from using these institutions for proselytization or for promoting sectarian attitudes and interests.

So far, this has not been particularly difficult. For although the country has an old tradition of denominational educational institutions -- dating back to Buddhist and Jain viharas, Sanskrit pathshalas, Muslim madrassas, and later Christian schools and colleges openly propagating their religious emphases and interests -- it also has a long tradition of curbing and containing such interests.

Perhaps this tradition helps. Or perhaps the memories of the partition of the country in 1947, the violence perpetrated in the name of religion at that time and earlier, and the martyrdom of Gandhi are still fresh enough to motivate tolerance. However, with the acceptance of denominational ownership and management of schools, the possibilities for their misuse for sectarian interests remain a potential threat to integration. With the growth of religious fundamentalism across the world this threat disturbs many Indians.

Meanwhile, language divides the Indian population today much more than religion does. There are 15 officially recognized languages in the country and more than 500 dialects. Since linguistic divisions happen also to be geographic, India has, since independence, been organized for administrative purposes into "states" consisting of linguistic regions. The language of the state is used for government and as the medium of instruction. Persons belonging to one state enjoy linguistic minority status in other states and, like the religious minorities, enjoy the minority right to "own and manage their own educational institutions."

All this has reduced the exclusive status of English and helped to broaden the base from which persons for positions of status are drawn. But it has also generated new parochialism and conflict. When the regional languages were reinstated, Hindi, the majority language in the country, was expected to function as the link language. English was to be retained as the language for advanced knowledge and international communication. Accordingly, the central government recommended to the states the adoption of the "three language formula" by which all school children would be required to be proficient in the language of the state, Hindi, and in Marathi. However, this created two major problems. First, Hindi, which is predominantly the language of North India, has been strongly rejected by the southern states. Second, the establishment of the regional language in the states has not solved the problem of inequality within each state. The language thus established happens, almost invariably, to be the language of the upper castes and upper classes, rarely the dialect of the masses. Therefore the latter continue to be disadvantaged in education. Meanwhile, the former gain not only because of the primacy accorded to their spoken language but because they are better placed to acquire proficiency in English and thus to gain access to advanced knowledge and to enter the international circuit.

A CRISIS OF CONFIDENCE IN EDUCATION

As may be gauged from the discussion so far, India faces a crisis of confidence in education as an instrument of equality. The deadline for the universalization of schooling, which was set for 1961 at the outset of independence, gets pushed farther with each official announcement on the issue. At present it is set for 2000. But observers are skeptical about this target. Some pioneers in development have already abandoned the notion that formal education is the first step to the betterment of the situation of the disadvantaged and they have moved on to programs of integrated action in which the entire concept of education has changed from that of "instruction" in formal or even nonformal settings to that of learning through and in the course of participation in multifaceted programs for change. In some cases this experiment has had such impressive results that the programs are seriously being considered as alternatives to schooling. As minority rights in education are misused and as the efforts to use the school system to promote Hindi as the link language fail, the faith in education as an instrument of integration is also shaken.

The quest for pedagogic and administrative strategies for more effective use of education to attain equality and integration continues. But it is recognized that at least three or four factors in the Indian situation will continue to render solutions difficult. The first of these is the problem of numbers. Of the population of about 700 million, almost 1.5 million are in the compulsory education age group of 5 to 14 years. The task of providing even rudimentary school facilities for such a large number is staggering in terms of its organizational implications.

The task becomes all the more difficult because of the paucity of funds and resources. In spite of its declared intention to spend at least 6 percent of its total budget on education, the central government is at present unable to spend anything more than 3.5 percent. Further, political pressures force the government to operate in contradiction to set objectives. For instance, the government allocates to higher education a disproportionately large share of the total allocation on education, whereas primary education receives much less than the objective of universalization warrants. This is partly because higher education, particularly technical education, is crucial to technological growth and industrialization, but even more because the sector that gains by higher education has a stronger political lobby. Similarly, linguistic and cultural chauvinists make it difficult for the government to use the school system as an instrument of national integration.

Yet it would be mistaken to conclude total failure of education as an instrument of equality and integration in India. There have been some major gains. Moreover, as the dynamics of inequality get to be better understood, it should be possible to wield the instrument with better success.

NOTES

1. These 1977-78 estimates are based on the thirty-second round of the National Sample Survey with the nutritional

norm of 2,4000 calories per day for the rural and 2,100 for the urban population.

2. V. M. Dandekar and N. Rath, Poverty in India (Bombay: Sameeksha Trust, 1978).

3. Fifty-one percent of the rural population as compared to 38 percent of the urban population lives below the poverty line. According to Sixth Plan (1980-83) estimates, about 40 percent of India's villages are without potable water, 24 percent are without electricity, and 8 percent are yet to be linked by all-weather roads. The number of landless labor households in dire need of housing assistance is estimated at 14.5 million.

4. According to the Fourth All India Survey of Education (New Delhi: National Council of Educational Research and Training [NCERT], 1980), 29 percent of the habitations in the country are without primary schools -- children have to walk .5 to 2 km to get to the nearest. Fifty percent of the habitations are without middle schools -- children have to walk 2 to 5 km to get to the nearest middle school.

5. Education and National Development Report of the Education Commission, 1964-66) (New Delhi: Ministry of Education, 1966).

6. For instance, Rita Britto, "Inequality Among Urban Schools," ongoing Ph.D. dissertation (Bombay: Tata Institute of Social Sciences); and J. K. Lindsey, Primary Education in Bombay: Introduction to a Social Study Evaluation in Education International Progress, vol. II, no. 1 (Oxford: Pergamon Press, 1978).

7. Suma Chitnis, "Dropout and Low Pupil Achievement Among the Urban Poor in Bombay," study conducted for the International Labor Organization (Bombay: Tata Institute of Social Sciences, 1982), mimeo.

8. Jacob Aikara, Educating Out of School Children. A Survey of the Dharavi Slum (Bombay: Municipal Corporation of Greater Bombay, 1982); also Chitnis, "Dropout and Low Pupil Achievement."

9. John Kurrien, Elementary Education in India: Myth, Reality, Alternative (New Delhi: Vikas Publications, 1983).

10. K. N. Sharma, Arithmetic of Social Inequality: A Study of Admission and Adjustment of IIT Students (Kanpur: Department of Humanities and Social Sciences, Institutions of National Importance, 1974), mimeo.; also Institutions of National Importance, Bombay Confidential Annual Reports submitted to the Senate.

11. S. Nurullah and J. P. Naik, History of Education in India During the British Period (Bombay: Macmillan, 1943), pp. 1-43.

12. Ibid., pp. 44-186.

13. Aparna Basu, The Growth of Education and Political Development in India, 1898-1920 (Delhi: Oxford University Press, 1974).

14. Nurullah and Naik, History of Education in India, pp. 98-129.

15. On the course of education in India during the eighteenth and nineteenth centuries, see ibid.

16. Over two and a half decades of independence, between 1947 and 1974, the number of primary schools increased almost fourfold -- from 14,105,418 to 63,193,358; middle schools increased from 11,162 to 97,356. But the increase in colleges for professional education was even larger, from 130 to 2,352.

17. M. N. Shrinivas, "Caste," in Encyclopaedia Britannica, vol. IV (London: Encyclopaedia Britannica, 1982), pp. 977-86.

18. Dhananjay Keer, Ambedkar Life and Mission (Bombay: Popular Prakashan, 1962).

19. For details see Report of the Commissioner of Scheduled Castes and Scheduled Tribes (New Delhi: Controller of Publications, Government of India, 1980).

20. The Indian Council of Social Science Research sponsored a major research program on this issue. Under this program, studies were conducted in 15 states. The findings have been documented in several mimeographs and publications. The consolidated findings are available in Suma Chitnis, A Long Way to Go (New Delhi: Allied Publishers, 1981), and in Vimal Shah, The Educational Problems of the Scheduled Caste School and College Students in India (New Delhi: Allied Publishers, 1982).

21. Suma Chitnis, "Education for Equality: The Case of Scheduled Castes in Higher Education," Economic and Political Weekly (Bombay) 7, nos. 31-33 (1977):1675-81; Suma Chitnis, "Education and Equality," in Education in a Changing Society, ed. A. Kloskawska and L. Martinotti (London: Sage Publications, 1977).

22. Suma Chitnis, "Reservations in Education: The Policy and the Practice," in Removal of Untouchability, ed. Vimal Shah (Ahmedabad: Department of Sociology, Gujarat University, 1980); Report of the Commissioner for Scheduled Castes

and Scheduled Tribes (New Delhi: Ministry of Social Welfare, Government of India, 1975-76 and 1976-77).

23. A. Yagnik, "Spectre of Caste War," Economic and Political Weekly (Bombay) 16, no. 13 (1981):553-55.

24. Chitnis, A Long Way to Go, pp. 16-20.

25. Article 30(1) of the Indian constitution says that "all minorities, whether based on religion or language, shall have the right to establish and administer educational institutions of their choice."

PART IV

CULTURAL SEGMENTATION AND STRUCTURAL COMMONALITY IN A HORIZONTAL RELATIONSHIP

11

SWITZERLAND: CONFLICT AND INTEGRATION

Gerhard Fatzer

During my two years as a visiting scholar in the United States, I received from Americans reactions of surprise or astonishment as I pointed out how complicated Switzerland's school system is. This is probably due to the fact that Switzerland is such a small country, and that from far away, others form the impression that it is characterized by a great deal of unity. I would like to suggest that the closer one is to the intricacies of Switzerland, the greater is the appreciation of the country's unbelievable varieties and differences.

Switzerland has four different national languages, of which the first three are "official" languages: German (or Swiss German) in northern, eastern, and central Switzerland (about 65 percent of the Swiss); French in the western part (about 25 percent); Italian in the southern part (9 percent); and <u>Romanash</u> (1 percent) in some mountain valleys of the eastern part (see Figure 11.1). The surprise is that the government structure does not follow these cultural linguistic boundaries at all; rather, there exists a mixture of centralist and decentralist tendencies (called "federalism"). An explanation for this arrangement can be found in the somewhat dramatic history of Switzerland.

Today, Switzerland's image is one of a neutral nation having survived two twentieth-century wars without damage, a nice miniature land of gorgeous mountains, expansive hotels, busy bankers, chocolate and cheese, yodeling farmers, and high-quality wristwatches. That this image is only partly true is affirmed by the news during the 1970s of violent youth riots in Zurich that startled much of the world. Reactions from outside Switzerland were very mixed: Most people had difficulty understanding the reason for these events. However, the few who did not subscribe to the aforementioned beautific image of Switzerland were not surprised. Nonetheless, they were probably impressed by the seriousness of the violence, which indicated the desparateness behind the tumult.

FIGURE 11.1
Switzerland: Different Language Areas, Cultures and
the Surrounding Cultural Influences

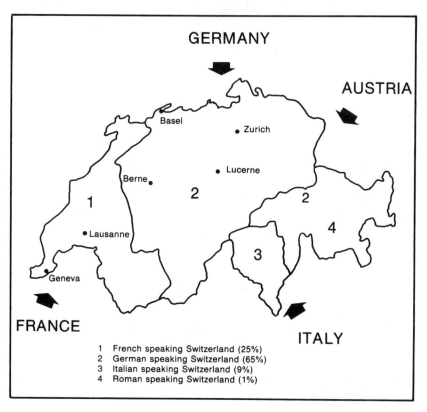

A reexamination of the protest events reveals that one of the main targets of the angry youth was the superficial image. In addition, Zurich, while taking care of the needs of visitors in its effort to be a "door to the world," was not attending to the cultural needs of its own youth. Money was not provided for the culture of the young, which, although not so perfect, was very much alive. This is one of the reasons that major destruction occurred in the famous Bahnhofstrasse and in the fancy stores along the River Limmat.

The riots made many people aware for the first time that the Swiss facade was hiding a great number of problems. On the other hand, the context that fostered the events serves to illustrate a political orientation typical of present-day German Switzerland. This orientation favors big business and, in the opinion of this author, has established wrong priorities. Big business was allowed to take over the city of Zurich, pushing up land prices and rents, and consequently the city became increasingly a town of banks and businesses. The city government was unwilling or unable to confront the trend. Politics was against the needs and interests of the people. The case of Zurich is representative of the present political situation in other big Swiss cities.

Contemporary realities combined with typical scenes from Swiss history offer much evidence contrary to the quiet and peaceful image. Swiss history consists of almost 700 years of outside wars. Switzerland began in 1291 with the three original cantons warring against Austria. Switzerland has been basically a conglomerate of cantons cooperating more for military reasons than because of cultural commonalities. Most difficulties and conflicts among and between the elements that make up the Swiss nation can be understood from this frame of reference.

Switzerland, as it exists today, grew over several centuries into a union of 26 states (or cantons). In 1291 the three original cantons united into one country; by 1353 there were eight cantons, in 1513 thirteen, in 1803 nineteen, and in 1815 twenty-five cantons. The Swiss Confederation, as it is known today, was established formally in 1948. In the 1970s the canton of Jura was separated from Bern, bringing the total number to twenty-six. This union of so many different states could only be governed by granting autonomy, especially in cultural and educational questions, to the cantons. The situation of considerable authority residing at the canton level has persisted to the present.

Before the Reformation (fourteenth century), education of the people was in the hands of church schools. In the cantons with a majority of Catholic inhabitants, church schools still exist and have even been expanded. In the cantons with Protestant majorities, church schools were changed into public schools. After the French Revolution, the movement to devel-op public schools spread throughout all cantons.

In the first half of the nineteenth century, new ideas and the idealism of famous Swiss educators, such as Johann Pesta-lozzi, Philipp Fellenberg, and Jean Girard, had a great influ-ence on the Swiss educational system. In the second half of the nineteenth and the first half of the twentieth century, general developments in Swiss education were similar to those in surrounding European countries. Switzerland distinguished itself in the psychological-educational area through the work of such famous Swiss scientists as Jean Piaget, Edouard Clapa-rede, and others. After the Second World War, when neigh-boring nations initiated major reform movements, most nota-bly the widespread efforts in Western Europe during the 1960s and early 1970s to replace highly articulated teaching systems with comprehensive secondary education, Switzerland did not follow, owing to its roots in traditionalism and also to its federalist form of government (autonomy of cantons).

Before we go into the details of our case study, a simpli-fied overview of Switzerland's government-supported educa-tional system will be discussed.

Although differences among the cantons can be found in the number of years that make up each step in the educational ladder, the structure of schooling throughout Switzerland is basically uniform (see Figure 11.2). Compulsory education be-gins between the ages of six and seven with the first grade of primary school. The first level of primary school, which pro-vides comprehensive instruction for all students "without dis-tinction for individual capacity," lasts from four to six years, depending on the canton, with three years in Vaud standing out as an exception.[1] Upon completing grade 4, 5, or 6, stu-dents pass through a selection screen that greatly influences their educational and occupational features. Approximately half of Switzerland's students is channeled into the first level of secondary school, and the other half remains in primary school throughout the duration of their nine years of compul-sory education.[2]

At the age of 15 or 16, upon completion of compulsory schooling, "the young person's future is determined almost ir-revocably."[3]

Most students at this stage enter into some form of vo-cational training, usually an apprenticeship with a mas-ter tradesman accompanied by further school (three

FIGURE 11.2
Overview of the Swiss Educational System

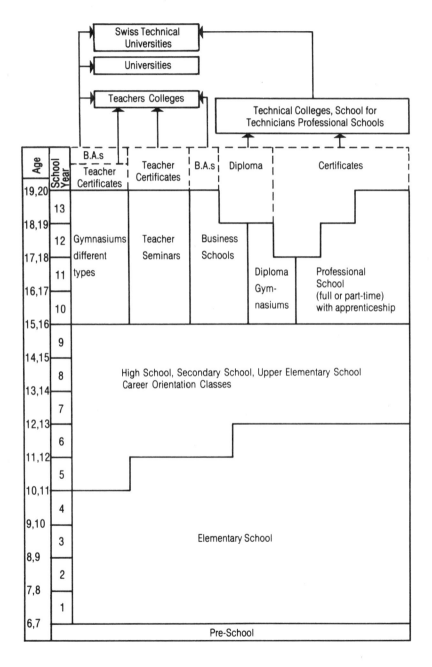

half days per week). A smaller number of students attend a full-time vocational school (teacher training college, commercial school, trade apprentices' school). About 10 to 20 percent (percentages depend on the canton) attend high school (Gymnasium, lycee), leading to the maturity examination (Maturitat, or maturite), generally taken after twelve and a half years of schooling. The student entering the maturite diploma gains access to one of Switzerland's ten universities.[4]

French-speaking Switzerland, with six cantons and 25 percent of the nation's population, has four universities -- at Lausanne, Neuchatel, Geneva, and Fribourg -- and the Federal Institute of Technology in Lausanne. German Switzerland, with 20 cantons and semicantons and 65 percent of the population, also has four universities -- at Zurich, Gallen, Bern, and Basel -- and the Federal Institute of Technology in Zurich. Italian Switzerland does not have a full university.[5] With its higher number of universities relative to the size of its population, the French region, in which every canton with the exception of Jura and Valais has its own university, clearly offers more opportunities for advanced study than does the German region.[6] The popular perception of greater educational opportunity is reflected in the pattern of higher gymnasium participation rates in French Switzerland as compared with that in German Switzerland.[7]

As with primary and secondary schools, "Swiss universities are cantonal institutions subordinated financially and administratively to the Department of Public Education in their canton."[8] However, the two institutes of technology are directly administered by the Swiss Confederation in keeping with the assignment by the constitution to the confederation of the responsibility for overseeing all scientific and technological development.

Until the 1960s, when the burden of supporting the universities became too great for the sponsoring cantons, the financing of higher education for the entire country was borne by only 62 percent of the population, that portion residing in the cantons with universities.[9] With dramatic expansion of university enrollments pushing up costs, combined with a relative diminishing of fiscal strength at the canton level, the confederation hastily stepped in to bail out the cantons with significant grants of aid. The confederation's contribution to higher education gradually became standardized.[10] Education in Switzerland is the single most costly budgetary item in the public expenditure at 20 percent of the confederate, canton, and subdivision combined revenues.[11]

Although universities are regulated by their cantons, a number of national bodies serve in a policymaking or consultative capacity, for example, the Swiss University Conference, the Swiss Scientific Council, and the Federal Department of the Interior.[12]

Switzerland has a rather extensive system of nonuniversity postsecondary institutions. These include technical colleges, colleges of economics and administration, and other vocational institutions with specializations in such areas as teacher training, special education, social work, advertising, and the arts. However, "this sector is weakly integrated into the general educational system and is largely neglected by the public authorities."[13]

EDUCATIONAL POLICIES IN SWITZERLAND

The purpose of this case study is to examine education in Switzerland by focusing on some of its most prominent characteristics and problems, as well as the attempts made to deal with them. The material is drawn from written sources and from interviews with key people in the school systems of the four different language areas. Thus the study presents a mixture of scientific, anecdotal, and historical data. The analysis will follow closely the guidelines set forth in Chapter 1 by La Belle and White. Specifically, in order to compare policies and actual practice, the six key policy areas identified by La Belle and White will be examined in turn: degree of school centralization; access to education; articulation (coordination and progression between the skills imparted at one level of the school system to those imparted at the next) and tracking (assignment of specialized curricula and the degree to which tracks are permeable); curriculum; training, selection, and placement of teachers and administrators; and language policies.

Degree of School Centralization

As already noted, there are important differences among the individual cantons, in some cases due not so much to cultural or language differences as to historical and political differences. Generally, in the French-speaking cantons (Geneva, Vaud, Neuchatel, Valais, Jura, and part of Fribourg) educational administration seems to be more centralized than in other regions. The directors of the education departments maintain a higher degree of control and coordination than do those in the German-speaking cantons, where strong community or city control is more often the norm. For instance, in the German-speaking canton of Zurich (the largest in terms of population), any attempt by the director of the education department to exert centralized decision making, for example, in the hiring of teachers, meets with much resistance.

Educational administration in the Italian-speaking part of Switzerland, the canton of Ticino, is even more highly centralized than in the French-speaking cantons. Although education in French and Italian areas is similarly characterized by centralism, only rarely are policies similar. It is as though Ticino were a separate and almost autonomous state.

The main reasons for the differences between the German-speaking and other areas are historical, demographic, and cultural ones. The French and Italian cantons are minorities in comparison to the German region. The main government offices are in Berne and Zurich, the financial center of Switzerland is in Zurich, and industry is concentrated in Zurich, Basel, and Berne. There are some industries in the French region (watches, machine industry), but the top management of these industries comes from the German zone. With Switzerland's major political and economic sectors based in the German region, this region can be described as superordinate in relation to the subordinate French and Italian regions. In only one dimension does the French-speaking district stand out: It contains the international diplomatic center of Geneva. The Italian region has little significance for Switzerland except as a center for tourism. Historically, the French cantons, which formerly belonged to France, joined the German sector in the nineteenth century. To the present, the Italian sector remains very much apart from the rest of Switzerland, separated geographically by the Alps, and in many ways Ticino seems to be more a part of Italy than of Switzerland.

The contrasting centripetal and centrifugal forces operative in Switzerland are illustrated in the case of the Romanash-speaking region. The Romanash-speaking region is almost integrated into the German part, as it is located in the German canton of Graubunden (where tourism is the main industry). On the one hand, the economic relationship between the Romanash- and German-speaking regions is one of structural interdependence. On the other, the recent movement to promote Romanash culture through the expansion of Romanash literature and by broadcasting romanash programs on national television provides evidence of segmentation. Educational policies in the Romanash region mirror those of the surrounding German zone in that administration is relatively decentralized. Decentralization in the Romanash region is not simply an institutional phenomenon; it is the dominant characteristic of life in this geographically fragmented mountainous region. The only centripetal force within the region is the movement toward a new cultural consciousness.

Access to Education

As was mentioned in the overview of the structure of Swiss schooling, with universal compulsory primary school initial access to education is high throughout the country. However, the picture changes dramatically after the first four to six years of schooling. Historically, only a fraction of those children who entered primary school advanced to gymnasium or lycee, the main gateway determining access to higher education. The selection pressure was reduced somewhat by the rapid expansion of secondary education in the 1960s, following the Swiss Scientific Council's determination that in order to sustain economic development 15 percent of Switzerland's youth should attend high school.[14]

In the different Swiss cantons, access to secondary education varies a great deal. In general, gymnasium participation rates are higher in the French-speaking region than in the German zone.[15] Even within the French region, Geneva is an extreme example of high general access to education, where approximately 20 percent of all secondary students earn the maturite diploma. In comparison, in the canton of Zurich, approximately 11 percent attain the maturitat. Further along this end of the continuum are Bern and Vaud, where selection begins early -- after the fourth year of school (age 10 -- and few pupils are able to attain the maturitat.

This general description of educational access obscures a certain amount of differentiation that does not arise from individual differences among students. Inequality based on sex has long plagued Swiss education. However, since the 1970s there has been a "gradual reduction in educational inequality between the sexes," such that, by 1979, female gymnasium students accounted for 44 percent of the enrollment.[16] National origin has also influenced access to education. Foreign students whose native tongue coincides with the local medium of instruction have no problem gaining access to education. However, for those students with language conflicts, notably Spanish, Turkish, and Italian, there is not equal educational opportunity.

Access to university is restricted across Switzerland, and because the 1960s expansion of secondary education was not followed by significant changes in university admissions, it has become more competitive over the past 15 years.[17] Differences between French and German regions in access to higher education mirror the imbalance at the lower levels of schooling. There is a higher degree of access in the French region, which contains a greater number of universities relative to the size of its population. Again, Geneva, where the university accepts students without a maturite in certain areas of study, is considered as having an exceptionally high degree of access to higher education.

La Belle and White note:

> Access in a type D relationship may be seen as an overt response to the demands (political, social, historical) of the various ethnic groups and a reflection of their power to make those demands on an equal footing with other groups in the society.[18]

In examining access to education in Switzerland, it becomes evident that with respect to this dimension of educational policy, the French-speaking area dominates the other regions. Through commanding a greater part of Switzerland's educational resources, it serves a greater proportion of its population. To use La Belle and White's phrasing, French-speaking Switzerland is clearly more "powerful" than German-speaking in ensuring that its "demand" for education is met.

Some of the differences among cantons can be attributed to deep-seated political antagonisms. The most striking example of this is the ongoing conflict between Geneva and Vaud (Lausanne). People in key positions in the educational systems of the two cantons disclosed that the pattern of the conflict is as follows: Educational policies that are implemented in Geneva, because of their association with this progressive canton, are automatically rejected by Vaud. Geneva traditionally has had a leftist government and it is an urban canton, whereas Vaud has had a rightist-liberal government and is a rural canton.

Articulation and Tracking

As shown in Figure 11.2, there are differences in the time at which tracking begins. In some cantons, children change from elementary to secondary school after four years, in other after five, and still others after six years. Once tracking begins there is limited opportunity for a student to change from one course of study to another. In general, education in Switzerland is highly articulated: Those students who attend lycee or gymnasium go on to university, and for the remainder there is comparatively early specialization in a variety of technical and professional fields. The apprenticeship program can be seen as the most explicit example of articulated schooling. In recent years the narrow path to university admissions, which was at one time totally dependent on the maturite or maturitat, "has been opened up by a Federal Maturity Examination, which corresponds to that held in the high schools."[19]

Efforts to promote comprehensive schooling have been most effective in the French- and Italian-speaking sections of Switzerland. For example, in the French region, the cycle d'orientation (circle of orientations) provides a high degree of permeability in higher education. In the Italian region, the scuola media serves as a model of integrated secondary schooling. German Switzerland's attempts to provide some form of comprehensive schooling beyond the primary level are still in the initial stages of development, policy proposals and experimental projects.

At the end of the 1960s, a movement toward coordination (Konkordat) of the French and German region systems began with an attempt to unify and coordinate the length of compulsory schooling, the beginning date of the school year, curricula, and the types of schoolbooks to be used; but in the practical solution of these problems little advance was made. The old conflicts remain. Italian-speaking Switzerland and the Romanash-speaking area tried to reach their own solutions to tracking and articulation. Resolution of problems was easier in these regions due to their smaller populations and their relative isolation from the rest of the country.

Curriculum

Curriculum in Swiss schools is influenced by the language-regional differences in degree of centralization of administration. Canton schools throughout the highly centralized French region use very similar curricula and schoolbooks. In contrast, in the schools of German Switzerland there is an incredible diversity of curricula and school texts. For example, about 20 different versions can be found of Swiss-German texts covering the history of Switzerland. There is little coordination in the curricula of successive grade levels in German-language schools. The freedom teachers have to implement different curricular approaches is reduced in practice by the unifying influence of the teachers associations, which maintain a high degree of control over their members. On the basis of differences in policies governing curriculum development and textbook selection, the German area can be divided into three subregions: In the eastern part, responsibility for this aspect of educational planning is assigned to the individual cantons; central Switzerland has a single curriculum development center; and, in northwest Switzerland, there is a form of intercantonal cooperative planning.

On one level, examination of Swiss education as a whole reveals the influence of strong centrifugal forces accounting for group-specific solutions to curriculum development. Equally interesting is the pattern of between-region differences that begins to emerge. Educational policies in the more populous and superordinate German-speaking region are characterized by diversity, whereas within the smaller subordinate French-, Italian-, and Romanash-speaking regions policies are more uniform. One explanation for this difference is that because of its dominant majority status, the German region can tolerate greater centrifugality whereas the minority regions cannot. Their power to exert demands on "an equal footing" with the German region derives from within-region consensus in educational policies, as well as a certain amount of between-region agreement.

Training, Selection, and Placement of Teachers and Administrators

As with the other policy areas, those determining the training of teachers vary across Switzerland. In the French region, teacher training centers in the universities. Prospective teachers begin to study at the universiy as soon as they receive their _maturite_. In the German region, grade level determines the form of teacher training: Kindergarten and elementary teachers are trained in "seminars," and secondary and gymnasium teachers are trained at the universities. In the Italian region, seminars are the only provision for teacher preparation.

In Switzerland, there are no nationwide or region-based policies for teacher selection. In general, canton education departments select teachers for their schools; however, in some Swiss-German cantons, including Zurich, teachers are selected by community-level school authorities.

Swiss school systems employ professional as well as lay administrators. For instance, in Zurich there is a lay supervisory system; in all the other German cantons there are professional supervisors; and in the French part of Vaud there are both. Differences in the type of school administrative personnel are not so much a reflection of cultural preferences as they are indicative of the different political orientations of the cantons. The training of administrators, which is organized by the cantons, is even less coordinated than the training of teachers.

Policies regarding Swiss school personnel exhibit generally the characteristics of type D group relations as described by La Belle and White. They state: "Language appears to act as a boundary between groups for purposes of dividing personnel into different programs of training and administration."[20] In the Swiss case, the clearest example is the difference between the French and German regions in the training of teachers.

Language Policies

Language policies is one of the few areas of potential conflict where coordination has been highly successful. Written-policies state very clearly the different languages to be used in instruction:

1. The official language of instruction is the language of the region.
2. The first foreign language, starting at the fourth and fifth years of elementary school, is a language spoken in another portion of Switzerland.
   a. In the Romanash section, the first foreign language is German.
   b. In the German section, the first foreign language is French.
   c. In the French section, the first foreign language is German.
   d. In the Italian section, the first foreign language is German or French.

Language policies were coordinated through a decision resulting from the Conference of Directors of the Education Departments (the most important instrument of coordination). The fact that policies governing medium of instruction were determined at the national level not only serves to legitimize the autonomy of the different language regions but in so doing diminishes the power of centrifugal forces. La Belle and White note: "The centrifugality of multiple languages is offset somewhat by the early introduction of at least one other language in the schools."[21] The adoption by the Romanash- and Italian-speaking regions of French or German as the first foreign language is evidence of integration through minority group compliance with dominant group values. At one time in the tourist centers of Geneva and Lucerne, there was a movement toward English as the first foreign language, but the movement was not successful. Although German dominates as the language of business and government in Switzerland, the near-parity of French and German in education demonstrates the strong influence of the French-speaking group's interests in the cultural life of the country.

CONFLICT AND COORDINATION

The structure of schooling, the form of teacher-pupil relationships, and even the architectural design of school facilities are relatively consistent throughout Switzerland. What, then, is the educational significance of the four language regions? And, conversely, what is the role of education in fostering or inhibiting cultural as well as structural equality among the German-, French-, Italian-, and Romanash-speaking segments of Swiss society? These questions guide the following discussion of conflict and attempts to resolve conflict in intergroup relations in Switzerland.

Sources and Arenas of Conflict

As already seen, the major conflicts do not exist among cultural areas, but within them, that is, among cantons. For instance, some of the cantons start their school year in the spring, others in the fall; attempts to coordinate the starting dates failed for political reasons. Differences in cantonal education systems are grounded in the history of Switzerland. As the cantons joined together in a loose federation, they retained considerable autonomy, most strikingly in the area of educational provision. Historically, there was little migration from one canton to the next; therefore there was no impetus to coordinate the assorted school systems established before amalgamation.

The secession some years ago of the French-speaking canton of Jura from Bern is the most prominent example of conflict among language interest groups. Before its actual separation, the French-speaking minority had planned to adopt the French school system (circle of orientation) as practiced in Geneva and Vaud. After separating from Bern, Jura inherited the entire Bernese system, with four years of elementary school ending in selection for further education. The sudden transfer of responsibility for school administration placed such a burden on the French-speaking community that it was unable to initiate reform. Only recently has the Swiss-French school system been implemented in Jura.

Is there any region or cultural group that in Swiss education dominates others? As with the arena conflict, the clearest cases of domination and subordination are to be found basically within cultural regions. For example, in German Switzerland three centers dominate the rest of the region: Zurich and Bern in the eastern part and Lucerne in central Switzerland. Zurich is the most dominant because of the prestige and number of its educational institutions; universities and continuing professional, technical, and art schools are located there. The French region is dominated by Geneva and Vaud, which vie for elite status.

The main reasons for conflicts between or within regions are economic, but political and cultural factors also contribute. Top government personnel are recruited mostly in the German area. The French and Italian regions can be said to function only as political satellites. In addition, they serve as markets for the German-dominated Swiss economy. Thus the areas in which conflict is most apparent -- economics and, to a lesser extent, politics -- are the very institutions that integrate Swiss society.

Cultural conflict is most evident between the French- and German-speaking sectors of the population. In general, the French-speaking Swiss have a great resistance toward learning German. French speakers feel that if they learn Swiss German, they will not be able to understand the "real" Germans and, if they learn "High German," they will not understand the Swiss. The Italian Swiss, prompted by the experience of being "colonized" by the tourists from German Switzerland and from Germany itself, also have an aversion toward the German Swiss. Minority group antipathy toward the German Swiss is explained in part by intergroup relations within Switzerland and in part it is influenced by the push and pull of shared interests with language communities bordering Switzerland.

The tendency for different parts of Switzerland to orient themselves toward their original cultures is accentuated generally during times of war. For instance, during World War II tensions between the different sectors of Swiss society escalated because the surrounding countries with which they identified were mutual enemies. An example of push and pull is the conflicting influences of attempts by German fascists to gain support in German Switzerland on the one hand and, on the other, a steady influx of refugees fleeing German domination.

In the French and Italian areas there is a positive inclination toward the influences of the original cultures. An example of direct influence is Geneva's move, inspired by the heavily centralistic French system, to centralize certain testing procedures, giving the same test at the same time in all schools. Nevertheless, in the French-Swiss case it is hard to identify the exact direction of educational change because the French politics of education change with every new government (about every five years). New developments toward an integrated <u>scuola media</u> in Italian Switzerland would not have been possible without having had the Italian model, which has no special schools for the handicapped and no segregation of the mentally retarded.

Unlike the other regions, the German reacts negatively to the influence of the original culture. Anything that comes from the German educational system has little chance of being implemented in German Switzerland. For example, when Germany launched the reform movement for integrated schooling, or <u>Gesamtschule,</u> a model similar to the French and Italian models, the establishment of a few experimental schools of this type was bitterly opposed by many German-speaking Swiss.

Although such trends should be seen primarily in a Western European context, the impact of local political orientations should not be underestimated. For instance, the extremely progressive system of "circle of orientation" would not have been possible in Geneva without its traditionally socialistic government.

Instruments of Coordination

Attempts to bring into compliance the disparate elements of Swiss society are made by integrative organs functioning at different levels of the educational apparatus. As mentioned, the main instrument for coordination at the national level is the Conference of Directors of Education Departments. Its function is to provide and collect information, to create goodwill, to heighten mutual understanding, and to give recommendations. The power of this body is limited because it functions primarily in an advisory and policymaking capacity; responsibility for policy implementations at most levels of schooling rests with the cantons.

Recommendations on various aspects of education, such as curriculum, articulation, and administration, are also made by other bodies. The different language regions, of which the French is the most advanced in coordination, sponsor regional conferences on education. There are as well working groups or "circles," called "meeting points." These groups consist of teachers and experts who explore new concepts and methods in the areas of mathematics and foreign languages.

The organization of funding for public education illustrates the balance of authority among the three tiers of the

Swiss educational bureaucracy: the nation, the canton, and the community. Government expenditure for education is shown in Figure 11.3 (not included are donations from private sources). It is obvious that the main responsibility for financing public elementary schools falls to the communities and, to a lesser extent, the cantons; for gymnasiums and professional schools, to the cantons; and for universities and research, to the state. In short, each administrative tier dominates one level of schooling.

FIGURE 11.3
List of Public Expenses for Research and Education (1974)

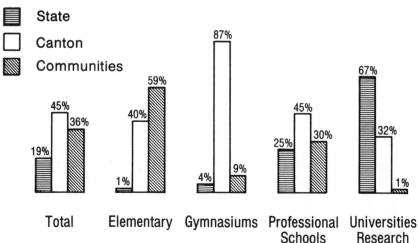

The most important decision-making process is consensus seeking. Thus, in order to serve the interests of all levels of schooling the three administrative tiers are forced to cooperate. The cantons, which once maintained absolute control over education, during the past 50 years increasingly lost autonomy in the areas of public works and social services, such as highway construction and the universities. At the same time, a new cultural consciousness in Switzerland has emerged. It finds expression in the current popularity of writing in Swiss German and in the increase of translated literature in the different Swiss tongues. The Romanash culture, which was dying out, has been revived through a growing literature and ethnological research at universities.

It can been seen that while economic interdependence forces cooperation among different sections of Swiss society, the expression of this cooperation often assumes cultural forms. Of particular interest to the discussion of education and intergroup relations is the recent nationwide project called SIPRI, meaning "an action approach to diagnose and change the situation of Swiss elementary schooling."

The SIPRI Project

First steps for an outline of the project were made in 1975, when the Conference of the Directors of the Education Departments recommended that the Swiss elementary schools start instruction of the first foreign language in the fifth year. In response, the Conference of the Swiss Teachers Association (Koslo), primarily out of fear that teachers would be overwhelmed by the imposition of increased responsibilities, demanded a general diagnosis of Swiss elementary schools.

The project had two goals: (1) to give an overview of the present state of the Swiss elementary school, and (2) to make recommendations for concrete improvements, to supply plans for implementing the different tasks, and to test implementation strategies in the so-called "contact schools" (model schools). Because the main goals were rather general, the project was divided into four investigatory subsections:

- Curricular and instructional objectives of the elementary school: ideal versus reality
- Functions and forms of selection (grading and tracking system)
- Transition from preschool to elementary school
- Contact and cooperation between teachers and parents

The dissemination of findings and diffusion of results took several forms:

- Recommendations to the Conference of Directors of Education Departments
- Interim reports (formative) to all schools and teacher associations
- SIPRI "contact schools" to serve as models of innovation
- SIPRI working groups formed with teachers, administrators, and parents from all parts of Switzerland

- Consultation services to be offered to all cantons and support given of related projects in all cantons
- SIPRI serving as the meeting point between cantons and the projects (collection and distribution of relevant information)

The organization chart in Figure 11.4 shows the different connections and partners involved.

To date, four workshop reports have been published. The first one (October 1981) described the contact schools, their project-type work, teachers' expectations, and first reports. It specified that for every project area in every canton there be at least one contact school. A second report (January 1983) described the research and the results of the working groups and projects in the area of "new forms of selection and grading." The third report (March 1983) presented findings and recommendations based on the most widespread forms of cooperation and ideas for new forms tested in the contact schools in the area of "cooperation between parents and teachers." It also described present teacher training activities and needs, including supervision and in-service training throughout Switzerland. The fourth report (March 1983) surveyed the present state of the project as a whole.

From the perspective of the author as consultant to different groups within the SIPRI project, many of the difficulties or conflicts discussed in this chapter have persisted in spite of the SIPRI effort. On the other hand, the very existence of the project, which is a large-scale venture, is indicative of a strong commitment to coordinate and strengthen the elementary school system. SIPRI is an attempt to foster greater integration through centrally coordinated research, planning, and implementation combined with considerable inputs from local units.

It is too soon to evaluate SIPRI success, for the criteria for success differ from canton to canton and from school to school. Participating in the project are 30 contact schools with about 300 teachers, four work groups with 80 participants, representatives of different organizations, four universities, and representatives of all cantons. A map (Figure 11.5) showing the location of the contact schools reveals the problem of the high concentration of participating schools in the German part (23) in comparison with the French (7), the Romanash (1), and the Italian sectors (0).

FIGURE 11.4
Organization Chart of the SIPRI-Project

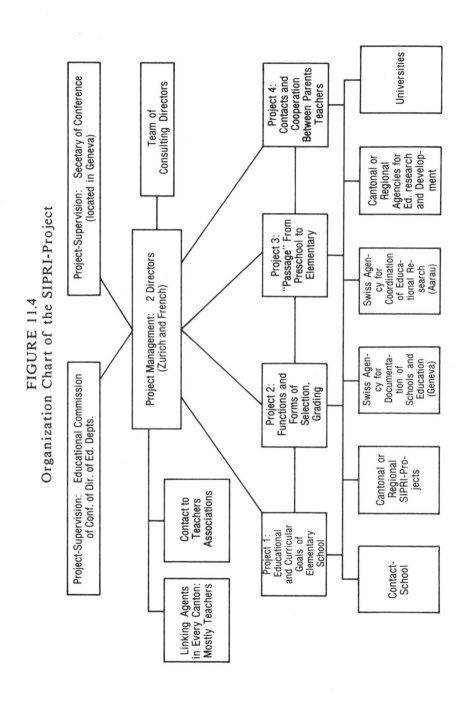

FIGURE 11.5
Switzerland: Location of Contact Schools in the SIPRI-Project

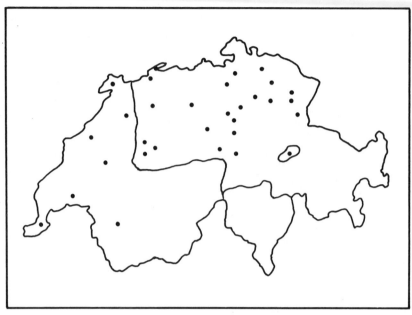

On first examination, this unequal distribution would appear to bode ill for the effectiveness of SIPRI as an integrative mechanism. Yet the numbers of facilities do not tell the entire story because the actual numbers of schoolchildren vary from region to region. If population distribution is taken into account, the discrepancies do not appear great. German Switzerland, with 65 percent of the population, has 74 percent of the project schools; the French region, with 25 percent of the population, has 25 percent of the project schools; the Romanash region, 1 percent and 3 percent; and the Italian, 9 percent and no project schools. The major inequality is in the absence of project schools in the Italian region; however, this region has the strong integrated <u>sculo media</u>. The attention given to the Romanash region by the SIPRI project can be considered an attempt at compensatory innovation to offset past neglect of this sector.

It will be interesting to observe in the future whether the SIPRI project will achieve a partial solution to some of the conflicts and problems described in this case study.

CONCLUSION

We shall conclude with a discussion comparing the Swiss educational system as described in the foregoing examination with some of the initial hypotheses on type D countries presented by La Belle and White.

The Swiss case evidences some features of the type D country (cultural segmentation and structural commonality in a horizontal relationship): "two or more groups that are roughly equal in prestige, political power, and economic power, and that participate in a single structural system of roles and positions."[22] The four ethnic groups of Switzerland are not as integrated as La Belle and White's ideal type D model would indicate; that is, all groups do not participate equally in all aspects of the economy. They are nevertheless interdependent. We see an alignment of structural and cultural divisions: The French-, Italian-, and Romanash-speaking minority regions are generally subordinate economically and politically to the dominant German region. In this context the international prestige of Geneva heightens the status of the otherwise basically subordinate French area and in so doing contributes to the interdependence of the regions.

The balance between groups in educational provision is achieved partly through decentralized administration, which allots each region considerable authority over primary, secondary, and to a lesser extent, postsecondary schooling. A countervailing movement is represented by the SIPRI project, which attempts to promote coordination among the traditionally autonomous cantonal schooling systems.

The complexity of centripetal and centrifugal tendencies in the Swiss case defies easy analysis. Within-group relations have been as important in our discussion as have between-group relations. For example, weak centripetal forces at the national level are especially clear in the case of Italian Ticino, yet Ticino and the French region are characterized by a high degree of internal centralization. In contrast, the most outstanding feature of the German region is the force of internal centrifugal tendencies.

Although the common structural system would suggest it, between-group permeability is not high in Switzerland. As La Belle and White predict, there is relative stability of group size and membership. The secession of Jura from Bern is the only significant instance of change in regional boundaries and crossover to a different educational system.

Push and pull factors have been determined by historical-political developments, such as the formation of Switzerland particularly for military reasons and the linkages to the wider European language and cultural communities. Italy's positive influence in the Italian portion of the Swiss educational system can be contrasted with the negative impact of fluctuations in Germany; any educational reform originating in Germany has little chance of being implemented in Switzerland.

Intergroup relationships rely on both political and economic interdependence to maintain internal cohesiveness. Educational policies are made through shared governance but with a great deal of autonomy for the individual cantons. Across Switzerland curricula are determined at various levels: the cantons, the regions, and the state through the Conference of the Directors of the Education Departments. While access to education is generally high for all people, postsecondary education in some French-Swiss cantons, notably Geneva, is extremely accessible. Teacher training is delegated to the cantons in the German region and to the universities in the French. The between-region diversity in the elementary and secondary schools is mitigated by unified policies governing teacher training and other forms of professional preparation. Careful attention is given to language differences; instructional media are the native tongues. This centrifugality is offset through the early introduction of one foreign language already spoken in Switzerland.

An important issue that has not been addressed in this chapter is the integration in Switzerland of a significant sized foreign-born population: Italian, German, Spanish, and Turkish. The presence of large numbers of foreign-born students -- in some cantons outnumbering Swiss born and comprising 30 percent of the University of Geneva enrollment (1980) -- raises critical questions for Swiss education and intergroup relations.[23] The foreign-born population is necessary for Switzerland's economy, but its presence has bred a series of largely unanticipated social and cultural conflicts in intergroup relations. An agenda for further research should include an examination of the impact of demographic changes, represented by this foreign-born influx since World War II, on the patterns of conflict and attempts at resolution in Swiss education.

In general, the problems can be understood more through economic and political analysis than cultural because most influences originate from general European developments. Nonetheless, they find expression in the cultural domain in which education plays a significant role as both an arena of conflict and a means of achieving a measure of cohesiveness in the complex plural society of Switzerland.

NOTES

1. "The Development of Higher Education in Switzerland" (Translation of <u>L'Enseignement Superieur en Suisse</u>, European Center for Higher Education [CEPES] (Bucharest: UNESCO, 1981), pp. 3-74; <u>Western European Education</u> 15, no. 2 (Summer 1983):15.

2. Rolf Deppeler, "Swiss Confederation," <u>The International Encyclopedia of Higher Education</u> (San Francisco: Jossey-Bass, 1977), vol. 8, p. 4039.

3. Ibid.

4. Ibid.

5. "The Development of Higher Education," p. 10.

6. Ibid., p. 11.

7. A. M. Gehring, H. Ochsenbein, G. Pillet, M. H. Poulet, and J. Prod'hom, "Demography and the Education System in Switzerland," <u>European Journal of Education</u> 16, nos. 3-4 (1981):291.

8. "The Development of Higher Education," p. 46.

9. Deppeler, "Swiss Confederation," p. 4037.

10. Ibid., p. 4041.

11. Gehring et al., "Demography and the Education System," p. 298.

12. Deppeler, "Swiss Confederation," p. 4040.

13. Ibid., p. 4038.

14. Ibid., p. 4039.

15. Gehring et al., "Demography and the Education System," p. 291.

16. Ibid.

17. Deppeler, "Swiss Confederation," p. 4039.

18. Thomas La Belle and Peter White, "Education and Multiethnic Integration: An interrelations Typology," <u>Comparative Education Review</u> 24, no. 2 (1980):170.

19. Deppeler, "Swiss Confederation," p. 4040.

20.　La Belle and White, "Education and Multiethnic Integration," p. 170.

21.　Ibid., p. 171.

22.　Ibid., p. 168.

23.　Gehring et al., "Demography and the Education System," pp. 275, 302.

12

MULTILINGUAL EDUCATIONAL PROVISION IN BELGIUM

Leslie Limage

AN OVERVIEW OF BELGIAN SOCIETY

Contemporary complexities of Belgian society are remote from the unitary, bourgeois, and Francophone state created in 1831. The National Congress that enacted the first constitution sought to unite provinces, with centuries of autonomous existence, on the basis of a highly centralized state system. Although it is beyond the scope of this discussion to go into a detailed examination of its evolution, no introduction to Belgian community relations in terms of education can neglect drawing attention to the political will to create unitary nation-states that swept Europe and attempted to defy the linguistic and cultural diversity of the actual societies involved. In the case of Belgium, even histories of this evolution are conflicting, and the author suggests that the reader consult the analyses drawn by Lorwin and Lagasse.[1]

As early legislators were quick to note, the centralized state was inadequate to deal with the emergence of special interest groups that were based on linguistic and economic differences. The state, as such, was modeled on a Rousseau-style laissez-faire system in which the nation related to individuals instead of groups. Nonetheless, these various groups -- trade unions and professional, religious, and agricultural associations -- developed to negotiate, in place of the individual, with the Belgian state. Political parties themselves developed along highly structured and compartmentalized lines. Antagonism between Catholics and liberals found its roots in this period, as did the third pillar of traditional Belgian political life, the Parti ouvrier belge, precursor of the Belgian Socialist party. The most striking characteristic of this political party, as of the others, was its all-encompassing nature. In a parallel fashion to the other political groupings, it provided all the services a member might require from birth to death. At this stage, these parallel structures were coming only into direct conflict on one point, which is in fact the focus of our discussion -- the school. As the <u>guerres scolaires</u> (scholastic wars) will be examined in detail later on, suffice it to say that lines were drawn opposing the so-called <u>ecole libre catholique</u> (free Catholic school) and the official nondenominational school system.

While on the surface the three major groupings to the French, the Flemish, and those from Flanders -- led a relatively peaceful coexistence, underlying linguistic and cultural diversity was seeking expression. From the beginning, Flanders sought its cultural identity while French was imposed for all official purposes. Flemish (or actually standardized Dutch) was admitted only in legal proceedings in 1873, in administration in 1878, in secondary education in 1883, in some university instruction in 1890, and in the army in 1913.

The Presence of Communities and Regions: Cultural and Linguistic Demands

The cleavage between French and Flemish speakers was accentuated by the First World War when the German occupational forces dealt on a preferential basis with the latter in the name of a <u>Flamenpolitik,</u> a phenomenon to be repeated during the Second World War with even greater repercussions for the tenuous social fabric of Belgium.

After the First World War, the political demands for recognition by the major cultural communities found acknowledgment in linguistic affirmation. In 1921 three unilingual linguistic regions were created. In 1932 linguistic laws reinforced the distinctiveness of the regions, and Brussels was given its special bilingual status. Children in Brussels only were required to learn both Dutch and French.

The Second World War further divided the north from the south of the country. Both areas provided collaboration and resistance, but the bulk of sympathy for German occupation was found in Flanders and the major forces of resistance developed in Wallonia and in Brussels. In addition, the majority of Flemish rallied to the neutrality of King Leopold III, which led, after the war, to bitter antagonism and the abdication of the king.[2] At the same time, Wallonia was becoming more aware of its cultural distinctiveness. There was even a point at which there was consideration of its being attached to France.

The 1947 census highlighted an increase in the Flemish population. Flanders continued to define itself as not only culturally and politically distinct, but independent economically as well. In fact, membership in a Flemish nation began to take precedence over traditional cleavages, such as employer/worker or conservative/socialist. The various political party divisions that followed can be understood only along these lines.

The French-speaking community was becoming progressively a minority in every sense of the term, in parliament in particular. Wallonia as an economic region began to decline from its earlier prestigious situation. Thus, while political consciousness in Flanders rose as a reaction to the unitary French state, Walloons and French speakers of Brussels developed their positions as a reaction against the loss of previous privilege. Parliament became the arena of continual community conflict. Communities and regions constituted sociopolitical reality.

A somewhat stereotypical dichotomy appears during this period. On the one hand, there was the youthful, primarily Catholic and conservative Flemish community, associated with a region at the peak of economic expansion, holding a belief in private enterprise and foreign investment. This community was confronted by a French population with a declining birth rate, much greater religious neutrality, and highly individualistic tendencies. Furthermore, the French constituted a majority in both Wallonia and Brussels, where the declining dynamism of early industrialization in the nineteenth century was producing growing unemployment.

Brussels continued to develop as a special case with a dominance of French speakers and, during the 1970s, a rising influx of migrant workers from the Mediterranean basin. Such was the impact of this immigrant population that one out of every three children born in the 1970s was of foreign origin, a rate that by the end of the century has been forecast to rise to 50 percent.

The original unitary state simply never existed in practice, and in terms of the aspirations of the communities in question, is a totally alien notion.

<u>Guerre Scolaire</u> and Sociolinguistic Complexities

In order to place the <u>guerre scolaire</u> of the 1950s in some context, other than political, attention must be drawn to the complex sociolinguistic map of Belgium. For a more complete understanding of the linguistic aspects of this discussion, the reader can consult the major work in the area by Verdoodt.[3]

A glance at the linguistic map of Belgium shows a rough division of the country into a northern half, in which Germanic dialects (Flemish, Brabantic, and Limburgisch) dominate; an eastern area, where Low German and Franco-Mosellan is spoken; and a southern area, in which Romance dialects prevail (Picard, Walloon, and Lorrain or Gaumais). Linguistic borders are vague and fluctuate. Hence, although Dutch and French are the languages of instruction in schools, along with a small German enclave, it would be utterly simplistic to state that the language issue is one dealing with two monolithic languages. Neither standard Dutch nor French is the spoken language of the linguistic community except among small groups.

The situation is further complicated by the massive presence in all the major industrial regions of Belgium, and in the Brussels area in particular, of migrant workers. As in other parts of Europe, children of migrant workers are concentrated in certain areas, hence in certain schools, and their education is highly problematic. Their specific problems are not the object of this discussion, but it is significant that their educational difficulties due to language problems are more readily discussed across Flemish/French borders than are the difficulties of indigenous cultural groups. There is already in this area a vast literature in Belgium, while an overall view of the Flemish/French conflict, in terms of educational provision, remains elusive.

FIGURE 12.1
Linguistic Map

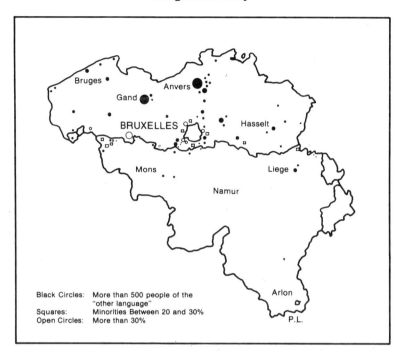

Source: Paul M. Levy, "Linguistic and Semantic Borders in Belgium" in "Belgium," ed. A. Verdoodt, International Journal of the Sociology of Language, no. 15 (The Hague: Mouton), p. 11.

Although three official languages are in use in schools in a unilingual manner, except for Brussels, which constitutes the single bilingual situation, the outer boundaries of Belgium in no way constitute linguistic frontiers. A glance confirms that beyond the region in which Dutch is the official language sits the Netherlands. Beyond the region in which French is taught sits France. Finally, adjacent to the German-speaking eastern sector extends Germany.

In addition to the major dialects mentioned, further local varieties exist. Yet it is increasingly customary to refer to the residents of the so-called Dutch-speaking area as Flemings and those of the so-called French-speaking region as Walloons. In fact, both classifications are extremely misleading. A further complication is added if one examines the impact of the creation of an official French-speaking state, as was the case in 1831. Standard French became an elite language by necessity and by prestige, even among Dutch speakers. Because French has remained a language of prestige and greater international acceptance, it has been the Dutch speakers who become bilingual. The French speakers have always been reluctant to learn the other official language and, although being privileged on an international basis, find themselves disadvantaged domestically whenever fluency in both languages is necessary, as in public and in the employment arena.

The Role of Education in Community Conflict and Coexistence

With these foregoing comments on the sociolinguistic background to the situation in Belgium, attention can be given now to the role of educational provision in community conflict and coexistence. The question of whether educational provision ought to favor religious or lay forms has been a major focus of community conflict since the nineteenth century. Indeed, the first guerre scolaire dates back to 1879, when an anticlerical minister of education presented a law requiring that each local authority provide at least one neutral primary school, with religious instruction to be purely an outside school affair. For the next five years, Catholics waged battle and finally succeeded in overthrowing the government. A new law in 1884 granted each local authority individual discretion to adopt either a denominational or a neutral primary school. Further conflict led to another government and another law in 1895 providing finance for all private schools and making religion an obligatory subject. In spite of high illiteracy rates in Belgium, school attendance was not yet compulsory.[4]

During the 1950s, a second guerre scolaire broke out on a much greater scale. On the one hand, the traditional cleavages were accentuated over the question of whether or not to subsidize "free" or Catholic education (enseignement libre). On the other hand, the heightened desire for cultural autonomy of the Dutch-speaking and French-speaking communities was reflected in the conflict over educational provision. From an ideological point of view, the proponents of a nondenominational schooling (l'ecole laique) demanded that the state monopolize control over education and rejected any provision for subsidy to private, that is, Catholic, schools. The latter demanded financial support without any state control.

In 1954, when socialists and liberals held the government amid much opposition, subsidies for Catholic schools were reduced. The Project Collard of 1955 responded with some attempt at compromise by providing:

- That each local authority have at least one nursery and one primary school and could adopt a private school only if it had already created public provision
- That public schools have at least 50 percent of their teaching staff holding recognized official diplomas
- That subsidies for both private and public schools be granted only in cases of proven economic and social need
- That diplomas granted by private teacher training colleges be considered valid after an examination before a jury composed partially of state-certified professors

Violent demonstrations led by clergy against this law did not prevent its passage in parliament. Nonetheless, Catholic opposition was such that a pacte scolaire was signed in 1958 leading to a 12-year agreement to provide a period free from conflict during which public instruction could be extended throughout the country. The resultant paix scolaire, or negotiated peace, involved

- Mutual nonaggression between proponents of the two types of instruction
- Uniform school years, but freedom in choice of programs, methods, and school hours
- Priority for employment in the public sector given to those holding official diplomas at all levels of instruction
- Freedom of choice between religious or moral instruction for two hours per week in public schools
- Financial assistance to public schools and the right for private schools to be built at the expense of local communities
- Identical rules governing the granting of diplomas

Efforts to democratize education in the 1950s included prolonging obligatory schooling to the age of 14; providing free education until 18 years of age; creating scholarships for secondary and university study; financially assisting all recognized forms of education, public or private; and controlling to some degree all subsidies.

As the pacte scolaire took effect, the community conflict assumed a more linguistic tone. Attention was turned to university provision in French and Flemish. In an abundantly documented series of negotiations and bitter conflict (which is beyond the scope of this discussion to amply reflect), the Catholic University of Louvain became two universities -- one Flemish speaking and the other French; in all, six universities provided the full range of courses, and partial studies were negotiated in the remaining institutions of higher learning throughout Belgium.[5]

The pacte scolaire came into question again in 1969 in all its aspects. Partial resolution followed: A ministerial decree of November 25, 1970 stipulated that the first foreign language taught in secondary school should be Dutch, English, or German in the French-speaking region; Dutch in Brussels; and French (or German) in the German-speaking region. Free choice of a second foreign language was also granted to the Dutch-speaking region. The law of July 21, 1971 created two cultural councils (French and Dutch), providing cultural autonomy to the Flemish in exchange for the right of heads of households in the Brussels area to choose freely the language of instruction of their children (Brussels is geographically, if not legally, in the Dutch-speaking region). A quarrel followed over the actual numbers of Dutch and French speakers in the Brussels area, as well as the corresponding finance of educational provision. At that stage, particular advantage was granted to the Dutch commission for school construction.

Since the early 1970s, it has continued to be abundantly clear that the paix scolaire depends on the peaceful coexistence of the two cultural communities. A cultural agreement was signed in 1971 to reaffirm this principle. In 1972, both major political parties in power (Christian-Socialists and Socialists) agreed to consolidate the paix scolaire by developing parental free choice, continuing the democratization of education and attempting to plan jointly the extension of educational provision along the lines of what came to be called a "pluralist school," or a school open to all philosophical or other backgrounds.

In 1973 a major revision of the pacte scolaire of 1958 was undertaken in the presence of all major parties, including those of the opposition. The first draft brought about major discord. Subsequently, a national commission drew up a second charter that included the following objectives: to offer parents the choice of a neutral school or a religious one, the former to include three-quarters of its staff with official diplomas; to continue the democratization of education through further in-service training for teachers; to eliminate discrimination between each system of education, that is, through school construction and salaries for subsidized personnel; and to encourage the creation of the pluralist school alongside the neutral and religious schools in order to draw both communities closer.

The entire reform proposal was seriously questioned and returned to its commission, so that the resultant law of July 11, 1973 limited itself to creating four funds for subsidizing school construction for the two educational systems and promising a recognized statute to teachers in each system.

The first point was intended only to be implemented on the basis of overall national planning. The new problems that arose were due to the nature of this planning and the role of the pluralist school. One camp was in favor of replacing neutral and religious schools by pluralist ones. The other group sought to ensure parental choice through the maintenance of two separate systems. The pluralist school was to be administered by representatives of all tendencies and views present in the community concerned. It was to have a full range of teaching and auxiliary staff (medical, social welfare, psychological, and so on). It was to cultivate the views of parents on religion, civics, and other subjects. Teachers were entitled to let their personal views be known as long as this did not interfere with pedagogical responsibilities. The pluralist school was also to include in its management all members of the educational community.

By January 25, 1975, one school considered itself to have conformed to the above criteria and became the first pluralist school in Belgium. It was a special education school for the handicapped.

The planning element, or "rationalization" as it was called, also met serious difficulty. By 1975, there were three systems administering instruction in Belgium: (1) the state, with an administrative hierarchy, including a French-speaking and a Dutch-speaking minister of national education; (2) the region and the local authority, organizing alongside the state the network of neutral or official schools; and (3) the private sector offering so-called "free" committed or religious instruction controlled by the Secretariate National de l'Enseignement Catholique for 80 percent of its provision. All systems were and are subsidized by the state.

The Tindemans government (1974-78) took up the various controversies surrounding educational provision: higher education, primary and nursery schooling, the status of the pluralist school, school transportation, and the status of teachers. The entire period was marked by various governmental crises: in December 1976, March 1977, and October 1978. The work of the school commission was almost entirely thwarted.[6]

By July 1980, under the Martens government, the six major political parties agreed on educational planning so that there were to be 285 secondary schools for the Francophone community and 340 for the Dutch-speaking community. These figures include official state instruction (105 Francophone schools), officially subsidized education divided between religious and nondenominational instruction (45 provincial and local authorities schools), and "free" subsidized private education divided between religious (125 schools) and nondenominational (5 schools). Five pluralist schools had come into existence. It was agreed that both Catholic and public education be equally financed, but the actual cost of the measure became a new cause for discord.

LANGUAGE POLICIES AND EDUCATIONAL PROVISION LANGUAGE

Quantitative Presence of the Flemish-, French-, and German-Speaking Populations in the School Systems

Against this historical background, current language usage and educational provision have particular significance. Although it would be difficult to affirm that Belgium advances to a fully formulated language policy, the trend appears to be more toward La Belle and White's notion of greater cultural pluralism, a series of compromises on the political and economic level that are rapidly translated into the educational arena. Demographic trends are also visible in the representation of language communities in schools.

According to statistics available for 1980 (Education in Belgium, 1981), the school population was as follows: French-language education system, 42 percent; Dutch-language education system, 57.50 percent; and German-language education system, 0.5 percent. The school population in both French and Dutch medium systems appears to be declining to a certain extent at the primary level but to a greater degree in the French-speaking area. Both systems appear to be expanding at the secondary level, undoubtedly due to some of the recent reforms in democratizing education. Table 12.1 gives some indication of present trends.

Changing Language Policies and the Balance of Power: The Case of Brussels

It cannot be said that a single coherent language policy has evolved in Belgium over the period described in the preceding discussion. The brevity of the presentation may not sufficiently emphasize that each successive agreement on educational provision has been the result of resolution on the basis of a political balance of power at the given historical moment. Each subsequent change in this balance has brought previous agreements into question.

This pattern of successive conflict and compromise distinguishes Belgium from other multilingual countries of type D described by La Belle and White. While an "inherent centrifugality" may be observed among Flemish, French, and German speakers, the decentralization and duplication of administrative bodies do not appear to be sufficient to counter more serious cleavages. The case of Brussels illustrates the continuing search for a new language policy consensus.

While the other major communities are only responsible for Dutch- or French-language usage, in Brussels, because of its bilingual requirements, administrations must provide all public documents and information in both languages. According to their status, all administrators at all levels must have some knowledge of the second language, which is not the case in the unilingual regions.

In terms of educational provision, a unilingual policy prevails in Flanders and Wallonia. A second language chosen from French (or Dutch), English, and German is taught from the first year of secondary school, as mentioned earlier. In Brussels, the situation is more complex. The head of the household residing in one of the 19 local authorities can choose from one or the other languages of instruction. Outside this area, the local language school must be accepted un-

TABLE 12.1
SCHOOL POPULATION 1969-1970 -- 1979-1980

EVOLUTION

Education	French + German			Dutch			Total		
	1969/70	1979/80	%	1969/70	1979/80	%	1969/70	1979/80	%
Pre-School									
Ordinary		159,936			222,500			382,436	
Special		749			1,716			2,465	
Total	182,912	160,685	87.84		224,216	78.93	466,994	384,901	82.42
Primary									
Ordinary	405,589	370,968	91.46	562,259	469,012	82.42	967,848	839,980	86.78
Special	22,896	15,392	67.22	22,675	21,766	85.99	45,571	37,158	81.53
Total	428,485	386,360	90.16	584,934	490,778	83.90	1,013,419	877,138	86.55
Lower Secondary									
General + Technical + Vocational + Special	206,499	234,437	113.52	286,584	294,286	102.69	493,083	528,723	107.22
Total	206,499	234,437	113.52	286,584	294,286	102.69	493,083	528,723	107.22
Upper Secondary									
General	44,537	53,860	120.93	57,084	88,125	154.38	101,621	155,481	153.00
Technical	27,503	26,767	97.32	44,849	68,238	152.15	72,352	99,119	136.99
Vocational	10,336	17,998	174.12	16,176	40,678	251.47	25,512	44,510	167.88
Total	82,376	98,625	119.72	118,109	197,041	166.82	200,485	299,110	149.19
Secondary									
Artistic	619	442	71.40	1,003	1,050	104.68	1,622	1,492	91.98
Special	4,479	12,912	288.27	5,172	13,112	253.51	9,651	26,024	269.65
Total	5,098	13,354	261.94	6,175	14,162	229.34	11,273	27,516	244.08
Higher Non-University									
Technical	19,298	30,154	156.25	22,164	40,789	184.03	41,462	70,943	171.10
Teacher Training	4,856	10,132	208.64	13,255	13,641	102.91	18,111	23,773	131.26
Artistic	992	1,097	110.58	1,030	1,032	100.19	2,022	2,129	105.29
Total	25,146	41,383	164.57	36,449	55,462	152.16	61,595	96,845	157.22

Source: Education in Belgium: 1978-1980, Ministry of National Education and French Culture, Ministerie van Nationale Opvoeding en Nederlandse Cultuur, Brussels, 1981, p. 79.

less it can be proven that the medium of instruction is not a child's native tongue. The head of the household must make an official declaration to this effect before a linguistic inspector. Schools accepting pupils who belong in another linguistic system may be penalized. Instruction is obligatory in the second official language starting from the third year of primary school. A further series of special conditions govern other aspects of cultural and linguistic expression in Brussels.[7]

Thus, with such a backdrop, we can turn to an examination of educational finance, administration, organization, curriculum, and teacher training. Because of the level of sensitivity to language issues, the following comments describe the various arrangements in each area but are rarely illustrated by cross-community research. It is striking that there is little possibility for Belgian research to cover the internal classroom experience in the three communities. (See Verdoodt's bibliographies on this point. Foreign researchers have been less cautious in this area.)

THE EDUCATIONAL SYSTEM: A HERITAGE OF RELIGIOUS AND ECONOMIC DISPARITY

Finance

We have discussed at some length the political overtones in recent years that have accompanied educational finance. The present situation in which all forms of education are highly subsidized is the result of the balance of power between proponents of Catholic instruction, subsidized without state control, and proponents of neutral public education for all; shifting regional disparities in which the previously advantaged French-speaking area is now declining economically and in population; and a definitie will among a majority to expand educational provision across cultural boundaries. Table 12.2 gives some indication of the growth in state expenditure.

Administration

Article 17 of the Belgian constitution stipulates: "There shall be freedom of education; any measure hindering such freedom shall be prohibited; penalization of infringement shall be governed by law." The administration of education is

TABLE 12.2
**TOTAL BUDGET OF EDUCATION AND CULTURE EXPRESSED IN
PERCENTAGE OF THE NATIONAL BUDGET AND THE GNP**

FINANCIAL STATISTICS

	Ministry of National Education and Culture Ordinary Budget	General State Budget	GNP	MEC B. State	MEC GNP
	in millions	in millions	in milliards	%	%
53	8,058	75,551	411.3	10.7	1.96
55	9,133	85,612	456.5	10.7	2.00
60	18,875	117,122	571.5	16.7	3.30
65	35,157	182,705	848.9	19.2	4.37
70	60,298	295,410	1,297.1	20.4	4.65
72	82,046	371,102	1,583.1	24.3	5.18
73	99,924	410,250	1,797.8	21.1	5.58
74	110,654	473,400	2,115.9	23.4	5.23
75	143,255	650,358	2,335.8	21.8	6.13
76	175,103	804,459	2,642.6	21.8	6.63
77	197,526	938.705	2,882.6	21.0	6.83
78	208,046	1,074,128	3,063.6	19.4	6.79
79	224,101	1,172,534	3,253.5	19.1	6.89
80	234,894	1,260,164	--	18.6	--

GENERAL TOTAL

Budget (in millions)	1978	1979	1980
A *National Education*	Adjusted Credits	Adjusted Credits	Initial Credit
French language sector	78,517.9	83,704.5	88,137.6
Dutch language sector	101,157.4	109,335.5	114,707.0
Common sector	15,706.6	16,673.8	17,162.5
Total	195,381.8	209,713.8	220,007.1
B *Culture*			
French culture	6,420.5	7,187.8	7,571.4
Dutch culture	7,631.3	6,198.0	6,298.0
Common sector	961.2	1,001.3	1,017.9
Total	15,013.0	14,387.1	14,887.3
General Total	208,046.3	224,100.9	234,894.4

Source: Education in Belgium: 1978-80, Ministry of National Education and French Culture, Ministerie van Nationale Opvoeding en Nederlandse Cultuur, Brussels, 1981, p. 21.

also a reflection of the complex balance of powers that have evolved in Belgium. In general, the system is administered by the legislative, the executive, decentralized public bodies, and private institutions at various levels of responsibility. The legislative functions refer to national parliament, the Cultural Council of the French Cultural Community, and the Cultural Council of the Flemish Cultural Community. Both of the latter bodies are responsible for education in its linguistic area.

National parliament determines the following:

Basic principles applying to all linguistic areas
School obligation
Structure of the educational system
Diplomas
Subsidies
Wages and salaries
All educational matters concerning the German cultural community, which does not possess the same relative autonomy as the other two linguistic groups

The executive refers to:

The king, acting as chief of state
The Ministry of National Education (French sector)
The Ministry of National Education (Flemish sector)
The Ministry of French Community
The Ministry of Flemish Community
The Ministry of Walloon
The Ministry of Brussels
The cultural councils

As stated earlier, administration is also handled at the provincial and local authority levels in an attempt at deconcentration of administration but not actual decentralization of decision making.

Organization

Belgium along with the United Kingdom, France, and other European countries, has been steadily shifting away from a highly selective secondary school system toward a more comprehensive, single school system. Nonetheless, as

Figure 12.2 indicates, very distinct tracking systems that are not easily penetrable still characterize Belgian schooling.

Curriculum and Teacher Training

Curriculum development and teacher training have remained relatively impervious to change for reasons that, to a large extent, call for further research. In spite of a movement to reform the entire secondary system in the 1970s, political will has been so fragmented that practical change has been thwarted. Symptoms of the difficulty in effecting change appear in the literature and in research. For example, Belgian participation in the International Education Association survey on instruction in the native tongue and reading attainment revealed that Belgium had the lowest percentage of university-trained teachers at all levels of education than any of the countries, industrialized or developing, that were included in the project.[8] On the other hand, when controlled for socioeconomic and other relevant criteria, the scholastic performance of Belgian children closely profiled that of other countries. Although in-service teacher training is highly developed, actual figures for participation are not readily available.

From this brief external structural examination, the discussion will now turn to some indication of the effect of present multilingual educational provision from the point of view of professional mobility and economic status of the various linguistic groups. Aspirations and attitudes of Belgian youth regarding language and education are also mentioned. They may constitute some indicator of actual awareness of the La Belle and White thesis concerning type D countries in terms of the lesser role of the education and inequality debate so prevalent in other countries that do not have multilingual institutional arrangements.

OUTCOME AND TRENDS

Effects of the System on Professional Mobility and Economic Status

A reexamination of the successive stages of the guerre scolaire of the 1950s and of recent Belgian education, in terms of cultural or linguistic conflict, can easily be linked to efforts

FIGURE 12.2
Description and Chart of the Education System

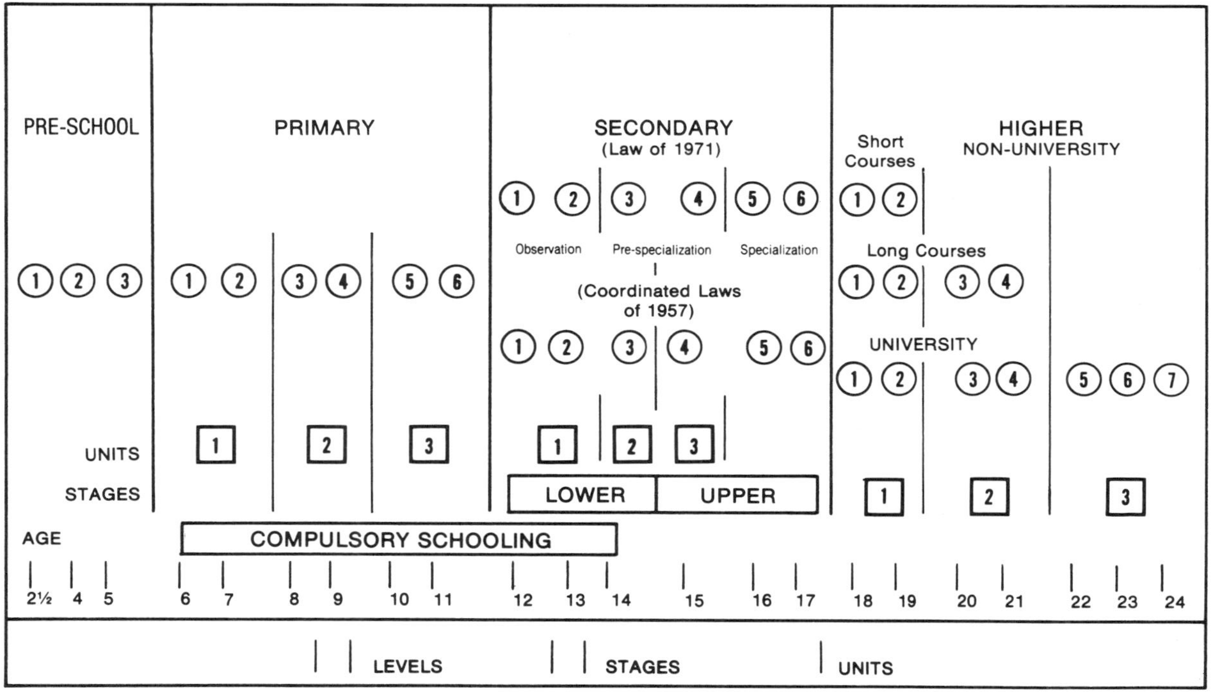

Source: Ministry of National Education and French Culture, Education in Belgium: 1978-1980, (Brussels: Ministerie van Nationale Opvoeding en Nederlandse Cultuur, 1981), p. 23.

309

toward economic equality. In particular, the creation of Dutch sections of universities, the split of the Catholic University of Louvain, and the transformation of the Dutch-language University of Gand testify to the struggle of the middle- and lower-class Flemish to obtain for their children real democratization of education. Their argument was not only one of cultural autonomy. The elite of the Flemish community had already succeeded for centuries in French-language higher education and hence in positions of power. The possibility to complete higher education in Flemish for young people entirely schooled in Dutch (representing the majority of the Flemish community) was perceived as a key to social and professional mobility.[9]

Further, when earlier community conflict was drawn along the lines of religious instruction or lay public provision, the linguistic element was not a primary concern. During the latter part of the nineteenth and early twentieth centuries, proponents of Catholic schooling were not questioning that instruction continue to be provided in French. The linguistic cleavage became central only as the community issues became mass issues and consequently had economic foundations.

Although substantial gains have been made in terms of equal but unilingual educational provision, another dimension has acted to determine professional mobility. French speakers have traditionally looked beyond their borders to the international prestige of the standard form of their language. They have been reticent to learn Dutch. On the other hand, the Flemish community has continued to learn standard Dutch and master French as well, gaining a significant market advantage, particularly in the civil service areas requiring bilingual skills and in important industrial and service sectors of the economy also requiring French- and Dutch-language use.

Aspirations and Attitudes of Youth

A small but growing body of research in Belgium is documenting the effects of the educational system on young people's attitudes and aspirations with respect to language acquisition and employment. Baeten and Verdoodt have examined a sample of both Dutch- and French-speaking youth. They found that French speakers studied Dutch for a shorter period (average 5 years) than Dutch speakers had undertaken

French (5.88 years).[10] When asked whether they considered that they had studied the other language sufficiently, again the Dutch speakers expressed greater satisfaction in learning French than did their French-speaking counterparts in learning Dutch. They also found that most French-speaking young people choose English as their first choice as a foreign language, while Dutch speakers choose both French and English on an equal basis.[11]

As section of the youth survey was also devoted to actual language contact in order to obtain some idea of the relevance of the second language to young people's daily lives. It again appeared that Dutch-speaking youth have more contact with French than did French speakers with Dutch. An example of such differential contact is that, of those surveyed, approximately 80 percent of Dutch-speaking young people watched a French-language television program at least once a month, whereas 50 percent of French speakers had monthly contact with Dutch programs. In both cases, however, young people felt that their mastery of the written foreign language was insufficient for their needs.[12]

Of particular interest for our discussion are Baeten and Verdoodt's findings regarding young people's expectations for the use they will make of the foreign language in the future. The findings show that once again Dutch speakers expected to make greater use of French in their future professions and further studies than did French speakers. Both groups, however, expected to use the foreign language equally rarely in leisure-time activities.

A small sample of German speakers was also compared to the larger groups of Dutch and French speakers. The German sample was highly satisfied with the obligation to learn French and expected to use it extensively in employment, studies, and leisure activities. Dutch was considered of secondary importance.

A general concluding finding of the study was that all groups -- Dutch, French, and German speakers -- favored at least a passive competence that young Belgians value a part of their heritage, in the other national languages. This finding appears a positive one in the light of the community conflicts described earlier.

In terms of the La Belle and White typology, it appears that equality remains an issue in Belgian education, both from a community and a socioeconomic standpoint. This partial study of aspirations and attitudes is highly innovative in examining the current balance in Belgian society as reflected among youth, but there is no indication that equality of opportunity or equality of condition are not central educational issues. Indeed, tentative conclusions in the following section indicate that "centrifugal" tendencies are taking the form of further demands for political and economic autonomy.

Demands for Further Autonomy

The community problems of previous generations have certainly left their mark on the forms of educational provision in Belgium. Current political trends are emphasizing a movement toward federalism of institutions.[13] Such a trend, were it to be confirmed, would imply a real decentralization of decision-making power in education, which is not presently the case. It would not be unreasonable to expect that such a turn of events would further compartmentalize already essentially unilingual educational provision. In a sense, the title of this chapter, "multilingual educational provision in Belgium," is more a statement of tendency rather than fact. Only the Brussels area provides obligatory second national language instruction at the primary level.

On the other hand, it is to be expected that the nature of Belgian society, its cultural diversity, strong migrant population, and the permeability of its economy to international presence can only increase the further need for a multilingually educated population. A 1983 survey conducted by Verdoodt and others examined the linguistic requirements of industry and public sector employment. The findings seem to indicate that there is a much greater need for knowledge of foreign languages in many employment areas than is actually being met by the kinds of language instruction young people are presently receiving. Responses to this inadequacy appear to vary. In many cases, private and public sector employers are seeking to redress the shortcoming through continuing education or through setting up language requirements for vacant posts.

Clearly, regardless of the political will toward a more federal system, economic realities seem to indicate that Belgium will require a multilingual population, or that the linguistic group most prepared to become multilingual will tend to dominate certain areas of employment and, possibly, power. This consideration leads us into an area of speculation.

It may be prudent to conclude, at least in terms of the great distance Belgian society has traveled from its initial unitary political conception, with two remarks made by prominent Belgians -- Jules Destree, Socialist minister, in his letter to the king in 1912: "No, Sire, there is no Belgian soul. The fusion of the Flemish and Walloons is not desirable; and if it were desirable, it would simply be necessary to note that it is not possible,"[14] and Prime Minister M. G. Eyskens in a declaration on February 18, 1970 notes: "The unitary State, as the laws prescribe it in terms of its structure and functioning, has been overtaken by events."[15]

And, in terms of Belgium's place among countries discussed along the intergroup relations typology, all groups' demands for a more truly federal state would seem to confirm the hypothesis that this shared centrifugal autonomy will lead to the search for an agreed-upon form of integration. Indeed, the history of Belgium is an apt illustration, placing it well along the path to a Swiss or Yugoslav federal system.

NOTES

1. V. Lowrin, "Linguistic Pluralism and Political Tension in Modern Belgium," in <u>Advances in the Sociology of Language,</u> vol. 2, ed. J. Fishman (The Hague: Mouton, 1973), pp. 386-412.   See also E. Lagasse, <u>La contre-reforme de l'etat, Panorama des institutions politiques de la Belgique</u> (Louvain: Ciaco, 1982).

2. See Lowrin, "Linguistic Pluralism and Political Tension in Modern Belgium."

3. A. Verdoodt, <u>Bibliographie sur le probleme linguistique belge</u> (Lavel: Centre International de recherche sur le bilinguisme, 1983). See also three earlier works by Verdoodt: "Belgium," issue no. 15 of the <u>International Journal of the Sociology of Language</u> (The Hague: Mouton, 1982); "Dix ans de recherches bibliographiques sur les problemes communautaires belges," <u>Recherches Sociologiques</u> no. 2 (1980):237-45; and <u>Les problemes des groupes linguistiques en Belgique</u> (Louvain: Bibliotheque des Cahiers de l'Institut de Linguistique de Louvain, 1977).

4. Henry Dorchy, <u>Histoire des Belges</u> (Brussels: A. de Boeck, 1982).

5. For bibliographic references on this major issue, see Verdoodt, <u>Bibliographie sur le probleme linguistique belge</u> and <u>Les problemes des groupes linguistiques en Belgique</u>.

6. See Verdoodt, <u>Bibliographie sur le probleme linguistique belge</u>; Francois Bouillon, "L'influence du probleme linguistique sure les partis politiques tradionnels en Belgique depuis 1968," thesis, Paris, 1979; and Dorchy, <u>Histoire des Belges</u>.

7. Lagasse, <u>La contre-reforme de l'etat</u>.

8. A. Grisay, <u>Rendement de l'enseignement de la langue maternelle en Belgique francophone</u>, in the series Recherche en education (Brussels: Direction generale de l'Organisation des Etudes, Ministere de l'Education Nationale et de la Culture Francaise, 1974).

9. For bibliographic references on the conflict over higher education, see Verdoodt, <u>Bibliographie sur le probleme linguistique belge</u> and <u>Les problemes des groupes linguistiques en Belgique</u>.

10. R. Baeten and A. Verdoodt, "L'interet des eleves de l'enseignement secondarie belge envers une autre langue nationale: Est-il reciproque a travers tout le pays?" <u>Recherches Sociologiques</u> 14, no. 1 (1983):75-93.

11. Ibid.

12. Ibid.

13. See prognosis, which is still relevant, in Lorwin, "Linguistic Pluralism and Political Tension in Modern Belgium."

14. Lagasse, <u>La contre-reforme de l'etat</u>.

15. Ibid.

13

INTER-ETHNIC RELATIONS AND EDUCATION IN YUGOSLAVIA

Val D. Rust

Yugoslavia provides a rich setting for the study of inter-ethnic and interrepublic relations. The country was created after World War II out of the ruins of a system that had disintegrated at the beginning of the war. The core of the new Yugoslavia was a disciplined partisan organization that spawned the idea of brotherhood and unity, which had been destroyed in the bitterness of the interethnic civil war that had raged between the world wars. The partisans were able to establish the beginnings of a multination state, but the task of consolidating and governing that state has been formidable.

It is declared to be one nation; but a multitude of languages (including Cryllic and Latin alphabets), religions (mainly Roman Catholic, Orthodox, and Muslim), as well as nations and nationalities exist. The nations include Croatians, Macedonians, Montenegrins, Muslims, Serbs, and Slovenians. Nationalities are constitutionally designated as those national groups whose parent nations are outside Yugoslavia. Most of these people come from the populations of the seven countries that border Yugoslavia (Italy, Austria, Hungary, Romania, Bulgaria, Greece, and Albania).

Structurally, the country is divided into six republics and two autonomous political provinces (Vojvodina and Kosovo). An important feature of this arrangement is the extent to which nations and nationalities reside in particular republics. We find that 97 percent of Slovenes live in Slovenia, 78 percent of Croats live in Croatia, 85 percent of Muslims live in

Bosnia-Herzegovinia, 96 percent of Macedonians live in Macedonia, 70 percent of Montenegrins live in Montenegro, and 74 percent of Serbians live in Serbia. The republic with other heavy concentrations is Serbia, where 90 percent of all Hungarians and 76 percent of all Albanians reside. However, Serbia accommodates these populations in the two autonomous provinces, with the Hungarians living in Vojvodina and the Albanians living in Kosovo.[1]

In spite of these divisions, the country emerged after World War II as a unified entity, mainly through the remarkable efforts of the communist leaders, who had been able to create -- with international recognition -- a total and all-pervasive political monopoly. The system that the partisans created exemplified type D in the typology proposed by La Belle and White.[2] The cultural axis of the typology consists of various groups that are segmented in a horizontal relationship because no single group is dominant. The structural axis of that typology is also horizontal and consists of a unified political apparatus. In Yugoslavia immediately after World War II, both state and party were highly centralized and hierarchical. Constitutionally, the republics were formally designated as sovereign possessors only of residual powers, while the real formal powers were vested in the federal government, specifically in the Federal Assembly's presidium. The single political party, the Communist party of Yugoslavia, exercised a conscious and deliberate policy of "democratic centralism."[3]

Such a centralized structure was necessary in the early postwar stages. There was little by way of natural cultural forces to bind the country together. Some sentiment toward reconciliation of national differences arose out of the threat of foreign domination, but it would not be unfair to suggest that the country was bound together mainly by the strong arm of its communist leaders. In other words, the major integrative mechanism was coercion as defined by La Belle and White.[4] In spite of this, a striking aspect of the postwar period was the relative absence of terror and violence. In fact, the only episode of terrorist-type action came immediately after the Tito-Stalin break in 1948 and was specifically designed to purge the Russian agents and supporters from the party.[5]

We must keep in mind, however, that the guerrilla war during the Nazi occupation period was as much a civil war as it was a war of resistance. During that time, 11 percent of the population was exterminated, and a significant portion of these people were members of groups that posed an internal threat to the partisans. If violence was held at a minimum in the early stages of the new Yugoslavia, the threat of internal military and police action was ever-present and pervasive.

If the threat of coercion was the dominant integrating mechanism, it was also accompanied by an ideal of brotherhood and interdependence. Rusinow, drawing from the slogan of the American Revolution, maintains that the leaders of the various national groups recognized that if they did not hang together they would end up hanging each other.[6] This awareness was accompanied by a deep conviction of unity based on community precepts. Marx, Lenin, and even Stalin connected nationalism with the so-called "bourgeois-capitalist" stage of historical development. They saw the proletarian movement as being inherently international in nature, and they maintained that with the passage of political and economic institutions to a socialist form, nationalism, with its divisive values, would be transcended.

Tito and his followers also believed, or at least claimed, that Yugoslavia was to lose its segmented form, which was seen as arising from the social division of labor in the epoch of capitalism. The people were expected to evolve a common Yugoslav consciousness. It was in this context that Tito would blandly declare that the "national question" had been settled.[7] However, the romantic view of the communist leaders was soon ruptured by a series of economic, social, and political events that required them to back away from their simplistic ideological position of unity and work to evolve a novel form of communism.

The very policies that the regime adopted in an attempt to contribute to a sense of integration seemed to have their shadow side, which set in motion countervailing attitudes. For example, the leaders attempted to forge a sense of unity by initiating a program of economic redistribution. The northern areas, economically dominant, were called on to assist the republics of Montenegro, Macedonia, and Bosnia-Herzegovinia and the province of Kosovo. This course of action, however, led to expressions of discontent on the part of the north, which was expected to give up a portion of its resources.

Even the idea of a unified Yugoslav culture created strong resentment. The nations and nationalities saw the idea as little more than a covert attempt on the part of the largest ethnic group, the Serbians, which constitutes approximately 40 percent of the population, to reestablish hegemony over the rest of the country. Yugoslavianism was identified with Serbia to the point that the notion had little currency with the other groups.

Specific events also contributed to a breakdown of centrism. These included the Tito-Stalin break in 1948 and the eventual ideological adjustments that the leaders were compelled to engage in. As a part of the break came a four-year economic blockade from Eastern Europe, which forced Yugoslavia to normalize relations with the West. Such an action reoriented trade and led to a network with the so-called democratic countries of the Western world that provided technical and industrial support. It also brought with it economic and political ideas that would facilitate a search for ideological alternatives. This search spawned the idea of self-management, which soon became the heart of Yugoslavian socialism.

The Marxist principle of self-management, with its antibureaucratic and antistate implications, allowed the Yugoslav leaders to remain true to Marx while initiating a radical alternative to the Russian version of Marxism. The basic idea of self-management is that "all those who work in an enterprise -- a factory, a business, a school -- share as equals in the authority and power of running it."[8]

Events such as those cited above forced the leaders to abandon the idea of Yugoslavism and accept the reality of a genuine federalism; a new constitution was ratified in 1964 to formalize that reality. The process of decentralization did not abate, however, as other events precipitated even further segmentation. The so-called Rankovic affair in 1965 wrenched the secret police out of its protected role and placed it under public control. Thus the threat of coercion and violence by the political elites was destroyed and signaled a formal declaration of respect for the autonomy of the individual.

The Croatian nationalist movement in the early 1970s symbolized a further step toward open and unrestrained feelings of nationalism and a corresponding declining identification of the nation-state. The process of accommodation by the centrist government was essentially completed with the 1974 constitution, which gave the central government little more than the role of orchestrating the interests of the composite republics/provinces. That constitution specifies that the central government assumes no special interests of its own and works simply to synthesize and regularize the interests of the republics and autonomous provinces. In fact, the practice of "mutual veto" has been incorporated into the federal system to ensure that no single nation or coalition of nations will be able to impose its will on the other groups.

The system that has emerged is one in which cultural boundaries now coincide by and large with structural boundaries. Because of the traditional cultural animosities that have existed, one would expect that a superstructure somewhat akin to the postwar arrangement would be necessary to counteract the centrifugal forces at work. Because no powerful centralized government exists, we must explore how integrative forces are maintained. Of course there are those who have claimed that the only glue holding the state together was the charisma of Tito. It has been predicted that his death would break those bonds, and it would only be a matter of time before the state blew apart. A brief span of time has passed since his death in 1980, but from all indications the system has maintained its viability; ethnic antagonism is held in check, and the government appears to be stable and orderly.

Among the factors contributing to this stability is the existence of the Communist Party of Yugoslavia. It is committed to a unified nation-state and is prepared to resort to any means to ensure that it remains unified, including coercion or the threat of coercion. For example, the party did not hesitate to employ armed troops and tanks during the nationalist demonstrations of Croatia in 1971 and Kosovo in 1981.

However, force alone is now inadequate to bind the state together. The Yugoslav leaders claim that their version of federalism has been responsible for diffusing interethnic distrust and rivalry. A claim that such arrangements facilitate integration would likely not find support by analysts of conflict regulation in divided societies, who feel that federalism and semiautonomous units are inherently centrifugal rather than centripetal in nature.[9] However, the mechanism that the Yugoslavs have developed may be specific enough to defy that generalization.

In moving from a condition of state ownership to so-called social ownership, Yugoslavia has created a country whose institutions and property simultaneously are nobody's and everybody's.[10] The system survives only if everybody assumes a joint responsibility to work, to participate in management and decision making, and to appropriate the means of individual and joint consumption. Yugoslavia has been partially successful in obtaining such a sense of responsibility. The degree of citizen participation in the economy and the government is

staggering. A recent Organization for Economic Cooperation and Development report indicated, for example, that
fully 7 percent of the province of Vojvodina (140,000 out of 2
million) were engaged as delegates in the four levels of government (commune, city or region, province, federation). Because most of these posts are restricted to a single two-year
term, it becomes necessary for most responsible citizens to
serve at one time or another in one or more offices.[11]

Participation is even more demanding in the economy.
The fundamental institution around which the economy is
structured is the so-called Basic Organization of Associated
Labor (BOAL). This is typically a small firm, business, or
subunit of a major firm. Every worker is expected to
participate in basic decisions regarding the BOAL to which he
or she belongs. The BOAL sends delegates to the next higher
organizational level, called the Organization of Associated
Labor, which in turn sends delegates to the Composite
Organization of Associated Labor. In a 1968 survey of firms
employing a total of 750,000 workers, it was found that
288,641 workers, or 38.5 percent, were involved in some form
of management.[12]

An important rule of the decision-making process is that a
delegate is bound to represent precisely the views and policies
of the unit that elected him or her. If compromise is necessary, then the delegate must obtain approval of the unit to
which he or she reports. In other words, higher units do not
dictate to the lower but serve as vehicles through which the
BOAL work to arrive at some operating consensus. Power re-
sides with the BOAL and even the individual. This arrangement replicates the political structure where the higher bodies
facilitate and organize the interests of the local units but are
unable to dictate to them.

A mechanism exists whereby the common interests of all
groups are identified and implemented. In the process, at
least in theory, alienation is reduced and a sense of brotherhood and responsibility for the total economy and the broader
politic of the nation-state is fostered. This mutual responsibility plays itself out in such a way that decisions at the local
level are refined and abstracted as they work their way
through the various levels of decision making until they reach
the federal level. Once agreement is obtained, these constitute boundaries and working agreements that must be adhered
to throughout the entire system. In other words, the local
level is constrained to function in accordance with the consen-

sus agreements that it contributed to at the higher levels. We see that a complex mixture of coercion, interdependence, and consensus has come to serve as an integrative mechanism in Yugoslav society.

In the remainder of this chapter we shall concentrate on specific social and educational issues to demonstrate how these mechanisms manifest themselves through the system. At this point, it is necessary to draw attention to a weakness in the La Belle and White typology. The authors attempt to accommodate all interethnic relations in a dyadic framework. In the case of Yugoslavia that becomes impossible, for two reasons.

First, no single republic is strong enough to force the others to accept its wishes. Coalitions are necessary, and the various republics and autonomous provinces align themselves in different constellations depending on the incident or issue. For example, Slovenia joined with Croatia against Serbia during the early 1960s as they succeeded in bringing about greater decentralization of the Communist party. However, after 1969, Slovenia sided with Serbia against Croatia because that republic's demands for decentralization appeared to go too far and signaled a breakup of the nation-state altogether. It would be inappropriate to look at only two groups when balance of power alliances shift from time to time.

Second, as we move from community to republic to nation-state, the relationships of any one ethnic group shift radically. On the one hand, Slovenia, for example, must accommodate itself to certain communities within the borders of its republic where the populations are not dominated by Slovenes but by Italians and Hungarians. On the other hand, Slovenia must deal with quite different national ethnic groups as it interacts as a republic.

We must, therefore, focus our discussion on more than a simple dyadic relationship. We shall concentrate mainly on the relationship of the Slovenes with other groups in order to simplify the discussion. We turn initially to the major social issue in Yugoslavia, that of language policy.

LANGUAGE POLICY

We are able to gain a keen sense of the way a nationality's policy works itself out at all levels of consideration by focusing on the language issue. Because of the mutual veto power of each nation and nationality, it has only been possible to establish a consensus about language policy by giving the special language of each ethnic group full recognition and giving it equal status with all other languages.

The language policy has been formulated in the federal constitution from a negative and a positive perspective. On the positive side, Article 247 guarantees each nationality "the right freely to use its language and alphabet, to develop its culture. . . ." On the negative side, Article 170 stipulates that "propagating or practicing national inequality and incitement of national, racial, or religious hatred and intolerance shall be unconstitutional and punishable." Although language is not specified, language choice is clearly implied, and any acts to create inequality with regard to cultural factors such as language are prohibited.

At the republic level, these same conditions hold. In fact, identical wording is generally used in the republic constitutions when referring to language policy. However, the republic constitutions make specific reference to the populations residing in their areas. Tollefson has made a detailed study of Slovenia, and we shall rely on his study for illustrative purposes.[13] The Slovene constitution gives special attention to the sizable Italian and Hungarian populations in the republic: "In areas inhabited by members of the Italian and Hungarian nationalities . . . the Italian and Hungarian languages are guaranteed equality with the Slovenian language" (Article 250). This same article not only guarantees equality but it requires the communes and work associations to develop more detailed policies that are consistent with the policy of equality but that fit local conditions.

The communal statutes of the city of Piran in Slovenia, for example, where 3,000 of its 5,000 inhabitants are Italian, reiterate the general principles spelled out in the republic and federal constitutions, but then declare that "citizens of the Italian nationality shall freely use their language in the Communal Assembly and its bodies, throughout public and social life, in discharging public functions and other public duties, as well as in exercising their legal rights and in using their legal benefits" (Article 64). Further articles of the statutes stipulate that all official documents are to be issued in Italian and Slovenian (Article 70); that all civil servants are expected to use Italian when dealing with Italians (Article 72); and that all public notices, materials for voters meetings, printed forms in the registry office, revenue office, health service, and social insurance service, industrial safety and social protection service, and the communal court are to be bilingual (Articles 73 and 74). Additional articles stipulate that official stamps and seals, traffic and place-name signs, and all public notice boards and kiosks must be in Slovenian and Italian.

The language policy outlined above illustrates how Yugoslav policy is designed at all levels. Policy deliberations take place at all levels of government, and the policies become more and more abstracted as the policy moves from the local to the regional to the federal level. Even though language issues penetrate almost every sphere of social activity, we have not mentioned language issues in specific institutions. However, we will describe how this comes to play in schools in our discussion of educational policies.

Of the six educational policy areas that La Belle and White highlight, four have been chosen as a focus: language policies in schools, degree of school centralization, structure of schooling and curriculum, and access to education.

Language Policy in Schools

The schools follow the general language principles laid down by the republic and federal constitutions, which means that members of nations and nationalities have a right to school instruction conducted in their own languages. It is at the local level that implementation takes specific form. For illustrative purposes, the community of Piran in Slovenia will once again be referred to. The commune statutes name four schools (of a total of ten) where Italian is the medium of instruction. These schools are expected to provide an educational program equivalent to those using Slovenian, not only with Italian-speaking instructors but textbooks, workbooks, and general literature written in Italian.

A similar story could be told about some 20 language groups throughout the country. For example, only four schools exist for the Rutherian population of Vojvodina; yet a full curriculum is provided children in that national group.[14] Even in the economically underdeveloped province of Kosovo, education is provided to the Turkish population on an equal footing with the two other nationalities, even though the Turks constitute only 3 percent of the population.[15]

Still another aspect of educational language policy has to do with bilingualism and multilingualism. In communities with mixed groups, it is taken for granted that the groups learn each other's language. Thus, in Piran, Slovene students are required to study Italian, while Italian students are required to study Slovenian. This policy appears to be fully enforced and functioning.[16]

When speaking of language provisions, included are not only the language of instruction but reading materials as well. Textbooks are controlled at the republic/province level, and officials jealously protect this right. A few textbook editions are used in schools in several republics and autonomous provinces, but, as a rule, they are written and published in each republic/province. In each republic/province, a textbook publishing institute is set up to accomplish the task. The institute itself is rather small because professional experts are contracted to write the texts.

The procedure used in the development of a textbook is as follows. General decisions are made by the Educational Council, which is a body of experts appointed by the republic/provincial assembly. Significantly, the Educational Council's authority is restricted to professional and pedagogical issues rather than political and cultural issues. The council charges the Textbook Publishing Institute to determine the specific contents of a textbook, invite bids, assess manuscript proposals, award contracts to authors, contract publishing houses to do the printing, and handle distribution.[17] Occasionally, more than one text will be approved so that schools do have limited choice. Every school is provided a full set of textbooks in the language of instruction, and the price for all textbooks is uniform, in spite of the great differences in their costs of production.

Yugoslav schools also have a tradition of having "books for obligatory school reading."[18] These books must be translated into some 20 languages and printed using appropriate alphabets so that all children may have access to them. Beyond these readings, general literature materials become problematic.

The national commitment to language equality is enormous; however, it is generally interpreted to mean that the proportion of titles of publications approximates the proportion of the total population of a particular nationality. For example, Italians constitute 0.2 percent of the population of Slovenia; therefore, the republic satisfies equity criteria if 0.2 percent of the titles published are in Italian.[19] Obviously, the minorities are greatly disadvantaged by this definition. We must hasten to add that literature sources from Italy compensate for this disadvantage, giving young people extensive foreign literature.

Degree of School Centralization

Schools and universities are organized into self-management communities in a similar fashion as are the BOALs in business and industry, with one major difference. A distinction has been drawn between productive enterprises and social service enterprises. The productive enterprises contribute directly to the production of economic goods, while social service enterprises are considered to be consumption enterprises, mainly because they are dependent on production enterprises for operating resources. It is therefore reasoned that the productive enterprises should participate in some level of decisionmaking regarding them. Thus there not only is a workers Council (the BOAL in education), consisting of workers in the school, but there is also a Governing Council, which includes workers and citizens of the community and parents. At the secondary and tertiary levels, the Governing Councils also include representatives of local work organizations and students. The Governing Council deals with more general issues, while the Workers Council deals with operating policy of the school.[20]

Educational policy emerges from the local level and is not dictated from above. There is a minimal centralized national activity in education, although some does take place. For example, because educational finances are locally determined, great disparity exists in the ability of some communities, regions, and republics/provinces to support education. The federal government maintains a grant-in-aid program as an expression of "solidarity," whereby funds are channeled to Bosnia-Herzegovinia, Macedonia, Montenegro, and Kosovo. These units then have control over their allocation to all social services, although education typically receives about one-third of these funds.[21]

The impact of federal funds is substantial. For example, the province of Kosovo has a per capita social income that is one-third that of the Yugoslav average and one-sixth that of Slovenia, but the difference in educational funds is only approximately half.[22] While this disparity remains a problem, federal support tends to cushion the difference.

Still another role played by the federal government is that of coordination. In the last decade an Inter-Republican Committee system has emerged in an attempt "to coordinate reforms among the federal units and to strive for a degree of synchronization."[23] In 1974 the Inter-Republican/Provincial Commission for Educational Reform was established; however, its efforts have had negligible consequences. The commission did submit a proposal for a system of uniform standards in teacher certification, and there has been some discussion about standardization of textbooks, but these discussions have never reached the level of consensus necessary for policy to be established. In fact, there is resistance on the commission itself to work toward greater standardization. The president of the commission cautioned in 1981 that "the tendency of creating some uniform system . . . is right now a greater problem than the problem of existing differences."[24] Indeed, in spite of the decentralized system, a high degree of educational uniformity exists throughout the country.

Two major factors appear to explain this consensus. First, just as the rest of society was centralized immediately after World War II, so was the educational system. All schools were declared state institutions, and the entire system was "rigidly centralized." Although the system has now become highly decentralized, a residue of the former mentality toward some central direction in education persists to this day.[25] Second, certain Yugoslavs claim that a major reason this consensus has evolved is that education has become a profession and has thereby alienated itself from an autonomous practice and theory, so that local cultural variations are largely overwhelmed in favor of more generally recognized professional standards.[26] In other words, education may have been able to extricate itself from cultural linkages to the point that it drives itself, rather than being driven by cultural norms.

This professionalization is reflected in the administrative mechanism of education at the republic level where professionals are appointed by the Educational Council to recommend for approval educational standards, textbooks, teaching aids and equipment, and provisions for preservice and inservice teacher training. The republic link with the local level comes mainly through the Institute for Promoting Education and Training and the corps of inspectors. These bodies consist of professionals who evaluate, give advice, and share information throughout the republic. Great deference is given to these professionals especially at the lower levels of the system, where the structure of schooling and the curriculum that is provided in that structure are almost completely centrally determined within each republic/province.

Structure of Schooling and Curriculum

At the elementary level, all children are expected to attend school in two phases. Phase one lasts four years, during which time the children have a single teacher who teaches all subjects. Phase two lasts another four years, but the children are exposed to subject specialists. The curriculum is centrally determined and consists of a long list of required subjects, which focus on basic skills, preparation for secondary school, and vocational training. While the languages of instruction are different, the curricular programs are rather uniform across republics and autonomous provinces, which is contrary to the condition predicted by La Belle and White.[27]

Secondary education represents a further four years' experience. The first two years consist of a continuation of a common required curriculum, mainly general studies. The last two years are intended to be occupationally oriented. The common curriculum at the secondary level remains rather conventional and reflects the traditional curriculum that one might expect professional educators to advocate. However, great diversity of schooling from community to community is found within the vocational education programs of secondary schools. This condition is also contrary to La Belle and White's prediction that secondary and higher education reflect more universal content and practices and can be easily explained.

A central feature of Yugoslav education is an insistence that all students learn about and gain practical experience in the world of work. The aim is that students leave school with some work qualification. Self-management comes to play mainly in that the local community defines what vocational training programs should be adopted. Such a policy has led to radically different types of vocational education configurations throughout the country. It is thought that by allowing the local community to define training, the vocational skills of school leavers would be better matched with the needs of business and industry. Major problems have emerged relating to the ability of students to gain access not only to desired vocational training programs but to all forms of higher education.

Access to Education

While educational access possibilities of all ethnic groups appear to be functioning well at the primary educational level, problems are found at the secondary level, especially with regard to vocational education programs. At the tertiary level, these problems become acute. We wish to elaborate on these problems.

Because of the extensive participation of the population in decision making, self-interest groups are typically inclined to make decisions reflecting narrow rather than general and more long-range viewpoints.[28] Consequently, training is often oriented to immediate, job-related needs. Even where interest groups are more enlightened, vocational training in the more remote areas encounters additional problems. While desired training assignments are easily satisfied where there are many industrial enterprises, young people face restricted options in communities where there is limited industry or where a community relies on a single industry, especially where these industries are conducted by a single ethnic group, as is often the case. Those who do not speak the appropriate language, who do not identify with the ethnic background of the firm in question, or who are not inclined to learn skills in that industry are extremely hampered.

One way in which communities attempt to overcome the obstacles presented by limited vocational choice is through exchange arrangements; guarantees are even made that vocational training will be conducted, if possible, in the native tongue. Obviously, that is not always possible.

Because of the costs of higher education, it is impossible to provide studies in an equal manner, at least as far as language is concerned. It might be argued that because nationalities must learn a national language, they are equipped to engage in higher education in that language. Tollefson provides shocking data on Italian-speaking students in Slovenia at the university, the art academy, and the theological faculty. In 1974-75, only 13 students, out of a total of 14,347, were Italian. This represents 0.09 percent of the student population, and Piran is an area where residents tend to proceed to higher education more than people from other areas of the republic.[29] The difficulty certain nationalities have in proceeding to higher education in the more depressed areas of Yugoslavia needs no elaboration.

The underrepresentation of certain nationalities in higher education has potentially explosive implications. The focus here shall be only on its implications for qualified teachers. Teacher training has been distinctly different for the first phase of elementary school, the second phase of elementary school, and for secondary school. First-phase elementary teachers have, until recently, been trained at special secondary schools called teacher training schools. Second-phase elementary teachers are typically trained at teacher colleges; and the secondary teachers are typically trained at the university. These standards have recently been shifted in that teacher training schools are being abolished, with aspirations to raise the qualifications of all teacher education to a university standard.

It is questionable if an adequate number of teachers belonging to minority nationalities can be trained who will qualify for the higher standards, if for no other reason than that they will have to do the studying in a language other than their own. The problem becomes even more acute when we realize that the teacher-pupil ratios are extremely low for most nationalities, which necessitates a higher proportion of the population to be teachers than with national groups. For example, the teacher-pupil ratio in elementary schools for most nationalities was as follows: Albanian (1:25), Bulgarian (1:12), Czech (1:12), Hungarian (1:15), Italian (1:6), Romanian (1:12), Rutherian (1:14), Slovak (1:17), and Turkish.[30]

A positive consequence of upgrading standards is the additional time available to deal with crucial attitudes about mutual understanding of different groups. Some evidence is available that indicates that the contents of teacher education programs are contributing to an attitude of "equality, brotherhood, and unity," but the record is far from consistent.[31] Some teacher training programs are now incorporating units of study designed to address these issues[32] and to help teachers develop attitudes that reflect national priorities.

CONCLUSION

Type D relationships are based on the notion of cultural segmentation with structural commonality. The evolution of

Yugoslav society during the past three decades indicates a great deal of structural segmentation as well. Whereas Yugoslavia maintained a centrist government in the years just after World War II, it has decentralized its political structure to the point that the main political units coincide largely with cultural, ethnic boundaries. The bonds that now hold the nation together are tenuous and complex; they relate mainly to the communist ideology and particularly to self-management practices.

Educational policies toward the various ethnic groups evolve out of a consensus orientation among the various groups. Educational policies are arrived at through a cumbersome decision-making process, which has only been able to function because of a genuine regard for certain cultural factors, particularly language. Ethnic groups appear to be disadvantaged mainly because of limited resources rather than overt attempts to discriminate. This is particularly so at the secondary and higher education levels of the system, where separate and equal programs in the appropriate languages become prohibitively expensive. The educational programs themselves do not appear to have a strong ethnic bias.

The La Belle and White model provides a valuable framework for assessing interethnic relations in Yugoslavia and their role in educational policy. It is especially valuable in providing a framework in which empirical data can be meaningfully sorted. La Belle and White are aware that the empirical data that were available to them from secondary sources were insufficient to substantiate some of their claims.[33] Even so, most of the type D projections that they made about educational policies have held firm, though a few of their claims are not accurate in the case of Yugoslavia. For example, the authors suggest that primary education programs would be culturally related in type D relationships. While language differences are addressed in Yugoslavia, the programs themselves appear to be unusually uniform from ethnic group to ethnic group.

We have identified two weaknesses in the model itself. First, the model is structured on the assumption that education is a dependent variable. That is, policies regarding education are dictated by political, economic, and cultural factors. Our interpretation of education in Yugoslavia is most meaningful when we accept the point of view that education as a professional field has been able to extricate itself especially from the more subtle cultural ties. It has a life of its own and may override, to some degree, the external factors that La Belle and White stress.

Second, the La Belle and White typology deals only with dyadic relationships. It is not possible to use that frame in a country such as Yugoslavia, where ethnic relationships shift depending on the administrative level under consideration and depending on the particular ethnic alignment that is at work on a given issue.

NOTES

1. D. Petrovic, "National Structure of the Yugoslav Population," Yugoslav Review 14, no. 2 (1973):1-22.

2. Thomas J. La Belle and Peter White, "Education and Multiethnic Integration: An Intergroup-Relations Typology," Comparative Education Review 24, no. 2 (June 1980):155-73.

3. D. Rusinow, The Yugoslav Experiment: 1948-1974 (Berkeley: University of California Press, 1977), p. 18.

4. La Belle and White, "Education and Multiethnic Integration," p. 156.

5. B. D. Denitch, The Legitimation of a Revolution: The Yugoslav Case (New Haven, Conn.: Yale University Press, 1976), p. 50.

6. Rusinow, The Yugoslav Experiment, p. 6.

7. J. B. Tito, "Concerning the National Question and Socialist Patriotism," Speech at Ljubljana, November 16, 1948, In J. B. Tito, Selected Speeches and Articles, 1941-1961 (Zagreb: Naprijed, 1963), p. 97.

8. Organization for Economic Cooperation and Development (OECD), Reviews of National Policies for Education: Yugoslavia (Paris, 1981), p. 37.

9. E. A. Nordlinger, Conflict Regulation in Divided Societies (Cambridge, Mass.: Harvard Studies in International Affairs, 1972).

10. N. N. Soljan, "The Concept of Self-Management and the Socio-Economic Background of Decision-Making in Education: The Yugoslav Model," Comparative Education 14, no. 1 (March 1978):66.

11. OECD, Reviews of National Policies for Education: Yugoslavia, p. 42.

12. D. Gorupic and I. Paj, Worker's Self-Management in Yugoslav Undertakings (Zagreb: Ekonomiski Institut Zagreb, 1970), pp. 206-07.

13.   Articles in the constitution are quoted in J. W. Tollefson, The Language Situation and Language Policy in Slovenia (Washington, D.C.: University Press of America, 1981).

14.   OECD, Reviews of National Policy for Education: Yugoslavia, p. 60.

15.   Ibid., p. 98.

16.   Tollefson, The Language Situation, p. 196.

17.   OECD, Reviews of National Policy for Education: Yugoslavia, p. 99.

18.   M. Knezevic, "The System of Primary Education," Yugoslav Survey 23, no. 2 (May 1982):101.

19.   Tollefson, The Language Situation, p. 204.

20.   Soljan, "The Concept of Self-Management," p. 67.

21.   S. Ristanovic, "Forms of Solidarity in Education," Yugoslav Survey 23, no. 3 (August 1982):97-188.

22.   OECD, Reviews of National Policy for Education: Yugoslavia, p. 121.

23.   P. Ramet, "Inter-republican Relations in Contemporary Yugoslavia," Ph.D. dissertation, University of California, Los Angeles, 1981, p. 190.

24.   Ibid., p. 191.

25.   OECD, Reviews of National Policy for Education: Yugoslavia, p. 115.

26.   Soljan, "The Concept of Self-Management."

27.   La Belle and White, "Education and Multiethnic Integration," p. 170.

28.   F. C. Kintzer, "Educational Reforms in Yugoslavia," Educational Record 59, no. 1 (1978):95.

29.   Tollefson, The Language Situation, p. 198.

30.   S. Peter, "Teaching Staff in Elementary and Secondary School," Yugoslav Survey 20, no. 2 (1979):155.

31.   M. Palav, "The Personality of the Teacher in the Realization of Educational Functions in Our Multi-National Community," in Contemporary Concepts and Perspectives of Teacher Training, summaries of papers submitted, published for a symposium held at Sombor, 1978, p. 59.

32.   D. Djuric, "The Psychological Pre-Service Training of Teachers for Mutual Understanding of Young People in a Multinational Community," in Contemporary Concepts and Perspectives of Teacher Training, p. 56.

33.   La Belle and White, "Education and Multiethnic Integration," p. 173.

14

CONCLUSION

John N. Hawkins, Thomas J. La Belle, and Peter S. White

In the preceding chapters the authors have discussed the relationship between education and intergroup relations in each of their case countries in accord with the typology presented in Chapter 1. In this concluding chapter we will review each of the four types presented and discuss the individual national studies in light of the analysis presented by each author.

We first turn, very briefly, to some of the specific educational policies found in the countries of our four intergroup types. The discussion will illustrate, first, how these policies reflect the centripetal/centrifugal tendencies and integrative mechanisms of each type. The second aspect of the discussion will be a comparison across types, focusing on those policy areas that most clearly highlight the differential influence of a particular intergroup context.

TYPE A

The vertically structured type A relationships, where ethnicity and socioeconomic participation are almost synonymous, can be generally characterized by centrifugal structural policies designed to keep distance between the dominant and subordinate populations. South African apartheid is the obvious example, but the nearly complete lack of infrastructural links (for example, roads, telecommunications, medical services) between Haiti's rural Creole/black areas and its essentially mulatto urban areas functions almost as effectively in this regard. Although subordinate populations may seek greater opportunity for participation, as with the blacks of South Africa, any such movement depends on dominant group acceptance. The structural centrifugality is often accompanied by cultural centripetality, indicating a subordinate demand for full assimilation rather than acculturation alone as the price for greater subordinate group participation in the society. In both Peru and Haiti the between-group barriers are so broad that geographic mobility, as well as cultural change (language, dress, and the like) are required for the subordinate individual's assimilation to be recognized.[1] As to mechanisms for societal integration, it is clear that except for token efforts at using consensus and interdependence, coercion predominates in enabling the dominant group in type A societies to continue its control over the integrative process.

The overall power differential, which has enabled the dominant group to establish socioeconomic lines that parallel ethnicity, is apparent in the combination of centripetal and centrifugal educational policies. Control of schools in all of our type A relations, for example, is vested in the central government, and access to all levels of schooling, as well as the patterns of articulation and tracking, coincide with ethnic group boundaries. Specifically, subordinate groups have less opportunity to enter schools and less chance of competing successfully in them. The geographic distribution of school sites works against the Creoles in Haiti and the blacks in South Africa, and a similar concentration of schools in urban areas has much the same negative effect on Indian enrollment in Peru. These initial structural barriers are often compounded within the few subordinate group schools by lack of materials, poorly trained personnel, and a hidden tracking toward low-wage skills, although Kinberg notes in Chapter 2 the tracking is not hidden.[2]

Haiti is a classic example of how these various groups are revealed in the differential access to education by the various groups in society. In 1961 only 25 percent of all elementary-age children were enrolled in school. And despite the concentration of the Haitian population in rural areas (90 percent), urban elementary students (overwhelmingly mulatto) outnumbered rural elementary students 3 to 2.[3] By 1967 the ratio was even more imbalanced; further, 60 percent of rural enrollment was in kindergarten alone, while 1 percent of rural enrollment was in the sixth year of primary school.[4] At the secondary level rural Creole students were at an even greater disadvantage. Of the approximately 70 general high schools, none was in a rural area; only 2 of the 105 secondary units (technical, agricultural, and so on) in Haiti were in the rural, that is, Creole, area.[5] Enrollment at that level means, almost by definition, prior residence in an urban area or the ability and motivation to move there. Creoles, then, are excluded. In fact, as Layne notes in Chapter 4, Haiti is a more strict case of verticality than is suggested by our typical type A society: "more like an old colonial show with new management."

Such policies in a type A context act to exclude most subordinate group members and to channel them back into the low-status occupational sphere. That is, schooling is often a dead end, terminating at a level or a track that leads directly back into the kind of closed occupations that are characteristic of the subordinate status. For the few academically successful subordinate group individuals, however, the same policies are clearly centripetal; success in school provides a confirmation of passage into the dominant group's cultural and structural circle.

School curricula and the language of instruction also evidence both centripetal and centrifugal tendencies in type A cases. In Peru, for example, the content and materials reflect a strong bias toward urban, upper, and upper-middle class experience and interests.[6] The Indian student lacks any familiar item to "grab onto" as he or she enters school. In much the same way, the most common complaint concerning Haitian education is its highly "classical" (humanities and social services) emphasis and its complete reliance on French as the language of instruction.[7] Since 90 percent of the population speaks no French (Creole and French are mutually unintelligible), the rural Creole and urban poor are at an immediate, and usually permanent disadvantage. In reality it is the source of the curriculum in a type A relationship that renders it a tool of continued intergroup separation; reflective as it is of only one experience in a heterogeneous society, the "centripetal" school content selects students according to their ability to grasp superordinate styles. It thus eliminates and channels the vast majority of subordinate group members into positions reserved for "failures" and the "noneducated."

Language of instruction is the final area of school policies in which our examples of type A intergroup relationships seem to indicate the strength of centrifugal tendencies in the maintenance of the unequal status quo. South Africa's Bantu Education Act requires that the vernacular be the medium of instruction throughout schooling. By learning a special curricula through the native tongue, the African child is exposed to little of the outside world and only enough English and Afrikaans to follow instructions as workers.[8] Cutting the Bantu off in this way also closes the door to social mobility except as it occurs in the tribal social system or at the lowest levels of dominant white society.[9] The monopolistic and exclusionary educational policies in South Africa may be tempered, however, if, as Kinberg suggests in Chapter 2, continued expansion of the economy necessitates increased black admission into the dominant power structure. Economic expansion needs then would create increased educational opportunities for blacks, thus making the access issue more complex than it has been in the past. Kinberg's study, however, confirms the cultural and structural segmentation suggested by the typology. By relying on one language -- that of the superordinate group -- the Peruvian and Haitian schools also reinforce the position of the superordinate group as a cultural model and thus act as a standardizing mechanism within a heterogeneous society. The overall effort, then, is one of the dominant control of the source and nature of educational experiences for the subordinates, holding out only limited possibility of individual assimilation while supporting a social system based on subordinate group economic and political dependency.

TYPE B

The vertical hierarchy of the type A society is tempered somewhat in the type B intergroup relationship, where ethnic dominance remains intact but structural permeability is more prevalent. In a type B context like Japan, New Zealand, or Britain, acculturation alone may provide the necessary entree to participation in the subordinate system because of the overlap between ethnicity and socioeconomic position. The culture question in Japan is somewhat more complex than suggested by the ideal type B. As Hawkins notes in Chapter 7, neither the Burakumin nor the Japanese minority consider the Burakumin as a separate ethnic group (although some minor cultural differences have been observed). Yet both groups like to think of the Burakumin as somehow "special," in either a negative or positive sense. This raises the issue of how caste fits into a type B situation and is an area for future research. In general, however, the subordinate group individual may retain his or her ethnic identity while occupying a higher status role or job. Overall, the dominant group in type A relationships evinces a generally centripetal tendency in its educational policies as it seeks to incorporate the subordinate populations into the social structure and into superordinate cultural patterns. This centripetal bias is characterized by a reliance on consensus and interdependence for societal integration. Again, however, it is the dominant group that controls the basic direction and rate of change in the relationship.

Centripetal tendencies in type B school policies can be identified in several areas. The educational systems are highly centralized; access is initially broad for all groups. In Britain, as in Japan and New Zealand, schooling is free and compulsory until age 15, or approximately until completion of nine years of education. Further, there are special government scholarships set aside for aiding Maori and Burakumin at the secondary and postsecondary levels, where subordinate enrollment typically drops off.[10] But success appears to require some accommodation to the cultural criteria of the dominant group. Those who do not meet such criteria are tracked into curricula leading to the lower socioeconomic roles and statuses of the wider society.

The barriers to school access, then, are not of a legal nature nor, for the achieving "elite" of the subordinate group, a financial one. For example, in 1962, 58 percent of Maori school leavers left before the fifth form year, whereas by 1969 this figure had been cut to some 36 percent. Yet nearly 60 percent of Maori school leavers in 1969 entered unskilled and less secure jobs compared with less than 25 percent of non-Maori school leavers.[11] Likewise, in Japan, although the prime minister's office reported that both Burakumin and non-Burakumin had achieved a 94 percent enrollment rate at the secondary school level, the vocational track, leading to lower-status positions, finds Burakumin enrolled in numbers far exceeding their proportion of total secondary enrollment.[12] Much the same mechanism is operative in Great Britain, where West Indians are quickly tracked into the virtually impermeable vocational and trades streams of secondary schooling. An exception to this form of articulated tracking occurs in the private sector, as Ginsburg and Sands note in Chapter 5. Far more disturbing, however, is the tendency to classify black immigrant children as "retarded," a form of tracking with obvious social-psychological implications as well as structural ones. Ogbu cites figures that show nearly one-quarter of all West Indian elementary students in London are in schools or classrooms for the retarded.[13]

Congruent with the overall structure of intergroup relations in type B situations, school access and tracking policies seek to incorporate subordinate group members into the society-wide system of roles and positions; but they do so by channeling those individuals into the lower echelons of the system. It is a centripetal tendency with clear upper limits for the subordinate group as a whole, even if the sheer numbers of that group served by education are greater than in type A relationships. In contrast to type A, however, the influence of class is not entirely synonymous with ethnic considerations; large numbers of the subordinate group are also tracked into the low-status positions. The case of Japan again deviates somewhat from the ideal type B in the sense that occupation and role are extremely salient features of the division between the Burakumin and the Japanese majority. Caste/status is largely occupation based and as such fixes the Burakumin into a majority of the low-income jobs. Neither class nor cultural differences fully explain the segmentation.

Although curricula in schools are principally centripetal in orientation, recognizing only dominant culture, there are some type B cases, as with the Maori in New Zealand, where both centripetal and centrifugal tendencies can be identified. This tendency is highlighted in Chapter 6 by Maclaren. The introduction of some Maori cultural aspects to New Zealand's Maori schools in the 1930s was in large part a dominant group attempt to institutionalize or co-opt the centrifugal Maori "revitalization movement" of that period. In so doing, the government also linked Maori education to "practical skills," thus further controlling the direction of the apparent concession to Maori demands.[14] With the return in the last decades to more openly centripetal tendencies in government educational policies, all New Zealand schools share the same curriculum, one part of which is Maori culture (dance, music, history). Rather than distinguishing the two major groups in society, the special cultural content of the curriculum is intended to blur the lines between them, making Maori culture only one strand of the national culture.

In Britain, by way of contrast, the centripetal tendency is much less flexible. The educational authorities have adopted the equivalent of an "immersion" approach, expecting West Indian children to adapt to and absorb standard British culture as well as British educational modes. There are, more recently, special remedial programs for the black population, attending to its "failure" in school achievement.[15] By taking no special curricular or pedagogical steps to accommodate the West Indians, acculturation is expected to be hastened.

School language policies in type B situations are also centripetal in orientation, even though at the younger age levels children may receive some initial exposure to the native language or the native language may be available for study in the secondary school. Basically, however, the use of the native language at the elementary level is designed to facilitate the learning of the dominant group language and culture. It is in New Zealand where we see the clearest example of between-group language differences in a type B relationship; in Japan the Burakumin speak the same Japanese as the rest of society, while in Britain the linguistic barrier is one of dialect rather than language per se. The verticality of the relationship in New Zealand and its overall centripetal tendency virtually dictate an English-only policy in all the public schools. The only exception in more than a century of this policy was the introduction of the Maori language as one facet of the Maori schools' effort in the 1930s to reflect more of the local culture. It has never been a required subject in non-Maori schools (if it was offered at all). Further, even in the parallel Maori schools the native language was one course of study; it was not used for instructional purposes.

The type A and B intergroup relationships, with their hierarchically ordered cultural and structural divisions, stand in sharp contrast to type C and D relationships, which tend toward greater horizontality among groups. The type C society is perhaps most complex of all, as vertical and horizontal lines crosscut the groups, and no particular ethnic population enjoys a monopoly of either political and economic power or cultural and social prestige.

TYPE C

As expected, the educational policies are no less complex than these other characteristics of type C societies. Because type C relationships reflect an elite-masses division as well as differences among value groups, there is some tendency to structure the schooling enterprise along one or both of these lines. Hence it is possible to find parallel school systems in accord with ethnic group differences as well as schools that are included to serve only the upper or lower classes. Malaysia, for example, has retained some ethnic group distinction by allowing essentially parallel primary schools for its Malay, Chinese, and Indian populations; but at the higher levels the politically dominant Malay sector imposes a national language and curricula on all groups.[16] As Thomas notes in Chapter 8 there are currently underway reforms to "Malayinize" the entire school system, thus suggesting a policy shift toward less cultural and structural segmentation and more unity -- in short, official government policies are centripetal.

India's public school system likewise reflects ethnic group differences through the regional decentralization of some aspects of educational decision making while overall supervisory and coordinative functions are maintained at the national level. This split governance pattern derives from the Indian constitution, which guarantees all religious and language groups the right to establish and administer their own schools. Although the decentralization in many cases encourages and reinforces societal divisions, with each ethnic group and subgroup setting up its own schools, the federal government seems to see it as the only realistic way to deal with the extreme, often tense, diversity in India.[17]

Both Kenya and India also reflect an emphasis on a parallel system of private schools, which reflect the vertical differences found in type C societies. In Kenya the elite-masses division of the wider society is found in the emphasis on local financial support of schools. This results in poorer groups being less able to raise adequate funds to support schools and less able to secure the political leverage needed to sanction their existence.[18] In India, private schools account for 24 percent of primary institutions, but 70 percent of high schools and universities. Although these institutions are funded largely by the government, they nevertheless reflect both value group and caste and class differences.[19] However, as Chitnis points out in Chapter 10, the most significant division is that between the mass and elite.

Initial access to schools is relatively broad for all groups in a type C relationship, but may later favor one ethnic group or class/caste. Likewise, articulation is most evident among academic curricula, the subject matter most often studied by those groups that possess economic and political power. The role of the schools in supporting these differences in access can be seen in the selection mechanisms used to restrict access to higher levels. In Malaysia, mastery of the Malay language has recently been required before individuals whose first language is Chinese or Tamil are permitted to enter secondary schools. In India, despite the elimination of primary school fees in the early 1960s and the long-standing policy of "positive discrimination" in favor of the most disadvantaged tribes, castes, and classes, only 25 percent of all enrollees reach the fourth year of primary school.[20] There is general agreement that economic and cultural barriers are the principal obstacles to higher rates of enrollment and school completion.[21]

Finally, both Kenya's public and private systems cut across ethnic boundaries, but their cost and location (especially the publicly supported secondary school in urban areas) limit the number and social class of people who can gain access to them. Hence, although the more urbanized Kikuyu are thereby most favored, the issue appears to be one of socioeconomic status as well.[22] In Chapter 9, Urch notes that recently the Kenyan government has sought to use education as an instrument for cultural consensus: a centripetal trend.

To overcome some of the cultural centrifugality present in these societies and to encourage a drawing together around the goals of the elites, the type C educational policies often seek greater uniformity in some areas of school curricula. One prominent area in which this can be seen is a school's language of instruction. Except in the cases of miniscule language groups, all primary education in India is to be given in the child's native tongue. Early on in a child's educational career, however, the local language of instruction must give way to the introduction of regional languages used at the secondary school level. In the universities, the language of instruction issue is again challenged, as regional languages must compete with English and Hindi.[23]

The language instruction issue in Kenya and Malaysia is less complex than in India, but the same influence from both the national level and the dominant groups is felt. All public schools in Kenya use either English or Swahili (increasingly so) as the language of instruction. In this case all of the separate ethnic groups are affected, as neither of the national languages -- chosen for reasons of national unity -- is spoken by any group in the country as a first language.[24] It may be that such a policy favors the Kikuyu over other groups simply because of their longer contact with the British and with Swahili-language traders. It is clear that the real effect, however, is a vertical one, favoring secondary and higher education over primary and the upper social classes over the lower ones. Language is further linked to curricular tracking because all academic secondary schools, including the self-help harambee, are in English, while only the village-technical institutes use Swahili or the vernacular.[25]

As the language of instruction examples demonstrate, the type C relationship builds on its heterogeneity by institutionalizing involvement at the local level even as it retains the ultimate decision-making capacity at the national level. The existence of parallel institutions, like schools, is sometimes congruent with particular ethnic groups in such societies, but more often the institutions reflect the interest of a cross-group class-based hierarchy. Those individuals who reap the greatest benefits from schools represent families and social groups that are traditionally better off in the larger society. The dominant elite in type C societies, as it is drawn from more than one cultural population, desires to pass on its heterogeneous cultural heritage to new generations; it typically does this through family- and community-based centrifugal mechanisms, including ethnic-specific elementary schools. In preserving its structural heritage and privileges, however, the multigroup elite relies on centripetal policies that draw all groups and social classes into closer coordination -- but not necessarily equality -- with the goals of the elites.

TYPE D

The strong elite and class divisions in type C intergroup relations give way to greater horizontal pluralism in type D. Such a model provides considerable permeability for socioeconomic mobility even though there are strong cultural ties and consequent centrifugal tendencies. This suggests the need for centripetal structural policies, as with the type C cases, to counter strong ethnic divisions.

Nevertheless, educational policies in the type D society go considerably beyond those of most type C countries in the extent of shared governance; decentralization in decision making closely follows ethnic group boundaries regionally with the central government intervening to provide a common ideology and national goals. In Switzerland, long-standing historical and ethnolinguistic diversity has been dealt with through delegating to individual cantons the responsibility of determining curricula and language of public instruction; in cantons that are themselves characterized by diversity, local areas or groups are often given power over their own public schools. Regional decentralization, often coextensive with ethnic group boundaries, is the approach in Belgium and Yugoslavia. In each of these countries there is a duplication of administrative bodies and functions; regional educational authorities all have their counterparts at the national/federal level, with the latter usually holding most of the final decision-making power. This situation is tempered somewhat in Switzerland, where, as Fatzer notes in Chapter 11 there is less sharing of power than is commonly thought.

The Yugoslav case in particular suggests that greater power equality between ethnic groups, as well as greater ethnic or cultural differences, is an important contributor to greater decentralization even within the context of a centralist political framework. In fact, Rust makes clear in Chapter 13 that there exists a trend toward structural segmentation. Belgium indicates, further, that a rough equality in between-group power coupled with the absence of a coherent countervailing centripetal force may indicate a continuing trend away from centralized control over the short run. Limage confirms this in Chapter 12. On the other hand, the interdependence of the two Belgian groups (economically within Belgium and politically within the Western European system) may provide that centripetal force when the centrifugality reaches some satisfactory (or perhaps unsatisfactory) equilibrium. We suggest that it is the balance between an inherent centrifugality among groups and the need for a common set of attachments to the nation-state that accounts for this shared decision making in type D contexts, with the central government typically holding final authority in many areas of curricula.

Such centralized authority as exists, however, is designed to complement interdependence rather than to promote assimilation. In each of our type D examples, there is a great deal of attention given to issues of educational access for all populations. Belgium has gone so far as to financially support what amounts to four school systems: church- and state-sponsored systems, each further divided into Flemish- and French-language schools.

As a structural question alone, access in a type D relationship may be seen as an overt response to the demands (political, social, historical) of the various ethnic groups and a reflection of their power to make those demands on an equal footing with other groups in the society. The uniformity in school structure between regions/groups (for example, equal number of vocational schools in all regions; universities in all regions) is another reflection of that group power. But it is also an indication of the inclusive nature of type D structural policies in general, which aim at an eventual participation in an economy and society that transcends group boundaries. Interdependence is probably at the root of this, with (at least at the higher levels of schooling) consensus building another strong factor. In areas of curricula, teacher training, and the school's language of instruction, a dialectic between centripetal and centrifugal policies emerges; we find, for example, that most of the type D countries employ group-specific practices at the elementary school stage, whereas secondary and higher education institutions tend to reflect more common national and international content and practices. This balance is clearly evident in Belgium, where it is the federal government alone that determines the extent of ethnic content in the local schools. Yugoslavia, in contrast, turns all curricular decision making over to the regions, but then retains the right to approve (or disapprove) certain aspects of those curricula. In all these type D relationships, however, the uniform curricular elements far outweigh the group-specific ones in time allotted to each.

Language, in contrast, appears to act as a boundary between groups for purposes of dividing personnel into different programs of training and administration. Belgium maintains separate training institutes for its Flemish and Walloon populations, as does Yugoslavia for each of its respective ethnic groups. Indeed, very careful attention to language differences is characteristic of type D relationships. National governments, reacting to powerful local interests, provide for native-language instruction at least through secondary school and often through university training.

This centrifugality of multiple languages is offset somewhat by the early introduction of at least one other language in the schools. In Yugoslavia students all study at least one of the other recognized languages of the country. Only in Belgium is there marked resistance to bilingualism as a school policy.[26] Despite the type D schools' scrupulous attention to language maintenance, economic forces in these societies tilt the language learning process in favor of one or another tongue in each country. Southern Yugoslavians lean toward learning Serbo-Croatian because of its predominance in the bureaucracy and in industry. Political interdependence may force a country to adopt a balanced language learning policy, but economic interdependence (for example, industries in one area but workers from another) may well work against this.

Not surprisingly, our analysis of these four types of inter-group relations finds overall societal tendencies to be re-flected in each nation's respective educational policies toward subordinate groups. It is necessary, however, to distinguish between short- and long-term tendencies as well as to assess the degree of dominant group commitment to a policy at any point in time. We find, for example, that all nations require some structural and cultural centripetality to exist as nations over time. Hence some educational policies are inevitably as-sociated with the need for a nation to achieve a minimal level of compliance and coordination among all groups in the popu-lation. This observation appears to hold, irrespective of the integrative mechanisms employed. Beyond this, however, short-term educational policies may very well mask long-term intentions. For example, a type B society's commitment to uti-lize a subordinate group language in the classroom (bilingual education) may actually be part of a long-term strategy to more effectively prepare the subordinates to use the dominant group's language later on.

We also note the importance of differentiating between structural and cultural tendencies in educational policies. Whereas politically and economically the total society in all types of intergroup relations is dependent on individuals and groups occupying appropriate occupational roles, certain types of relationships appear to offer a somewhat greater tolerance for cultural heterogeneity or even pluralism, for example, sub-ordinate group adherence to linguistic, religious, and other ethnic-specific practices. Particularly in our types C and D we find examples of societies that show what otherwise would be considered "contradictory" or "opposing" tendencies in structural concerns on the one hand and cultural matters on the other.

Such a balance, we feel, contributes directly to the relative scarcity of educational policies designed to absorb and assimi-late subordinate groups to the ways of the dominant popula-tion. Rather, the general trend in societies with type C and D relationships appears to be toward policies that promote acculturation or accommodation in the shape of either greater cultural pluralism or greater horizontality in power and prestige. This is an example of the importance of viewing societal integration from both the dominant and subordinate perspectives, as such trends appear to be general compromises reflecting the interests of all parties. In these cases, the centripetal preferences of the dominant group are tempered by the resistance offered by subordinates, who tend to seek greater ethnic group autonomy. The result is pressure for further cultural centrifugality by constituent ethnic groups and a greater cultural pluralism evinced in educational policies.

CONCLUSION

The value of a typology of intergroup relations is twofold. As we have indicated in the discussion above, the first value is that it directs the researcher's attention to societal features that place individual cases in a context broader than national borders and particularistic traits. We can thus examine intergroup processes in Britain -- or Malaysia or Peru -- as examples of general trends or principles. A reading of our type descriptions certainly suggests that there do exist strong similarities among cases in each of the four types, and our concluding remarks have attempted to outline what we see as some of the more important of those similarities. The second value of a typology such as the one presented here is that it provides a framework -- a lens, as it were -- through which the researcher can examine and compare individual policies as they occur across a variety of intergroup settings. Just as we would expect a specific British school policy to resemble its Japanese counterpart in form, intent, and potential effect because of their similar type B context, so would we expect that same policy to vary in form, intent, and effect when manifested in Peru (type A), Malaysia (type C), or Yugoslavia (type D).

It is to this second value of the typology that we now briefly turn. From our country examples, policies related to educational tracking and between-level articulation appear to be among the areas most clearly reflective of distinct intergroup processes, especially integrative processes. In type A case, for example, explicit tracking follows group lines and thereby acts centrifugally, reinforcing the existing between-group differences. Blacks in South Africa are channeled into vocational and service careers, Haitian Creoles find their school opportunities limited to primary education and agricultural training, while Peruvian Indians may find no schools at all. In contrast, the equally rigid academic versus vocational tracking that one finds in Belgium -- type D cases -- operates across group lines and thus acts centripetally, drawing members from all groups into a structurally homogeneous system.

Other differences between our four types also shape the variations we have noted in school language policies. Policies that aim at one-language use at higher levels of education are culturally centripetal but structurally centrifugal in type A cases, such as Peru and Haiti. That is, individual assimilation to dominant group behaviors and values is encouraged by single-language practices at the same time that the margination of the great majority of the subordinate group is further reinforced. In the very different type C setting, on the other hand, single-language policies tend to be much more structural than cultural in their centripetal intent. The recognized position of the nondominant ethnic groups and, usually, their languages, makes assimilation an unlikely or untenable goal; the one-language policy for upper-grade levels appears to aim at providing a lingua franca (albeit an elite-biased language) that cuts across ethnic groups and thus leads to greater structural uniformity.

A third area of educational policy in which we can observe the differential effect of intergroup type is that of curriculum. The common (across all ethnic groups) curriculum of type A or B reflects the experience of one group only. It is centripetal in its cultural facet, presenting as it does one picture of national reality and national identity. In the type A and B examples, the structure of society and its limited rewards for subordinate groups also make this kind of policy part of a consensus-building mechanism in the process of integration; that is, the superordinate group seeks agreement without necessarily providing full structural outlets or participation for such agreement (especially in type A cases). Common curriculum in the type D context is more limited in scope; the balance among ethnic groups precludes the presentation of only one group's cultural perspective, in effect reducing the commonality to neutral or structural elements, for example, society-wide requirements in science or technical courses. This kind of curricular uniformity is also centripetal in intent but has structural goals rather than cultural ones as its objective. Further, in a type D setting, curricular uniformity is likely to reflect an emphasis on interdependence rather than consensus; societal integration here does depend on some level of agreement, but the agreement is usually based on mutual need and concrete trade-offs rather than simple acceptance of one group's propositions.

The framework presented in Chapter 1, the separate case studies, and the discussion in this conclusion lead us to the position that there is value in conducting further research to test some of the assumptions associated with the typology. The cases have provided us with an initial test of the framework as a whole, and for the most part the typology appears to be a useful heuristic device for both ordering data and in predicting some aspects and features of each case in each type. What is perhaps needed now is work on linking the types through some dialectical mechanism to predict shifts from one type to another, as was suggested by some of the contributors.

We would hope that this volume has tempered many educators' advocacy positions on behalf of particular groups and instead directed attention to providing explanations for those advocacy positions. Likewise, we hope that the work here demonstrates the value of comparative and international perspectives on cases that are often considered unique because they occur in one's home country. In this regard, it is important to recognize that all societies must develop educational policies for the societal integration process. We hope that this volume is a step toward analyzing such policies for the enlightenment of policymakers and of course for the members of the groups involved.

NOTES

1. P. Van den Berghe, "Ethnicity and Class in Highland Peru," in Ethnicity and Resource Competition in Plural Societies, ed. L. Despres (The Hague: Mouton, 1975); and J. Leyburn, The Haitian People (New Haven, Conn.: Yale University Press, 1966).

2. E. Ballon Echegaray, et al., Educacion Basica Laboral: Proceso a un Proceso (Lima: DESCO [Centro de Estudios y Promocion del Desarrollo], 1978); and E. Erickson, et al., eds., Area Handbook for Peru (Washington, D.C.: American University Press, 1965).

3. V. Rubin and R. Schaedel, eds., The Haitian Potential (New York: Teachers College Press, 1975).

4. T. Weil, et al., eds., Area Handbook for Haiti (Washington, D.C.: American University Press, 1973).

5. Ibid.

6. A. Boggio, et al., Cuesta Arriba o Cuesta Abajo? Un Analisis Critico de los Textos de Lectura de Primaria (Lima: DESCO, 1973).

7. H. Mitchell, Contemporary Politics and Economics in the Caribbean (Athens: Ohio University Press, 1968).

8. M. Whately, "Educating the Bantu for Serfdom," America, September 24, 1955, pp. 618-19.

9. H. Bernstein, "Schools for Servitude," in Apartheid, ed. A. La Guma (London: Lawrence and Wishart, 1972), pp. 43-79.

10. T. Brameld, Japan: Culture, Education and Change in Two Communities (New York: Holt, Rinehart and Winston, 1968).

11. A. C. Walsh, "Developments Since the Hunn Report and Their Bearing on Education," in Polynesian and Pakeha in New Zealand, ed. D. H. Bray and C. G. N. Hill, Vol. 1, The Sharing of Cultures (Auckland: Heinemann Educational Books, 1973), pp. 18-29.

12. Brameld, Japan.

13. J. Ogbu, Minority Education and Caste: The American System in Cross-Cultural Perspective (New York: Academic Press, 1978).

14. Ibid.

15. Ibid.

16. C. L. Sharma, "Ethnicity, Communal Relations and Education in Malaysia" (Greensboro: University of North Carolina, n.d.).

17. H. Gould, "Educational Structures and Political Processes in Fauzabad District, Uttar Pradesh," in Education and Politics in India, ed. S. Rudolph and L. Rudolph (Cambridge, Mass.: Harvard University Press, 1972), pp. 94-120.

18. J. Anderson, The Struggle for the School (London: Longman Kenya, 1970).

19. Gould, "Educational Structures and Political Processes in Fauzabad District, Uttar Pradesh."

20. J. Sargent, Society, Schools and Progress in India (Oxford: Pergamon Press, 1968).

21. Ibid. J. Laska, Planning and Educational Development in India (New York: Teachers College Press, 1968).

22. Z. Ergas and F. Chege, "Primary School Education in Kenya: An Attempt at Evaluation," Education in Eastern Africa 4, no. 2 (1974):235-49.

23. J. Dakin, B. Tiffin, and H. G. Widdowson, Language in Education (London: Oxford University Press, 1968).

24. R. Mutua, Development of Education in Kenya (Nairobi: East African Literature Bureau, 1975).

25. D. Court, "Dilemmas of Development: The Village Polytechnic Movement as a Shadow System of Education in Kenya," in Education, Society and Development: New Perspectives from Kenya, ed. D. Court and D. Ghai (Nairobi: Oxford University Press, 1974), pp. 219-41.

26. M. P. Herremans, The Language Problem in Belgium (Brussels: Belgian Information and Documentation Institute, 1967).

BIBLIOGRAPHY

ARTICLES/CHAPTERS IN BOOKS AND PAPERS

Aikara, J. "Educating Out of School Children." In <u>A Survey of the Dharavi Slum</u>. Bombay: Municipal Corporation of Greater Bombay, 1982.

Altbach, P. G. "Higher Education in Singapore: A Permanent Revolution." <u>Phi Delta Kappan</u> 64 (November 1982):200-01.

Archer, D., and M. Archer. "Race Identity, and the Maori People." <u>Journal of the Polynesian Society</u> 79 (1970):201-18.

Aziz, A. A., and C. T. Yow. "Malaysia." In <u>Schooling in the ASEAN Region</u>, edited by T. N. Postlethwaite and R. M. Thomas. Oxford: Pergamon Press, 1980.

Baber, Z., and E. G. Balch. "Problems of Education." In <u>Occupied Haiti</u>, edited by E. G. Balch, pp. 93-108. New York: Writers Publishing Co., 1927.

Baeten, R., and A. Verdoodt. "L'interet des eleves de l'enseignement secondaire belge envers una autre langue nationale est-il reciproque a travers tout le pays!" <u>Recherches Sociologiques</u> 14 (1983):75-93.

Balch, E. G. "Notes on the Land Situation in Haiti." In <u>Occupied Haiti</u>, edited by E. G. Balch, pp. 65-81. New York: Writers Publishing Co., 1927.

————. "Something of the Background." In <u>Occupied Haiti</u>, edited by E. G. Balch, pp. 1-14. New York: Writers Publishing Co., 1927.

Barrington, J. M. "From Assimilation to Cultural Pluralism: A Comparative Analysis." Comparative Education 17 (March 1981):59-69.

Barth, F., and D. Noel. "Conceptual Frameworks for the Analysis of Race Relations: An Evaluation." Social Forces 50 (March 1972):333-48.

Belding, R. E. "Lapps: An Educational Study of a Minority Group." The Clearinghouse 48 (April 1974):501-07.

Benn, C. "A New 11-Plus for the Old Divided System." Forum for the Discussion of New Trends in Education 22 (Spring 1980):36-42.

Benton, R. A. "Policy Implications for English-Maori Bilingual Education in New Zealand." Paper presented at the symposium on New Zealand's Language Future. ANZAAS Congress (49th Auckland, New Zealand). Wellington: New Zealand Council for Educational Research, 1979.

Bernheim, C. T. "The Problem of Democratizing Higher Education in Latin America." Prospects 9 (1979):78-84.

Bernstein, H. "Schools for Servitude." In Apartheid, edited by A. La Guma, pp. 43-79. London: Lawrence and Wishart, 1972.

Berreman, G. D. "Race, Caste, and Other Distinctions in Social Stratification." Race 23 (1972):39-56.

Berry, P. "Literacy and the Question of Creole." In The Haitian Potential: Research and Resources of Haiti, edited by V. Rubi and R. P. Schaedel, pp. 83-113. New York: Teachers College Press, 1975.

Biggs, B. "The Maori Language Past and Present." In The Maori People in the Nineteen-Sixties, edited by E. Schwimmer, pp. 65-84. Auckland: Blackwood and Janet Paul, 1968.

Bouillon, F. "L'influence du probleme linguistique sur les partis politiques traditionnels en Belgique depuis 1968." Thesis. Paris, 1979.

Broadfoot, P. "Accountability in England and France: The Centralist Alternative." Education Policy Bulletin 10 (Spring 1983):55-68.

Brock, C. "Problems of Articulation Between Secondary and Higher Education in England and Wales." European Journal of Education 16 (1981):157-73.

Brook, M. R. M. "The Mother-Tongue Issue in Britain: Cultural Diversity or Control." British Journal of Sociology of Education 1 (October 1980):237-56.

Bunting, B. Education for Apartheid (pamphlet). London: Christian Action for the Southern Africa Education Fund, 1974.

Buraku Kaiho. "Organization of Education in Japan 1971-1973." Report presented at the 34th International Conference on Education. Geneva, 1973.

Butler, R. "The Politics of the 1944 Education Act." In Decision Making in British Education, edited by G. Fowler, V. Morris, and J. Ozga, pp. 1-28. London: Heinemann, 1973.

Capelle, G. "A temps nouveaux, solutions nouvelles: Quelques propositions." Francais dans le monde, August to September 1983, pp. 70-76.

Chancy, M. "Education et developpement en Haiti." In Symposium: Culture et Development en Haiti. Montreal: Lemeac, 1972.

Chancy, M., and C. Pierre-Jacques. "Problemes scolaires et conditions socio-economiques des familles." In Enfant de migrants Haitiens en Amerique du Nord. Montreal: Centre de Recherches Caraibes, Universite de Montreal, 1982.

Chevalier, F. "Official Indigenismoin Peru in 1920: Origins, Significance and Socioeconomic Scope." In Race and Class in Latin America, edited by M. Morner, pp. 184-96. New York: Columbia University Press, 1971.

"The Child and Learning in a Multi-Cultural Society." In New Zealand Official Yearbook. Wellington: Department of Statistics, 1979.

Chitnis, S. "Education and Equality." In Education in a Changing Society, edited by A. Kloskowska and K. Martinotti, pp. 73-106. London: Sage, 1977.

_____. "Education for Equality: The Case of Scheduled Castes in Higher Education." Economic and Political Weekly 8 (1977):1675-81.

_____. "Reservation in Education: The Policy and the Practice." In Removal of Untouchability, edited by V. Shah, pp. 1-13. Ahmedabad: Department of Sociology, Gujarat University, 1980.

Chung, I. "The Korean Minority in Manchuria (1900-1937)." Ph.D. dissertation, American University, 1966.

Churchill, S. "National Linguistic Minorities: The Franco-Ontarian Educational Renaissance." Prospects 6 (1976):439-49.

_____. "The Stages of Development of Policies for Education of Linguistic Minorities: A Cross-National Model." Paper presented at the American Educational Research Association Annual Meeting. Montreal, April 11-15, 1983.

Clinton, R. L. "Military-Led Revolution in Peru: A Postmortem." Latin America Review 15 (1980):198-205.

Corbett, A. "Education in England." In Education in Great Britain and Ireland, edited by R. Bell and K. Little, pp. 2-8. London: Routledge and Kegan Paul, 1973.

Court, D. "Dilemmas of Development: The Village Polytechnic Movement as a Shadow System of Education in Kenya." In Education, Society and Development: New Perspectives from Kenya, edited by D. Court and D. Ghai, pp. 219-41. Nairobi: Oxford University Press, 1974.

Dedic, M. "Organizations for Adult Education and Cultural and Educational Activity." Yugoslav Survey 23 (August 1982):109-18.

Degregori, C. I. "Indigenismo, clases sociales y problema nacional." In CEPES (Centro Peruano de estudios sociales), Indigenismo, clases sociales y problema nacional: La discusion sobre el problema Indigena en el Peru, pp. 17-51. Lima: Ediciones CELATS, 1980.

Delius, A. "The Educated African, from Separate but Equal on the Veld." The Reporter, December 1959.

Deppeler, R. "Swiss Confederation. In The International Encyclopedia of Higher Education, pp. 4036-42. San Francisco: Jossey-Bass, 1977.

"The Development of Higher Education in Switzerland." Western European Education 15 (Summer 1983):1-92.

DeVos, G. A. "Japan's Outcasts: The Problem of the Burakumin." In The Fourth World: Victims of Group Oppression, edited by B. Whitaker, pp. 307-27. Eight Reports from the Field Work of the Minority Rights Group. New York: Schocken Books, 1973.

_____. "Ethnic Adaptation and Minority Status." Journal of Cross-Cultural Psychology 11 (March 1980):101-24.

Djuric, D. "The Psychological Pre-Service Training for Teachers for the Mutual Understanding of Young People in a Multilingual Community." In Contemporary Concepts and Perspectives of Teacher Training. Summaries of papers submitted (published at a symposium held in Sombar), 1978.

Donald, J. "Green Paper: Noise of Crisis." Screen Education 30 (Spring 1979):13-49.

Dorn, A., and B. Troyna. "Multiracial Education and the Politics of Decision-Making." Oxford Review of Education 8 (1982):175-85.

Dorsinville, M. "Haiti and Its Institutions: From Colonial Times to the Present." In Haitian Potential: Research and Resources of Haiti, edited by V. Rubin and R. P. Schaedel, pp. 183-220. New York: Teachers College Press, 1975.

Douglas, P. "History of the Occupation." In Occupied Haiti, edited by E. G. Balch, pp. 15-36. New York: Writers Publishing Co., 1927.

Dunn, E. "Education of the Small Peoples of the Soviet North: The Limits of Cultural Change." Arctic Anthropology 5 (1968):1-31.

Ekstrand, L. H. "Migrant Adaptation -- A Cross-Cultural Problem. A Review of Research on Migration Minority Groups and Cultural Differences with Special Regard to Children." In Educational and Psychological Interactions. Malmo, Sweden: School of Education, Department of Educational and Psychological Research, 1977.

Epstein, C. "Intergroup Education in Australia." Integrated Education 11 (July 1973):38-41.

Epstein, E. H. "Education and Peruanidad: Internal Colonialism in the Peruvian Highlands." Comparative Education Review 15 (June 1971):188-201.

_____. "Peasant Consciousness Under Peruvian Military Rule." Harvard Educational Review 52 (August 1982):280-300.

Ergas, Z., and F. Chege. "Primary School Education in Kenya: An Attempt at Evaluation." Education in Eastern Africa 4 (1974):235-49.

Femmes Haitiennes. Montreal: Maison d'Haiti, 1980.

Finn, D., N. Grant, and R. Johnson. "Social Democracy, Education and the Crisis." Working Papers in Cultural Studies 10 (1977):147-98.

Foster, C. R. "Creole in Conflict." Migration Today 8 (1980):8-13.

Foster, P. "Ethnicity and Schools in Ghana." In Schools in Transition, edited by A. Kazamias and E. Epstein, pp. 236-47. Boston: Allyn & Bacon.

Foundation for Change. "White Control and Minority Oppression." In Fact Sheets on Institutional Racism. New York: Foundation for Change, 1975.

Fourth Malaysia Plan. Kuala Lumpur: National Printing Department, 1981.

Franke, E. "Problems of Chinese Education in Singapore and Malaysia." Malaysian Journal of Education 2 (December 1965):182-91.

Fullante, L. Language Policy in Philippine Education. Los Angeles: University of California, Graduate School of Education, 1976.

Fulton, O. "Strategies for Revival: Increasing Demand and Improving Access." Education Policy Bulletin 9 (Spring 1981):39-49.

Gabor, J. "Textbooks for Schools for Ethnic Minorities." Yugoslav Survey 13 (1972):81-86.

Garvin, P. L., and M. Mathiot. "The Urbanization of the Guarani Language: A Problem in Language and Culture." In Proceedings of the Fifth International Congress of Anthropological and Ethnological Sciences, edited by A. Wallace, pp. 783-90. Philadelphia: University of Pennsylvania Press, 1960.

Gehring, A., H. Ochsen, G. Pillet, M. Poulet, and J. Prod'hom. "Demography and the Education System in Switzerland." European Journal of Education 16 (1981):287-306.

Ginsburg, M., R. Meyenn, and H. Miller. "Teachers, the 'Great Debate' and Education Cuts." Westminister Studies in Education 2 (1979):5-33.

Ginsburg, M., G. Wallace, and H. Miller. "Professionals Responding to Reduced Financial Resources and to Increased Government Control." Paper presented at the World Congress of Sociology, Mexico City, August 16-21, 1982.

Gonzalez, C. E., and V. Galdo. "Historia de la educacion en el Peru." In Instituciones, edited by J. Bracamonte, pp. 11-123. Lima: Editorial Juan Mejia Baca, 1980.

Gould, H. "Educational Structures and Political Processes in Fauzabad District, Uttar Pradesh." In Education and Politics in India, edited by S. Rudolph and L. Rudolph, pp. 94-120. Cambridge, Mass.: Harvard University Press, 1972.

Gupta, J. D. "Language Education and Development Planning." Prospects 6 (1976):382-87.

Habermas, J. "Conservatism and Capitalist Crisis." New Left Review 115 (May-June 1979):73-84.

Hall, S. "Racism and Reaction." In Five Views of Multi-Racial Britain: Talks on Race Relations. BBC-TV Broadcast, pp. 23-35. London: Commission on Racial Equality, 1978.

Halls, W. D. "Belgium: A Case Study in Educational Regionalism." Comparative Education 19 (1983):169-77.

Harker, R. K. "Research on the Education of Maori Children." Paper presented at Research in Education in New Zealand. A Balance Sheet. First National Conference of the New Zealand Association for Research in Education, December 7-10, 1979. Wellington: Victoria University, 1979.

_____. "Multiculturalism and Multicultural Schools." Paper presented to the Joint NZARE-AARE Special Interest Seminar, Palmerston North, New Zealand, December 2, 1981. Wellington: New Zealand Association for Research in Education, 1981.

Hartshorn, K. "The Unfinished Business: Education for South Africa's Black People." Optima, July 1981.

Hawkins, J. N. "Educational Demands and Institutional Response: Dowa Education in Japan." Comparative Education Review 27 (1983):204-26.

Heggoy, A. A. "Education in French Algeria: An Essay on Cultural Conflict." Comparative Education Review 17 (June 1973):180-97.

Hermans, P. "Case Study on Skovde Municipality and Its Ethnic Minorities (Sweden)." CDCC Project No. 7. The Education and Cultural Development of Migrants. Strasbourg, France: Council for Cultural Cooperation, 1983.

Hirasawa, Y. "The Burakumin: Japan's Minority Population." Integrated Education 20 (November to December 1983):3-8.

Hirschman, C. "Political Independence and Educational Opportunity in Peninsular Malaysia." Sociology of Education 52 (April 1979):67-84.

Hollick, J. E. "The Influence of Apartheid on Educational Policies in South Africa." Master's thesis, University of California, Los Angeles, 1970.

Honna, N. "Cultural Pluralism in Japan: A Sociolinguistic Outline." Jalt 2 (1980):5-29.

Houis, M. "The Problem of the Choice of Languages in Africa." Prospects 6 (1976):393-405.

Humphrey, R. A. "The Fall of the Spanish American Empire." History (October 1952), pp. 244-54.

Hunt, J. "Education and Bilingualism on the Language Frontier in Switzerland." Journal of Multilingual and Multicultural Development 1 (1980):17-39.

Ireland, R. "Specialized Educational Facilities for the Bantu in South Africa." Intellect 102 (January 1974):265-69.

Jackson, A. C. "A Model of Social Work Education for Multiracial Practice in Great Britain." Journal of Education for Social Work 17 (Winter 1981):102-10.

Jacobson, P. L. "The Future Past: The Social Context of Franco-American Schooling in New England." Paper presented at the Annual Meeting of the American Educational Research Association, Montreal, April 11-15, 1983.

"Japan." Integrated Education 20 (November-December 1983):18-22.

Jeffcoate, R. "Why Multicultural Education?" Education 9 (Spring 1981):4-7.

Johnson, R. "Educational Policy and Social Control in Early Victorian England." Past and Present 49 (1970):96-119.

Jones, J. "Access to University Education in New Zealand." Studies in Higher Education 7 (1982):159-68.

Juhas, M. "Educational Reform in Yugoslavia." Yugoslav Survey 19 (1978):75-98.

Keech, W. R. "Linguistic Diversity and Political Conflict in Switzerland." Comparative Politics 4 (April 1972):387-404.

Kelly, G. P. "Education and Participation in Nationalist Groups: An Exploratory Study of the Indochinese Communist Party and the VNQDD 1929-31." Comparative Education Review 15 (June 1971):227-36.

Kelman, H. C. "Language as an Aid and Barrier to Involvement in the National System." In Can Language Be Planned? edited by J. Rubin and B. H. Jernudd, pp. 21-51. Honolulu: University Press of Hawaii, 1971.

King, K. "Development and Education in the Narole District of Kenya: The Pastoral Masai and Their Neighbors." African Affairs 71 (October 1972):389-407.

Kintzer, F. C. "Educational Reforms in Yugoslavia." Educational Record 59 (1978):87-104.

Kitwood, T., and C. Borrill. "The Significance of Schooling for an Ethnic Minority." Oxford Review of Education 6 (1980):241-53.

Knezevic, M. "The System of Primary Education." Yugoslav Survey 23 (May 1982):81-96.

Kowalczewski, P. S. "Race and Education: Racism Diversity and Inequality: Implications for Multicultural Education." Oxford Review of Education 8 (1982):145-61.

La Belle, T. J., and P. White. "Education and Multiethnic Integration: An Intergroup-Relations Typology." Comparative Education Review 24 (June 1980):155-73.

Latortue, F. "Reflections on the Haitian Labour Face." In The Haitian Potential: Research and Resources of Haiti, edited by V. Rubin and R. P. Schaedel, pp. 221-39. New York: Teachers College Press, 1975.

Laughlin, M. A. "A Political Focus on Issues in Bilingual Education: Comparative Views from Selected Countries Around the World." Paper presented at the Annual Meeting of the National Association of Interdisciplinary and Ethnic Studies, Santa Clara, Calif., April 16, 1982.

Le Grand, K. R. "Perspective on Minority Education: An Interview with Anthropologist John Ogbu." Journal of Reading 24 (May 1981):680-86.

Lelyveld, J. "Pretoria and Black Education: Status Change?" New York Times, December 1982, p. 33.

Lester, M. "Bilingual Education in the United States, the Pacific and Southeast Asia." In Topics in Culture Learning, edited by R. W. Breslin, pp. 137-46. Honolulu: Culture Learning Institute, 1974.

Little, A. "Schools and Race." In Five Views of Multi-Racial Britain: Talks on Race Relations. BBC TV Broadcast, pp. 56-65. London: Commission on Racial Equality, 1978.

Loh, P. "Some Current Problems in Primary Education in Malaysia." Masa'alah Pendidekan (Educational Problems) 1 (1965):20-21.

Lorwin, V. "Linguistic Pluralism and Political Tension in Modern Belgium." In Advances in the Sociology of Language, edited by J. Fishman, pp. 386-412. The Hague: Houton, 1973.

McBeath, G. Political Integration of the Philippine Chinese. Ann Arbor: University of Michigan Microfilms, 1970.

McLean, M. "Cultural Autonomy and the Education of Ethnic Minority Groups." British Journal of Educational Studies 28 (February 1980):7-12.

MacPherson, C. "Do We Need a Theory of the State?" In Education and the State. Vol. 1. Schooling and the National Interest, edited by R. Dale, G. Esland, R. Ferguson, and M. MacDonald, pp. 61-76. Sussex: Open University and Falmer Presses, 1981.

Male, G. "Multicultural Education and Educational Policy: The British Experience." Comparative Education Review 24 (1980):291-301.

Malpica, C. "Education and the Community in the Peruvian Educational Reform." International Review of Education 26 (1980):356-67.

Minaya-Rowe, L. "A Comparison of Latin American and the United States Bilingual Education Programs." Paper presented at the I. N. Thut World Education Center Centennial Colloquium, Hartford, Conn., October 23, 1980.

Mir de Cid, M. "Language and Cultural Discrimination as Related to Bilingual Education." Metas 2 (Spring 1982):61-67.

Mukherjee, T. "Multicultural Education: A Black Perspective." Early Child Development and Care 10 (February 1983):275-81.

Naik, J. P. "Equality, Quality, and Quantity: The Elusive Triangle in Indian Education." International Review of Education 25 (1979):167-85.

National Institute of Education. "Hispanic Migrations from the Caribbean and Latin America: Implications for Educational Policy, Planning and Practice: Conference Proceedings." In Urban Diversity Series 65. Washington, D.C.:

Department of Health, Education, and Welfare, NIE/New York: Columbia University, 1979.

New Zealand Commission on Education. Report. Wellington: Government Printer, 1962.

"New Zealand Unveils the Secondary School of Tomorrow." Education News 1 (October 1975).

Offe, C. and V. Ronge. "Theses on the Theory of the State." In Education and the State. Vol. I. Schooling and the National Interest, edited by R. Dale, G. Esland, R. Ferguson, and M. MacDonald, pp. 77-86. Sussex: Open University and Falmer Presses, 1981.

Ogden, J. D. "Teaching French as a Multicultural Language: The French-speaking World Outside of Europe." In Language in Education: Theory and Practice. Washington, D.C.: National Institute of Education, 1981.

Palov, M. "The Personality of the Teacher in the Realization of Educational Functions in Our Multi-National Community." In Contemporary Concepts and Perspectives of Teaching Training: No. 7. Summaries of papers submitted (published for a symposium held at Sombor), 1978.

Parekh, B. "Asians in Britain: Problem or Opportunity." In Five Views of Multi-Racial Britain: Talks on Race Relations. BBC TV Broadcast, pp. 36-55. London: Commission on Racial Equality, 1978.

Parker, W. "Maori Education." Education 9 (October 1962):56-59.

Pattison, M. "Intergovernmental Relations and the Limitations of Central Control: Reconstructing the Politics of Comprehensive Education." Oxford Review of Education 6 (1980): 63-89.

Paulston, C. B. "Las escuelas bilingues in Peru: Some Comments on Second Language Learning." International Review of Applied Linguistics in Language Teaching 10 (November 1972):351-56.

Paulston, R. "Ethnicity and Educational Change: A Priority for Comparative Education." Comparative Education Review 20 (October 1976):269-80.

Petar, S. "Teaching Staff in Elementary and Secondary Schools." Yugoslav Survey 20 (1979):149-58.

Petrovic, D. "National Structure of the Yugoslav Population." Yugoslav Survey 14 (1973):1-22.

Pike, K. L., and S. C. Tuggy. "Social Linguistics and Bilingual Education." System 7 (August 1979):99-109.

Premfors, R. "National Policy Styles and Higher Education in France, Sweden and the United Kingdom." European Journal of Education 16 (1981):253-62.

Quijana, A. "Contemporary Peasant Movements." In Elites in Latin America, edited by S. M. Lipset and T. Solari, pp. 301-40. New York: Oxford University Press, 1967.

Ramet, P. "Inter-Republican Relations in Contemporary Yugoslavia." Ph.D. dissertation, University of California, Los Angeles, 1981.

Raynor, P. "Race and Education: Interpreting British Policies in the 1960s and 1970s." In Different People: Studies in Ethnicity and Education, edited by E. Gumbert, pp. 75-99. Atlanta: Center for Cross-Cultural Education, Georgia State University, 1983.

Reid, D. M. "Turn-of-the-Century Egyptian School Days." Comparative Education Review 27 (October 1983):374-93.

Rex, J. "Race in the Inner City." In Five Views of Multi-Racial Britain: Talks on Race Relations. BBC TV Broadcast, pp. 9-22. London: Commission on Racial Equality, 1978.

Roy, A. "Schools and Communities: An Experience in Rural India." International Review of Education 26 (1980):369-78.

Rubaiy, A. A. "A Case Study of Unsuccessful Political Integration: The Education of the Kurdish Minority in Iraq." Paper presented at the Comparative and International Education Society, San Antonio, Tex., 1973.

_____. "Failure of Political Integration in Iraq: The Education of the Kurdish Minority. Intellect 102 (April 1974): 440-44.

Samuda, R. J. "Placing Immigrant Students in the Ontario School System." Journal of Special Education 6 (Fall 1982): 249-62.

Saunders, M. "The School Curriculum for Ethnic Minority Pupils: A Contribution to a Debate." International Review of Education 26 (1980):31-47.

Schwimmer, E. "The Maori Education Foundation." Comment 3 (1962):7-11.

Shuster, D. R. "Schooling in Micronesia During Japanese Mandate Rule." Educational Perspectives 18 (1979):20-26.

Silver, H. "Education Against Poverty: Interpreting British and American Policies in the 1960s and 1970s." In Poverty, Power and Authority in Education, edited by E. Gumbert, pp. 13-34. Atlanta: Center for Cross-Cultural Education, Georgia State University, 1981.

Simon, B. "Marx and the Crisis in Education." Marxism Today, 1977, pp. 195-205.

Singham, A. "The Political Socialization of Marginal Groups." In Majority and Minority: The Dynamics of Racial and Ethnic Relations, edited by N. Yetman and C. Steele, pp. 102-16. Boston: Allyn & Bacon, 1972.

Soljan, N. N. "Some Problems of Educational Theory and Policy in Yugoslavia." Prospects 8 (1977)184-93.

_____. "The Concept of Self-Management and the Socioeconomic Background of Decision-Making in Education: The Yugoslav Model." Comparative Education 14, (1978):65-74.

_____. "The Reform of the System of Pre-Service and In-Service Teacher Training in Yugoslavia: Towards Educating the Community." International Review of Education 24 (1978):75-80.

_____. "Educational Needs and the Philosophy of Democratization in Higher Education in Yugoslavia." Prospects 9 (1979):58-68.

"Southern African Universities Oppose Plan to Set Up Quota for Blacks." New York Times, November 1983, pp. 21-22.

Sparks, A. Black Education in South Africa: The Current Situation. New York: Institute of International Education, 1983.

Stafford, K. "Early Educational Development in East Africa: A Case Study." Comparative Education Review 23 (1979): 66-81.

Storm, M. "Development Education and Multi-Ethnic Education: Some Tension." Development Education Paper No. 21. New York: United Nations Children's Fund, 1981.

Teske, Jr., R. and B. Nelson. "Acculturation and Assimilation: A Clarification." American Ethnologist 2 (1974):351-68.

Thomas, M., G. K. Leong, and R. W. Mosbergen. "Singapore." In Schooling in the ASEAN Region, edited by T. N. Postlethwaite and R. M. Thomas, pp. 187-95. Oxford: Pergamon Press, 1980.

Times Educational Supplement. "Extracts from the Green Paper." July 1977, pp. 5-8.

Tito, J. B. "Concerning the National Question and Socialist Patriotism. Speech at Ljublijana, November 16, 1948. In J. B. Tito Selected Speeches and Articles, pp. 97-98. Zagreb: Naprijed, 1963.

To, C. Y. "Education of the Aborigines in Taiwan: An Illustration of How Certain Traditional Beliefs of a Majority People Determine the Education of a Disadvantaged Minority." Journal of Negro Education 41 (1980):183-94.

Tollefson, J. W. "The Language Planning Process and Language Rights in Yugoslavia." Language Problems and Language Planning 4 (1980):141-56.

Toma, P. "The Educational System of Czechoslovakia." Washington, D.C.: Department of Health, Education, and Welfare, Office of Education, Bureau of Post-Secondary Education, U.S. Government Printing Office, 1976.

Tomlinson, S. "Inexplicit Policies in Race and Education." Education Policy Bulletin 9, (1981):149-66.

"Trends in Education." Unpublished. Singapore: Ministry of Education, 1979.

Tsow, M. "Ethnic Minority Community Languages: A Statement." Journal of Multilingual and Multicultural Development 4 (1983):361-84.

Ulrih-Atena, E. "National Linguistic Minorities: Bilingual Basic Education in Slovenia." Prospects 6 (1976):430-38.

UNESCO. "Languages of Instruction in Ceylon Schools for Minorities." Education Abstracts 13 (1961):75-76.

UNESCO. "Languages of Instruction in Schools for Minorities in Israel." Education Abstracts 13 (1961):90-91.

United Nations. "Summary of the Country: Presentation for Haiti." Paris: United Nations Conference on the Least Developed Countries, September 1981.

Valdman, A. "The Language Situation in Haiti." In The Haitian Potential: Research and Resources of Haiti, edited by V. Rubin and R. P. Schaedel, pp. 61-82. New York: Teachers College Press, 1975.

Van den Berghe, P. "Ethnicity and Class in Highland Peru. In Ethnicity and Resource Competition in Plural Societies, edited by L. Despres, pp. 71-85. The Hague: Moulton, 1975.

Versoerd, H. F. "Bantu Education -- Policy for the Immediate Future." Statement in the Senate of the South African

Parliament. Pretoria: Information Service of the Department of Native Affairs, 1954.

Vielot, K. "Primary Education in Haiti." In The Haitian Potential: Research and Resources of Haiti, edited by V. Rubin and R. D. Schaedel, pp. 114-43. New York: Teachers College Press, 1975.

Wagatsuma, H. "Political Problem of a Minority Group in Japan: Recent Conflicts in Buraku Liberation Movements." In Case Studies on Human Rights and Fundamental Freedoms, edited by W. A. Veehoven. The Hague: Foundation for the Study of Plural Societies, 1975-76.

Walker, R. "Culture Gap." New Zealand Listener. November 1973.

Wallace, G., H. Miller, and M. Ginsburg. "Teachers' Responses to the Cuts." In Contemporary Education Policy, edited by J. Ahier and M. Flude, pp. 109-38. London: Croom Helm, 1982.

Walsh, A. C. "Developments Since the Hunn Report and Their Bearing on Education." In Polynesian and Pakeha in New Zealand. Vol. 1. The Sharing of Cultures, edited by D. H. Bray and C. G. N. Hill, pp. 18-29. Aukland: Heinemann Educational Books, 1973.

Wang, B. C. "Positive Discrimination in Education: A Comparative Investigation of Its Bases, Forms and Outcomes." Comparative Education Review 27 (June 1983): 191-203.

Watson, J. K. P. "Education and Cultural Pluralism in South East Asia, with Special Reference to Peninsular Malaysia." Comparative Education 16 (June 1980):139-58.

Watson, K. "Educational Policies in Multi-Cultural Societies." Comparative Education 15 (1979):17-31.

Weigand, P. "Educational and Social Class, Disparity, and Conflict in Latin America with Special Reference to Minority Groups in Chile." Comparative Education 19 (1983):213-18.

Whately, M. "Educating the Bantu for Serfdom." America 93 (1955):618-19.

Wirt, F. M. "The Stranger Within My Gate: Ethnic Minorities and School Policy in Europe." Comparative Education Review 23 (1979):17-40.

Yagnik, A. "Spectre of Caste War." Economic and Political Weekly (Bombay) 16 (1981):553-55.

Zolberg, A. "Transformation of Linguistic Ideologies: The Belgian Case." In Multilingual Political Systems: Problems and Solutions, edited by Jean-Guy Savard and R. Vigneault, pp. 445-72. Laval, Que.: Les Presses de l'Universite, 1975.

Books

Advisory Council on Educational Planning. Directions for Educational Development. Wellington: Government Printer, 1974.

Alberti, G., and J. Cotler. Aspectos sociales de la educacion rural en el Peru. Lima: Instituto de Estudio Peruanos, 1972.

Alfageme, A., and M. Valderrama. El debate sobre la cuestion agraria y el problema indigena y nacional a comienzos del siglo XX. Lima: Universidad Catolica, 1977.

Allen, S. New Minorities, Old Conflicts: Asian and West Indian Migrants in Britain. New York: Random House, 1971.

Anderson, J. The Struggle for the School. London: Longman Kenya, 1970.

Anderson, R. Education in Japan: A Century of Modern Development. Washington, D.C.: U.S. Department of Health, Education, and Welfare, Office of Education, U.S. Government Printing Office, 1975.

Archer, M. Social Origins of Educational Systems. Beverly Hills, Calif.: Sage, 1979.

Arestegui Moras, M. Nuclearizacion educativa: Teoria y practica. Lima: Impreso en los Talleres de ITAL-Peru, 1976.

Arista, M. L. El curriculum y la dependencia educativa peruana. Colecion mundo Latino Americano. Editorial Litografia La Confianza, 1973.

Atkinson, N. Educational Cooperation in the Commonwealth: An Historical Study. Salisbury: University of Rhodesia, 1972.

Auerbach, F. E. The Power of Prejudice in South African Education. Cape Town, 1965.

Ausubel, D. P. The Fern and the Tiki. Sydney: Angus and Robertson, 1960.

_____. Maori Youth. Wellington: Price Milburn, 1961.

Ballon Echegaray, E., et al. Educacion basica laboral: Proceso a un proceso. Lima: Centro de Estudios y Promocion del Desarrollo, 1978.

Banks, J. A. and G. Gay. Ethnicity in Contemporary American Society: Towards the Development of a Typology. Washington, D.C.: National Academy of Education, 1975.

Barrantes, E. Pedagogia. Lima: Universidad Nacional Mayor de San Marcos, 1966.

Barrington, J. M., and T. H. Beaglehole. Maori Schools in a Changing Society. Wellington: NZCER, 1974.

Barth, F., ed. Ethnic Groups and Boundaries. Bergen: Universitets Forlaget, 1969.

Basu, A. The Growth of Education and Political Development in India 1898-1920. Delhi: Oxford University Press, 1974.

Bates, R. J., ed. Prospects in New Zealand Education. Auckland: Hodder and Stoughton, 1970.

Baucke, W. Where the White Man Treads. Auckland: Wilson and Horton, 1928.

Bender, B. W. Linguistic Factors in Maori Education: A Report. Wellington: Council for Educational Research, 1971.

Bertsch, G. K. Values and Community in Multi-National Yugoslavia. New York: Columbia University Press, 1976.

Beteille, A., ed. Castes: Old and New. New York: Asian Publishing House, 1969.

Bienen, H. Kenya: The Politics of Participation and Control. Princeton, N.J.: Princeton University Press, 1974.

Boggio, A., et al. Cuesta arriba o cuesta abajo? Un analisis critico de los textos de lectura de primaria. Lima: Centro de Estudios y Promocion del Desarrollo, 1973.

Bohanan, P. Africa and Africans. Garden City, N.Y.: Natural History Press, 1963.

Bolton, F. Education for a Multi-Racial Britain. London: Fabian Society, 1972.

Bourricaud, F. Poder y sociedad en el Peru contemporaneo. Buenos Aires, Argentina: Editorial Sur, 1967.

Brameld, T. Japan: Culture, Education and Change in Two Communities. New York: Holt, Rinehart and Winston, 1968.

Brembeck, Cole, and H. Walker. Cultural Challenges to Education. Lexington, Mass.: Lexington Books, 1973.

Broadbent, R. F., ed. Education Policy Making in Australia. Selected papers from the Annual Conference of the Australian College of Education, Hobart, Tasmania, Australia, January 10-14, 1982. Victoria: Australian College of Education, 1982.

Bugen, E., et al. Das schulwesen in der schweiz. Geneva, 1976.

Busch, P. A. Legitimacy and Ethnicity: A Case Study of Singapore. Lexington, Mass.: Heath, 1974.

Carlson, R. A. The Quest for Conformity: Americanization Through Education. New York: Wiley, 1975.

Carnoy, M. Education as Cultural Imperialism. New York: David McKay, 1974.

Centro de Informacion, Estudios y Documentacion. Peru: La reforma educativa en una sociedad de clases. Lima: CIED, 1980.

Charles, R., et al. National Education Policies for Aboriginal Peoples. Ottawa: Department of Manpower and Immigration/Toronto: Ontario Indian Education Council, 1981.

Chitnis, S. A Long Way to Go. New Delhi: Allied Publishers, 1981.

_____. Dropout and Low Pupil Achievement Among the Urban Poor in Bombay. Bombay: Tata Institute of Social Sciences/International Labor Organization, 1982.

Cobo, B. History of the Inca Empire: An Account of the Indians, Customs and Their Origin Together with a Treatise on Inca Legends, History and Social Institutions. Austin: University of Texas Press, 1979.

Conquest, R. A. Soviet Nationalities Policy in Practice. London: Badley Head, 1967.

Coppieters, F. The Community Problem in Belgium. Brussels: Institut Belge d'Information et de Documentation, 1974.

Court, D., and D. Ghai, eds. Education, Society and Development: New Perspectives from Kenya. Nairobi: Oxford University Press, 1974.

Cox, C., and A. Dyson, eds. Right for Education: A Black Paper. London: Critical Science Society, 1969.

Cox, C., and R. Boyson, eds. Black Paper. London: Dent, 1975.

Cox, C., and R. Boyson, eds. Black Paper. London: Maurice Temple Smith, 1977.

Cross, M., ed. West Indian Social Problems. Port-of-Spain, Trinidad: Columbus Publishers, 1970.

Crowder, M. Senegal: A Study of French Assimilation Policy, rev. ed. London: Methuen, 1967.

Cummings, W., I. Amano, and K. Kazayuki, eds. Changes in the Japanese University. New York: Praeger, 1979.

Cumper, G. The Social Structure of the British Caribbean. Millwood, N.Y.: Kraus Reprint Co., 1978.

Curtis, M., and M. Chertoff, eds. Israel: Social Structure and Change. New Brunswick, N.J.: Dutton, 1973.

Dakin, J., B. Tiffen, and H. G. Widdowson. Language in Education. London: Oxford University Press, 1968.

Dandekar, V. M., and N. Rath. Poverty in India. Bombay: Sameeksha, 1978.

Degler, C. N. Neither Black nor White: Slavery and Race Relations in Brazil and the United States. New York: Macmillan, 1971.

Del Busto, J. A. Peru Incaico. Lima: Libreria Studium, 1978.

Deloff, E. L'enseignement en Belgique. Brussels: Institut Belge d'Information et de Documentation, 1977.

Denitch, B. D. The Legitimation of a Revolution: The Yugoslav Case. New Haven, Conn.: Yale University Press, 1976.

de Reuck, A., and J. Knight, eds. Caste and Race: Comparative Approaches. London: Churchill, 1967.

De Vos, G., and H. Wagatsuma, eds. Japan's Invisible Race. Berkeley: University of California Press, 1972.

Diederich, B., and A. Burt. Papa Doc: The Truth About Haiti Today. New York: McGraw-Hill, 1969.

Doeringer, P., and M. Piore. Internal Labor Markets and Manpower Analysis. Lexington, Mass.: Heath, 1971.

Dorchy, H. Histoire des Belges. Brussels: A. de Boeck, 1982.

Dore, R. Diploma Disease. Los Angeles: University of California Press, 1976.

Dorotich, D., ed. Education and Canadian Multiculturalism: Some Problems and Some Solutions. Eighth Yearbook 1981. Ottawa: Department of the Secretary of State/Saskatoon: Canadian Society for the Study of Education, 1981.

Dowa Taisaku Shingikai Toshin. Tokyo: Japanese Government Printing Office, 1965.

Edgerton, B. The Individual in Cultural Adaptation: A Study of Four East African Peoples. Berkeley: University of California Press, 1971.

Education and National Development Report of the Education Commission 1964-66. New Delhi: Ministry of Education, 1966.

Enloe, C. Ethnic Conflict and Political Development. Boston: Little, Brown, 1973.

Epstein, E., Politics and Education in Puerto Rico: A Documentary Survey of the Language Issue. Metuchen, N.J.: Scarecrow Press, 1970.

Erickson, E., et al., Area Handbook for Peru. Washington, D.C.: American University, 1965.

Esman, M. J. Administration and Development in Malaysia. Ithaca, N.Y.: Cornell University Press, 1972.

Fafunwa, A. B., and J. V. Aisiku, Education in Africa: A Comparative Survey. London: Allen and Unwin, 1982.

Figueroa, J. Society, Schools and Progress in the West Indies. Elmsford, N.Y.: Pergamon, 1971.

Finnan, A. Multicultural Education: An Annotated Bibliography. New York: Fordham University Component of the New York State Teacher Corps Network, 1976.

Fishman, J. A. Language in Socio-Cultural Change. Stanford, Calif.: Stanford University Press, 1972.

Foner, N. Status and Power in Rural Jamaica: A Study of Education and Political Change. New York: Teachers College Press, 1973.

Fornaciari, D. El campesino tucumano, education y cultura. Sierie estudios y documentos 4. Tucuman, Argentina: Centro de Documentacion e Informacion Educativa, 1974.

Fourth All India Survey of Education. New Delhi: NCERT, 1980.

Franklin, J. H., ed. Color and Race. Boston: Houghton Mifflin, 1968.

Fraser, S. E., and K. L. Hsu. China: The Cultural Revolution: Its Aftermath and Effects on Education and Society. A Select and Partially Annotated Bibliography. Nashville, Tenn.: George Peabody College for Teachers, Peabody International Center, 1972.

Furnivall, J. S. Colonial Policy and Practice: A Comparative Study of Burma and Netherlands India. Cambridge: Cambridge University Press, 1948.

Gall, N. La reforma educativa Peruana. Lima: Mosca Azul Editores, 1976.

Gerhard, F. Gruppe als methode. Weinheim, Basel, 1980.

Giles, R. The West Indian Experience in British Schools. London: Heinemann, 1977.

Golan, G. <u>Reform Rule in Czechoslovakia: The Dubcek Era 1968-1969</u>. Cambridge: Cambridge University Press, 1973.

Gold, M., et al., eds. <u>In Praise of Diversity: A Resource Book for Multicultural Education</u>. Washington, D.C.: Association of Teacher Educators, 1977.

Gorupic, D., and I. Paj. <u>Workers' Self-Management in Yugoslav Undertakings</u>. Zagreb: Ekonomiski Institut Zagreb, 1970.

Government of India. <u>Report of the Commissioner for Scheduled Castes and Scheduled Tribes</u>. New Delhi: Ministry of Social Welfare, 1975-76.

_____. <u>Report of the Commissioner for Scheduled Castes and Scheduled Tribes</u>. New Delhi: Ministry of Social Welfare, 1976-77.

_____. <u>Report of the Commissioner of Scheduled Castes and Scheduled Tribes</u>. New Delhi: Controller of Publications, 1980.

Grace, G. <u>Teachers, Ideology and Control</u>. London: Routledge and Kegan Paul, 1978.

Graham, M. A. <u>Acculturative Stress Among Asian, American and Polynesian Students on the Brigham Young University-Hawaii Campus</u>. Hawaii: Brigham Young University, 1981.

Grisay, A. <u>Rendement de l'enseignement de la langue maternelle en Belgique fraxophone</u>. Recherche en Education series. Brussels: Direction Generale de l'Organisation des Etudes, Ministere de L'Education Nationale et de la Culture Francause, 1974.

Grove, C. <u>The Intensively Annotated Bibliography on Cross-Cultural Problems in Education</u>. New York: Columbia University, Institute of International Studies, September 1975.

Habermas, J. <u>Legitimation Crisis</u>, trans. by T. McCarthy. London: Heinemann, 1976.

Hall, S., C. Critcher, T. Jefferson, J. Clarke, and B. Roberts. <u>Policing the Crisis: Mugging, the State, and Law and Order</u>. London: Macmillan, 1978.

Hawkins, I. <u>The Changing Face of the Caribbean</u>. Bridgetown, Barbados: Cedar Press, 1976.

Heine, B. <u>Status and Use of African Lingua Francas</u>. Munich: Weltforum Verlag, 1970.

Hensey, F. G. <u>The Sociolinguistics of the Brazilian-Uruguayan Border</u>. The Hague: Mouton, 1972.

Herremans, M. P. and F. Coppieters. <u>The Language Problem in Belgium</u>. Brussels: Belgian Information and Documentation Institute, 1967.

Heyneman, S. P. <u>The Conflict over What Is to Be Learned in Schools: A History of Curriculum Politics in Africa</u>. Syracuse, N.Y.: Program of East African Studies, Syracuse University, 1971.

Hill, C. <u>Immigration and Integration: A Study of the Settlement of Coloured Minorities in Britain</u>. Oxford: Pergamon Press, 1970.

Hippolyte-Manigat, M. <u>Haiti and the Caribbean Community</u>. Kingston, Jamaica: Institute of Social and Economic Research, University of the West Indies, 1980.

Hirschman, C. <u>Ethnic and Social Stratification in Peninsular Malaysia</u>. Washington, D.C.: American Sociological Association, 1975.

HMSO. <u>Norwood Report</u>. Board of Education's Departmental Committee on Curriculum and Examinations in Secondary Schools. London, 1943.

_____. <u>Fifteen to Eighteen. Crowther Report</u>. Ministry of Education's Central Advisory Council for Education. London, 1959.

_____. <u>Half Our Future. Newsom Report</u>. Central Advisory Council for Education. London, 1963.

_____. Higher Education. Robbins Report. London, 1963.

_____. English for Immigrants. London: Ministry of Education, 1964.

_____. Second Report on Commonwealth Immigrants. London, 1964.

_____. Teacher Education and Training. James Report. London, 1972.

_____. Language for Life. Bullock Report. London, Department of Education and Science, 1974.

_____. Educating Our Children: Four Subjects for Debate. A Background Paper for Regional Conferences. London, Department of Education and Science, 1977.

_____. Education in Schools: A Consultative Document. Green Paper. London, Department of Education and Science, 1977.

_____. Report of the Committee of Enquiry into the Education of Handicapped Children and Young People. London, 1978.

_____. Report on the Brixton Disorders. Scarman Report. Cmnd. 8427. London, 1981.

_____. West Indian Children in Our Schools. Rampton Report. Committee of Enquiry into the Education of Children of Ethnic Minority Groups. London, 1981.

Holloway, J., and S. Picciotto. State and Capital: A Marxist Debate. London: Edward Arnold, 1978.

Holtham, G., and A. Hazlewood. Aid and Inequality in Kenya. London: Overseas Development Institute, Croom Helm, 1976.

Horrell, M. A Decade of Bantu Education. Johannesburg: South African Institute of Race Relations, 1964.

_____. Bantu Education to 1968. Johannesburg: South African Institute of Race Relations, 1968.

_____. Laws Affecting Race Relations in South Africa 1948-1976. Johannesburg: South African Institute of Race Relations, 1978.

Hunn, J. K. Report on Department of Maori Affairs. Wellington: Government Printer, 1960.

Hurn, C., and B. Burn. An Analytic Comparison of Educational Systems: Overview of Purposes, Policies, Structures and Outcomes. Comparative Overview/Comparative Assessment. Washington, D.C.: Department of Education, National Commission on Excellence in Education, 1982.

Inter-American Development Bank. Economic and Social Progress in Latin America 1980-81 Report. Washington, D.C., 1981.

Jackson, P. M., ed. Maori and Education. Wellington: Ferguson and Osborn, 1931.

ahan, B. Pakistan: Failure in National Integration. New York: Columbia University Press, 1972.

James, C. L. R. The Black Jacobins, 2nd ed. rev. New York: Random House, 1963.

Jemuovic, R. Education in Yugoslav. Belgrade: Medunariodna Politika, 1964.

Jost, L., ed. Alternative schulen. Zurich, 1980.

_____. Schulsituation schweiz. Zurich, 1981.

Kapsoli, W. Los movimientos campesinos en el Peru 1879-1965. Lima: Delva Editores, 1977.

Karimi, J., and P. Ochieng. The Kenyatta Succession. Nairobi: English Press, 1980.

Keer, D. Ambedkar Life and Mission. Bombay: Popular Prakashan, 1962.

Kenya Education Commission Report. 1664-65. Kenya Government Report. Nairobi: English Press, 1964-65.

Kenyatta, J. Harambee: The Prime Minister of Kenya's Speeches 1963-1964. Nairobi: Oxford University Press, 1964.

King, E. Other Schools and Ours, 5th ed. New York: Holt, 1979.

Kirp, D. Benign Neglect: Race and Schooling in Britain. Berkeley, Graduate School of Public Policy, University of California, 1977.

_____. Doing Good by Doing Little. Berkeley: University of California Press, 1979.

Kitchen, H., ed. The Educated African. New York: Praeger, 1962.

Kobeyashi, T. Society, Schools and Progress in Japan. New York: Pergamon Press, 1976.

Krausz, E. Ethnic Minorities in Britain. London: MacGibson and Kee, 1971.

Krejci, J. Social Change and Stratification in Postwar Czechoslovakia. London: Macmillan, 1972.

Kurrien, J. Elementary Education in India: Myth, Reality, Alternative. New Delhi: Vikas Publications, 1983.

La Belle, T. J., ed. Education and Development: Latin America and the Caribbean. Los Angeles: University of California Press, 1971.

Lagasse, C. E. La Contre-Reforme de l'etat, panorama des institutions politiques de la Belgique. Louvain: Ciaco, 1982.

Larson, M., and P. M. Davis, eds. Bilingual Education: An Experience in Peruvian Amazonia. Washington, D.C.: Center for Applied Linguistics, 1981.

Laska, J. Planning and Educational Development in India. New York: Teachers College Press, 1968.

Leyburn, J. The Haitian People. New Haven, Conn.: Yale University Press, 1966.

Leys, C. Underdevelopment in Kenya. Berkeley: University of California Press, 1974.

Lindsey, J. K. Primary Education in Bombay: Introduction to a Social Study Evaluation in Education International Progress. Oxford: Pergamon Press, 1978.

Logan, R. W. Haiti and the Dominican Republic. New York: Oxford University Press, 1968.

Long, A. Fikiran-Fikiran Tentang Pendidkan (Thoughts on Education). Kuala Lumpur: Dewan Bahasa dan Pustaka, 1979.

Lowenthal, D., and L. Comitas, eds. Consequences of Class and Color: West Indian Perspectives. Garden City, N.Y.: Doubleday, 1973.

McCully, B. English Education and the Origins of Indian Nationalism. New York: Columbia University Press, 1940.

Mahar, J. M., ed. The Untouchables in Contemporary India. Tucson: University of Arizona Press, 1972.

Maitland-Jones, J. F. Politics in Africa: The Former British Territories. New York: Norton, 1973.

Marchandisse, G. L'Evaluation pratique pars les professeurs enseignant la langue maternelle en premiere annee de l'enseignement secondaire renove. Brussels: Direction Generale de l'Organisation des Etudes, Ministere de L'Education Nationale et de la Culture Francaise, 1974.

Mariategui, J. C. Siete ensayos de interpretacion de la realidad peruana. Lima: Biblioteca Amauta, 1973.

Marquard, L. People and Policies of South Africa. London: Oxford University Press, 1952.

Marshall, D. The Haitian Problem: Illegal Migration to the Bahamas. Kingston, Jamaica: Institute of Social and Economic Research, University of the West Indies, 1979.

Megarry, J., et al., eds. World Yearbook of Education 1981. Education of Minorities. New York: Nichols, 1981.

Milliband, R. The State in Capitalist Society. London: Quartet, 1973.

Millspaugh, A. C. Haiti Under American Control 1915-1930. Boston: World Peace Foundation, 1931.

Mitchell, H. Contemporary Politics and Economics in the Caribbean. Athens: Ohio University Press, 1968.

Mitchell, R. H. The Korean Minority in Japan. Berkeley: University of California Press, 1967.

Mohamad, M. B. The Malay Dilemma. Singapore: Donald Moore Press for Asia Pacific Press, 1970.

Mombusho Dowa Kyoiku Shiryo. Tokyo: Japanese Government Printing Office, 1981.

Moore, O. E. Haiti: Its Stagnant Society and Shackled Economy. New York: Exposition Press, 1972.

Mukerji, S. History of Education in India. Barada: Acharya Book Depot, 1966.

Mutiso, G. C. Kenya: Politics, Policy and Society. Nairobi: East African Literature Bureau, 1975.

Mutua, R. Development of Education in Kenya. Nairobi: East African Literature Bureau, 1975.

National Advisory Committee on Maori Education. He Huarahi. Wellington: Department of Education, 1980.

National Manpower Commission. High Level Manpower in South Africa. Pretoria: Department of Manpower Utilization, 1980.

New Zealand Department of Education. Parent-School Communication. Wellington, 1973.

New Zealand Educational Institute. Report and Recommendations on Maori Education. Wellington, 1967.

Ngata, A. The Past and the Future of the Maori. Christchurch, New Zealand: Christchurch Press, 1863.

Nordlinger, E. A. Conflict Regulation in Divided Societies. Cambridge, Mass.: Harvard Studies in International Affairs, 1972.

Nurullah, S., and J. P. Naik. History of Education in India During the British Period. Bombay: Macmillan, 1943.

Ogbu, J. Minority Education and Caste: The American System in Cross-Cultural Perspective. New York: Academic Press, 1978.

Organization for Economic Cooperation and Development. Reviews of National Policies for Education: Yugoslavia. Paris, 1982.

Parkin, D. The Cultural Definition of Political Values. New York: Academic Press, 1978.

Passin, H. Society and Education in Japan. New York: Teachers College Press, 1965.

Paulston, R. Society, Schools, and Progress in Peru. New York: Pergamon Press, 1970.

_____. Conflicting Theories of Social and Educational Change: A Typological Review. Pittsburgh: University of Pittsburgh Press, 1976.

Pennar, J. Modernization and Diversity in Soviet Education with Special Reference to Nationality Groups. New York: Praeger, 1971.

Pezo, C., E. Ballon, and L. Peirano. El magisterio y sus luchas 1985-1978. Lima: DESCO.

Poulantzas, N. <u>Political Power and Social Classes</u>. London: New Left Books, 1973.

_____. <u>Classes in Contemporary Capitalism</u>. London: New Left Books, 1975.

Prewitt, K., ed. <u>Education and Political Values</u>. Nairobi: East African Publishing House, 1971.

Quijano, A. <u>Dominiacion y cultura: lo cholo y el conflicto cultural en el Peru</u>. Lima: Mosca Azul Editores, 1980.

Republic of Kenya. <u>African Socialism and Its Application to Planning in Kenya</u>. Nairobi: Government Printer, 1965.

_____. <u>Development Plan 1966-70</u>. Nairobi: Government Printer, 1966.

_____. <u>Primary School Syllabus, Ministry of Education</u>. Nairobi: Government Printer, 1967.

_____. <u>Development Plan 1974-78</u>. Nairobi: Government Printer, 1974.

_____. <u>Report of the National Committee on Educational Objectives and Policies</u>. Nairobi: Government Printer, 1976.

_____. <u>Educational Trends 1973-77</u>. Nairobi: Central Bureau of Statistics, 1980.

Rex, J. <u>Race, Colonialism and the City</u>. London: Routledge and Kegan Paul, 1973.

Rice, F. A., ed. <u>Study of the Role of Second Languages in Asia, Africa and Latin America</u>. Washington, D.C.: Center for Applied Linguistics, 1962.

Rivera Serna, R. <u>Historia del Peru-Republica</u>, 2nd ed. Lima: Editorial Juridica, 1974.

Robushka, A. <u>Race and Politics in Urban Malaysia</u>. Stanford, Calif.: Hoover Institution Press, 1973.

Rose, E. Colour and Citizenship. A Report on British Race Relations. London: Oxford University Press, 1969.

Rothchild, D. S. Racial Bargaining in Independent Kenya: A Study of Minorities and Decolonization. London: Oxford University Press, 1973.

Rubin, V., and R. Schaedel, eds. The Haitian Potential. New York: Teachers College Press, 1975.

Rudolph, S., and L. Rudolph, eds. Education and Politics in India. Cambridge, Mass.: Harvard University Press, 1972.

Runnymeade Trust and the Radical Statistics Race Group. Britain's Black Population. London: Heinemann Educational Books, 1980.

Ryan, S. Race and Nationalism in Trinidad and Tobago: A Study of Decolonization in a Multi-Racial Society. Toronto: University of Toronto Press, 1972.

Salazar Bondy, A. La educacion del hombre nuevo: La reforma educativa Peruana. Buenos Aires: Editorial Paidos, 1975.

Salter, B., and T. Tapper. Education, Politics and the State. London: Grant McIntyre, 1981.

Sargent, J. Society, Schools and Progress in India. Oxford: Pergamon Press, 1968.

Sarup, M. Education, State and Crisis: A Marxist Perspective. London: Routledge and Kegan Paul, 1982.

Schermerhorn, R. A. Comparative Ethnic Relations: A Framework for Theory Research. New York: Random House, 1970.

_____. Ethnic Plurality in India. Tucson: University of Arizona Press, 1978.

Shah, V. The Educational Problems of the Scheduled Caste School and College Students in India. New Delhi: Allied Publishers, 1982.

Sharma, K. N. Arithmetic of Social Inequality: A Study of Admission and Adjustment of IIT Students. Kanpur, India: Department of Humanities and Social Sciences, 1974.

Sheffield, J. R. Education in Kenya. New York: Teachers College Press, 1973.

Sher, J. P., ed. Rural Education in Urbanized Nations: Issues and Innovations. Westview Special Studies in Education. An OECD/CERI Report. Paris: Organization for Economic Cooperation and Development, 1981.

Shields, J. A Selected Bibliography on Education in East Africa 1941-1961. Kampala, Uganda: Makerere University College, 1962.

Shuy, R., and R. W. Fasold, eds. Language Attitudes: Current Trends and Prospects. Washington, D.C.: Georgetown University Press, 1973.

Simpson, G. E. Religious Cults of the Caribbean: Trinidad, Jamaica and Haiti, enl. 3rd ed. Rio Piedras, P.R.: Institute of Caribbean Studies, University of Puerto Rico, 1980.

Singleton, J. Nichu: A Japanese School. New York: Holt, Rinehart and Winston, 1967.

Stockholm International Peace Research Institute. Project. Kontaktschulen. Geneva, 1981.

_____. Project. Die vorbeitung der lehrer auf pie pflege der eltern kontakte. Geneva, 1983.

_____. Project. Gedanken zum therma schulerbeurteilung. Geneva, 1983.

_____. Project. SIPRI-Informationen. Geneva, 1983.

Skolnik, R. L. The Nation-Wide Learning System of Singapore. Singapore: Institute of Southeast Asian Studies, 1976.

Smock, D. R. Black Education in South Africa. Brussels, Belgium: Institute of International Education, January 1983.

Snodgrass, D. R. Inequality and Economic Development in Malaysia. Kuala Lumpur: Oxford University Press, 1980.

Snyder, P., and F. Stone, eds. Minority Education in Global Perspective. Storrs: University of Connecticut, 1972.

South African Institute of Race Relations. Survey of Race Relations in South Africa. Johannesburg, 1980.

Srivastava, G. N. The Language Controversy and the Minorities. Delhi: Atma Ram, 1970.

Sulmont, D. Los movimientos populares en el Peru. Lima: Pontifica Universidad Catolica, 1983.

Tabata, I. B. Education for Barbarism in South Africa. London: Pall Mall Press, 1960.

Tawney, R. Secondary Schools for All. London: Allen & Unwin, 1922.

Taylor, F. Race, School and Community: A Study of Research and Literature. Atlantic Highlands, N.J.: Humanities Press, 1974.

Third Malaysia Plan. Kuala Lumpur: Government Press, 1976.

Tollefson, J. W. The Language Situation and Language Policy in Slovenia. Washington, D.C.: University Press of America, 1981.

Uchendu, V. C., ed. Education and Politics in Tropical Africa. New York: Conch Magazine, 1979.

UNESCO. Workshop on Problems Relating to the Language of Instruction in Multilingual Countries in Asia and the Pacific, Mysore, India, December 8-12, 1980. Final Report. Paris, 1980.

————. Statistical Yearbook 1982. Paris, 1982.

UNICEF. Primary Education in Rural India: Participation and Wastage. Bombay: McGraw-Hill, 1971.

Urry, J. The Anatomy of Capitalist Societies. London: Macmillan, 1981.

Vakil, K., and S. Natarajar. Education in India During the British Period. Bombay: Oxford University Press, 1951.

Valcarcel, E., and D. Carlos. Historia de la educacion Incaica. Lima: Universidad Nacional Mayor de San Marcos, 1961.

_____. Breve historia del la educacion Peruana. Coleccion Ciencias Historico Sociales. Lima: Editorial Educacion, 1975.

Van den Berghe, P. Race and Ethnicity. New York: Basic Books, 1970.

Verdoodt, A. Les problemes des groupes linguistiques en Belgique. Bibliotheque des Cahiers de l'Institut de Linguistique de Louvain. Louvain: Peeters, 1977.

_____. "Dix ans de recherches bibliographiques sur les problems communautaires belges." Recherches Sociologiques 2 (1980:237-45.

_____. "Belgium." In International Journal of the Sociology of Language. The Hague: Moulton, 1982.

_____. A bibliographie sur le probleme linguistique belge. Laval: Centre International de Recherche sur le Bilinguisme, 1983.

_____. "Entreprises et services publics: Besoins en langues modernes etrangeres." Unpublished summary of a survey undertaken by the Centre de Recherches Sociologiques de l'Universite de Louvain with the Centron voor Mathematics Psychologie en Psychologrsche Methodologie of the Katholieke Universiteit de Leuven, 1983.

Verma, G., and C. Bagley. Race and Education Across Cultures. Stanford, Conn.: Greylock Publishers, 1975.

Verwey, C. T., R. R. Brazelle, and F. J. Wilkinson, eds. Education and Manpower Production. Bloemfontein: University of the Orange Free State, 1982.

Vodkinsky, S. Schools in Czechoslovakia. Prague: State Pedagogical Publishing House, 1965.

Wardle, D. The Rise of the Schooled Society: The History of Formal Schooling in England. London: Routledge and Kegan Paul, 1974.

Watson, J. E. Horizons of Unknown Power. Wellington: NZCER, 1967.

Weil, T., et al., eds. Area Handbook for Haiti. Washington, D.C.: American University Press, 1973.

Willis, P. Learning to Labour. London: Saxon House, 1977.

Wilson, J. M. P. The Development of Education in Ecuador. Hispanic-American Studies. Miami: University of Miami Press, 1970.

Wirt, F. M., and M. W. Kirst. Political and Social Foundations of Education. Berkeley, Calif.: McCutchan, 1967.

Wong, F. H. K., and T. H. Lee. Education in Malaysia. Kuala Lumpur: Heinemann, 1975.

Young, C. The Politics of Cultural Pluralism. Madison: University of Wisconsin Press, 1976.

INDEX

ABOUT THE AUTHORS

Suma Chitnis, currently a Jawaharlal Nehru Fellow, is professor and head of the unit for research in the sociology of education at the Tata Institute of Social Sciences, Bombay, India. She has researched and published extensively on the education of the scheduled castes in India. She is also director of a major women's studies program sponsored by the Ford Foundation at the Tata Institute.

Gerhard Fatzer is a lecturer at the Adult Education Training Center, Migros, and a trainer at the Institute for Applied Psychology in Switzerland, University of Zurich. He is the author of several studies on humanistic education in institutions.

Mark B. Ginsburg is an associate professor of education at the University of Houston and is the author of several works on ideology and education and the sociology of education.

John N. Hawkins is professor of comparative and international education and chairman of the department of education in the Graduate School of Education at the University of California, Los Angeles. He has conducted research on educational policy and planning in the Asia region for the past 15 years and is a specialist on education and national development in China and Japan. He is the author of five books on education in China and Asia, the most recent being <u>Education and Social Change in the People's Republic of China</u> (Praeger, 1983). He holds degrees from the University of Hawaii, the University of British Columbia, and a Ph.D. from George Peabody College, Vanderbilt University.

M. E. Kinberg is a doctoral student in comparative and international education at UCLA, California. Interests include adult, nonformal education, the effects of television on the ecology of education, and the politicization of education in various parts of the world.

Thomas J. La Belle is a professor of education and associate dean of the Graduate Division at UCLA. His interests are in educational anthropology, inter-group relations, and nonformal education. Many of his publications concern Latin America and the Caribbean, including his most recent book entitled <u>Nonformal Education and the Poor in Latin America and the Caribbean: Stability, Reform or Revolution?</u>

Anthony Layne is a lecturer in comparative and developmental studies at the School of Education, University of the West Indies. He received his Ph.D. in sociology of education from the University of Calgary. He was formerly employed as a program officer with the International Development Research Centre in Ottawa. His publications have appeared in leading journals in Canada and the United States, Germany, Colombia, and the Caribbean.

Leslie J. Limage is currently assistant editor of UNESCO's quarterly <u>Review of Education</u>. He has been a consultant to the Organization for Economic Cooperation and Development, the International Labor Office, and UNESCO in projects and research on educational provision for linguistic minorities, migrants in Europe, and disadvantaged groups, as well as a secondary teacher and an adult education tutor and organizer in the United Kingdom. Limage received degrees from the University of Paris and the University of London Institute of Education, obtaining his doctorate in comparative education and sociology of education. His research and publications include "Illiteracy in Industralized Countries" (UNESCO, 1979), "Language and Literacy Policy: Education for Multicultural Societies, the Case of France" (OECD-CERI, 1979), "The Situation of Young Women Migrants in Europe" (ILO, 1981), and "Second Generation Migrants in Europe: Education and Employment Prospects" (forthcoming, 1983).

Professor Ian Maclaren is a graduate of the University of New Zealand and the University of Chicago. At present he is head of the education department, University of Waikato, Hamilton, New Zealand, where his main teaching and research interests are in educational history and in aspects of comparative education that have a bearing on educational development in the South Pacific region.

Jorge M. Nakamoto is a doctoral student in comparative and international education at UCLA.

Val D. Rust is an associate professor in the Graduate School of Education at UCLA. He is a specialist on education and modernization with a focus on Europe and Eastern Europe.

Judy K. Sands is a doctoral candidate at the University of Houston.

R. Murray Thomas, head of the program in international education at the University of California, Santa Barbara, has served as a university professor and educational consultant in Southeast Asia for the past 25 years. He wrote the chapter on education in Malaysian Studies: Present Knowledge and Research Trends (1979) and is co-author of Schooling in the ASEAN Region (1980) and Political Style and Education Law in Indonesia (1980).

Dr. George Urch is professor of comparative international education at the Center for International Education, University of Massachusetts. He has lived and worked in Europe, Asia, and Africa. Dr. Urch holds the Ph.D. in comparative education from the University of Michigan.

Peter S. White is a doctoral student in comparative and international education at UCLA.